Lecture Notes in Computer Science 3184

Commenced Publication in 1973
Founding and Former Series Editors:
Gerhard Goos, Juris Hartmanis, and Jan van Leeuwen

T0223566

Sokratis Katsikas   Javier Lopez
Günther Pernul (Eds.)

Trust and Privacy in Digital Business

First International Conference, TrustBus 2004
Zaragoza, Spain, August 30 - September 1, 2004
Proceedings

 Springer

Volume Editors

Sokratis Katsikas
University of the Aegean
Department of Information and Communication Systems Engineering
Karlovassi, 83200 Samos, Greece
E-mail: ska@aegean.gr

Javier Lopez
University of Malaga, Computer Science Department
Campus de Teatinos, 29071 Málaga, Spain
E-mail: jlm@lcc.uma.es

Günther Pernul
University of Regensburg, Department of Information Systems
Universitätsstr. 31, 93053 Regensburg, Germany
E-mail: pernul@wiwi.uni-regensburg.de

Library of Congress Control Number: 2004110771

CR Subject Classification (1998): K.4.4, K.4, K.6, E.3, C.2, D.4.6, J.1

ISSN 0302-9743
ISBN 3-540-22919-1 Springer Berlin Heidelberg New York

Springer is a part of Springer Science+Business Media

springeronline.com

© Springer-Verlag Berlin Heidelberg 2004
Printed in Germany

Typesetting: Camera-ready by author, data conversion by Olgun Computergrafik
Printed on acid-free paper   SPIN: 11312376   06/3142   5 4 3 2 1 0

Preface

Sincerely welcome to proceedings of the 1st International Conference on Trust and Privacy in Digital Business, Zaragoza, Spain, held from August 30th to September 1st, 2004. This conference was an outgrowth of the two successful TrustBus international workshops, held in 2002 and 2003 in conjunction with the DEXA conferences in Aix-en-Provence and in Prague. Being the first of a planned series of successful conferences it was our goal that this event would initiate a forum to bring together researchers from academia and commercial developers from industry to discuss the state of the art of technology for establishing trust and privacy in digital business. We thank you all the attendees for coming to Zaragoza to participate and debate the new emerging advances in this area.

The conference program consisted of one invited talk and nine regular technical papers sessions. The invited talk and keynote speech was delivered by Ahmed Patel from the Computer Networks and Distributed Systems Research Group, University College Dublin, Ireland on "Developing Secure, Trusted and Auditable Services for E-Business: An Autonomic Computing Approach". A paper covering his talk is also contained in this book.

The regular paper sessions covered a broad range of topics, from access control issues to electronic voting, from trust and protocols to digital rights management. The conference attracted close to 100 submissions of which the program committee accepted 29 papers for presentation and inclusion in the conference proceedings. The authors of the accepted papers come from 12 different countries. The proceedings contain the revised versions of all accepted papers.

We would like to express our thanks to the people who helped put together the program: the program committee members and external reviewers for their timely and rigorous reviews, the DEXA organizing committee, in particular Mrs. Gabriela Wagner for her help in the administrative work, and, last but not least, Mr. Christian Schläger who was the main organizational force behind most of the involved tasks in making the conference possible.

Finally we would like to thank all authors who submitted papers, those who presented papers, and the attendees who made this event an intellectually stimulating one. We hope they enjoyed the conference.

Athens, Malaga, Regensburg   Sokratis Katsikas
August 2004   Javier Lopez
                                               Günther Pernul

Program Committee

General Chairperson
Sokratis Katsikas, University of the Aegean, Greece

Conference Program Chairpersons
Javier Lopez, University of Malaga, Spain
Guenther Pernul, University of Regensburg, Germany

Program Committee Members
Peter Bramhall, HP Labs, Bristol, UK
Mike Burmester, Florida State University, USA
David W. Chadwick, University of Salford, UK
Frederic Cuppens, ENST Bretagne, France
Jorge Davila, Polytechnic Univ. of Madrid, Spain
Ed Dawson, Queensland University of Technology, Australia
Hannes Federrath, University of Regensburg, Germany
Eduardo B. Fernandez, Florida Atlantic University, USA
Elena Ferrari, University of Como, Italy
Simone Fischer-Huebner, Karlstad University, Sweden
Steven Furnell, University of Plymouth, UK
Rüdiger Grimm, University of Technology, Ilmenau, Germany
Stefanos Gritzalis, University of the Aegean, Greece
Dimitrios Gritzalis, Athens Univ. of Economics and Business, Greece
Ehud Gudes, Ben-Gurion University, Israel
Sigrid Guergens, Fraunhofer, Germany
Sushil Jajodia, George Mason University, USA
Kamal Karlapalem, IIIT Hyderabad, India
Dipak Khakhar, Lund University, Sweden
Hiroaki Kikuchi, Tokai University, Japan
Antonio Lioy, Politecnico di Torino, Italy
Diego Lopez, RedIRIS, Spain
Peter Lory, University of Regensburg, Germany
Masahiro Mambo, Tohoku University, Japan
Olivier Markowitch, Université Libre de Bruxelles, Belgium
Martin Olivier, University of Pretoria, South Africa
Eiji Okamoto, Universisty of Tsukuba, Japan
Rolf Oppliger, eSecurity Technologies, Switzerland
Ahmed Patel, University College Dublin, Ireland
Andreas Pfitzmann, University of Technology, Dresden, Germany
Birgit Pfitzmann, IBM Zurich Research Lab., Switzerland
Hartmut Pohl, FH Bonn-Rhein-Sieg, Germany
Karl Posch, University of Technology, Graz, Austria
Bart Preneel, Katholieke Universiteit Leuven, Belgium
Gerald Quirchmayr, University of Vienna, Austria
Kai Rannenberg, University of Frankfurt, Germany

Arnon Rosenthal, MITRE Corporation, USA
Carsten Rudolph, Fraunhofer, Germany
Pierangela Samarati, University of Milan, Italy
Jose M. Sierra, Univ. Carlos III, Spain
Mikko T. Siponen, University of Oulu, Finland
Adrian Spalka, University of Bonn, Germany
Leon Strous, De Nederlandsche Bank, Netherlands
Stephanie Teufel, University of Fribourg, Switzerland
Bhavani Thuraisingham, MITRE Corporation, USA
Ivan Visconti, ENS, France
Michael Waidner, IBM Zurich Research Lab., Switzerland
Marianne Winslett, University of Illinois, USA
Jianying Zhou, I2R, Singapore

External Reviewers

Angelis, George
Balopoulos, Thodoris
Bergmann, Mike
Boehme, Rainer
Bouabdallah, Ahmed
Boyd, Colin
Chen, Shiping
Clauss, Sebastian
D'Arco, Paolo
Erat, Andreas
Franz, Elke
Gilberg, Jörg
Guo, Huiping
Iliadis, John
Julisch, Klaus
Klimant, Herbert

Koepsell, Stefan
Kriegelstein, Thomas
Kühn, Ulrich
Lambrinoudakis,
Costas
Martucci, Leonardo
Monahan, Brian
Muschall, Björn
Nikova, Svetla
Olson, Lars
Otenko, Sassa
Paul, Souradyuti
Pearson, Siani
Peng, Kun
Plank, Kilian
Priebe, Torsten

Proudler, Graeme
Rossnagel, Heiko
Rosulek, Mike
Roy, Sankardas
Schläger, Christian
Schlienger, Thomas
Schmidt, Nikita
Steinbrecher, Sandra
Steinert, Martin
Wang, Guilin
Westfeld, Andreas
Woelfl, Thomas
Yao, Chao
Zuccato, Albin

Table of Contents

Invited Talk

Trust

Access Control

e-Business Issues

Privacy

e-Voting

Protocols

Copyright Protection

Multicast

PKI, Signature Schemes

Developing Secure, Trusted and Auditable Services for e-Business: An Autonomic Computing Approach

Ahmed Patel

Computer Networks and Distributed Systems Research Group,
Department of Computer Science,
University College Dublin,
Belfield, Dublin 4, Ireland
apatel@cnds.ucd.ie

Abstract. Why have e-business trust and security often been evasive and un-successful? This keynote paper attempts to answer this question by looking at an autonomic approach to communications services for on-line businesses. It reviews the issues and challenges, and presents a rationale for security, privacy, interception, forensics of digital evidence and trust in an autonomic communications and computing environment. A combination of security, privacy enhancing technologies, trustworthy computing interfaces and techniques, advocacy, and greater understanding of the socio-economic and technical aspects of this new electronic phenomena must be covered to establish a sound e-business operating environment on a global level. Some possible solutions pertaining to this environment are also reviewed and examples of some key research areas outlined. Finally a brief overview of directions for innovative research is presented and followed by concluding remarks.

1 Introduction

The e-business industry has changed dramatically in recent years. The explosive growth of the Internet, the proliferation of mobile networks and the increasing difficulty in managing multi-vendor environments and the services that they are meant to provide have altered forever the dynamics of this industry, the expectations of its customers and the business models under which it operates. The impact of Moore's Law has had a profound effect across all sectors of the industry – equipment manufacturers, network operators, service providers and e-businesses continually strive to rapidly deploy the latest technology in order to gain competitive advantage. Although recent economic upheavals have had a drastic effect on certain sectors, the level of innovation has been impressive and the industry is again poised to drive another wave of economic growth. Further, as much as e-business rests on the benefits obtained from personalisation and customisation, it also requires that client and system privacy and security risks be effectively minimised. Eradicating these risks and maximising the client's confidence level is a key e-business requirement, as it not only influences the acceptance of e-business by clients, but also opens the avenues for effective design of e-business processes and supporting systems.

S. Katsikas, J. Lopez, and G. Pernul (Eds.): TrustBus 2004, LNCS 3184, pp. 1–10, 2004.

However, the challenges posed by the complexity of modern communications environments, which link businesses and clients, are potentially overwhelming. A gulf has emerged between the communications infrastructure and the capabilities of the services and applications deployed across it. This is manifested in the inflexible nature of current service offerings: they are rigidly defined, closely coupled to the network, possess static functionality, and are prone to a variety of security breaches and mandatory interception of traffic. Critically, current service offerings are manually deployed and managed, requiring highly labour intensive support structures, with a consequent inflexibility and significant time to market constraints.

The heart of this problem is the inability of service providers, communications operators and e-business applications to adapt, in a dynamic fashion, their offered services to the changing needs of their customers in a seamless and secure fashion. An approach to solving this problem is through envisaging an Autonomic Communications Environment (ACE) underpinning or supporting an autonomic computing user base, an idealistic service-centric environment exhibiting self-governing behaviour with independent auditability. Within an ACE, services will be created that are self-aware and self-healing. In their deployment, they will be self-adapting, self-optimising and self-configuring, and in operation they will be self-protecting, self-managing and self-composing. These features enable ACE services and the associated resources to adapt to changing business needs and environmental conditions without manual intervention. The proposed answer is the development of a secure, trusted and auditable Autonomic Communications Framework (ACF), whose mission is to support the development of different ACEs targeted at different business needs but in a global e-business interlaced Net environment.

At the heart of the ACF will be a new methodology for managing objects. It is required because different stakeholders have different views of a managed object, and current approaches do not take this into account. For example, the business analyst looks at a 'Service Level Agreement' object and sees an entity that represents a contractual agreement, whereas a network administrator looks at the same object and sees the different network services that must be supported using different vendor-specific functions, such as interception and audit rules, security functions and other algorithms such as queuing, routing, etc. This methodology cannot be built in either private industry or fora, and requires the combination of academic, scientific, technical and industrial advances which must be produced through a combination of fundamental basic, applied and strategic research.

The security issues that are of concern and urgent today will be even more urgent in the new world of autonomic systems that will also bring new and as yet undefined security issues of its own, issues that may not be significant or present at all today. It is envisaged that autonomic technology will offer new opportunities – new ways and means of securing e-business systems against attacks and with a level of trust that will minimise the level of tolerance in loss of revenue or non-economic function.

The growing awareness, coupled with an expanding number of new initiatives in the area internationally, is leading to a great deal of exciting research and development in the areas of security, privacy enhancing technologies, trustworthy computing interfaces and techniques, advocacy, and greater understanding of the socio-economic and technical aspects of the these new electronic phenomena.

This keynote presentation attempts to explore with you what are the issues, possible solutions and directions for research in this challenging area.

2 Issues and Challenges

The autonomic communications approach, proposed as a facilitator of e-business development on the Internet and other networks (mobile, 3G), is intrinsically tied to a variety of security challenges. The term 'security' is understood here in the broad sense and includes protection from unauthorised intervention, privacy, trust and forensics. Security in an ACE plays a dual role: to *protect autonomic facilities* of the ACE and to *offer security services to e-businesses*. Therefore, it can no longer be developed as an afterthought; it must be built in from the outset.

System and network security are vital parts of any autonomic computing solution, key to the achievement of the goals of self-protection, self-healing, and self-optimisation. Additional security challenges arising in autonomic systems include the establishment of trustworthy identities, automatically handling changes in system and network configuration, and greatly increased configuration complexity. Elements of autonomic systems will need to both establish and follow security policies in an understandable and fail-safe manner.

The fields of information technology security and telecommunications security are characterised by the existence of many technologies, services and concepts with little, if any, cohesive architecture. Furthermore, many existing protocols and systems were designed without security. In addition, there are complex interactions between society's needs (as expressed in laws, regulations etc.) and what is technologically possible. Conflicts arise between users' reasonable expectations of privacy and other reasonable expectations of law enforcement, network owners and similar stakeholders to access and control information in the telecommunications system [8]. At present, these areas are developing in an *ad hoc* manner without a clear model of how the different issues relate to one another, and how the telecommunications infrastructure should address them.

Security and reliability issues are rarely considered at the initial stages of system development. In fact, security technology is still erroneously considered as supplementary, and engineering of security techniques are not integrated within software engineering processes, with negative consequences. As a result of recent computer security crises, operating system designers have realised this need for integrated security but are constrained by the original design of their systems and the networks they are connected to – a fundamental change in system security design is needed. It is no longer sufficient to rely on rigid traffic filtering and periodic updates to protect systems from computer intruders and virus infections. Increased awareness of service and network level activities is needed to enable human analysts and automated agents to detect and respond to major problems. However, to reduce the latency between detection and response, a more organic approach to security must be developed. In addition to improving our awareness of system activities at the macro level, we need services to be resilient (self-aware and self-healing) to defend themselves against injury at the micro level to protect individuals against identity theft, privacy violation and financial loss [2,4,9].

Modern telecommunication systems are very challenging from a security and privacy perspective due to their complexity, distributed nature, diverse components, and rapid growth. Managing security is even more difficult when systems are being regularly altered to provide improved or new services. The associated lack of control over these systems must be compensated by identifying and mitigating weaknesses prior to an incident and detecting problems when prevention is not successful.

Existing approaches to security management (reconfiguration, dissemination of updates) are designed for relatively static computing environments and are not well suited to a dynamic system such as the ACE. Therefore, new security management techniques and tools must be developed for resilient autonomic systems. Similarly, vulnerability assessment must be rethought when dealing with systems that adapt and protect themselves.

Little attention has so far been paid to the usability of secure services. At present it is often the case that 'secure' equates to 'too complicated for the average user'. Security that is too complicated for the average user is likely to be turned off, undermining the protective mechanisms. In the future, security must be present as default behaviour without special knowledge or actions by users.

For the concept of autonomic communications to succeed, its target environments must be *secure enough to be trustworthy* in the eyes of their users. They must also provide services such as privacy protection and authentication to their users in an autonomic fashion, i.e. with minimum human involvement. While no functioning system is perfectly secure, the goal for ACEs is to be secure enough that their benefits outweigh the risks. The autonomic systems infrastructure must provide reliable identity verification, integrity and access control. To satisfy privacy policies and laws, the system and its elements must also appropriately protect private and personal information that comes into their possession. Data segregation according to their origin or purpose is needed to satisfy policy and legal requirements [6].

3   Possible Solutions

As discussed above, the challenges can be classified into three main groups: provision of *security services* to ACE users, maintaining the *security of an ACE* itself, and ensuring *usability* and transparency of security mechanisms to the end user.

3.1 Security Services in an Autonomic Communications Environment

Business scenarios envisaged in an ACE will depend on a variety of security services provided by the environment. Such services include reliable authentication (and single sign-on) of users, confidentiality (e.g. when sensitive information such as financial data or credit card numbers is transmitted), proof and non-repudiation of transactions, and trust management. Given the power of information, access to it must be protected to preserve our freedom and to defend against abuse. Since some autonomic systems deal with personal information about individuals, they need to be able to represent and demonstrably obey privacy policies required by national and international law and reinforced by proper business ethics. More powerful authorisation methods, that are context-aware and policy-driven, are required.

A methodology needs to be defined to incorporate single sign-on, as well as authentication, authorisation, accounting, and auditing of services delivered and resources used. Particular emphasis will be placed on federating security resources and services into a set of 'zones' that each provides security according to the business requirements of their context as policy-based. This combination facilitates a distributed architecture for supporting the special security needs of users. Management of end-user privacy and profiles will enable the end-user to control what information should be provided to what resource when, where, why and how.

A major challenge in the specific to ACE is to make its security services autonomic. Autonomic computing offers a host of new abilities that include ways and means to make our systems more secure and our private data better protected. Building and administering secure computing systems is well known to be a difficult task, especially so if they are heterogeneous and highly distributed. Autonomic systems offer us the opportunity to semi-automate such processes.

Making security resources and services autonomic depends largely on the underlying model of the autonomic communications architecture. For instance, they can be modelled through some kind of 'resource abstraction layer', like any other services and resources in autonomic networks. However, it is important to ensure that specific requirements of security services are met: for instance, that autonomic service management mechanisms will not undermine security of the managed services.

3.2 Security of an Autonomic Communications Environment

The aim is to create resilient systems that enable the ACE to bounce back and self-heal after an injury. This type of resilience exists in biological systems in the form of adaptive immune systems [1,5]. The concept of self-healing communication systems harks back to the early conceptions of the Internet but was not fully accomplished because sensing and response capabilities were not integrated. Our aim is to implement this resilience in more complex global, mobile communication environments, where security problems are compounded by increasing distribution and openness, with a design goal of allowing anyone to connect from anywhere.

In part resilience in ACE depends on internal sensors and alarms but also on internal triggers and responses similar to antibodies in biological systems. A biological analogy can be further explored by considering nervous and immune systems. A nervous system is responsible for sensing (and problem detection) and self-protection through reflexes and smart responses. An immune system is responsible for anomaly detection ('self' vs 'not self', 'legitimate' vs 'illegal' or 'harmless' vs 'harmful') and self-healing. The success depends on integration, reliable data, and proper response.

Prevention of unauthorised access to communication systems along with auditing individual activities are requirements of a modern communications infrastructure [3]. These functions require some form of authentication of individuals and devices. Additionally, the protection and reliability of system-generated data such as audit trails and alerts is important for system operation and forensic purposes.

The autonomic communications framework will need to provide facilities to ensure that services and resources are designed with security in mind, as well as address existing security exposures and deficiencies in current resources, services, and protocols. It will also enable business and legal concerns to be addressed (Fig. 1).

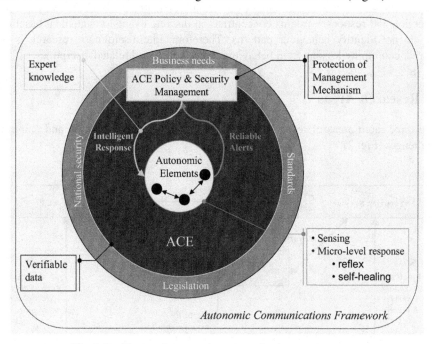

Fig. 1. Resilience of autonomic communications environments

3.3   Usability and Human-Computer Interaction

A key weakness in today's security systems usage is the failure to accommodate the end user or system processes in a seamless and transparent way to use security functions and features. This is one of the main reasons that powerful existing security services and mechanisms are not only not used but also not used effectively today. There is a dire need to sit back and take a deep look at this failure and come clean with new approaches of using security functions and features by studying human–computer interaction issues with respect to security in ACE and devising new seamless and transparent solutions. The goal is to find security mechanisms that would be both effective and usable. User-centred design techniques may be employed, which *places the user at the centre of the process*, investigating user experience across all stages of the development lifecycle.

This requires developments in human-computer interaction techniques as well as careful integration of the security and privacy services within the reference architecture. It probably also requires that psychologists and computer scientists will need to work together to strike the right balance between overwhelming humans with too many questions or too much information and under-empowering them with too few options or too little information [6]. Assistance coming from techniques such as location and context awareness, smart labels and cards, and biometrics can be used to improve this situation.

From an ACE protection point of view, an understanding of human behaviour can help distinguish between accidental injuries and malicious attacks. Current intrusion detection and response systems concentrate on discrete events or statistical baselines but do not identify behaviour patterns. Therefore, interdisciplinary research is required, combining lessons from behavioural, biological and related disciplines.

4 Research Areas

The three main areas of research in this domain have strong linkages and common challenges (Fig. 2).

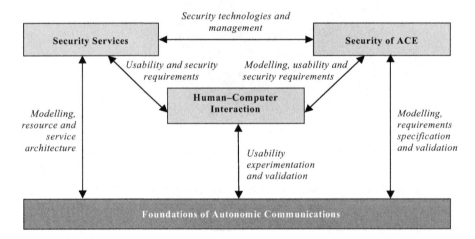

Fig. 2. Research areas in autonomic security

There are other critical domains with similarly important issues such as privacy, interception, trust management and forensic digital evidence of events that must be incorporated into the holistic solution for an all encompassing secure autonomic environment.

The following key areas of application will be used for advanced problem resolution:

- Behavioural science
  - Assessing and predicting human–system interaction.

- Machine learning
  - Knowledge bank of past problems and solutions.
- Data mining
  - Taking into account human behaviour.

Data identification and collection, forensics and digital evidence will form research sub-areas needed to support the concept of ACF.

Data Identification and Collection

Key data identification and collection of actual (real) values pertaining to all aspects of security, privacy, trust, interception and forensic digital evidence presentation should be specified with the sole purpose of collecting data as part of a process for system awareness and problem detection and prevention. The data collected will be used both for autonomic resilience and for forensic purposes.

Forensics and Digital Evidence

Forensics and digital evidence is presently an inexact science with little rigorous formalism. Research in this area is in its infancy. It poses some real challenges for researchers. Primarily, it is envisaged that major studies and new forms of forensic techniques and digital evidence gathering and presentation should be devised that can be used to investigate incidents in ACEs in exact ways regardless of the number of times that such incidents are investigated by different systems, process or persons. In other words, an incident of breach should investigated by multiple sources should come to the same result or outcome. One research direction here is how to ensure integrity of evidence to make it suitable for internal investigations and, if necessary, court proceedings. Another direction is to employ formal models to recreate the chain of events leading to an incident together with a formal proof. This is a fascinating area of untapped research.

5   Directions for Innovative Research

There are a number of challenges facing those defining, designing and developing secure and trusted e-business autonomic systems. There are also a number of autonomic principles that can be used to make systems more secure and trustworthy than they are today. However, there is a significant need for further research in many key areas such as:

- ways to present and reason about security, privacy, interception, trust and forensic digital evidence policies that govern autonomic systems and their total operating environment;
- ways to recognise, represent and reason about security states, and the trust relationships between elements;
- criteria, procedures and methods for effectively differentiating between normal system failures or glitches and failures or glitches caused by unwanted malicious attacks;

- policies and algorithms for constructing autonomic elements that are resistant to evasion, fraud and persuasion;
- ways to define and construct individual autonomic elements so that their overall collective behaviour is both trustworthy and trusted;
- a common nomenclature, languages and taxonomies for communicating and negotiating about security, privacy, interception, trust, and forensic digital evidence states and policies in a unified and global manner;
- human–computer interaction issues with respect to security, including usability requirements for seamless and transparent to end user security and development of models satisfying these requirements;
- standards-based data mining to ensure interoperability and cross-domain cooperative usage of data mining.

6 Conclusions

The growing complexity of business scenarios in a modern networked setting makes their management increasingly labour-intensive and prone to human error. A promising approach, based on autonomic computing principles, is to move this burden onto the computing systems involved in implementing these scenarios. This can be done by introducing autonomic features into communications systems on top of which businesses operate.

A group of issues which must be immediately taken into consideration are those related to security: protection, trust, privacy, forensics and legal. Security is inherently interwoven into the fabric of autonomic communications. The three major challenges that can be identified are: provision of autonomic security services; protection of autonomic communications environments; and the right balance of trustworthiness and transparency of security to the end user.

While, at the technological level, many useful and tried security mechanisms already exist, things are not so clear at higher conceptual levels. Models and architectures need to be developed which define how these mechanisms can be used in a complex autonomic system. A paradigm shift in security thinking is needed, from cryptography and mathematical methods to business, conceptual and social issues. An important conclusion is that 100% security will no longer be even theoretically achievable; the goal is to make systems which are *secure enough* and which can *bounce back* after a security incident. To what extent this is feasible is not known yet. Autonomic security opens a new challenging research avenue, full of exciting opportunities.

Acknowledgements

The author would like to express his sincere gratitude to Eoghan Casey, John Strassner and Nikita Schmidt for their insightful comments on the draft versions of this paper.

References

1. D.L. Chao, S. Forrest (2003). Information Immune Systems, *Genetic Programming and Evolvable Machines*, 4(4): 311–331.
2. D.M. Chess, C.C. Plamer, S.R. White (2003). Security in an autonomic computing environment, *IBM Systems Journal*, 42(1): 107–118
3. T.E. Daniels (2002). *Reference Models for the Concealment and Observation of Origin Identity in Store-and-Forward Networks*. Ph.D. dissertation, Purdue University.
4. R. Gopalakrishna, E.H. Spafford (2001). A framework for distributed intrusion detection using interest driven cooperating agents. Presented at the 4th International Symposium on Recent Advances in Intrusion Detection (RAID 2001).
5. S.A. Hofmeyr, S. Forrest (2000). Architecture for an artificial immune system, *Evolutionary Computation*, 7(1): 1289–1296.
6. J.O. Kephart, D.M. Chess (2003). The vision of autonomic computing, *IEEE Computer*, 36(1): 41–50.
7. The Open Group (2001). *CDSA Explained*, 2nd edition. Electronic publication.
8. A. Patel, S. Ó Ciardhuáin (2000). The impact of forensic computing on telecommunications, *IEEE Communications*, 38(11): 64–67.
9. K. Shanmugasundaram, N. Memon, A. Savant, Hervé Bronnimann (2003). ForNet: A distributed forensic network, in *Proc. 2nd International Workshop MMM-ACNS 2003*, Lecture Notes in Computer Science 2776, pp.1–16, Springer.

A Mechanism for Trust Sustainability
Among Trusted Computing Platforms[*]

Zheng Yan[1] and Piotr Cofta[2]

[1] Nokia Research Center, Nokia Group, Helsinki, Finland
zheng.z.yan@nokia.com
[2] Media Lab Europe, Dublin, Ireland
piotr.cofta@medialabeurope.org

Abstract. Trust plays an important role in social life as well as in cyberspace. Trust establishment in cyberspace relies on human beings as well as digital components. Trusted computing platform (TCP) was proposed to improve the trust between users and their devices. However, current TCP lacks solutions for trust sustainability among TCPs, so that trust relationship might be broken after a period of time. In order to solve this problem, this paper presents a mechanism for sustaining trust among TCPs. The mechanism builds up the trust relationship based on the root trust module (RTM) at a trustee and ensures the trust sustainability according to pre-defined conditions approved at the time of trust establishment and enforced through the use of the pre-attested RTM until the intended purpose is fulfilled. The paper also presents the applicability of the trust sustainability mechanism in several application areas.

1 Introduction

With the rapid growth of internetworking and electronic commerce, trust plays a crucial role in cyberspace in order to provide various digital services [1-3]. However, establishing trust relationship in cyberspace is more complicated than in social world. This is because communication in the cyberspace relies not only on human beings but also on digital components. Moreover, it is also more difficult to accumulate accurate information for trust purpose in remote digital communications. Generally, it is reasonably easy to initiate trust based on many existing technologies and structural regulations, but hard to sustain the trust during the fulfilment of the whole services.

Trust in digital information society, called digital trust, introduces two major challenges. The first one is to establish trust between users and their devices (e.g., PC and mobile phone) that is necessary to start the communication. With the increasing complexity of devices and various software running on the devices, it is very difficult for users to verify that their devices work properly. Trusted computing platform (TCP) has been proposed to solve the problem [7].

The other challenge is that the trust has to be sustained over time. For example, trustor A's trust on trustee B at one moment does not mean A could trust B at the next moment. The trust relationship built at the beginning of the communication should be maintained at least until the service is completed. It is essential to monitor and control

---

[*] The work reported in this paper has been entirely funded by Nokia Group.

S. Katsikas, J. Lopez, and G. Pernul (Eds.): TrustBus 2004, LNCS 3184, pp. 11–19, 2004.
© Springer-Verlag Berlin Heidelberg 2004

the conditions to sustain the trust for the final success of the service. This paper will mainly focus on solving the second challenge that has not been yet properly explored.

This paper mainly presents a mechanism for sustaining trust among TCPs. The mechanism can automatically inform the trustor about any distrustful behaviour of the trustee according to pre-defined conditions. Thereby, the original established trust relationship would be regulated accordingly. The paper contributes in three aspects. Firstly, issues for sustaining trust relationships are discussed. Secondly, a mechanism for trust sustainability is presented. Thirdly, the mechanism is applied for many real applications, e.g., MIDlet applications' trust on mobile information device (MID).

The rest of the paper is organized as follows. Section 2 presents related work. Section 3 describes the problem considered in the paper. Section 4 presents the trust sustainability mechanism and its applications are discussed in Section 5. The conclusions and future work are given in the last section.

2 Related Work

There is a large range of existing work on trust in information technology. The concept of trust is defined in various ways in the literature [1-3]. It is widely understood that the trust itself is a comprehensive concept, which is hard to narrow down. The trust is subjective because the level of trust considered sufficient is different for each entity. The trust is also dynamic as it is affected by many factors that are hard to monitor.

In order to figure out the trust in digital space, many people believe that some metrics should be defined to state various degree of trust [4]. A number of computational trust models were presented in [9-13]. These models compute the trust based on trustors direct or indirect experience. However, these models only pays attention to the influence of previous knowledge on the trust, but ignore future changes that may destroy the established trust. Thereby, it lacks support for cases that demand the trust for a longer period of time.

There is also a lot of work done on trust management [17-19]. Trust management systems provide trust assessments based on some trust root e.g. on policy assertion and trust specifications, which is also a major foundation of this paper as well.

Another important work in the literature is Digital Rights Management (DRM) [15]. It deals with client-side control of the usage of digital information. The trust model of traditional DRM solution can be described as a reference monitor (generally a software application) existing at a user's system for controlling usage of disseminated digital information in lieu of an information issuer. Not only DRM poses significant technical and operational challenges but none of existing DRM solutions considers how to sustain the trust relationship.

The paper is highly related to work on trusted computing platforms [5-8]. All work on TCP is based on the hardware security and cryptography to provide a root trust module at a digital computing platform. However, as described in next section, current work on TCP still lacks support on trust sustaining over the network. This is the key problem that the paper tries to solve. We believe trust management in the cyberspace should be extended not only for trust assessment, but also for trust sustainability.

3 Problems with Trust Sustainability in TCP

The intention of this section is to clarify one of the problems of current TCP used for remote digital services. In TCP the trust is built upon a root trust, which is enforced by sound technologies, and realized through secure hardware [5, 6]. Every time a computer is reset, the root trust module steps in, checks itself, and then verifies the OS loader (e.g. BIOS) before letting the boot-up continue. Through checking the integrity metrics of different components, the OS loader is assumed to verify the operating system, then, the operating system is assumed to verify every piece of software, and so on. A remote computing platform can be trusted by challenging its integrity metrics, verifying and comparing them with expected values that represent components that are trusted enough to perform the intended purpose. If compared values match the expected values, trusted interaction with the remote computing platform can be commenced. Anomalous metrics indicate that the platform is not operating as expected and further communication with the platform should be reconsidered.

However, the trust in the remote platform (remote device) neither necessarily remain intact for an extended period of time, nor does it remain intact after hardware or software configuration changes. Actually, as the trusted remote computing platform is built up during system boot, the root trust module can only verify OS within the previously identified configurations, thus failing to verify the trust for any newly added hardware or software components. This also means that the trust on remote platform cannot be sustained even though the platform could have been trusted at some moment. Therefore, one disadvantage of the current TCP paradigm is that it does not provide a dynamic solution and is thus unable to sustain its protection in changeable environment.

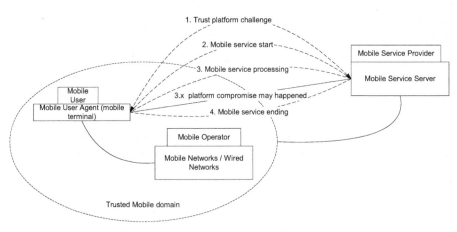

Fig. 1. An example of trust in mobile services

In order to illustrate the problem, we take mobile service as an example. The term 'mobile services' can be vaguely defined as services that are provided to mobile users via mobile terminals [16]. Specifically, mobile terminals such as mobile phones are considered to be the user agents of mobile services. As shown in Figure 1, a mobile phone already has the trust relationship with its operator through the existence of SIM

(Subscriber Identity Module) and relevant authentication methods. A mobile service provider (SP) stays out of the usual trust relationship. Based on the TCP technology, it is possible for both the mobile SP server and the mobile terminal to verify each other as trusted computing platforms at the beginning of the service. However, as time passes, the SP server cannot guarantee that trust is sustained since hardware or malicious software can be installed in the mobile terminal

One simple solution is to periodically re-challenge the remote platform. This however requires frequent communication between the remote device and the server, the communication that is neither feasible nor economical in the mobile environment. Further, the remote device bears the burden of frequent and unnecessary computationally-intensive operations. Still, this method may be subject to some forms of the man-in-the-middle attacks.

4   Mechanism for Trust Sustainability in TCPs

In order to overcome the above problem, we introduce a mechanism for sustaining the trust among TCPs. We first present the trust formula used in the mechanism, and then the root trust module (RTM) on which the mechanism is based. We also describe the state machine of the mechanism in the final sub-section.

4.1   Trust Form

The proposed mechanism uses the following trust formula: "Trustor A trusts trustee B for purpose P under condition C based on root trust R". The difference between this formula and others is in the element C - conditions to trust. The element C is defined by A to identify the rules for sustaining the trust for purpose P, the conditions and methods to get signal of distrust behaviours, as well as the mechanism to restrict any changes at B that may influence the trust relationship. The root trust R is the foundation of A's trust on B and its sustainability. Since A trusts B based on R, it is rational for A to sustain its trust on B based on R controlled by the conditions decided by A. This formula makes it possible to extend one-moment trust over the longer period of time.

4.2   Root Trust Module

The proposed mechanism is based on a root trust module (RTM), which is also the basis of TCP. The RTM could be an independent module embedded in the computing platform. It could also be a build-in feature in the current TCP's Trusted Platform Module [6].

The root trust module at the trustee is most possibly a hardware security module that has capability to register, protect and manage the trust conditions, monitor any computing platform's change including any alteration or operation on hardware, software and their configurations, check changes and restrict them based on conditions, as well as notify the trustor accordingly. Herein, a trusted community refers to a trust relationship established between the trustor A and the trustee B and sustained for an intended purpose. Figure 2 illustrates a basic structure of this module.

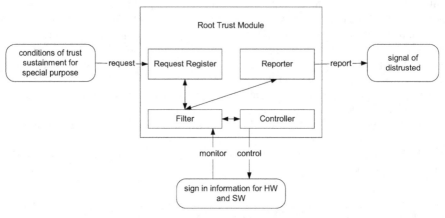

Fig. 2. Root trust module

4.3 Mechanism for Trust Sustainability

As postulated, the trust relationship is controlled through the conditions defined by the trustor, which are executed by the RTM at the trustee on which the trustor is willing to depend. The reasons for the trustor to depend on the RTM at the trustee can be various. Herein, we assume that the RTM at the trustee can be verified by the trustor as its expectation for some intended purpose and cannot be compromised by the trustee or other malicious entities later on. This assumption is based on the work done in industry and in academy [5-8].

As shown on Figure 3, the proposed mechanism comprises the following procedures.

a) Root trust challenge and attestation for ensuring the trustor's basic trust dependence at the trustee in steps 1- 2;
b) Trust establishment by specifying the trust conditions and registering them at the trustee's root trust module for the trust sustainability in steps 3-6;
c) Sustaining the trust relationship in the trust community through the root trust module monitor and control in steps 7-8;
d) Re-challenge the trust relationship if necessary when any change against trust conditions are reported.

As it can be seen from the above protocol, the trust is based on the trustor's dependence on the RTM. Although the RTM is located at the trustee, its execution for trust maintenance and sustainability is based on the agreed conditions and rules approved by both the trustee and trustor at the time the trust is built.

5 Applications

The mechanism proposed above provides a way to sustain the trust. It can be used to support any services that are using remote digital communications. It could also be applied for building up personalized trusted computing platform. This section presents some of its applications.

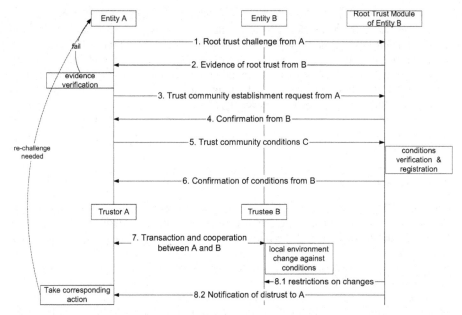

Fig. 3. Protocol for trust sustainability

5.1 Trusted MIDlet

One of the most popular mobile terminal applications is Java MIDP (Mobile Information Device Profile) application – MIDlet. There are certain measures to evaluate trust in MIDlets at the time they are loaded into the device. However as the MIDlet may be modified from its original state or illegally copied, its provider can no longer trust it after the installation. This introduces security problems in mobile services that interact through MIDlet with the service provider. Digital signatures and Digital Rights Management (DRM) procedures are currently unable to solve all the problems successfully. As shown in Figure 4, the current MIDP 2.0 can support the trust attestation from MID (Mobile Information Device) to MIDlet, but lacks support on building up and sustaining the essential trust from the MIDlet or MIDlet providers to the MID running environment.

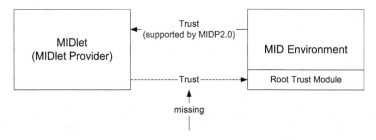

Fig. 4. One-way trust relationship between MID and MIDlet

With the proposed mechanism, the trust relationship could be sustained between a MIDlet provider (or a MIDlet) and a mobile information device. The method comprises attaching trust conditions to a MIDlet suite, downloading the MIDlet suite with attached trust conditions to the MID's RTM (already trusted by the MIDlet provider), checking the trust conditions against any alteration of the MID to determine a violation of the trust conditions and restrict changes accordingly, as well as reporting the violation to the MIDlet provider if necessary.

Complementary to DRM solutions that control the lifecycle of the MIDlet itself, this solution allows to express flexible rules associated with the execution environment of the MIDlet.

5.2 Personalised TCP

Current TCP technology forces users to accept pre-set rules defined by service providers, with no ability to personalise them according to their preferences. This kind of 'blind trust' is one of the biggest barriers that delays the acceptance of TCP, especially by end users. With the help of the proposed mechanism, the trust can be built according to the user's personalized conditions and based on the same root trust module already built into the digital device. In this case, the user is the trustor while the digital device is the trustee. The root trust module will behave as a crucial component in the future TCP compliant devices. It will inform the user about any distrustful behaviour of the device or restrict some changes at the device according to the user's personal trust specifications. Potentially such mechanism may alleviate also some of the privacy issues commonly associated with TCP.

5.3 Trusted Ad Hoc Networking

A mobile ad hoc network (MANET) is a collection of autonomous nodes or terminals that communicate with each other over relatively bandwidth-constrained wireless links. It is a new paradigm of networks where all network activities including discovery of the topology and delivery of messages must be executed by the terminals themselves. The MANETs are generally more prone to physical security threats, such as eavesdropping, spoofing, denial-of-service, and impersonation attacks.

With the proposed mechanism embedded into the ad hoc network terminals, it is possible for those devices to build the trusted community for autonomous communications. The trusted community is composed of a number of nodes following a common intended purpose, as shown in Figure 5. By imposing identical trust conditions on members of the community the required trusted behaviour could be assured.

5.4 VPN Trust Management

Trust plays a key role in the context of virtual private networking (VPN). However, providing advanced trust into VPN networks has proven to be problematic as none of existing VPN systems can ensure that data or components on a remote user terminal can be controlled according to the VPN operator's security requirements even though the user verification is successful, especially during the VPN connection and after disconnection. Nowadays, the VPN operators depend on user's responsibility to address this potential security problem.

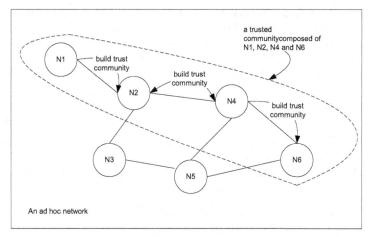

Fig. 5. Establishing trusted community in ad hoc networks

The proposed mechanism provides a solution for the above problems. In this case, a VPN management server is the trustor, while VPN a client terminal is the trustee. The VPN management server identifies the client terminal and specifies the trust conditions for that type of terminal at the VPN connection. Thereby, the VPN client terminal could behave according to the VPN operator's expectation.

6   Conclusions and Future Work

This paper presented a mechanism to sustain the trust among TCPs on the base of the root trust. The formula of trust used throughout this paper takes on the form "A trusts B for P under C based on R". The formula creates the trust based on the attestation of the RTM at the trustee and controls its sustainability according to the pre-defined conditions C. Those conditions are approved by both the trustor and the trustee at the time of trust establishment and enforced through the use of the pre-attested RTM until the intended purpose is fulfilled.

The paper extends the trust model from static to dynamic. Thus, it develops the notion of using trust management not only for the trust assessment but also for the trust sustainability. The proposed mechanism could be applied in many real applications for the trusted services and communications. It could work as an extension of future trusted computing platform to support various applications with greater flexibility.

Our future work will focus on developing the theory of trust model and prototyping the mechanism for trusted mobile Java applications.

References

1. Kari Chopra, William A. Wallace: Trust in Electronic Environments. Proceedings of the 36th Hawaii International Conference on System Sciences (HICSS'03), 2003.
2. McKnight, D. Harrison, Chervany Norman L.: The meanings of Trust. UMN university report. 2003.

3. McKnight, D. Harrison, Chervany Norman L.: What is Trust? A Conceptual Analysis and An Interdisciplinary Model. In Proceedings of the 2000 Americas Conference on Information Systems (AMCI2000). AIS, Long Beach, CA (August 2000).
4. Peter Herrmann: Trust-Based Protection of Software Component users and Designers. In Proceedings of the First International Conference of Trust Management (iTrust 2003), Crete, Greece, May 2003.
5. Davis P T, TCPA: who can you trust. EDPACS: the EDP Audit, Control and Security Newsletter, Dec. 2002.
6. Vaughan-Nichols, S.J., How trustworthy is trusted computing? Computer, Volume 36, Issue 3, March 2003.
7. Paul England, Butler Lampson, John Manferdelli, Marcus Peinado, Bryan Willman: A Trusted Open Platform. IEEE Computer Scciety, p55-62, July 2003.
8. Adrian Baldwin, Simon Shiu: Hardware Security Appliances for Trust. In Proceedings of the First International Conference of Trust Management (iTrust 2003), Crete, Greece, May 2003.
9. Daniel W. Manchala: Xerox Research and Technology. E-Commerce Trust Metrics and Models. IEEE Internet Computing, vol.4, no.2 p.36-44 (2000).
10. Mui Lik, Mohtashemi Mojdeh, Halberstadt Ari: A Computational Model of Trust and Reputation. In Proc. Of the 35th Annual Hawaii International Conference on System sciences, 7-10 (Jan. 2002), Big Island, HI, USA.
11. A. Jøsang and S. J. Knapskog: A metric for trusted systems. In Proceedings of the 21st National Security Conference, NSA 1998.
12. A. Jøsang: An Algebra for Assessing Trust in Certification Chains. In J.Kochmar, editor, Proceedings of the Network and Distributed Systems Security (NDSS'99) Symposium, The Internet Society, 1999.
13. A. Jøsang: A Logic for Uncertain Probabilities. International Journal of Uncertainty, Fuzziness and Knowledge-Based Systems. 9(3), pp.279-311, June 2001.
14. Yao-Hua Tan, Thoen, W.: Toward a generic model of trust for electronic commerce. International Journal of Electronic Commerce vol.5, no.2, p.61-74.
15. Jaehong Park, Ravi Sandhu: Towards usage control models: beyond traditional access control. Proceedings of the seventh ACM symposium on Access control models and technologies, Monterey, California, USA, 2002.
16. Zheng Yan, Piotr Cofta: Methodology to Bridge Different Domains of Trust in Mobile Communications. The First International Conference on Trust Management (iTrust2003), Crete, Greece, May 2003.
17. A. Jøsang, N. Tran: Trust Management for E-Commerce. In proceedings Virtual Banking 2000. DSTC university report, 2003.
18. Matt Blaze, John Ioannidis, Angelos D. Keromytis: Experience with the KeyNote Trust Management System: Applications and Future Directions. In Proceedings of the First International Conference of Trust Management (iTrust 2003), Crete, Greece, May 2003.
19. Tyrone Grandison, Morris Sloman: Trust Management Tools for Internet Applications. In Proceedings of the First International Conference of Trust Management (iTrust 2003), Crete, Greece, May 2003.
20. Felten, E.W.: Understanding trusted computing: will its benefits outweigh its drawbacks? IEEE Security & Privacy (May-June 2003) vol.1, no.3, p.60-2.

Enabling Trust-Awareness in Naming Services[*]

Nicola Mezzetti

Dept. of Computer Science, University of Bologna
7, Mura Anteo Zamboni
40127 Bologna, Italy
nicola.mezzetti@cs.unibo.it
http://www.cs.unibo.it/~mezzettn

Abstract. In a distributed system entities perform their respective activities by consuming or providing each other services. For the entities deployed in a global computing scenario it is important to be aware of the trustworthiness of each other. Trust-awareness enables entities to decide either which service provider to refer to or whether to accept a service request from a client; additionally, trust degrees enable entities to negotiate which security measures to employ for interacting with each other.

This paper describes TAw, an implementation of the social reputation model described in [11,12]; TAw is a peer-to-peer architecture designed to maintain the notion of reputation in a global computing environment and integrate existing naming technologies. A TAw peer is transparently interposed between a client application and the naming service. TAw peers proactively gossip with each other exchanging trust information; the gossiping technique allows the whole system to scalably and flexibly maintain trust information in a human-like manner.

1 Introduction

In a global network, entities (e.g., service consumers and producers) are deployed and interact with each other so as to complete their respective tasks. For both service consumers and producers, trust plays a crucial role; currently, service consumers and producers interact with each other without having any idea as to the other's trustworthiness. This lack of information makes service consumers and providers distrust the wide-area deployment of services in a manner that depends on the nature of such services.

When reading the literature on reputation modeling [1–4, 6, 8, 14, 15], it is clear that current technologies do not provide any general-purpose solution for transparently managing reputation and trust; additionally, the Openprivacy framework [13] requires a specific distributed object middleware to be employed, and the model in [5] does not currently model trust issues which, to our opinion, have to be considered.

---

[*] This work has been partially supported by the European FP5 RTD project TAPAS (IST-2001-34069) and by the base project "WebMiNDS" under the FIRB program of the Italian Ministry of Education, University and Research.

S. Katsikas, J. Lopez, and G. Pernul (Eds.): TrustBus 2004, LNCS 3184, pp. 20–29, 2004.

Currently, enterprise application developers still have to code into their applications all the logic needed to support trust-aware decisions. In order for a common and scalable trust infrastructure to be designed and deployed in a large-scale environment, a common trust semantics is necessary; starting from the social reputation model developed in [11, 12], in this paper we employ that model in designing TAw, a peer-to-peer middleware that enables any existing naming service with a notion of trustwothiness.

TAw has not been designed to play any active role in managing computer security, it only provides every entity in the system with information about other entities dependability; however, TAw services can be exploited by any consumer or producer to meet a better degree of dependability when dealing with other entities in the system. TAw can be employed in a variety of scenarios; for instance, it can be employed for maintaining information pertaining the reliability of a service's replicas in a cluster as well as for triggering security mechanisms in B2B interactions (i.e., based on the trust degree each part places on the other's dependability, different security mechanisms can be agreed and exploited by both of the parties so as to prevent one's illegitimate behaviour producing the lower most-reasonable overhead). Due to the adoption of the peer-to-peer design principle and the epidemic dissemination model (also called gossiping) [7, 10], employed for supporting information propagation, TAw is expected to provide service consumers and producers with a scalable and flexible trust-awareness service that also enables an high degree of interoperability.

This paper is structured as follows. Section 2 describes the design of a distributed peer-to-peer architecture that implements the aforementioned trust semantics. Section 3 examines related research contributions. Finally, Sec. 4 concludes this work.

1.1   Trust, Trustworthiness and Reputation

In this paper we make intensive use of terms such as trust, trustworthiness and reputation; we adopt the definitions from [12] since we find them to be appropriate for the purpose of this work. First, we define a principal to be an entity that can be granted access or affect access control decisions; the set of all principal will be referred to as $\mathcal{P}$. A principal can consume or produce more than one interface; thus, it can be trusted within more than one context. Second, we say Alice trusts Bob within a given context if Alice expects Bob to exhibit a dependable behaviour when acting within that context; thus, trust is a measure of how much reliance a trustor (e.g., Alice) can justifiably place on the dependability of a trustee (e.g., Bob) behaviour within a specific context. Third, we say that an entity is trustworthy, within a given context, if it actually justifies reliance on the dependability of its behaviour within that context; thus, we define trustworthiness to be a private and secret property of any entity and, therefore, neither known to other entities nor provable. Finally, we define reputation within a specific context to be the subjective perception of trustworthiness that is built from a given, possibly partial, amount of information that describe the behaviour that a specific entity exhibited in the past within the specified context.

1.2   A Reputation's Metric and Model

In this paper we adopt the trust model described in [12]; here, trust is defined as in (1), where $\mathcal{P}$ is the set of principals, $\varPhi$ the set of contexts, and τ is time.

$$\mathcal{T} : \mathcal{P} \times \mathcal{P} \times \varPhi \times \tau \longrightarrow [0,1] \tag{1}$$

Trust evolves according to time and events (e.g., an interaction between two principals); without any event happening, the owned information become obsolete and, as a consequence, trust decays. However, on an event occurrence, trust adapts so as to reflect both the aging of the previously achieved information and the trust degree associated with the occurred event, as in (2) where is defined the direct trust between a trustor α and a trustee β; here, the trust stability parameter, represented with the notation ω, indicates how much the result of a new interaction affects a given trust degree. In principle, the trust stability should depend on how much the fresh trust value differs from the expected one and on whether that difference is positive or negative: as much that difference is higher, a positive one will be discounted while a negative one will be counted.

$$\mathcal{T}(\alpha,\beta,\phi,t') \;=\; \omega(tv)\,\mathcal{T}(\alpha,\beta,\phi,t) \cdot \eta(\phi)^{t'-t} + (1-\omega(tv))\,tv \tag{2}$$

The indirect trust degree (3) is defined to be the average trust-degree that a set $\varGamma$ of known principals, namely recommendors, associate with the trustee (within a given context at a specific time). Evaluating the trustworthiness of a principal within the context $J(\phi)$ means evaluating its trustworthiness in providing recommendations within context ϕ.

$$\mathcal{I}(\alpha,\beta,\phi,t) = \frac{\sum_{\gamma \in \varGamma} \mathcal{T}(\alpha,\gamma,J(\phi),t)\,\mathcal{R}(\gamma,\beta,\phi,t)}{\sum_{\gamma \in \varGamma} \mathcal{T}(\alpha,\gamma,J(\phi),t)} \tag{3}$$

Finally, reputation, $\mathcal{R}(\alpha,\beta,\phi,t)$, is defined as a linear combination in $[0,1]$ of direct trust and indirect trust; it describes the trustworthiness that a trustor α associates with a trustee β within context ϕ at time t. In (4), ψ is a real parameter in $[0,1]$ that indicates the subjective weight a specific principal assigns to direct trust with respect to indirect trust; it is individually decided by each principal.

$$\mathcal{R}(\alpha,\beta,\phi,t) = \psi\,\mathcal{T}(\alpha,\beta,\phi,t) + (1-\psi)\,\mathcal{I}(\alpha,\beta,\phi,t) \tag{4}$$

Let any two principals carry out an interaction; after that interaction, each of them can associates a trust value with the other principal, according to his behaviour during that interaction. A new trust value does not only contribute to compute the direct trust between a trustor and a trustee; it is also used for computing the direct trust between the trustor and the recommendors, within the context of providing recommendations. Basically, the less the recommendation differs from the direct trust the trustor associates with the specific trustee, the better reputation will be associated with that recommendor by the trustor. Thus, the trust value tv_d associated with that recommendor is 1 if the recommendation is equal to the interaction's trust value and will go towards 0 as the difference becomes larger; the new direct trust degree between the trustor and the recommendor will be computed according to (2) and tv_d.

2   The TAw Architecture

TAw enables trust-aware interactions among distributed service consumers and producers, enabling a principal either to refer to the most trustworthy provider in a specific context or to trigger adequate security mechanisms to support a further interaction. It also provides principals with fault tolerance and good performance by maintaining and computing trust information in a highly distributed manner; for this purpose, it implements both a peer-to-peer interaction paradigm and an epidemic information dissemination model (see below). In TAw each principal is provided with a specific TAw peer that locally maintains trust information, computes reputations and propagates them on his behalf. A piece of trust information that is collected by a peer is either originated by the owner principal (after an interaction with another principal), or obtained via the trust propagation protocol described further in this section. To enforce only legitimate principals to access to the TAw services, another entity, namely the Virtual Society Service (VSS), is introduced. Additionally, it manages principals groups based on the services each principal is intended to consume or produce. For the sake of conciseness, it was impossible to insert UML diagrams of the interaction patterns discussed in this section; however, they are included in the extended version of this paper available for downloading at the author's web page.

2.1   TAw Peer

A TAw peer is a proxy client which mediates between a principal and a specific naming service. According to this scheme, the peer provides the associated principal with the `bind` and `lookup` operations; the first allows a service provider to register itself to a naming service so as to make its services available to remote consumers, whereas the latter allows a client of the naming service to obtain the reference to a service provider. The TAw peer also provides a `getTrust` operation that returns the reputation of a specific principal within a given context. Additionally, each peer implements a peer interface that is used by other peers for propagating trust information. When a principal invokes the `lookup` operation on its own peer for a trustee in context ϕ, this looks into its trust repository T for tuples matching that context. Then, for each known possible trustee, it computes the reputation, chooses the most trustworthy and returns its reference. If the peer cannot itself provide information about a trustee in that context, the naming service is queried for a trustee that is added to the trust repository (with direct trust degree set to 0, which also mean completely unknown principals) and returned to the calling principal.

Each peer maintains a data structure, namely the trust repository, that is used to store trust information; basically, it is a collection of tuples $(\alpha, \beta, \phi, t, p)$ where $\alpha \in \mathcal{P}$ is the trustor, $\beta \in \mathcal{P}$ is the trustee, $\phi \in \Phi$ is the context, t is the time to which the trust degree refers and $p \in [0, 1]$ is the trust degree associated with $\mathcal{R}(\alpha, \beta, \phi, t)$. A peer acquires trust information both when the associated principal consumes (provides) services from (to) other principals, and when the trust degrees are collected from the other peers, via the trust propagation protocol (see below). In order to reduce the maximum size of trust repositories, a constant ρ is introduced such that, each time reputation about a specific principal is being computed, if that reputation is less than ρ then data about that principal will be removed from the table.

2.2 Virtual Society Service

So far, we described the TAw peer which is the basic abstraction that implements our trust model; however, no criteria has been given about how such peers connect with each other to form a social network and exchange trust information. The Virtual Society Service (VSS) is responsible for such a task; additionally, for the system to implement a correct and efficient behaviour, it enforces the following constraints:

– So as to reduce the communication overhead due to reputation dissemination, peers have to be grouped according to the interfaces they are intended to produce or consume.
– In order to prevent a principal to illegitimately influence the reputation computed by the other principals in the system, it is important that each principal is not associated with multiple peers in the TAw architecture.

As a principal wants to join the TAw reputation infrastructure, it has to authenticate to the VSS; in turn, the VSS will manage its membership within the social network and will providing it with references to the peers with which it has to exchange reputations.

When a new peer joins the virtual society, the VSS provides it with the knowledge of its neighborhood, a random set of individuals which are intended to produce or consume the same set of service interfaces and towards which that peer will gossip trust information; in this case we say that the size of the neighborhood corresponds to the fan-out of the gossiping protocol. As shown by the experimental results in [10], for the trust propagation to behave efficiently, the fan-out has to depend on the logarithm of the number of principals in the system which consume and provide the same interfaces.

Due to the dynamical nature of B2B scenarios, peers that dynamically join and leave the system may enforce frequent changes in the gossiping fan-out and, thus, may require all the peers in the system to update their neighborhood in order to maintain the gossiping properties. We prevent the peers to require frequent neighborhood updates by enforcing the neighborhood size to be twice the gossiping fan-out, only requiring the peers to be notified of changes in the fan-out.

Further, to improve TAw's resilience against reputation-based attacks (i.e., neighbors that continuously send incorrect trust degrees in order to either get advantages over or disadvantage a specific set of individuals), the VSS periodically updates the neighborhood of every individual; for the same purpose, a similar technique has previously been adopted in [16, 17]. Neighborhood update both enforces an upper bound on the possible duration of a reputation based attacks towards a specific principal.

Essentially, the VSS makes the system to start from scratch, enabling the peers to connect with each other forming a social network; although it may appear like a centralized service, it can be implemented in a distributed and trustworthy manner. For instance, in a scenario in which principals are deployed over different security domains, the VSS can be implemented as a cluster of servers, one for each domain, which have to agree (e.g., by voting) on the decisions about the management of TAw system (e.g., which principals can legitimately access TAw services).

Within TAw, each legitimate principal is uniquely identified by a long-term PK certificate that will be used for providing authenticity of exchanged informations. In order to group TAw principals based on the services they produce or consume, the mentioned long-term certificates are enriched with two attributes, namely `provides` and `consumes`, that respectively indicate the interfaces the associated principal is intended to produce or consume.

2.3   TAw Trust Propagation Protocol

In order to distribute trust information over the system, TAw implements an epidemic information dissemination technique. If such an approach prevents the principals from building a global state about trust information, and thus computing more precise and consistent trustworthiness estimations, on the other hand it significally reduces the communication overhead due both to the construction and the maintenance of a global trust-information status. According to the experimental results that are discussed in [12], after an initial time in which the system principals collect a set of trust information which describes the other principals' behaviour, each principal in the system is expected to request services to the principals which he associates with better reputations. Moreover, such trust information can also be employed for triggering reconfigurations when a currently referred provider loses reputation or a new provider, with a better reputation than the known ones, is discovered.

So as to disseminate trust information over the TAw architecture, each individual periodically sends the newly computed reputations to a random subset of its neighborhood, whose size corresponds to the gossiping fan-out. The receiving neighbors will store these tuples in the respective trust repositories where they will be employed for computing fresh reputations.

The gossiping propagation model gives probabilistic guarantee to spread reputations over all the group in $O(\log n)$ propagations, with n being the number of peers in the group. Never in two successive propagation rounds the same information is propagated. At each round each individual propagates its own opinion about the known principals, according to the social human behaviour; however, it is worth noting that such a gossiping technique allows a fresh trust information to reach all the TAw peers within a number of propagation rounds that depends on the logarithm of group size. The adoption of such an epidemic model for trust information spreading does not provide the guarantee that all the principals compute the same trust degree about a specific principal; however, according to the preliminary results in [12], we expect trust degrees to tend towards the mathematical ideal described in Sec. 1.2, in a manner that depends on the social distance between the trustor and the trustee (i.e., the average number of recommendors which stand between the trustor and the trustee).

2.4   Interoperability

Interoperability is a key issue to address in a wide area system; in this section we outline some design issues that enable TAw (i) to be suitable for extending every existing naming and directory service and (ii) to allow a global virtual society to be built upon several domains which make use of different naming and directory technologies. Both of the mentioned interoperability aspects are addressable by having a common underlying trust semantics; this semantics also allows a common internal representation of trust information. Thus, we address interoperability by dividing the individual in two logical units:

TAw core peer: The core peer implements the trust semantics described in Sec. 1.2. Each peer implements both a generic naming interface and a peer interface. The former enables a principal to query the trust repository for service providers according to the semantics explained in Sec. 2.1. The interface is called "generic" because each specific naming-and-directory service interface can be mapped into a sequence of invocations to this interface. The peer interface implements the trust propagation protocol; this interface is not affected by the underlying naming and directory service. In fact, the common trust semantics and representation allow peers to exchange trust information independently from the interface implemented by the underlying naming service.

Interface layer: The interface layer implements the underlying service specific interface with a set of invocations to the generic naming interface that is provided and implemented by the core peer. In addition, this layer possibly translates the results returned by the invocations of the generic naming interface into a set of invocations on the actual instance of the underlying naming service.

Figure 1 shows two peers are interacting with each other; the first is deployed on JNDI whereas the second is deployed on Corba IR. The common trust semantics enables the TAw Core peers to communicate with each other, exchanging trust information. The peer interface layer enables the respective applications to transparently manage trust information, providing the same interface of the underlying naming and directory services. This design approach addresses the second concern as well; because of the common trust semantics and representation, the core peers are able to exchange trust information with each other directly as long as they are able to identify each principal by resource identifiers that are independent from any specific naming and directory service.

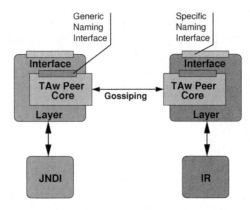

Fig. 1. Interoperability among TAw peers.

3   Related Work

3.1   Trust and Reputation

In [1], Aberer and Despotovic propose a formal model of trust to enforce a trust-worthy document retrieval mechanism in a file sharing peer-to-peer architecture; in this work, global trust information is maintained in a distributed decentralized data structure and computed by querying this data structure and combining the obtained values. In order for one to query that structure, the trustee identity has to be known a priori. In TAw, each principal is maintains a local set of trust information, specific of its tasks, so as to reduce the communication overhead; moreover, the only context information enables a principal to retrieve the most-trustworthy known principal.

In [2–4], Azzedin and Maherswaran develop a socially inspired reputation management framework to be applied to resource management in Grid middleware. By relying on a distributed trust server that computes and returns reputations computed on a global state, this architecture introduces a higher communication and computational overhead than TAw does.

In [5], a precise and well founded model for reputation is presented; however, this model does neither consider trust decay with time nor describe the trustworthiness associated with recommendations and, thus, it does not allow one to isolate bad recommendors.

The SECURE European Project is studying a reputation based system specifically for ubiquitous computing [6]; they make use of knowledge degrees to disambiguate between principals that present the same trust levels and to bootstrap the trust acquisition mechanism in an unknown environment. Although the trust model they develop is very precise, still it is not clear the dynamic behaviour of their trust model.

Both Dragovic et al [8] and the OpenPrivacy project [13] implement reputation management systems; the former for trust-aware selection of application servers, and the latter for disseminating and computing trust information within a specific distributed object middleware. However, no detailed information about the trust architecture and semantics were available to the authors.

In [14, 15], Abdul-Rahman and Hailes present a reputation-based infrastructure to be applied for information retrieval. The trust model they implement is not time dependent; in TAw, we assume time to affect trust degrees.

3.2   Gossiping Dissemination Model

In the gossiping dissemination model [7], entities perform local update operations and then propagate the effects lazily. Entities operate in a manner that maintains the casual order of information dissemination and update over the system, in a way that is similar to how information propagates in a social environment. However, these systems do not support transactional properties, they only offer single operation semantics.

Gossiping is often exploited for designing reliable and fault tolerant probabilistic multicast protocols [9, 10] that rely on a peer-to-peer interaction model, distributing the protocol load among all the peers. Gossiping protocols have been proven efficient [7, 10]; in these works, the experimental results provide probabilistic guarantees of disseminating information among a community's members in $O(\log n)$ protocol rounds (where n is the number of participants to the protocol).

4   Concluding Remarks and Future Work

To the best of our knowledge, TAw represents the first general-purpose middleware architecture for reputation management. TAw transparently manages trustworthiness of physical and logical resources in middleware systems deployed over large scale distributed contexts as well as for managing the trustworthiness of principals that interact or collaborate via application level services in a business-to-business context.

We expect TAw to efficiently and robustly scale in wide area networks. A discrete-event simulator is being implemented so as to evaluate how the adopted trust semantics captures the complex behaviour of social trust and TAw's resilience against the malicious dissemination of false trust information. A TAw prototype is being developed as an extension of Java Naming and Directory Interface (JNDI) to be employed within an open source J2EE application server.

Although our current research firstly aims at evaluating a practical application of our reputation model, further efforts will be spent on relaxing the assumptions made on the VSS and on researching a distributed architecture which implements its functions in a flexible, scalable and secure manner.

Acknowledgements

The author thanks Licia Capra, David Hales, Vance Maverick, Lucian Wischik and the anonymous reviewers for the useful discussions and comments.

References

1. Aberer, K., Despotovic, Z.: Managing Trust in a Peer-2-Peer Information System. In Proceedings of 10th International Conference on Information and Knowledge Management (2001)
2. Azzedin, F., Maheswaran, M.: Integrating Trust into Grid Resource Management Systems. In Proceedings of International Conference on Parallel Processing (2002)
3. Azzedin, F., Maheswaran, M.: Evolving and Managing Trust in Grid Computing Systems. In Proceedings of IEEE Canadian Conference on Electrical and Computer Engineering (2002)
4. Azzedin, F., Maheswaran, M.: Towards Trust-Aware Resource Mnagement in Grid Computing Systems. In Proceedings of First IEEE International Workshop on Security and Grid Computing (2002)
5. Buchegger, S., Le Boudec, J.-Y.: The Effect of Rumor Spreading in Reputation Systems for Mobile Ad-hoc Networks. In Proceedings of Modeling and Optimization in Mobile, Ad Hoc and Wireless Networks (WiOpt'03), Sophia-Antipolis, France, March 2003 (2003)
6. Carbone, M., Nielsen, M., Sassone, V.: A Formal Model for Trust in Dynamic Networks. In Proceedings of International Conference on Software Engineering and Formal Methods (2003)
7. Demers, A., Greene, D., Hauser, C., Irish, W., Larson, J., Shenker, S., Sturgis, H., Swinehart, D., Terry, D.: Epidemic Algorithms for Replicated Database Maintenance. In Proceedings of the 6th Symposium on Principles of Distributed Computing (1987)
8. Dragovic, B., Hand, S., Harris, T., Kotsovinos, E., Twigg, A.: Managing Trust and Reputation in the XenoServer Open Platform. In Proceedings of First International Conference on Trust Management (2003)
9. Eugster, P., Guerraoui, R., Handurukande, S., Kermarrec, A., Kouznetsov, P.: Lightweight Probabilistic Broadcast. In Proceedings of the The International Conference on Dependable Systems and Networks (2001)
10. Kermarrec, A., Massoulié, L., Ganesh, A.: Probabilistic and Reliable Dissemination in Large Scale Systems. IEEE Transactions on Parallel and Distributed Systems $14(2)$ (2003)
11. Mezzetti, N.: Towards a Model for Trust Relationships in Virtual Enterprises. In Proceedings of 14th International Workshop on Database and Expert Systems Applications, pp. 420–424, September 1–5 2003, Prague, Czech Republic, IEEE Computer Society (2003)
12. Mezzetti, N.: A Socially-Inspired Reputation Model. In Proceedings of the 1st European PKI Workshop (EuroPKI 2004), June 25–26, 2004, Samos Island, Greece, Springer-Verlag, Lecture notes in Computer Science vol. 3093, pp. 191–204, (2004)
13. The Openprivacy Project. http://www.openprivacy.org/
14. Abdul-Rahman, A., Hailes, S.: A Distributed Trust Model. In Proceedings of New Security Paradigms Workshop (1997)
15. Abdul-Rahman, A., Hailes, S.: Supporting Trust in Virtual Communities. In Proceedings of 33rd Hawaii International Conference on System Sciences (2000)
16. Zhoh, L., Schneider, F., van Renesse, R.: APSS: Proactive secret sharing in asynchronous systems. Cornell Computer Science Department. Technical report 2002-1877. Submitted to ACM Transactions on Information and System Security (2002)
17. Zhoh, L., Schneider, F., van Renesse, R.: COCA: A secure distributed online certification authority. ACM Transactions on Computer Systems $20(4)$ 329–368 (2002)

Virtual Trust in Distributed Systems

Semir Daskapan, Ana Cristina Costa, Willem G. Vree, and Amr A. Eldin

Faculty of Technology Policy and Management,
Delft University of Technology, PO Box 5015,
2600 GA Delft, The Netherlands
{Semird,Anac,Wimvr}@tbm.tudelft.nl

Abstract. This paper raises two problems of trusted services in distributed organizations. First, on a global scale trust becomes a hard issue to solve for many multinationals since there is no such thing as a global PKI, although many efforts try to overcome this gap. We propose an alternative non-institutionalized trust model to overcome this global trust dilemma. Second, trust prohibits real-time concurrent replication of the trusted service on redundants to increase dependability. We argue why the fuzzy concept trust does not permit replication techniques and propose an indirect approach to trust by indicators.

1 Introduction

The Achilles' heel of security and privacy is trust since trust models plays a vital role in securing business transactions. As the Internet is growing and the type of applications and transactions between systems change, new trust mechanisms emerge with different certificate formats and/or different roots. The difference in certificate formats does not only appear between certification formats of other trust concepts, but also within the same implementation of a standard. Besides the difference in formats a more disturbing problem is the institutionalized approach of many certification models relying on different institutional (governmental) roots. Digital trust becomes a representation of real trust, locally controlled by governments at the root and globally prearranged by international treaties. The world of trust is as such divided in several conglomerates with hierarchical and meshed structures of certification authorities (CA). The consequence is that cross-boundary trust management is usually cleared between settled (almost monopolistic) companies and governmental institutions. The many drawbacks, like complexity of the certification process, technological overhead for achieving trust between institutionally rooted entities, limited coverage due to the limited bilateral agreements, political hurdles and high costs for or no entrance for new independent entrants in the trust service market, frustrate global transactions.

Another problem in the intersecting domain of global business and trust is dependability. Globally distributed organizations like multinationals exploit wide area networks to interconnect their business and have several protected (public) access points. The forefront security bastions of such a large-scale distributed system suffer from different type of failures, like due to denial of service attacks. The security services are therefore replicated on a limited low number of local redundants to resist attacks with a limited effect. An attacker can succeed when he plans repeated attacks from

S. Katsikas, J. Lopez, and G. Pernul (Eds.): TrustBus 2004, LNCS 3184, pp. 30–39, 2004.

different locations by a distributed denial of service attack. Not only is the security service unavailable for a time then, but also after the recovery the trustworthiness or trust authority is harmed. The fuzzy trust is harder to restore in the minds of the clients.

In this paper we will elaborate on the two problems. A better understanding of what trust means would ease the quest for solutions. We will start in the second chapter with describing the meaning of trust in an interpersonal context and slowly make the transition to virtual trust. Here we try to discover how real trust can manifest in the virtual world. In the third chapter we will discuss the trust models with respect to their lack to solve global trust issue and propose an alternative. In the fifth chapter we elaborate on the dependability problem and pose a directive to 'commoditize' trust.

2   Trust: An Interpersonal Perspective

For human and computer entities spread over different places that have to cooperate in order to achieve a valuable aggregated service, an inevitable success factor is trust [1]. Trust is central to human life and is considered to be essential for maintaining cooperation, vital to any exchange, and necessary for even the most routine of everyday interaction. Trust functions can be seen as a catalyst for those interactions. The higher the importance of the exchanged goods, the more critical trust becomes between the negotiating end points. However, trust is not something that can be described easily; it rather depends on the context [2]. As trust is ultimately an interpersonal matter, we can understand trust in the virtual world by looking first in the real world. The question is whether trust though can manifest as an independent object.

A major impetus for research on trust has been the growing evidence of its varied and substantial benefits of trust for teams and organizations [3]. Numerous studies have demonstrated how increases in trust result directly or indirectly in more positive workplace behaviors, attitudes, better team processes and superior levels of performance (see [4]). Considerable efforts have also been made to apply emerging trust theory to a variety of important organizational problems, some being the result of the increase of distrust in systems, institutions, policies and management [5]. Although trust may not be the ultimate solution for all problems, as organizations have moved towards flatter and flexible forms of organized activity, interpersonal dynamics, and trust in particular, have become critical elements in achieving effective collaboration. Perhaps more than ever organizations need to invest in conditions that facilitate trust among members in order to survive and remain effective.

Trust becomes a vital concept when there are significant risks involved in trusting (i.e., vulnerability) and when there is objective uncertainty about future consequences of trusting [2]. In organizations uncertainty and vulnerability arise from different reasons. Consequently, trust has been studied with regard to different respects and has been approached through different perspectives. Because trust is so central to human relations many definitions have been put forward from a variety of perspectives, but to date no general definition has been agreed.

As one-dimensional phenomenon, trust has been conceptualized as either a psychological state or a choice behavior. The *psychological state* point of view defines trust in terms of interrelated cognitive processes and orientations towards beliefs or positive expectations in relation to others. Some definitions apply to contexts where these others are identifiable, such as in [6] "trust is a psychological state comprising the intention to accept vulnerability based upon positive expectations of the intentions or behavior of another". In other definitions trust is presented as a more general attitude or expectancy about other people or about the general social system. Common to these definitions is the reference to states of "vulnerability", "confidence", and "positive expectations". Trust as *a choice behavior* can be seen as the willingness to take risks by acting on the basis of words, actions or decisions of others [7]. In some definitions trust is viewed as a more or less rational decision, motivated primarily by perception of risks, concerning either the probability of successful cooperation or the possibility of transaction cost-reduction. More recent definitions argue the need to conceptualize trust not only as calculative orientation towards risk but also as a social orientation toward other people and societies as a whole [8]. As recent research has demonstrated, one does not only 'think' but also 'feels' trust. Throughout research various behaviors have appeared indicative of trust such as cooperative behaviors including open communication, acceptance of influence, forbearance from opportunism, and lack of monitoring ([9]; [10]; [11]).

In discussing how expectations underlying trust affect subsequent behaviour, several scholars have alluded to the fact that an adequate analysis of trust begins by recognizing its multi-faceted character. Trust is a highly complex phenomenon with distinct cognitive, emotional and behavioural dimensions [12]. People trust by acting as if uncertain future actions of other were certain. This decision is made based on a cognitive process that discriminates others as being trustworthy, untrustworthy or unknown as well as on emotional bonds [12]. Several authors describe trust as a function of different inter-related components, including individual propensities, interpersonal assessments of trustworthiness, and behaviours of cooperation and lack of monitoring. For instance, [10] refers to trust as a psychological state that manifests it self in the behaviours towards others in situations entailing risk. Others [1] explicitly connect positive expectations with cooperation.

More than defining trust in different ways, trust may be composed of different elements, each of a different nature. Individual predispositions, characteristics and intentions of the trustee(s) and situational conditions such the degree of risk can determine both the level and the potential form that trust takes. The relative importance of these factors is determined by the type and course of the relationships where trust occurs.

According to [6] vulnerability and uncertainty arise under conditions of risk and interdependence. Risk is considered to be the probability of loss as perceived by the trusting person(s). When trust is not fulfilled, the trusting party suffers from an unpleasant consequence, which is greater than the gain he would have received [13]. Assessing the risk before trusting involves considering other peoples' motives and intentions and the situational factors that weight the likelihood of the possible positive and negative long-term effects of the trust. Interdependence refers to the extent to which the interests of one person cannot be achieved without relying upon another. According to [14] interdependent relationships vary according to type and depth, and entail distinctively different risks. These differences suggest that in different situations people will look for different attributes in order to trust. For example, in superficial dependence relationships it is necessary to look for partners that have a history of reliable behavior, whereas in situations of deep dependence people will look for additional attributes such as honesty, integrity [14].

Regarding the previous, a conclusion we can draw is that trust is too fuzzy and depends on too many independent social psychological factors to make a simple transition into the virtual world. As we cannot simply define a general method to convert real trust into a virtual (software) object, an option could be to define derived indicators. In the real world derived indicators are for example police uniforms that indicate the profession and as such the services you might expect and rely on. As we cannot simply 'commoditize' trust in the virtual world, we can also build trust models to be able to deal with real trust in the virtual world. These models are explained next.

3 Translating Interpersonal Trust into Virtual Trust

In the virtual world trust is not created for the first time; it is a derivative of trust in the real world. As trust is not something absolute and tangible it is in the virtual world addressed by reference between unknown entities, like x trusts y, because x trusts z and z trusts y. Z functions here as a point of reference (POR). Several trust models exist in which they differ in the way they include this POR. When examining trust models, they can be distinguished according to many dimensions, ranging from technical issues like certification formats and key management to legal issues like international treaty laws for global e-business. *Topology* and *status* of the PORs are chosen here as a solution on an abstract level is looked for. Topology refers to the structure (i.e. degree of decentralization and number of participants) in which all the end-entities interact with each other indirectly via the POR like in a hub-and-spoke system. Social status refers to the degree of social acceptance and authorization consisting of two discrete values: low for institutionalized and high for anarchistic principles.

Table 1. Trust models

		Topology	
		Central	Decentral
	High	1. Central hierarchical	4. Meshed hierarchical
Status	Low	2. Central Peer	3. Decentral peer

The first cell represents the class of trust models, in which trust depends on a single central institutionalized authority. According to the **central hierarchical authority** trust principle, one or more superior entities grant credentials to the computing peers. A typical instance of this class is the public key infrastructure (PKI) [15]. PKI is the process and structure of using digital certificates to authenticate, encrypt and decrypt information that is transmitted over an open network like the Internet. Typical example of an X.509 [16] based PKI model is PEM [17].

In the third cell the POR is also centralized, but in contrast with the first cell it has a low status equal to the peer end-entities. This class relies on the **central peer** trust principle. The POR in this case is just a peer-entity with a special duty, i.e. mediating credentials between all the peers who want to interact with each other. It might as such be responsible for example for key management in Kerberos [18] and Kryp- toKnight [19]. Other examples of such systems are KeyNote and PolicyMaker [20].

The decentralized peer trust principle in the fourth cell the POR has also a low status, but this time not one, but all entities can function as a POR. As each peer chooses it self which other peers to trust as PORs, it relies on peer-to-peer computing principle. Examples are PGP [21] and Poblano [22].

Now hybrid PKI approaches exist in which the hierarchical concept partly is con- figured according this decentralization principle by issuing cross-certificates [23] and bridge certification authorities [24], which tends to the **meshed hierarchical models** of the second cell. The second cell consists of models representing trust by decentral- ized PORs with a high status. Some initiatives and tests have been carried out with bridge certification authorities (BCA), trust lists [25] and cross certification authori- ties (CCA) [23]. In a BCA model a new central interconnecting CA is set up to func- tion as an institutional bridge between CAs that do not necessarily trust each other but though trust the BCA. The Bridge CA essentially acts as a non-hierarchical facilitator or introducer of one organization or enterprise to another. Cross-certification is the act of one CA issuing a certificate to another CA. The trust lists model is actually not a general solution as it is an informal linkage of CAs by the peers themselves. The peers subscribe to and maintain a list of the many CAs they trust. As each is identi- fied by a hash of the public key certificate of the subject CA, they can function as a verification list for the browser.

4   Global Distrust

Here we will discuss the shortcomings of the models with respect to global trust and propose a hybrid alternative.

4.1   Discussion

Central Hierarchical Authority. Although the certification chain is unidirectional and rather simple it is unpractical, because of some assumptions. It assumes that there is globally one superior certification authority (CA) that can bind al the lower authori- ties. This implicates that all end-entities (companies, individuals) are also globally related via an institutional tree. Because of this singular POR the hierarchy tree can be very long, causing intensive maintenance of the CA–lists of the end-entities. Be- cause of this tree chaining the structure becomes more critical the higher in the tree. When keys of a high authority are confiscated, all the lower entities will suffer. Also private key infrastructures are thinkable to be modeled in this way, but suffer from the same. Despite of those drawbacks this model represents highly trusted services in theory, when a real binding between identity and the keys is guaranteed (registration POR). As even no consensus can be reached about a supranational authority in the real world (UN is just administrative), a supranational POR is not likely to exist in the near future. For overcoming global distrust and interoperability this model works well in theory, but unfortunately it will remain an utopia.

Central Peer. It suffers from the same drawback that all entities can rely on a single POR. Such a global POR does not exist and if it exists it would become too critical. When there is a binding between the real identity and the assigned keys, after a real registration, this model works enough for a limited amount of entities. Like the models of cell 1, this one cannot overcome the problems of global interoperability and distrust.

Decentralized Peer. As this is an easy anarchistic and simple model and more in the line of the Internet thought, it can overcome global distrust and interoperability. It is however not to be recommended for high value transactions, as it is considered the least reliable. As trust is determined by a group of peers, each as an unofficial POR as a real binding between identity and key is unavailable, this group can fake the truth.

Meshed Hierarchical. Although, meshed models offer more possibilities to overcome the global distrust there are some limitations. First, BCA and CCA are still the domain of the real institutionalized world, which is rejected by the average Internet user. Secondly, verification paths become now multidirectional require complex algorithms and large storage list of PORs at the client side. Thirdly, setting up a CCA requires a lot of management overhead per bilateral agreement about social, legal, technical and economical issues. Those inter-hierarchy models serve well in small numbers of CA (n), but not with large numbers with n(n-1) links for all countries. Regional agreements and CCAs between the developed countries are more likely. Fourthly, a BCA is logically a step towards a supranational POR and therefore suffers at the end from the same drawbacks as the models in the first cell.

4.2 The Proposal: Trust Service Broker

Regarding the above models some key issues are evident that make global trust a hard problem. Despite the described drawbacks of the trust models, current researchers accept or ignore the mentioned drawbacks and expect a formal (institutionalized) solution for global trust and interoperability to be found with models of the fourth cell [26]. We rather derive a hybrid model that adopts the positive elements from the models without going into the nasty administrative miseries. In this section a non-institutionalized trust service broker (TSB) is therefore proposed to overcome the described problems. The credibility of this TSB is not based on delegation and mandating by other trust brokers (CA's), but rather on derivation, so that the TSB does not need an explicit approval from the CA's. The TSB functions then as a mediator in situations where end-entities cannot trust each other directly neither can they agree on one CA nor on a bridge or cross certificate.

The TSB provides interoperability by matching different certificates either by using the flexible extensions of the current standards (like in PKIX) or by providing an interface for non-standard certificates to an own homogeneous format. Moreover it provides a bridge between the unlinked CA's, without drowning in the trust chain of certification authorities. The TSB would then not only be subjected to the higher institutional boundaries, but also lose its impartial role, which is of crucial importance on the anarchistic Internet. Ironically however, it derives its credibility from CAs and from the Internet community. The TSB owes after all multiple certificates from the different CAs and it is chained in web of trust of the individual peers. The trust broker architecture is not only of importance for e-business transactions between global organizations with heterogeneous CAs, but also for trust developments in small devices as the TSB relieves many trust related tasks. It partly relies on the existing certification standards as it makes use of the currently available flexible extensions, but it also issues an own format converter for non-standard certificates. However it does not submit itself to any institution, respecting the anarchy of the Internet. Although the TSB model reaches some complexity, it is deployable as a web service. This web service mediates not only trust between the different models, but also takes care of the interoperability problem as it portals trust assertions.

5 Fault Tolerant Trusted Services

As we have explained in the introduction many organizations suffer from failures of their forefront security systems due to several reasons, among them denial of service attacks. It is then important to have a cluster of instant up-to-date redundant systems to too increase dependability [27,28,29]. Redundancy means that (in parallel or serial) similar systems are ready to replace the main system. Services are therefore frequently replicated on the redundants and recovered after a failure. However, deploying replicated servers has a limited scalability, as it requires costly dedicated hardware. As such its effectiveness to resist failures is also limited to the fixed number of replicas - 1. It is also considered inefficient, as most of the time the redundant is hibernating.

Especially, due to the possibility of multiple sequential attacks it is important not to be limited in the number of redundants and preferably have infinite redundant resources. Only then it is possible to achieve perpetual availability of security servers and to resist numerous multiple attacks. A well-known technique to decrease inefficiency and to increase effectiveness is resource-sharing. Resource sharing techniques enable multiple servers with different purposes and superfluous capacity to share each other's resources and as such gain economies of scale. The collaborating servers are then able to host data and/or execute programs on other hosts to achieve fault tolerance [30]. Assuming that a multinational owes n different servers, he can resist n-1 attacks, without having to invest in n-1 redundants for each server. If n is very large it approaches perpetual availability as the time between the first attack and the last attack is assumed sufficient enough to recover the first server. As such multiple attacks could be resisted. To achieve a very large number all servers of a company or multiple companies (joint ventures, mergers, etc) have to be included. However, concurrent real time replication of the service with remote redundants via asynchronous open networks like the Internet remains an utopia due to some problems, like Byzantine failures. The main concern lies however in the fact that replicating the data (content) does not implicate that the clients also trust the succeeding redundant server.

The main reason lies in the fact that 'trust' cannot simply be treated as any software object that can be exchanged between the remote computers when failures occur [31]. Due to the fuzziness of trust and the impossibility to 'commoditize' trust, as we have described in the second section, trust does not permit replication techniques. As such we proposed to use trust indicators. Like in the real world unique distinctive personalized indicators should be agreed on. The fact that we rely on a man with a police uniform is because we agreed on the color, type and so on of that uniform. In the virtual world we should as such define a unique distinctive personalized indicator. In cryptography it is common to use secrets for different techniques. As such we should define a unique distinctive personalized secret that will represent the trustworthiness of one entity in an intercourse between two entities. As such we pose the next agreement: If CEx trusts CEy this trust assertion can be 'commoditized' when CEx shares his unique, personalized and distinctive secret with CEy. We might append to this assertion also expected services, like we have with the policeman in uniform. We might agree on the fact that who knows the secret s is implicitly mandated to perform some tasks on the behalf of the originator (owner). A task could be in our case to mediate security services. Representing trust as a secret enables us thus to replicate the secret and as such, considering the made agreements about the holder, the trust authority.

6 Conclusion and Future Work

In this paper we have raised two problems concerning dependable trust. First we explained how the problem of global distrust might frustrate global transactions. We have depicted the importance of interpersonal trust that precedes virtual (technical) trust between the remote entities. Trust models have been presented and their limitations to clear global distrust have been discussed. A non-institutionalized trust service broker as an alternative to the formal approaches has been proposed. This model does not, in contrast with the previous, require formal hierarchical bindings with certification authorities. It reuses the granted certificates from the different local CA's as a user to set up a trust broker via a web service in which middleware will take care of matching the different formats from the several CA's. Although it is technically achievable, we expect that other type of problems might rise. Due to decreasing market share and thus their (often) monopoly the existing CA's mighty try to forbid (legally) their users to exploit the certificates for commercial reuse. In future work we aim at implementing this (web)service with a limited number of CA's.

The second problem we raised was the frustrating role of trust in replicating trusted security servers to achieve low cost dependability by means of resource sharing techniques. The fuzziness of trust does not permit replication techniques. As such multinational organizations have to invest more in dedicated servers and achieve relatively less dependability due to limited budgets. We proposed to use secrets to frame the fuzzy concept of trust as a software object. In future work we intend to develop specific replication schemes for trust in asynchronous environments.

References

1. Gambetta, D. (Ed.): Trust: Making and breaking cooperative relations. Oxford, UK: Basil Blackwell (1988)
2. Morris, J.H., Moberg, D.J.: Work organizations as contexts for trust and betrayal. In: R. Theodore Sarbin, Ralph M. Carney, Carson Eoyang (Eds.): Citizen espionage: Studies in trust and betrayal, US. Praeger Publishers/Greenwood Publishing Group (1994) 163-187
3. Kramer, R.M.: Trust and Distrust in Organizations: Emerging Perspectives, Enduring Questions. Annual Review of Psychology, Vol. 50. (1999) 569-598
4. Dirks, K.T., Ferrin D.L.: The role of Trust in Organizational Settings. Organization Science, Vol. 12(4). (2001) 450-467
5. Shaw, R. B.: Trust in the balance: building successful organizations on results, integrity, and concern. San Francisco, Jossey-Bass (1997)
6. Rousseau, M.T., Stikin, S.B., Burt, S.B, Camerer, C.: Not so different after all: a cross-discipline view of trust. Academy of Management Review, Vol. 23. (1998) 393-404
7. Zand, D.E.: Trust and managerial problem solving. Administrative Science Quarterly, Vol. 17, (1972) 229-239
8. Cummings, L.L., Bromiley, P.: The Organizational Trust Inventory (OTI): Development and validation, Trust in organizations. Frontiers of theory and research (1996)
9. Smith, J.B., Barclay, W.B.: The effects of organizational differences and trust on the effectiveness of selling partner relationships. Journal of Marketing ,Vol.61, (1997) 3-21
10. Costa, A.C., Roe, R.A., Taillieu, T.: Trust within teams: the relation with performance effectiveness. European Journal of Work and Organisational Psychology, Vol. 10(3), (2001) 225-244
11. Costa, A.C.: Work team trust and effectiveness. Personnel Review, Vol.32(5), (2003) 605-622
12. Lewis, J.D., Weigert, A.: Trust as a social reality. Social Forces, Vol.63, (1985) 967-985.
13. Giffin, K., Patton, B.R.: Personal Trust in Human Interaction. Basic Readings in Interpersonal Communication, New York, Harper & Row (1971)
14. Sheppard B.H., Sherman, D.M.: The grammars of trust: A model and general implications. Academy of Management Review, Vol. 23, (1998) 422-437
15. Adams, C., Lloyd, S., Understanding PKI: Concepts, Standards, and Deployment Considerations. Second Ed. Addison-Wesley (2002)
16. Housley, R., Ford, W., Polk, W., Solo, D.: Internet X.509 Public Key Infrastructure-Certificate and CRL Profile. IETF RFC 2459 (January 1999)
17. Kent, S. T. RFC-1422 Privacy Enhancement for Internet Electronic Mail: PartII: Certificate-Based Key Management. Network Working Group (February 1993)
18. Steiner, J.G. , Neuman, B.C., Schiller, J.I.: Kerberos: An Authentication Service for Open Network Systems. Usenix Conference Proc., Dallas (1988) 191-202
19. Bird, R., Gopal, I., Herzberg, A., Janson, P., Kutten, S., Molva, R., Yung, M.: The KryptoKnight Family of Light-Weight Protocols for Authentication and Key Distribution. IEEE/ACM Transactions on Networking. Vol 3(1), (February 1995) 31-41

20. Blaze, M., Feigenbaum, J., Ioannidis, J., Keromytis, A.D.: The Role of Trust Management in Distributed Systems Security. In Secure Internet Programming, J.Vitek, C. Jensen, Ed., Springer-Verlag (1999) 185-210
21. Zimmermann, P.: PGP User's Guide. MIT Press, Cambridge, USA (1994)
22. Chen, R.:Poblano- A Distributed Trust Model for Peer-to-Peer Networks. Sun (2002)
23. Elley, Y., Anderson, A., Hanna, S., Mullan, S., Perlman, R., Proctor S: Building Certification Paths: Forward vs. Reverse. NDSS Symposium, (2001)
24. A&N Associates, Phase II Bridge Certification Authority Interoperability Demonstration Final Report. National Security Agency (2001)
25. Freeman Trevor: Certificate Trust List. Microsoft, Unpublished (1999)
26. Lee, S-L, Lee, J.I, Lee, H-S, Global PKI Interoperability; Korean Endeavour. proc. of the first International Workshop for Asian PKI, Korea (2001)
27. Barbour, A.E., Wojcik, A.S.: A General Constructive Approach to Fault-Tolerant Design Using Redundancy. IEEE Transactions on Computers, Vol. 38(1), (1989) 15-29
28. Hiltunen, M.A., Schlichting, R. D., Ugarte, C. A.: Building Survivable Services Using Redundancy and Adaptation. IEEE Transactions on Computers, vol. 52(2), (2003) 181-194
29. Dutertre, B., Crettaz, V., Stavridou, V.: Intrusion-Tolerant Enclaves, IEEE Symposium on Security and Privacy. California, (2002) 216-226
30. Daskapan, S., Vree, W.G.: Self-organizing trust principle for survivable systems. Proc. of the IASTED/ACI, Tokyo, (2002) 7-12
31. Daskapan, S., Verbraeck, A., Vree, W.G.: The merge of computing paradigms. 5th International Conf. on computer and information technology, Dhaka (2002) 553-558

Modelling Trust Relationships
in Distributed Environments

Weiliang Zhao[1], Vijay Varadharajan[1,2], and George Bryan[1]

[1] Centre for Advanced Systems Engineering
University of Western Sydney
Locked Bag 1797
Penrith South DC, NSW 1797, Australia
{wzhao,g.bryan}@cit.uws.edu.au
[2] Department of Computing
Macquarie University
NSW 2109, Australia
vijay@ics.mq.edu.au

Abstract. Trust management and trustworthy computing are becoming increasingly significant at present. Over the recent years there have been several research works that have addressed the issue of trust management in distributed systems. However a clear and comprehensive definition that can be used to capture a range of commonly understood notions of trust is still lacking. In this paper, we give a formal definition of trust relationship with a strict mathematical structure that can not only reflect many of the commonly used extreme notions of trust but also provides a taxonomy framework where a range of useful trust relationships can be expressed and compared. Then we show how the proposed structure can be used to analyze both commonly used and some unique trust notions that arise in distributed environments. This proposed trust structure is currently being used in the development of the overall methodology of life cycle of trust relationships in distributed information systems.

1 Introduction

The concept of trust has been used and studied in social science for a long time [1, 2]. Trust was originally used in human and social issues in day-life relationships, laws, regulations and policies. In the computing world, the trust was originally used in the context of trusted computing such as trusted system, trusted hardware and trusted software [3]. Recently, trust has been used in the context of trust management in distributed computing [4–7]. When the Internet and web technologies are broadly and increasingly used in daily life for electronic commerce, trust becomes a very hot topic [8,9]. The trust between customers and e-vendors includes not only technical aspects but also social aspects. In this paper, we will provide our definition of trust relationship. Most of the issues relating to social aspects of trust is beyond the scope of this paper, but we hope that our general definition of trust relationship can cover both aspects. The trust relationships of involved entities or computing components in distributed computing are our major concern.

S. Katsikas, J. Lopez, and G. Pernul (Eds.): TrustBus 2004, LNCS 3184, pp. 40–49, 2004.

XML-based Web Services technologies have been rapidly evolving since 1999. Web Services technologies address the challenges of distributed computing and B2B integration. There are huge number of service oriented applications on the Internet and they are coupled loosely. Web Services technologies target at loosely-coupled, language-neutral and platform-independent way of linking applications for business process automation within organizations, across enterprizes, and across the Internet. There is no centralized control and the users are not all predetermined. Normally, the computing components involved in a e-service can belong to different security domains and there is no common trusted authority for the involved entities. How to define/model trust relationships between computing components is an important and challenging issue in the design of web services. The draft of WS-Trust was proposed in 2002 [10]. Unfortunately, the current WS-Trust only touches the issue of trusted message exchange and has not provided more details for dealing with trust relationships.

Many researchers have recognized the trust management as a distinct and important component of security in distributed systems. Several automated trust management systems have been proposed such as PolicyMaker[4], KeyNote[5, 6], and REFEREE [7]. In all these trust management systems, trust and its related concepts are assumed in a specific way relating to the specific topics. There is no consensus on the definition of trust. In PolicyMaker and KeyNote, M. Blaze *et al* provided clear definition of trust management system and there are many clues to understand what is trust but they did not comment on the concept of trust directly. In REFEREE, Y. H. Chu *et al* described trust as "to trust is to undertake a potentially dangerous operation knowing that it is potentially dangerous". Tyrone *et al* [11] gave a definition of trust as "the firm belief in the competence of an entity to act dependably, securely, and reliably within a specified context". Y. H. Chu *et al* and Tyrone *et al* talked about trust in a kind of general terms, however trust is difficult to express without a strict mathematical structure. In Policy-Maker, KeyNote and REFEREE, a new trust management layer has been successfully built but the concept of trust and how to model trust has not been considered carefully. It is necessary to have a solid understanding of the concept of trust relationship and to develop a powerful set of tools to model the trust relationships for trust management in distributed information systems.

The starting point of this research is trust in the context of distributed environments. Here we have not separated the traditional distributed computing and the Web Services. Web Services are included when we talk about distributed computing for the consideration of trust issues.

The rest of the paper is structured as follows. In section 2, we give the definition of trust relationship and discuss some extreme cases. In section 3, we give a series of definitions, propositions and operations about trust relationships. The mathematical properties of trust relationships are embedded in these definitions, propositions and operations. In section 4, we provide two scenario examples of trust relationships and we give some analysis of trust relationships using the definitions, propositions and operations in section 3. In section 5, we provide concluding remarks.

2   Definition of Trust Relationship

Most of the researchers agree that a trust relationship is the relationship between a set of trusters and a set of trustees in a specified context, but it is not clear enough, especially when it is used in the computing world. There is a need to convert the generally used terms into strict mathematical structure in algorithms of real systems. In this paper, we will provide our definition of trust relationship with a strict mathematical structure.

In trust management of distributed information systems, we believe that the definition of trust should have the following characteristics:

- The definition of trust is unique and can be used for different computing purposes.
- The definition of trust has strong expressive power and makes the system as simple as possible.
- The definition of trust has a strict mathematical structure.
- The definition of trust provides the solid foundation for discussing the properties of trust relationships.
- The definition of trust follows hard security mechanisms.

Hard security assumes complete certainty and it allows complete access or no access at all. Here we only model the static status of trust in distributed environments.

We believe that it is not enough to understand trust as a simple bilateral relation between trusters and trustees. The whole syntax of trust relationship should be "under a set of specified conditions, a set of trusters trust that a set of trustees have a set of specified properties (the set of trustees will/can perform a set of actions or have a set of attributes)". The definition is expressed as follows:

Definition 1 *A trust relationship is a four-tuple $T = < R, E, C, P >$ where:*

- *R is the set of trusters. It contains all the involved trusters. It can not be empty.*
- *E is the set of trustees. It contains all the involved trustees. It can not be empty.*
- *C is the set of conditions. It contains all conditions (requirements) for the current trust relationship. Normally, trust relationship has some specified conditions. If there is no condition, the condition set is empty.*
- *P is the set of properties. The property set describes the actions or attributes of the trustees. It can not be empty. The property set can be divided into two sub sets:*
  - *Action set: the set of actions what trusters trust that trustees will/can perform.*
  - *Attribute set: the set of attributes what trusters trust that trustees have.*

Anywhere, a trust relationship must be used with full syntax(four-tuple $< R, E, C, P >$. Trust relationship T means that under the condition set C, truster set R trust that trustee set E have property set P. There are some extreme cases of the trust relationship when some involved sets included nothing(empty set) or anything(whole set of possible entities). The extreme cases have special meanings and are crucial in the understanding of the definition of trust relationship. These extreme cases will play important roles in the real world. The followings are the five extreme cases of trust relationship:

1. R is ANY. Truster set includes all possible entities. All possible entities trust that the set of trustees E have the set of properties P under the set of conditions C.

2. E is ANY. Trustee set includes all possible entities. All possible entities can be trusted to have the set of properties P by the set of trusters R under the set of conditions C.

3. C is $EMPTY$. There is no condition in the trust relationship. The set of trusters R trust that the set of trustees E have the set of properties P without any condition.

4. P is ANY. The property of the trustee can be anything. The set of trusters R trust that the set of trustees E have all possible properties under the set of conditions C.

5. C is $EMPTY$ and P is ANY. The set of trusters R trust that the set of trustees E have all possible properties without any condition. This case happens when the set of trusters R trust the set of trustees E by default.

When the full syntax of the trust relationship is not used, trust relationship is easily misunderstood. Normally, there are many implicit assumptions and some parts of full syntax are usually omitted. When we analyze the true meaning of a trust relationship, the full syntax must be recovered. Our definition of the trust relationship has strict mathematical structure with the full syntax in any case. There is no confusion when the full syntax trust relationship is used in any information system.

It is straightforward to use the set of conditions in the definition of trust relationship. When a trust relationship is used, trusters, trustees and properties are normally involved individually. The trust relationship can always be evaluated based on one truster, one trustee and one property. In our definition of trust relationship, the trusters, trustees and properties turn up as sets are based on the following concerns (1) The concept of security domain is broadly used and related technologies are quite mature. The role-based access control is broadly used and well understood by programmers and business people. When a set of trusters, a set of trustees and a set of properties are used in the definition of trust relationship, the similar ideas in security domain and role-based access control can be employed easily. It is convenient to define some abstraction characteristics based on a group of trusters, a group of trustees and a group of properties. We hope that a set of trusters, a set of trustees and a set of properties in the definition of the trust relationship have better abstraction and it is easier to use the definition. (2) The set theory can provide formal mathematical notion and handy tools to discuss the relationships of sets. (3) An individual truster (or trustee, or property) is a special case of the set of trusters (or trustees, or properties). (4) It is convenient to discuss special cases of trust relationship when truster (or trustee, or property) is anyone.

3   Mathematical Properties of Trust Relationships

In this paper, we will discuss the mathematical properties of trust relationship based on our strict definition of trust relationship. The trust relationship has a full syntax with truster set, trustee set, condition set and property set. It is incorrect to only talk about the trust relationship between trusters and trustees without mention of the condition set and property set. The discussions of properties of trust relationship should be based on the full syntax of trust relationship in its definition. In the following part of this section, we will give some definitions, propositions and operations related to trust relationships. The mathematical properties of trust relationships are embedded in these definitions, propositions and operations. These mathematical properties focus on some relations of trust relationships and they will be used as tools in the analysis and design of trust relationships in real systems.

From the nature of trust relationship and its mathematical structure, some new trust relationships can be derived based on the existing trust relationships. In the follows, we will define the operations of using two existing trust relationships to generate a new trust relationship under specific constraints and operations of decomposing one existing trust relationship into two new trust relationships under specific constraints.

Operation 1 *Let* $T_1 = (R_1, E_1, C_1, P_1)$ *and* $T_2 = (R_2, E_2, C_2, P_2)$. *There is a set* $T = (R_1 \cap R_2, E_1 \cap E_2, C_1 \cup C_2, P_1 \cup P_2)$. *If* $R_1 \cap R_2 = \emptyset$ *or* $E_1 \cap E_2 = \emptyset$, $T = \emptyset$.

If $R_1 = R_2$ and $E_1 = E_2$, the operation becomes:

Operation 1A *Let* $T_1 = (R, E, C_1, P_1)$ *and* $T_2 = (R, E, C_2, P_2)$. *There is a set* $T = (R, E, C_1 \cup C_2, P_1 \cup P_2)$.

If $R_1 = R_2$, $E_1 = E_2$ and $C_1 = C_2$, the operation becomes:

Operation 1B *Let* $T_1 = (R, E, C, P_1)$ *and* $T_2 = (R, E, C, P_2)$. *Then there is a set* $T = (R, E, C, P_1 \cup P_2)$.

Operation 2 *Let* $T_1 = (R_1, E_1, C, P)$ *and* $T_2 = (R_2, E_2, C, P)$. *There is a set* $T = (R_1 \cup R_2, E_1 \cap E_2, C, P)$.

If $E_1 = E_2$, the operation becomes:

Operation 2A *Let* $T_1 = (R_1, E, C, P)$ *and* $T_2 = (R_2, E, C, P)$. *There is a set* $T = (R_1 \cup R_2, E, C, P)$.

Operation 3 *Let* $T_1 = (R_1, E_1, C, P)$ *and* $T_2 = (R_2, E_2, C, P)$. *There is a set* $T = (R_1 \cap R_2, E_1 \cup E_2, C, P)$.

If $R_1 = R_2$, the operation becomes:

Operation 3A *Let* $T_1 = (R, E_1, C, P)$ *and* $T_2 = (R, E_2, C, P)$. *There is a set* $T = (R, E_1 \cup E_2, C, P)$.

Operation 4 *Let* $T = <R, E, C, P>$. *If there are* R_1, R_2 *and* $R = R_1 \cup R_2$, *then there are trust relationships* $T_1 = <R_1, E, C, P>$ *and* $T_2 = <R_2, E, C, P>$.

Operation 5 *Let* $T = <R, E, C, P>$. *If there are* E_1, E_2 *and* $E = E_1 \cup E_2$, *then there are trust relationships* $T_1 = <R, E_1, C, P>$ *and* $T_2 = <R, E_2, C, P>$.

Operation 6 *Let* $T = <R, E, C, P>$. *If there are* P_1, P_2 *and* $P = P_1 \cup P_2$, *then there are trust relationships* $T_1 = <R, E, C, P_1>$ *and* $T_2 = <R, E, C, P_2>$.

This operation has the following special case:

Operation 6A *Let* $T =< R, E, C, P >$. *If there are* P_1, P_2, C_1, C_2 *and* $P = P_1 \cup P_2$, $C = C_1 \cup C_2$, *then there are trust relationships* $T_1 =< R, E, C_1, P_1 >$ *and* $T_2 =< R, E, C_2, P_2 >$.

All operations can be used to generate new trust relationships from the existing trust relationships under some specific constrains. The **Operation 1** deals with any two trust relationships and a new trust relationship is possibly generated(if the result is not $\emptyset$). The **Operation 1A, 1B, 2A, 3A** deal with how to use two trust relationships to generate one trust relationship under some specific constraints. The **Operation 4, 5, 6 and 6A** deal with how to decompose one trust relationship into two trust relationships under some specific constraints. **Operation 1A** and **Operation 6A** are inverse operations. **Operation 1B** and **Operation 6** are inverse operations. **Operation 2A** and **Operation 4** are inverse operations. **Operation 3A** and **Operation 5** are inverse operations.

In the following part of this section, we will focus on the relation of trust relationships, especially we will discuss and define the equivalent, primitive, derived, direct redundant and alternate trust relationships. We will classify the direct redundant trust relationships into different types as well.

Definition 2 *Let* $T_1 =< R_1, E_1, C_1, P_1 >$ *and* $T_2 =< R_2, E_2, C_2, P_2 >$. *If and only if* $R_1 = R_2$ *and* $E_1 = E_2$ *and* $C_1 = C_2$ *and* $P_1 = P_2$, *then* T_1 *and* T_2 *are equivalent, in symbols:*

$$T_1 = T_2 \iff R_1 = R_2 \text{ and } E_1 = E_2 \text{ and } C_1 = C_2 \text{ and } P_1 = P_2$$

Definition 3 *If a trust relationship can not be derived from other existing trust relationships, the trust relationship is a primitive trust relationship.*

Definition 4 *If a trust relationship can be derived from other existing trust relationships, the trust relationship is a derived trust relationship.*

Note: Trust relationships are predefined in information systems. A derived trust relationship is always related to one or more other trust relationships. For an independent trust relationship, it is meaningless to judge it as a derived trust relationship or not.

Proposition 1 *If a derived trust relationship exists, there is information redundancy.*

Proof. When the derived trust relationship is moved out of the system, the information of the derived trust relationship has not been lost. The derived trust relationship can be built when it is necessary. From the view point of information, there is redundancy.

Definition 5 *Let* $T =< R, E, C, P >$. *If there is trust relationship* $T' =< R', E', C', P' >$ *and* $T \neq T'$, $R \subseteq R'$, $E \subseteq E'$, $C \supseteq C'$, $P \subseteq P'$. T *is a direct redundant trust relationship.*

In the following part of this section, we discuss several special cases of direct redundant trust relationships based on the single tuple of trust relationship. We believe that these special cases play important roles in the analysis and design of trust relationships in information systems.

Direct Redundancy Type 1 *: DLR-redundant trust relationship*
Let $T =< R, E, C, P >$. *If and only if there is a trust relationship* $T' =< R', E, C, P >$ *and* $R' \supset R$, *T is a DLR-redundant trust relationship.*

T is DLR-redundant trust relationship means that there is another trust relationship with super set of trusters and all other tuples are same as peers in T.

Direct Redundancy Type 2 *: DLE-redundant trust relationship*
Let $T =< R, E, C, P >$. *If and only if there is a trust relationship* $T' =< R, E', C, P >$ *and* $E' \supset E$, *T is a DLE-redundant trust relationship.*

T is DLE-redundant trust relationship means that there is another trust relationship with super set of trustees and all other tuples are same as peers in T.

Direct Redundancy Type 3 *: DMC-redundant trust relationship*
Let $T =< R, E, C, P >$. *If and only if there is an alternate trust relationship* $T' =< R, E, C', P >$ *and* $C' \subset C$, *T is a DMC-redundant trust relationship.*

T is DMC-redundant trust relationship means that there is another trust relationship with sub set of conditions and all other tuples are same as peers in T.

Direct Redundancy Type 4 *: DLP-redundant trust relationship*
Let $T =< R, E, C, P >$. *If and only if there is a trust relationship* $T' =< R, E, C, P' >$ *and* $P' \supset P$, *T is a DLP-redundant trust relationship.*

T is DLP-redundant trust relationship means that there is another trust relationship with super set of properties and all other tuples are same as peers in T.

Definition 6 *Let* $T =< R, E, C, P >$, $T' =< R, E, C', P >$ *and* $C \neq C'$. T *and* T' *are alternate trust relationships of each other.*

An alternate trust relationship means that there is an alternate condition set for the same truster set, trustee set and property set. Perhaps, there are multiple alternate trust relationships. In distributed computing, multiple mechanisms and multiple choices are necessary in many situations and it is the main reason why we define and discuss alternate trust relationship here.

Proposition 2 *If* T *is a DMC-redundant trust relationship, there is one or more than one alternate trust relationships which are not DMC-redundant trust relationship.*

Proof. If T is a DMC-redundant trust relationship, there is $T' =< R, E, C', P >$ and $C' \subset C$. T' is an alternate trust relationship of T. If T' is not DMC-redundant trust relationship, the proposition is proved. If T' is a DMC-redundant trust relationship, the next T'' can be found, $T'' =< R, E, C'', P >$ with $C'' \subset C'$. Such a process will continue until the set of conditions includes minimum number of conditions. In every turn of the process, one or more conditions are removed from the condition set. Because C contains limited conditions, the process can finish when no condition can be removed from the condition set. The final set of conditions is C^f. $T^f =< R, E, C^f, P >$ is an alternate trust relationship with non-redundant conditions.

A DMC-redundant trust relationship may have multiple alternate trust relationships with different sets of non-redundant conditions.

4   Scenario Examples of Trust Relationships

In this section, we make up two scenarios for discussing trust relationships in the real world. We hope that these examples can be helpful in understanding the definition of trust relationship and mathematical properties of trust relationships expressed in section 2 and section 3.

Scenario 1: When people want to change their names, they need to apply to a specific organization (In Australia, the organization is the Registry of Birth Deaths & Marriages). The officers in the organization and the requesters are involved in this scenario. Using the full syntax of our definition of trust relationship, some trust relationships may be modelled as follows:

TS1- 1 *Officers trust requesters if requesters have their Birth Certificate & Driver's Licence that requesters have the right for the change.*

TS1- 2 *Officers trust requesters if requesters have their Citizenship Certificate & Driver's Licence that requesters have the right for the change.*

TS1- 3 *Officers trust requesters if requesters have their Birth Certificate & Citizenship Certificate & Driver's Licence that requesters have the right for the change.*

If **TS1-1**, **TS1-2** and **TS1-3** are all the trust relationships in this information system, based on the definitions and operations in section 3, we can have the following analysis:

- **TS1-1** and **TS1-2** are primitive trust relationships.
- **TS1-1** and **TS1-2** are alternate trust relationships of each other.
- **TS1-3** is a derived trust relationship which can be derived by **Operation 1A** with **TS1-1** and **TS1-2**.
- **TS1-3** is a DMC-redundant trust relationship and it should be removed out of the system.

Scenario 2: An online e-commerce service is called FlightServ which can provide flight booking and travel deals. FlightServ is designed based on the new technologies of web services. FlightServ connects with customers, airlines, hotels and credit card services (some of them maybe web services). The whole system could be very complicated, but we only consider some of trust relationships in the system. In the system, customers are classified into normal flyers and frequent flyers. Originally, some trust relationships are modelled as:

TS2- 1 *Airlines trust normal flyers if they have address details & confirmed credit card information that normal flyers can make their airline bookings.*

TS2- 2 *Airlines trust frequent flyers with no condition that frequent flyers can make their airline bookings.*

TS2- 3 *Hotels trust normal flyers if they have address details & confirmed credit card information that normal flyers can make their hotels booking.*

TS2- 4 *Hotels trust frequent flyers if they have address details & confirmed credit card information that frequent flyers can make their hotels booking.*

TS2- 5 *Credit card services are trusted by all possible entities without any condition that the credit card services will give the correct evaluation of credit card information.*

TS2- 6 *Credit card services are trusted by all possible entities without any condition that the credit card services will keep the privacy of credit card information.*

For the above trust relationships in the system, based on definitions and operations in section 3, we have the following analysis:

- All above trust relationships are primitive.
- Using the **Operation 3A**, trust relationships **TS2-3** and **TS2-4** can be merged to a new trust relationship **TS2-(3)(4)**: "Hotels trust customers if they have address details & confirmed credit card information that customers can make their hotels booking". If **TS2-(3)(4)** has been defined in the system, **TS2-3** and **TS2-4** becomes DLE-redundant trust relationships and will be removed out of the system.
- Using the **Operation 1B**, trust relationships **TS2-5** and **TS2-6** can be merged to a new trust relationship **TS2-(5)(6)**: "Credit card services are trusted by all possible entities without any condition that the credit card services will give the correct evaluation of credit card information & the credit card services will keep the privacy of credit card information". If **TS2-(5)(6)** has been defined in the system, **TS2-5** and **TS2-6** becomes DLP-redundant trust relationships and will be removed out of the system.

Obviously, the definition of trust relationship in section 2 and the mathematical properties of trust relationships in section 3 provide terminologies and helpful tools in the analysis of the two scenarios. In the analysis of the two scenarios, we only employ some definitions, propositions and operations expressed in section 3. We hope that these examples can provide a general picture for the usage of the definitions, propositions and operations. In these two scenarios, we only choose some trust relationships as examples and there are more trust relationships. The systematic methodologies and strategies for modelling trust relationships are beyond the scope of this paper as well and will be discussed elsewhere.

5   Concluding Remarks

The definition of the trust relationship provided in this paper has a strict mathematical structure and broad expressive power. The definition is suitable for any computing purpose. The mathematical properties of trust relationships are shown in a series of definitions, propositions and operations. We believe that these definitions and mathematical properties of trust relationships provide useful tools for enabling the analysis, design and implementation of trust in distributed environments.

This research only provides a starting point for the analysis and design of trust relationships in distributed information systems. How to model trust relationships in distributed information systems and how to merge the trust relationships into the over-all distributed information systems provides lots of challenges for further research. We believe that our definition of trust relationship and the associated mathematical proper-ties described in section 3 could be used as helpful tools to model the trust relationships. The definitions and operations in section 3 provide some starting points and tools for the analysis and design of the trust relationships in a system. We are currently working on using the proposed definition of trust relationship and mathematical properties of trust relationships to develop a methodology for modelling trust in distributed systems. This involves several stages such as extracting trust requirements in system, identify-ing possible trust relationships from trust requirements, choosing the whole set of trust relationships from possible trust relationships and implementing and maintaining trust relationships in systems. We will describe them in details in a separate paper.

References

1. M. Deutsch, "Cooperation and trust:some theoretical notes", Nebraska Symposium on Mo-tivation, Nebraska University Press, 1962.
2. D. Gambetta, "Can we trust trust?", In Trust:Making and Breaking Cooperative Relations, Basil Blackwell, Oxford, pp.213-237, 1990.
3. J. Landauer, T. Redmond, et al. "Formal policies for trusted processes", Proceedings of the Computer Security Foundations Workshop II, 1989.
4. M. Blaze, J. Feigenbaum, and J. Lacy, "Decentralized trust management", Proceedings of the IEEE Conference on Security and Privacy, Oakland, 1996.
5. M. Blaze, J. Feigenbaum, and J. Lacy, "KeyNote:Trust management for public-key infras-tructure", LNCS 1550, pp.59-63, 1999.
6. KeyNote web page, "The KeyNote Trust-Management System", http://www.cis.upenn.edu/ keynote/.
7. Y. H. Chu, J. Feigenbaum, B. LaMacchia, P. Resnick and M. Strauss, "REFEREE:Trust Management for Web Applications", AT&T Research Labs, 1997, http://www.research.att.com/ mstraus/pubs/referee.html.
8. A. Kini and J. Choobineh, "Trust in electronic commerce:defintion and theoretical consider-ations", 31st Annal Hawaii International Conference of System Sciences, Hawaii, 1998.
9. D. W. Manchala, "Trust metrics, models and protocols for electronic commerce transac-tions", Proceedings of 18th International Conference on Distributed Computing Systems, 1998.
10. G. Della-Libera et al, "Web Services Trust Language (WS-Trust)", http://www-106.ibm.com/developerworks/library/ws-trust/, December 18th, 2002.
11. T. Grandison and M. Sloman, "A survey of trust in Internet application", IEEE Communica-tions Surveys, Fourth Quarter, 2000.

Dynamically Changing Trust Structure in Capability Based Access Control Systems

Sandra Wortmann, Barbara Sprick, and Christoph Kobusch

Information Systems and Security, Department of Computer Science,
University of Dortmund, Germany
{sandra.wortmann,barbara.sprick,christoph.kobusch}@udo.edu

Abstract. The functioning of modern IT-systems with autonomously acting components requires an elaborate access control system in which each participant can maintain her own trust structure.
In this work, we discuss ideas for an extension of capability based access control systems that allow the specification of dynamically changing trust of participants. We propose a classification of credentials and distinguish between credentials that have a positive and those that have a negative impact on access decisions. Furthermore, we investigate, how our ideas can be implemented in existing approaches for capability based access control systems.

1 Introduction

The functioning of distributed IT-systems requires an elaborate access control system. In a distributed IT-system with autonomous components, a fixed global or even hierarchical trust stucture is not suitable. In such a system, every participant maintains her own trust structure autonomously. Capability based access control systems are well suited to capture the individual and dynamically changing trust structure of each participant.

In a capability based access control system, access to a resource is granted or denied on the basis of the requester's capabilities rather than on the basis of her identity. Existing approaches for capability based access control systems such as [1–3] are monotonic: more certified properties usually imply more access permissions.

However, we believe that such a monotonic approach is too simple to reflect a substantial set of real world applications. Owners of resources might for example wish to explicitly prohibit other participants from accessing their resource or might wish to formulate exceptions from their general access control policy. In such cases, issued certificates can have a negative impact on the access decisions of owners of resources. In particular, we believe that not only certified properties and access permissions need to be considered: Each participant of a capability based access control system needs to dynamically maintain her own trust structure (concerning the trustworthiness of other participants). Consequently, revocation of already certified properties, explicit access prohibitions

S. Katsikas, J. Lopez, and G. Pernul (Eds.): TrustBus 2004, LNCS 3184, pp. 50–59, 2004.

and statements about trust and distrust concerning other participants need to be considered as well.

For these reasons we claim for an extended property based access control framework that is able to deal with a dynamically changing trust structure and with the potentially negative impact of certified properties. In our paper, we identify requirements for such a framework and suggest implemetation mechanisms.

Our paper is structured as follows. Section 2 describes the main roles in which participants of a credential based system may act and discusses their different interests and actions on the basis of an application scenario. Section 3 discusses aspects of time dependent, dynamically changing trust structures of participants. Section 4 analyses, how current approaches handle certificates with a potentially negative impact on access decisions. If certificates can have a negative impact on access decisions, one important question is how to enforce that all appropriate certificates are shown by a requester? Section 4 suggests implementation mechanisms as solution to this question. A discussion about related literature can be found in section 5. Finally, a conclusion is drawn in chapter6.

2   Capability Based Access Control

In capability based access control systems, access to resources is granted or denied on the basis of proven capabilities of the requester. Controllers of resources define the security policy of the resource in terms of capabilities or properties, participants of the access control system can certify properties to other participants who in turn can use the certified properties and capabilities to prove their eligibility for accessing a resource.

In the following we briefly introduce an application scenario and discuss the various roles in which participants of a capability based access control system can act and various types of certificates that can be issued.

2.1   Application Scenario

Consider a conference with two attached workshops. The conference as well as each of the workshops have their own online registration service. To register for the conference, one needs to prove membership of a university. To register for a workshop one has to be registered for the conference as well. Furthermore, it is only possible to register for one workshop. Consequently, if a person wants to register for a workshop, she needs to prove that she has registered for the conference but has not yet registered for the other workshop. People that verifiably have violated the guidelines for good research are excluded from participation in the conference and in the workshops. After successful registration, each of the registration services returns a registration receipt. Such a registration receipt can be used to request access to the respective conference or workshop site. Furthermore, a conference registration receipt is needed when registering for a workshop.

2.2   Roles and Their Interests

We distinguish among four different roles which the participants of the system can hold, namely controller, assigner, grantee and verifier.

Controllers are either owners of resources or their delegates. The main interest of a controller is to restrict access to the respective resource only to authorized participants. To do so, the controller defines the security policy of the resource in terms of capabilities and properties that authorize requesters for accessing the resource. Further, the controller certifies capabilities concerning access to this particular resource to other participants of the system. In our example, the organizing chairs of the conference or workshops acts the role of the controller when defining the access control policy of the registration web sites or issuing conference or workshop registration receipts.

Assigners act independently of particular resources. They autonomously certify properties to participants of the access control system. Usually, assigners do not have particular interests concerning the use of issued certificates. In our example, universities act as assigners when they certify university membership. These certificates are not bound to any particular purpose by the university.

Grantees collect certificates about their properties issued by the controller and assigners. Their main interest is to gain access to resources. When requesting access, grantees either present required certificates about their attributes or directly present authorization certificates. In our example, university members act as grantees when they collect certificates about their university membership or about conference and workshop registration.

Verifier grant or deny access to the particular resource on the basis of the resource's security policy and the requesters' certificates. In our example, the conference and workshop organizers act as verifiers. However, they have delegated the role of the verifier to the conference and workshop registration tools, respectively.

2.3   Certified Properties

As described in the previous paragraph, controllers and assigners issue certificates about certain properties to grantees. According to [4], we can distinguish between two different types of properties:

1. Free properties are certified by assigners. Their certification is not bound to any particular purpose and they do not directly entail an access permission at a particular resource.
2. Bound properties are certified by controllers of resources. Their certification is to be seen in the context of the respective resource. They express a promise about some specific access permission.

Note, that the distinction between free and bound properties is context dependent: In our example scenario, a registration receipt issued by the conference registration service certifies a bound property in the context of the conference web site. However, it can also be considered as a free property in the context of the workshop registration services.

3   Dynamically Maintained Trust Structure

As described in the previous section, in a capability based access control system, access to resources is granted to requesters on the basis of certified properties. Usually, an increase of certificates issued to a grantee implies an increase of access permissions, i.e. capability based access control systems are monotonic. However, we believe that a monotonic access control system is too restrictive to enable the specification of security policies of a substantial subset of real world applications.

The controller of a resource defines the resource's security policy, which in turn reflects the controller's trust structure of the access control system. In a monotonic capability based access control system, the controller defines the properties required for accessing a resource and constitutes which assigners are trusted to certify the required properties. However, the controllers also need a possibility to explicitly exclude holders of certain properties from access and to define a trust structure concerning assigners.

Apart from credential revocation mechanisms, there hardly exist any mechanisms in credential based access control systems that facilitate above mentioned non monotonic aspects of the controller's trust structure.

In many real world applications, the controller's trust structure is more complex and should reflect modalities such as trust, distrust, belief and doubt (concerning other participants and concerning certified properties). Often, the trust structure is not static but changes over the time. It is therefor desirable to have a time dependent notion of a trust structure that can be dynamically maintained by the respective controllers.

By certifying a free property, the assigner expresses her firm belief that the certified property holds for the grantee. As in monotonic capability based access control systems, a controller trusts certain assigners to certify certain free properties. This trust is reflected in the access control policy defined by the controller. If the controller certifies a bound property to a grantee, she expresses her trust in the grantee to appropriately use the access permission.

In some cases, a controller has reservations or doubts against participant for whom certain properties hold or against assigners of certain properties. These doubts should be expressed in the access control policies of the respective resources controlled by the controller.

If a controller explicitly distrusts particular participants, access for these participants should be explicitly prohibited.

In section 2.3, we distinguished between free and bound properties. Speaking in terms of SPKI/SDSI, certificates about free properties are called attribute credentials and certificates about bound properties are called authorization credentials. Attribute credentials refer to belief of assigners concerning properties of grantees, authorization credentials refer to trust of controllers concerning eligible and appropriate use of resources.

To be able to additionally express doubt and distrust in a credential based way, we suggest to consider another type of credentials, namely prohibition credentials.

As we have argued before, the trust structure of controllers may change over the time, an appropriate credential based access control framework should allow to dynamically maintain trust structures and in particular, to allow to revoke previously issued credentials. We thus suggest to consider a fourth type of credentials called revocation credentials.

3.1   Types of Credentials

Attribute Credentials

By issuing an attribute credential, an assigner certifies that the grantee holds the specified free property. If the assigner wants to certify the absence of a particular free property p, she issues an attribute credential certifying, that the grantee has property **not** p. This type of attribute credential, whether it certifies a property p or the absence of property p is not bound to a particular resource. It can be used for requesting access at any arbitrary resource, depending on the resources security policy. Note, that a certificate about the absence of a particular property does not necessarily have a negative impact on the access decision. It might well be, that exactly the absence of the property is required for access. Recall the example about the conference management scenario. Only users who can prove that they have **not** registered for workshop a are entitled to register for workshop b.

Authorization Credentials and Prohibition Credentials

By issuing an authorization credential, a controller explicitly certifies that the grantee is eligible to access the resource. For instance, the users holding a conference registration receipt are entitled to use the conference web site. By issuing a prohibition credential, a controller explicitly certifies that the grantee is prohibited from accessing the resource. A prohibition credential has a negative impact for the grantee on the access decision to the resource. If, for example, a user has verifiably violated the guidelines of good research, the organization chair explicitly excludes the user from registration.

Revocation Credentials

As motivated before, assigners and controllers may want to revoke previously issued credentials as their trust structure may change over the time.

We can distinguish between two cases of changing belief: In the first case, the issuer of a credential knows at issuing time, that the certified property is valid only until a particular point in time or at least, that she wants to certify the association between the grantee and the property only for a particular time period. In this case, she can simply certify this by issuing a credential which is valid only for this particular period in time. For example, a university issues student certificates only for one semester and membership certificates for scientific staff only for the time of their contract. In the second case, the issuer of a credential learns only after certifying a property, that the grantee of the credential does no longer hold the certified property. In this case, the issuer of the credential will want to revoke the issued certificate. For this purpose, a revocation credential can be issued stating that the formerly issued credential is no longer valid. For example, when learning, that a user who has already registered for the conference has violated the guidelines for good research, the conference chair may want to revoke the previously issued registration receipt. Note, that not only authorisation credentials and attribute credentials can be revoked but also prohibition credentials. Thus, a revocation credential can have both positive and negative impacts on access decisions.

Negatively Used Attribute Credentials
The access control policy of a resource should not only define necessary access conditions but also conditions that exclude from access. It is desirable to be able to define a policy that allows access for all requesters having property a except for those having property b. By issuing attribute credentials, an assigner subsumes groups of grantees that have the same property. In order to exclude a subset of such a group from access, the controller can again identify the subset that is to be excluded by a set of attribute credentials. In such a case, an attribute credential can have a negative impact for the grantee on the access decision. The controller subtracts the group of grantees determined by the attribute credentials from the group of grantees eligible for access to a resource. If a grantee holds a workshop registration certificate for workshop b, this attribute credential has a negative impact on the access decision for the registration service of workshop a.

4   Implementation of Doubt and Distrust

This section surveys how doubt and distrust can be implemented in current public key infrastructures ([3, 1, 5, 2]).

Revocation Credentials
M echanism s Suppose, an issuer wants to revoke a previously issued credential as she does no longer belief, that the grantee of the credential holds the certified property. The KeyNote Trust Management System does not currently provide credential revocation mechanisms. However, an issuer of a KeyNote credential may specify and implement revocation policies. In other public key infrastructures, e.g. X.509 or SPKI/SDSI, the issuer of a credential may give further validity conditions. The revocation of credentials is usually specified in certificate revocation lists (CRL). Such lists need to be checked by the verifier of a resource for access decisions: revoked credentials should not have any impact on the access decision.

Im plem entation CRLs are usually placed on designated servers. Because of the potential length of such lists it is sometimes more appropriate to issue signed δ-CRLs that contain only the difference between the current CRL and the previously issued CRL. The Online Certificate Status Protocol (OCSP), [6], improves standard CRLs by avoiding the transmission of long CRLs and by providing more recent revocation information. To do so, it uses so-called status requests for credentials. In [7], Kocher suggested Certificate Revocation Trees. Such a data structure is a hash tree where the leaves denote the currently revoked credentials.

Prohibition Credentials

A prohibition credential explicitly prohibits the holder of the credential from accessing the respective resource. Existing public key infrastructures do not currently provide mechanisms to implement prohibition credentials. One of the main questions to answer is why would a user present a prohibition credential to the verifier?

Negatively Used Attribute Credentials

M echanism s The access control policy of a resource specifies access requirements on the basis of attribute credentials. Note, that attribute credentials can have both positive and negative impacts on the access decision: While some attributes are mandatory, others may not desirable and thus exclude form access. Again, the question arises why users would present credentials that have a negative impact on the resource's access decision? Existing public key infrastructures do not provide appropriate mechanisms for enforcing such "negatively used" credentials.

Im plem entation. On the specification side, we suggest, that the controller defines the security policy through algebra expressions built from free properties and operators. To specify negatively used credentials, the controller may use a subtraction operator. Roughly speaking, the semantics of such an algebra expression would be to interpret attribute credentials, certifying free properties, as groups of grantees having the respective properties. The operators are then evaluated as set-theoretical operations applied to sets of grantees. Negatively used attribute credentials are standard attribute credentials, but are negatively interpreted when used as subtrahend in the underlying security policy.

As mentioned before, on of the main problems is how to enforce grantees to show attribute credentials when thy have a negative impact on access decisions. Biskup and Wortmann ([8]) propose a solution to this problem: The authors suggest a new kind of online test of a credential as so-called bcation that is used in combination with a new kind of subject of a credential as so-called ■rst-of-two. An alternative approach to prevent grantees from hiding negatively used attribute credentials, investigated in [9], introduces so-called not credentials that certify a grantee her "not membership" of a particular group.

5   Related Work

We have focused on credentials that certify participants non identifying capabilities. While SPKI/SDSI and KeyNote are based on public keys of the participants and allow for a non identifying approach, the X.509 public key infrastructure [1] does not fully support this non identity based approach as credentials are inevitably identifying in X.509.

We analyzed attribute credentials, authorization credentials, prohibition credentials and revocation credentials. The differentiation between attribute credentials (certifying free properties) and authorization credentials (certifying bound properties) leads us to the public key infrastructure SPKI/SDSI, because the KeyNote trust management system [3] does not support attribute credentials.

SPKI/SDSI was invented in 1996 and results from a name definition part called Simple Distributed Security Infrastructure (SDSI [5]) and an authorization part called Simple Public Key infrastructure (SPKI [2]). A lot of work contributed to a semantics for SPKI/SDSI. Comparing Abadi's logic, introduced in [10], to the requirements and aspects identified in our paper, his modal operator *says* expresses the belief of an issuer (controller or assigner) about the properties of other participants. Translated to our setting, Abadi's relation $A \Rightarrow B$, read as "(participant) A speaks for (controller) B", expresses controller B's promise of an access right towards participant A, or controller B's trust towards participant A. Howell and Kotz [11] extend Abadi's logic by (restricted) delegation and authorization. In their extension, belief of an issuer (controller or assigner) is modeled by the modal operator `believes`. The formula A `believes` σ, where A is an issuer and σ is a certificate certifying a grantee to have a certain property, can be interpreted as "Issuer A believes the binding expressed in certificate σ to be true". Howell et.al. further introduce a relation $A \overset{T}{\Rightarrow} B$, read as "(participant) A speaks for (controller) B regarding (the set of access permissions) T". Interpreted in our setting, this formula expresses controller B's trust in (participant) A regarding the set of access permissions T. In [12], Halpern and van der Meyden develop a logic to deal with SPKI authorization credentials. However, their logic does not provide an mechanism for the specification of attribute credentials. Thus, it only supports the specification of certificates about bound properties, but not about free properties. logic programming based semantics for SPKI/SDSI and in [13] Li and Mitchell introduce a first order logic semantics of SPKI/SDSI. Most of the logics are able to express belief and (restricted) trust of participants of a capability based access control system. Some of the languages provide mechanisms for treating a dynamically changing trust structure, see e.g.[11]. However, none of the logics explicitly formalizes prohibition or revocation credentials.

Some work has been done about the meaning of credentials and their revocation, see for instance [14–17]. In particular [17] introduces a language for creating and manipulating, i.e. issuing and revoking, credentials. All approaches deal with revocation of credentials, some of them treat issues of time, e.g. [14]. However, as to our knowledge, there do not exist any approaches that deal with negatively used credentials in general or prohibition credentials in particular.

6   Conclusion

Capability based access control systems have shown to be appropriate for access control in highly distributed systems where a global controlling instance cannot be assumed. However, current implementations of capability based access control systems, such as [3], [2] or [1] are monotonous and have significant limitations when it comes to access prohibitions. In this paper, we first analyzed various roles in a capability based access control systems and discussed their interests. We pointed out the need for appropriate mechanisms for assigners of credentials and controllers of resources to dynamically and autonomously maintain their trust structures. Further, we suggested new types of credentials that are suited to help assigners and controllers specifying and maintaining their trust structures. Finally, we discussed how credentials with a potentially negative impact on access decisions can be implemented in current credential based access control systems.

Acknowledgements

We thank Joachim Biskup and Torben Weibert for helpful discussions and proof reading. A part of this work was funded by the DFG German Research Council (DFG) under grant number BI 311/11-1.

References

1. IETF: public key infrastructure (x.509).
   http://www.ietf.org/html.charters/pkixcharter.html (1998) IETF X.509 Working Group.
2. Ellison, C., Frantz, B., Lampson, B., Rivest, R., Thomas, B., Ylonen, T.: SPKI certificate theory. Internet RFC 2693 (1999)
3. Blaze, M., Feigenbaum, J., Ioannindis, J., Kermytis, A.: The keynote trust management system version 2. http://www.cis.upenn.edu/~keynote/Papers/rfc2704.txt (1999) IETF RFC 2704.
4. Biskup, J., Karabulut, Y.: A hybrid pki model: Application to secure mediation. In: Research Directions in Data and Application Security. 16th Annual IFIP WG 11.3 Working Conf. on Data and Application Security, Kluwer, Boston etc. (2003) 271–282
5. Rivest, R., Lampson, B.: SDSI – a simple distributed security infrastructure. http://theory.lcs.mit.edu/~cis/sdsi.html (1996)
6. Myers, M., Ankney, R., Malpani, A., Galperin, S., Adams, C.: X.509 internet public key infrastructure online certificate status protocol – OSCP. http://www.ietf.org/rfc/rfc2560.txt (1999) IETF RFC 2560.
7. Kocher, P.: On certificate revocation and validation. In: Proceedings of the 2nd Internation Conference on Financial Cryptography (FC'98). Volume 1465 of LNCS., Springer Verlag, Berlin (1998) 172–177
8. Biskup, J., Wortmann, S.: Towards a credential-based implementation of compound access control policies. In: Proceedings of the 9th ACM Symposium on access control and models (SACMAT), Yorktown Heights, New York, USA, ACM (2003) To appear.
9. Kobusch, C.: Mechanismen zur durchsetzung negativ wirkender zertifikate in zugriffskontrollsystemen. Master's thesis, University of Dortmund (2003) http://ls6-www.cs.uni-dortmund.de/dpa.html.
10. Abadi, M.: On SDSI's linked local name spaces. In: Proceedings of the 10th IEEE Computer Security Foundations Workshop, IEEE Computer Society (1997) 98–108
11. Howell, J., Kotz, D.: A formal semantics for SPKI. In: Proceedings of ESORICS 2000. Volume 1895 of LNCS., Springer Verlag, Berlin (2000) 140–158
12. Halpern, J., van der Meyden, R.: A logic for SDSI's linked local name spaces. Journal of Computer Security 9 (1–2) (2001) 47–74
13. Li, N., Mitchell, J.: Understanding spki/sdsi using first order logic. In: Proceedings of 16th IEEE CSFW, Boston, Mass., ACM Press, New York (2003) 182–189

14. Li, N., Feigenbaum, J.: Nonmonotonicity, user interfaces, and risk assessment in certificate revocation. In: Proc of the 5th Int. Conf. on Financial Cryptography (FC'01). Volume 2339 of LNCS., Springer Verlag, Berlin (2001) 166–177

15. Rivest, R.: Can we eliminate certificate revocation lists? In: Proceedings of the 2nd Internation Conference on Financial Cryptography (FC'98). Volume 1465 of LNCS., Springer Verlag, Berlin (1998) 178–183

16. Myers, M.: Revocation: options and challenges. In: Proceedings of the 2nd Internation Conference on Financial Cryptography (FC'98). Volume 1465 of LNCS., Springer Verlag, Berlin (1998) 165–171

17. Gunter, C., Jim, T.: Generalized certificate revocation. In: Proceedings of the 27th ACM SIGPLAN-SIGACT symposium on Principles of programming languages, ACM (2000) 316–329

18. Myers, M., Malpani, A., Pinkas, D.: X.509 internet public key infrastructure online certificate status protocol, version 2. http://www.ietf.org/proceedings/02mar/ID/draft-ietf-pkix-ocspv2-02.txt (2002) Network Working Group.

On the Design of a New Trust Model
for Mobile Agent Security

Ching Lin[1], Vijay Varadharajan[1], Yan Wang[1], and Yi Mu[2]

[1] Department of Computing
Macquarie University, Sydney, NSW 2109, Australia
{linc,vijay,yanwang}@ics.mq.edu.au
[2] School of Information Technology and Computer Science
University of Wollongong, Wollongong, NSW 2522, Australia
ymu@uow.edu.au

Abstract. Recently, the notion of trust has been recognized as an important aspect of the mobile agent security. However, the current research on trust models focuses only on the hard trust relationships that are usually established via cryptographic mechanisms assuming the availability of Trusted Third Parties (TTPs) and cryptographic protocols for trust verification. We argue that in order to harness the benefits of open network operations securely, the above assumptions need to be relaxed. Thus it is necessary to build a trust model that can be extended beyond the reliance of cryptography based protocols and TTPs, and is capable of managing soft trust relationships in addition to the hard ones in mobile agent systems. We propose a new trust model which provides solutions to meet the above requirements with hybrid trust mechanisms. We analyze the properties of the new trust model and show how they can help improve the effectiveness of hard and soft trust and thus raise the security levels of mobile agent systems.

1 Introduction

Mobile agent computing is a promising paradigm for distributed computing that offers numerous benefits comparing to conventional client-server model. However, mobile agent based systems which are capable of free roaming in open network environments violate the usual security assumptions made on traditional distributed computer systems such as identity and origin of participating entities, and operating system protected execution of programs. Therefore, mobile agent systems are vulnerable to a number of attacks in an open network [3]. These include attacks on the host by malicious mobile agents and attacks on the mobile agent by the malicious hosts. The fundamental issues that need to be addressed before full commercial viability can be achieved lie in the areas of security and robustness of the mobile agent system. Presently, the mobile agent security research focuses primarily on the designs of cryptography based mechanisms for the protection of mobile agents and hosts[9, 4].

Recently, some initial research effort has been directed towards the development of a trust model for mobile agent security [11]. However, the current

S. Katsikas, J. Lopez, and G. Pernul (Eds.): TrustBus 2004, LNCS 3184, pp. 60–69, 2004.

research focuses mainly on the trust relationships that are established via cryptographic means. Such solutions often assume the availability of some form of Trusted Third Parties (TTPs) for trust verification. We argue that in order to harness the true benefits of open network operation in terms of enabling interactions and co-operations while ensuring acceptable level of security, it is necessary to have a trust model that can be extended beyond the reliance on cryptography and TTPs. This is because in open networks, TTPs may not be always available. Social control mechanisms (using soft trust) [10] often may be the only option in evaluating the security related trust relationships in a mobile agent system when a TTP can not be located.

In this paper we propose a new hybrid trust model employing soft trust mechanisms with constructs such as recommendation, direct experiences via interactions and observations to complement hard trust for enhancing the mobile agent security in situations where full authentication trust is not available due to absence or unavailability of TTPs in the mobile agent systems.

The main contributions of this paper are: 1) identifying the need and proposing a hybrid trust model combining soft trust relationships which is based on non-cryptographic mechanisms (with mechanisms like observation, direct interaction and recommendation), with the hard trust relationships are based on conventional cryptographic mechanisms; 2) proposing solutions to overcome the shortcomings of previously proposed trust evaluation formalisms (such as trust saturation and low trust evaluation) and improve the overall levels of security for mobile agents.

The rest of the paper is organized as follows: Section 2 discusses the related work on trust model for distributed systems. In Section 3 we identify the need for a hybrid trust model, derive the relevant types of trust relationships between entities in a secure mobile agent system, describe our trust evaluation methods. Section 4 analyzes the properties of the new model. Finally, concluding remarks and future research directions are provided in Section 5.

2   Related Work

Following is a brief review of some of the previously proposed trust models. First let us look at one of the first trust models proposed by Marsh. His trust model can be considered as a soft one in that it captures situational trust in different situations taking into account of trustor's own utility preference [8]. However, the original model does not consider hard trust. Another soft trust example is the social control system proposed by Rasmusson et al. [10] where each participant in the system takes responsibility for security, rather than leaving it to some external authorities such as TTPs. The main idea of Rasmusson's theory is to use social control to demand certain group behaviors, i.e. to indirectly force the group members to behave in certain ways such that interactions with malicious entities can be avoided. Abdul-Rahman et al. [1] propose a trust model along with a protocol for trust recommendation queries in distributed system based on PGP. Yu et al. [14] present a distributed reputation based social control mechanism using evidential theory to combine direct experiences with recommendations (witness) on evidences of trustworthiness from distributed sources to make trust decisions and weed out malicious entities from the system - in line with the main idea of social control proposed by Rasmusson [10]. In general, these soft trust models do not consider the issues of hard trust or authentication trust which is important to security properties of distributed applications such as the mobile agent systems.

One of the hard trust example is the trust model proposed by Tan et al. [11] developed for mobile agents, where the authors have identified six types of trust and belief relationships specific to mobile agent systems and developed a trust derivation algorithm for mobile code security, using TTPs (verification servers) for execution trace verification. However, the trust transitivity used in the inference rules for trust derivation is based on the availability of TTPs. This assumption seems to be too strong in our opinion for a mobile agent based application in an open network where such a structure of a grouped verification servers may not always be available. Wilhelm et al. [13] give a more comprehensive treatment on the issue of trust in mobile agent systems. They have identified what they referred as the four foundations of trust, namely: blind trust, trust based on (a good) reputation, trust based on control and punishment and trust based on policy enforcement. Their solution to the trust in mobile agent systems problem was the CryPO protocol, based on tamper-proof hardware to provide tamper-proof environments, which are the foundation for the agent executor and agents can assert which environment manufacturers they trust. The protocol uses certificates and encryption technology to ensure security and is essentially an extension of the certification framework. However, the authors of CryPO did not consider soft trust in their proposal.

A more general example is the trust formalism proposed by Beth et al. [2] where they identify and apply different types of trust for authentication protocols. Even though the authentication trust (i.e. hard trust) is the main goal, social control mechanisms such as recommendations and direct observations are used for evaluation and the associated drawbacks have been reported by Jøsang in [5].

3   A New Trust Model for Mobile Agent Security

3.1   Definitions

Definition 1 (Trust) Trust is the belief of honesty, competence, reliability and availability of an entity in a context of interaction and co-operation in social and technical settings.

In the mobile agent security context we extend this trust concept into hard trust and soft trust.

Definition 2 (Hard Trust) Hard trust is the trust that is established via cryptographic mechanisms.

Definition 3 (Soft Trust) Soft trust is the trust that is derived from non-crypto-graphic mechanisms such as social control via recommendation protocols, observation and direct experiences.

As mentioned in Section 1, social control mechanisms often may be the only option in evaluating trust in an open network environment as TTPs may not always be available. It therefore follows that a more comprehensive trust model is needed to represent the soft trust in addition to the hard trust. Furthermore, the new trust model provides a means of trust evaluations via trust dynamics (based on social control mechanisms) using notions of positive and negative experiences. In general, a trust model must address the following issues in mobile agent system security: 1) Trust Abstraction: How to capture the fundamental trust assumptions and the trust relationships among different principals that exist in the mobile agent systems. 2) Trust Establishment: How to formally represent the known trust relationships explicitly and update them dynamically in light of experiences. 3) Trust Derivation: How to derive new trust from existing trust relationships. We cover these issues in the following sections.

3.2   A Hybrid Trust Approach

We propose a new trust model where we combine the notions of hard and soft trust thereby enabling a wide range of trust relationships to be established. These include the trust relationships established in closed systems such as in an intra-domain operation where trust are chained and rooted from the domain trusted entities (such as a domain manager) to various member principals; full trust evaluation is possible once authentication and authorization is completed [12]. On the other hand, in an inter-domain operation in open networks, domains may not trust or know of each other or even TTPs may not always be available. This thus indicates the absence of authentication trust. In such cases we propose the use of soft trust based on social control mechanisms such as direct observation history or recommendations from other entities in the system (given that these entities are trusted to offer such recommendations) in conjunction with any hard trust (authentication trust) to form an informed opinion (ie the combined opinion) on the trustworthiness of an entity in question. Naturally, such an approach enables us to gain the benefits of both the hard and soft trust mechanisms in a scalable and flexible way that fits well with characteristics of extremely distributed nature of mobile agent systems. We will analyze and show the useful properties of our new trust model in Section 4. In the following section we will discuss the trust relationship modelling issues for mobile agents.

3.3   Mobile Agent Trust Relationships

Broadly speaking, in the context of mobile agents, we believe two types of trust that need to be addressed to cater for host and mobile code security issues. From the mobile agent owner point of view, we have trust on execution defined as the belief that the hosts will faithfully run mobile code and then migrate it to next destination; this trust is related to the underlying mechanisms for mobile code security, which provide preventive measures using TTPs to verify and certify the hosts' capacity for running the mobile code [11]; this trust is also related to the detection mechanisms such as signed security tags and chained hashing algorithms for mobile agent data integrity [12]. From the executing host point of view, we have the trust on mobile code defined as the belief on the ability of the agent owner principal to produce good code and on the honesty of the prior interim sender principals for not tampering with the code or making it malicious; this trust is related to the countermeasures employed in secure mobile agent systems such as the passports for mobile agent credentials and signed security tags for code integrity which can be verified by executing hosts [12]. We have refined these two types of trust using the Security Enhanced Mobile Agent (SeA) [12] as an example. We have derived several security related trust questions that should be answered at different stages of the life cycle of a typical mobile agent operation [7]. In the remaining part of this paper we focus on evaluation problems on such trust relationships.

3.4   Trust Evaluation

The trust valuation aids the decision making in the face of uncertainty in open network operations. Currently, the evaluation of trust relationships are mainly done by a single trust type, typically a hard trust relationship [11]. Such approaches suffer from drawbacks of higher access barriers, lack of ability in dealing with the uncertainties of post authentication and authorization behaviors in an inter-domain operation as entities in this situation will have different degree of trustworthiness for each other. One thus needs to set up proper metrics to evaluate such varied degrees of trust worthiness. Provided in Section 3.4.1 is a brief review on a well-known evaluation method and our new evaluation method is presented in Section 3.4.2.

3.4.1   Existing Trust Evaluation Methods.

As introduced in Section 1 Beth et al. [2] have developed a now well-known formalism for trust evaluation which takes into consideration trust dynamics such as trust evaluation via recommendation and direct experiences. In this paper we adopt and extend Beth's approach for trust valuation for mobile agent system. First let us consider some key results from Beth's trust evaluation formalism [2,5].

– A distinction is made between direct trust which consists of trusting an entity to perform a specific task, and the recommended trust which consists of trusting an entity to recommend another entity for a specific task. Definition of trust level V is based on the confidence level according to the conceptual formula:

$$v = \int_{\alpha}^{1} f_x(\theta)d\theta \quad 0 < \alpha < 1 \tag{1}$$

where θ is the trust and $f_x(\theta)$ can be called trust density function of an entity with regard to trust class x.

– Estimation of direct trust V_d, based on p positive observations, is done according to Formula 2. This trust value is the probability that a trustee has a reliability of more than α ($\alpha = [0, 1]$) when entrusted with a single task (i.e. a trust class such as execution or mobile code):

$$V_d = 1 - \alpha^p \qquad (2)$$

– Estimation of recommended trust V_r, based on p positive and n negative experiences, is done according formula:

$$V_r = \begin{cases} 1 - \alpha^{p-n} & if \ p > n \\ 0 & else \ 0 \end{cases} \qquad (3)$$

– Estimation of new trust V_n, based on a sequences of recommended trust V_r, and direct trust V_d is done using special ring-dot product defined as below:

$$V_n = V_r \odot V_d = 1 - (1 - V_d)^{V_r} \qquad (4)$$

3.4.2 Our New Evaluation Method Using the New Trust Model.
Before we propose our new trust model, let us first look at the problems associated Beth's Model.

Problem 1: While soft trust has the advantages of enabling interactions without full hard trust (authentication trust), it does has some problems of its own. One of the issues raised by Jøsang [5] is the trust saturation problem which arises due to long history of positive experiences. For example, in Formula 2 trust value for direct trust can only increase since only positive experience is used, and as a consequence, a long history either implies absolute trust or none at all. This can be misused by a malicious entity by cooperating during a certain period in order to accumulate high trust from another entity and then defecting on a transaction of sufficiently high value. We have simulated these behaviors in Fig. 1 and Fig. 2.

Problem 2: Another problem is the lack of ability to adapt to changing trustworthiness in the calculation of recommended trust observed also by Jøsang [5]. This is treated differently from direct trust in that negative experiences are accepted according to Formula 3, which makes it possible to have a relatively low trust value after a long history when same level of positive and negative experiences have been observed. However, when the entity changes its behavior so will the related number of the positive and negative experiences. Hence it is possible after a long history of positive observations the new observations will hardly have any influence at all on the trust value at both end of the shape. Fig. 2 shows the shape of the saturation and low evaluation regions. Now we describe in the following the solutions to the above problems using our new trust model:

Proposed Solution to Problem 1: A possible solution is to derive a new model whereby the soft trust V_s (a set of trust containing direct trust V_d, recommended trust V_r, or derived trust V_n) can be combined with the hard trust

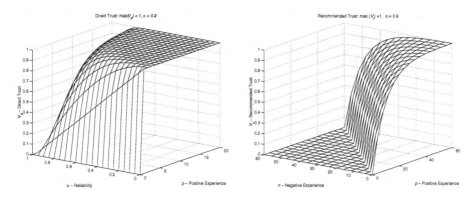

Fig. 1. Direct trust V_d.   **Fig. 2.** Recommended trust V_r.

V_h(e.g. a set of authentication trust V_{auth}) into a new set of hybrid trust V_c using a combining function f_{com}:

$$V_c = f_{com}(mV_s, nV_h) \tag{5}$$

Where: m and n are scaling factors allocating the weighting for V_s and V_h in the combining function, such that $m, n \in \mathcal{R}$ and $m + n = 1$ and a simple instantiation of Formula 5 can be defined as below:

$$V_c = mV_s + nV_h \tag{6}$$

This simple additive combining function is chosen for illustrative purpose only. As for a practical implementation, there are more developed trust combining operators proposed such as the Consensus Operator offered by the Subjective Logic [6]. With reduced allocation to soft trust (say 50 % allocation), the saturation is no longer possible even without the presence of authentication trust (V_h=0), but the drawback is that the full trust evaluation is also lost by the reduced trust allocation and thus put a high access barrier. Fig. 3 and Fig. 4 show better examples where 50 % of trust is allocated for the authentication trust and 50 % to the observation based direct trust, i.e. $V_c = 0.5 * V_d + 0.5 * V_{auth}$, where $V_d \in V_s$ and $V_{auth} \in V_h$. These simplified examples show the idea that the combined trust can be used as a practical solution to above-mentioned trust saturation problem.

Proposed Solution to Problem 2: Again this trust low trust evaluation problem with a recommended trust V_r can be improved in a similar fashion as for the direct trust solution discussed above by combining the recommended trust with authentication trust(see Fig. 4), i.e. $V_c = 0.5 * V_r + 0.5 * V_{auth}$, where $V_r \in V_s$ and $V_{auth} \in V_h$. After adding the required amount of authentication trust to the recommended trust one can see that the recommended trust's low evaluation regions (see Fig. 2) has been elevated. This sets a certain level of combined trust initially and thus enables controlled interactions. This therefore provides an opportunity for the recommended trust to evolve.

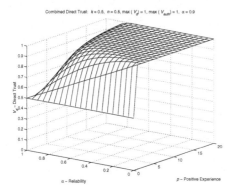

Fig. 3. Combined direct trust.

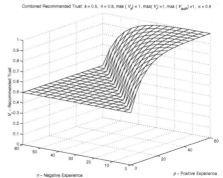

Fig. 4. Combined recommended trust.

4   Properties of the New Trust Model

The new trust model possesses several new properties that can not be achieved by hard security mechanisms alone. These new properties provide synergies between the hard trust and soft trust mechanisms yielding desirable mutual improvement.

First, whilst hard trust can provide assurance on security properties such as authentication, authorization, integrity protection and non-repudiation, it has high demands on the presence of TTPs [13, 11]. This can put server constraints on the scalability and flexibility of the security system design. By combining the hard trust with soft trust, the requirements for the availability on TTPs can be relaxed, as trust can now be evaluated via soft trust mechanisms in situations where none or only partial authentication trust exists. This improves the scalability and flexibility of the security design. For example, the verification sever based model proposed by Tan et al. [11] only accepts the code execution verification from fully trusted servers (based on boolean trust relationships), which is a very strong constraint that may restrict the scalability of the system. With the help of the proposed hybrid model, the verification servers can now be evaluated with different trustworthiness, and selections of verification servers will be far more flexible and fine-gained. The hard trust model by [13] can also be improved in a similar way by enabling the agent owner host to specify trust policies for Tamper-Proof Environment (TPE) based on different trustworthiness on the TPEs and thus improve the flexibility and scalability of TPE model. Equally important is that in a soft trust environment trustworthiness can be evaluated dynamically and even in the post authentication stage and thus the over-all security level can be raised.

Second, hard trust, in addition to its usual function mentioned in the previous paragraph, can also play a role in providing improvement to the soft trust. As discussed in Section 3.4.2, by insisting on certain portion of authentication trust in the system (providing the required amount of hard security assurance) one can avoid the trust saturation region introduced by the flat contour (See Fig. 1 and Fig. 2) in the soft trust evolution based on recommendation and direct trust alone. This provides a means to combat the trust saturation problem introduced in Section 3.4.2. In a practical implementation, for example, a malicious entity may explore a soft trust only system by accumulating trust through certain number of interactions and only to defect on a high value transaction [5]. With the hybrid model, trust policies can be used to specify the required amount of authentication trust for each access decisions. In the case of defection, the hard trust demanded by the trust policies will provide a certain level of assurance for non-repudiation. Another example is the low trust evaluation problem [5] associated with soft trust alone, where it is possible to have a relatively low trust value after a long history when same level of positive and negative experiences have been observed (see the flat contour in Fig. 2). This low evaluation problem can hinder the open network operation by putting up an unnecessary higher barrier, which is contradictory to the original goal of soft trust. With the hybrid trust model the low evaluation area can be eliminated by adding authentication trust (see Fig. 4).

It is thus worth noting that at an application level, with our hybrid model, trust policies can be set up for different application contexts, which will assert the required amount of authentication trust as a threshold for any access control decisions on the resources in the case of host protection. For agent owner hosts, similar trust policies can also be implemented for assembling mobile agent itinerary list, initiating appropriate recommendation protocols, and selecting security patterns before deploying the agent into the open network for the itinerant computing. As can be seen from the above application scenarios that one can use the hybrid trust model to make more accurate and fine-grained security decisions.

5   Conclusions and Future Work

This paper proposes a new approach for the design of mobile agent trust model. The notion of hybrid trust for mobile agent security is introduced by combining both the hard and soft trust. We illustrated the use of the new hybrid model to describe relevant trust relationships explicitly in an existing security enhanced mobile agent system. We have analyzed the properties of the new model such as the ability to allow controllable level of interactions in situations where authentication trust is absent or partial. The proposed model has provided significant improvement for hard and soft trust models in terms of trust dynamics, and ability to guard against known problems of trust saturation/low evaluation which can occur if only a single form of trust is used. The hybrid model enhances the security of mobile agent systems by eliminating the possibility of attacks against the known flaws of existing trust models and furthermore it can help make more accurate and fine-grained security decisions. Therefore, the hybrid trust model can help raise the security levels of mobile agent systems.

The new model presented in this paper is only a starting point into researching a new approach of using hybrid trust based security techniques for mobile agents. We are currently working on the formalization of the model and integrating it into a comprehensive mobile agent security framework; in particular, modelling the new trust model formally in a variety of mobile agent systems with hierarchical, non-hierarchical and mixed domain structures and integrating it into a practical mobile agent application [12].

References

1. Alfarez Abdul-Rahman and Stephen Hailes. A distributed trust model. In *Proceedings of the 1997 New Security Paradigms Workshop, pages 48–60. ACM*, 1997.
2. T Beth, M Borcherding, and B Klein. Valuation of trust in open networks. In *Computer Security - ESORICS '94, D. Gollmann (Ed), Lecture Notes in Computer Science, Berline: Springer-Verlag*, volume 875, pages 3–18, 1994.
3. D. M. Chess. Security issues in mobile code systems. In *Mobile Agents and Security, Editor Vigna*, volume LNCS1419. Springer-Verlag, 1998.
4. W. Jansen. Mobile agents and security. *NIST*, 1999.
5. Audun Jøsang. The prospectives of modelling trust in information security. In *Proceedings of 1997 Australasian Conference on Information Security and Privacy.* Springer-Verlag, 1997.
6. Audun Jøsang. A logic for uncertain probabilities. *International Journal of Uncertainty, Fuzziness and Knowledge-Based Systems*, 9(3):279–311, 2001.
7. Ching Lin and Vijay Varadharajan. Modelling and evaluating trust relationships in mobile agent based systems. In *Proceedings of First International Conference on Applied Cryptography and Network Security (ACNS03)*, volume LNCS2846, pages 176–190, Kunming, China, October 2003. Springer-Verlag.
8. S. Marsh. Formalising trust as a computational concept. *PhD thesis, University of Stirling*, 1994.
9. R. Oppliger. Security issues related to mobile code and agent-based systems. *Computer Communications*, 22(12):1165–1170, July, 1999.
10. L. Rasmusson and S. Jansson. Simulated social control for secure internet commerce: Position paper at the new security paradigms workshop. 1996.
11. Hock Kim Tan and Luc Moreau. Trust relationships in a mobile agent system. In Gian Pietro Picco, editor, *Fifth IEEE International Conference on Mobile Agents*, volume LNCS2240, Atlanta, Georgia, December, 2001. Springer-Verlag.
12. Vijay Varadharajan. Security enhanced mobile agents. *Proc. of 7th ACM Conference on Computer and Communication Security*, 2000.
13. Uwe G. Wilhelm, Sebastian Staamann, and Levente Buttyán. Introducing trusted third parties to the mobile agent paradigm. *Secure Internet Programming, Jan Vitek, Christian D. Jensen (Eds.)*, pages 469–489, 1997.
14. Bin Yu and Munidar P. Singh. Distributed reputation management for electronic commerce. *First International Joint Conference on Autonomous Agents and Multiagent Systems, Bologna, Italy*, 2002.

Balancing Privacy and Trust
in Electronic Marketplaces

Sandra Steinbrecher

Technische Universität Dresden, Fakultät Informatik, D-01062 Dresden, Germany
steinbrecher@acm.org

Abstract. Person-to-Person marketplaces have become quite popular on the Internet. Members of the communities established by these marketplaces may sell and buy items within the community. Naturally they have certain security requirements on every trade conducted within the community. We investigate these requirements and the possibility to fulfill them to guarantee multilateral security. eBay, one of the greatest auction providers, uses a reputation system to enhance trust in its marketplace. Unfortunately this system does not address privacy. We suggest how the use of other pseudonym types can increase privacy within a marketplace community like eBay while maintaining the same level of trust.

1 Introduction

On the Internet person-to-person marketplaces, especially auctions, have become quite popular during the recent years. Numerous providers offer platforms which initiate so-called 'communities' whose members are allowed to sell and buy arbitrary items within the community. To become a member a user has to register at the provider by choosing the pseudonym he wants to use and declaring some personal information (e.g. his age, postal and e-mail address) that may be verified by the provider. One of the greatest providers with nearly 95 million registered members worldwide at the end of 2003 [9] is eBay (http://www.ebay.com/).

If a member of the community wants to sell an item he has to set up an offer which will be linked by the provider's web site. Usually the offer at least contains the seller's pseudonym and a description of the item. Typically selling/bidding period and selling/reserve price are added.

After the item has been sold seller and buyer somehow have to exchange the item purchased and the reward pursuant to its price. This exchange must be fair, i.e. seller and buyer both have to receive what they have agreed upon. If the item is a digital good (e.g. information) and for the reward electronic money is available, the exchange can be realized by electronic fair exchange [2]. In the project SEMPER [18] a framework for an optimal electronic marketplace which allows trade with digital goods was developed. But most items are physical goods that can be exchanged either directly between seller and buyer or via a trusted third party that guarantees the correct transfer. Many providers offer or mediate an appropriate transfer service against a charge. Some specialty providers already

S. Katsikas, J. Lopez, and G. Pernul (Eds.): TrustBus 2004, LNCS 3184, pp. 70–79, 2004.
© Springer-Verlag Berlin Heidelberg 2004

collect the item from the seller beforehand and set up the offer themselves. This is only utilizable for easy describable and comparable goods.

But because the price of many items sold within marketplace communities is quite low (e.g. books, CDs, computer games) many buyers and sellers decide to exchange money and item directly. The provider provides them with the other member's personal data necessary to do this. Usually the buyer transfers money from his account to the seller's account and after the money has been credited his account the seller sends the item by mail to the buyer.

This exchange needs trust in each other that own expectations and the other's behaviour are equivalent. Many of these exchanges are successful, but unfortunately some are not. In the eBay community continuously frauds are discovered where a member pretended to sell items, collected money from buyers, but did not deliver the items offered. In 2002 more than 51,000 complaints about Internet auction frauds in the U.S. were reported to the Federal Trade Commission [7]. Although the money lost might be little the victim usually is annoyed.

So-called feedback forums or reputation systems have been introduced to the provider's service to handle problems that might occur during the interactions between sellers and buyers. After the direct exchange of money and item is completed (satisfying or not) both may give comments or/and marks to each other. These are added to the member's feedback profile (usually together with the annotator and the exchange considered). Before buying from or selling to a person every member of the community can inform himself about the other's profile. His past behaviour usually might indicate his behaviour in the future.

Unfortunately the currently used reputation systems[1] allow to generate interest and behaviour profiles of pseudonyms (e.g. time and frequency of participation, valuation of and interest in specific items). If the pseudonym becomes related to a real name, as it typically does for trading partners, the profile becomes related to this real name as well.

Section 2 gives a more detailed overview of the requirements members and providers of marketplace communities usually have. We concentrate on privacy requirements because recent surveys [15, 11] indicate that a lack of privacy seems to reduce the success of electronic commerce. Every member wants to determine himself how much and when he wants to reveal data about his person, behaviour and interests. Possible measures that help to fulfill the security requirements are outlined. In Section 3 we investigate to what extent the auction provider eBay makes use of these measures. In section 4 we describe how identity management can help to reach a compromise between different requirements in the sense of multilateral security. Section 5 describes the use of reputation systems to increase trust in electronic marketplace communities. In Section 6 we present simple ad-hoc measures to realize the privacy requirements users might have while not decreasing the trust in other security requirements the system should provide. The measures presented should be understood as possible suggestions that have to be elaborated further but can easily be implemented in existing platforms. Due to space limitation they cannot be described in detail.

---

[1] An overview of common reputation systems currently in use can be found in [13].

2   Requirements on Electronic Marketplaces

Let an electronic marketplace community be given with a set of members at a specific time who are allowed to take the role seller, prospect or buyer. Within the community a seller-iniated trade consists of the following actions:

1. **Offer:** By taking the role seller and offering an item under specific conditions (including usually a minimum price) a member initiates a new sale.
2. **Bidding:** By bidding on an item and specifying his conditions for the buying a member (who is not the seller of this item) takes the role prospect.
3. **Sale:** If the sale ends one of the prospects in the sale might get the role buyer. Which prospect gets this role is determined by the provider by comparing the prospects' conditions with the seller's and choosing the optimal one for the seller (if there is one).
4. **Exchange:** After the sale buyer and seller have to exchange item and reward pursuant to the price. The order of paying the reward and delivering the item has to be negotiated between them.

In a buyer-initiated trade the buyer publishes the item he is interested in under specific conditions and waits for prospects who want to sell this item to him.

Members and provider of the community want to benefit by participating in resp. providing it: The provider wants his service to succeed and give him an economical benefit. The buyer wants to receive the item bought and the seller wants to receive the reward pursuant to the price.

Members and providers necessarily have security requirements on the principles of the community and the trades transacted within it that have to be negotiated and as far as possible fulfilled to guarantee multilateral security [14]. Usual security requirements as listed in [19]) distinguish between protection of content and circumstances. In the case of electronic marketplace communities content means every information regarding a trade members might give. Correspondingly circumstances cover every (explicit and implicit) action regarding a trade that might be performed. Protection of unauthorized access to information regarding content (confidentiality) and circumstances (anonymity)[2] and unauthorized modification of information regarding content (integrity) and circumstances (accountability) are described in subsection 2.1 and 2.2. Security and cryptography provide us with a lot of measures which help to reach these requirements. Our favourites are outlined briefly in these subsections as well.

As additional security requirements unauthorized impairment of functionality regarding content (availability) and circumstances (reachability, legal enforceability) have to be mentioned. But we do not outline them in detail here. We assume that the community provider is interested in guaranteeing reachability and availability, because as we already noted he wants his service to succeed. Further the community provider is liable for the service he offers but may transfer a part of liability for trades to the members involved. For this reason the community provider has to link an artificial person to every member.

---

[2] We neglect as well hiding of content as unobservability of circumstances that are listed in [19] as security requirements.

2.1 Unauthorized Access to Information

We assume that members do not interact with each other except from trades to prevent outside information flows between them.

– **Confidentiality:** This requirement seems to contradict usual trades which at least need a detailed description of the item offered and its actual price. But members might only want to buy from or sell to specific other members and keep a trade secret from others. Also there could be the wish to keep bids made and digital items exchanged secret from everyone not involved in a trade or for a specific time. Using public key encryption with a convenient distribution of public keys can help to do so. Additionally secret sharing schemes might be used to prevent misuse of data deposited at the provider.
– **Anonymity/Pseudonymity:** A member wants to specify which personal information about him other members or the provider get. One is anonymous resp. his role as a `seller`, `prospect` or `buyer` of an item if this particular action he performs under the role is not linkable to him (cf. the definition in [12]). This cannot be reached in this strict sense because during a trade a member has to be identified under a certain pseudonym. But by the usage of pseudonyms members can control the linkability of the trades they are involved in. This results in the following pseudonym types as listed in [12]:
  - A person pseudonym only is a substitute for the member's real name. All his actions within the community are linkable
  - A role pseudonym is used just in one role of the roles `seller`, `prospect` or `buyer`. If a `prospect` becomes the `buyer` of an item his pseudonyms used become linkable for everyone noticing this change.
  - A relationship pseudonym can be used by a member for every participation in a trade with the same other member. This is only possible as `prospect` or `buyer`. For a `seller` other member's participation in his trades are linkable. A `seller` cannot use a relationship pseudonym when offering an item because he does not know a future `prospect` or `buyer`.
  - A role-relationship pseudonym can only be used as `prospect` or `buyer` for the same reason. But the for the `prospect` becoming the `buyer` his pseudonyms used for these roles become linkable.
  - A transaction pseudonym guarantees optimal unlinkability of a member's actions within the community. Every member uses a different pseudonym for every trade he is involved in what makes his participations unlinkable. But the change of role `prospect` to `buyer` still might be linkable.

2.2 Unauthorized Modification of Information

– **Integrity:** Members want to be certain that every modification within the actions of a trade will be detected.
– **Accountability:** Every member wants other members to be responsible for the actions they are allowed to perform within the community, especially offering/delivering items as `seller`, bidding on items as `prospect` and paying

for items as `buyer`. No member should be able to deny an action he executed. Accountability guarantees that everyone taking part in a trade and not following its protocol is accountable for his misbehavior. Members want other members and the provider to follow the trade protocol correctly. The provider has to determine the outcome of a sale correctly. Especially he has to determine the `buyer` correctly[3]. Ideally the members are able to verify the correctness of the provider's actions. The exchange between `seller` and `buyer` has to take place in a fair manner that means both get what they expected.

All digital available information can be made integer and accountable by adding a digital signature and if necessary a time stamp. Every member accusing another member to have taken the role `seller` or `prospect` for a trade must show the corresponding signature to prove his accusation. A secure implementation of electronic auctions using these primitives to guarantee accountability and integrity has been presented in [17]. The techniques used can easily be adapted to general electronic marketplaces.

The exchange within a trade often is not executed under the control of the marketplace provider. For this reason other proofs have to be collected that the members' actions are integer. Examples are receipts of bank transfers or shipping via mail. But this is outside the scope of this paper.

Note all measures only provide proofs to members and provider that others did not execute an action correctly. But any dispute between them has to be solved outside the system in a legal proceeding. Legal enforceability naturally depends on the grade the cryptographic and security measures or other proofs are recognized as legally binding in national and international law.

3   Realization by eBay

The choice on which of the measures is the best one to realize a certain requirement depends on several factors. According to multilateral security [14] members should be able to negotiate a compromise between their requirements. Usually in current implementations of marketplaces communities the provider determines the requirements. Communities will often start with no or only simple measures depending on the money that should be invested in the community's infrastructure. With the community's growth and the members security requirements' increasing after some of them might have been disappointed by dishonest members the measures often become stronger. The provider's interest in benefit hopefully reaches that he provides a service acceptable for the majority of his members. He necessarily has to assure that members and potential members trust in the community and his kind of organizing sales. Electronic marketplaces currently in use and successful on the Internet neglect some security requirements and use

---

[3] There might be sellers or prospects who cooperate with the provider to influence the outcome to get additional benefit. But usually at least one of the other prospects or the seller involved in the auction wants the provider to work correctly.

weaker measures than the ones described in section 2 for the benefit of usability and lower costs of providing the framework and participating in it.

One of the greatest providers of an electronic marketplace community is eBay. eBay charges a fee for every item offered and sold. To assure that the members pay this fee since 2001 becoming a member of eBay is only possible for people who are willing to declare a bank account or credit card the fee will be paid with. eBay delegates all liability for trades within the community to the members involved. In the following we analyze in extracts to what extent the security requirements users have are realized.

3.1 Unauthorized Access to Information

– **Confidentiality:** A member is free to set up a trade with the information he likes to reveal. But there is no possibility to restrict the access to the trade to other members, only taking the role `prospect` might be limited.
– **Anonymity/Pseudonymity:** Person pseudonyms are in use. For eBay as provider every member of the eBay community is linkable to his pseudonym. All purchases, sales and their circumstances (e.g., time, business partner, reputation) of a pseudonym are linkable to this pseudonym for every member of the community.

  Even after the change of a pseudonym that is offered by eBay all previous changes of pseudonyms are linkable for all members.

  eBay allows a seller to set up trades which hide the link between an item and pseudonyms bidding on or buying it from every member except the seller (so-called 'private auctions') and eBay. After a sale `buyer` and `seller` get their corresponding real names and addresses.

3.2 Unauthorized Modification of Information

– **Integrity:** Bidding on and selling an item within the eBay community has to be confirmed by the buyer by logging in with his pseudonym and a password. The default used is unencrypted transmission to the eBay server, but the member may choose SSL and afterwards the password will be stored in a cookie.
– **Accountability:** eBay offers a transfer service for the exchange of item and reward pursuant to the price against an extra charge. If the members decide to execute the exchange on their own both seller and buyer have the possibility to complain about an unfair behaviour to eBay. The dishonest member gets an admonishment from eBay. After multiple admonishments he might be excluded from the eBay community.

  eBay Germany aligns the address a member provides with his application to the community with the Schufa database of addresses where all data about bank credits and accounts is collected in Germany.

  The bids made are published speedily. This helps the members to verify that their own bid is considered. But the members have to trust eBay that the time of every bid or sale is recorded correctly and the bids listed were made by the members listed.

4   Identity Management

User-controlled privacy-enhancing identity management gives the possibility to reach pseudonymous trading within a marketplace community that tries to satisfy both provider's and members' security requirements. The user can protect against unauthorized access to information while by the use of credentials the server can be sure pseudonymous users are reliable and can be made accountable for misbehaviour. The use of an identity management system for the scenario of classical e-Commerce on the Internet is outlined in [6]. In contrast to electronic marketplace communities in this scenario the roles of seller ('shop') and buyer resp. prospect ('visitor') are fixed and not interchanged. One of of the possible additional scenarios for identity management mentioned briefly in [6] are Internet auctions (a special case of electronic marketplace communities) but not addressed with respect to the change of roles.

The project PRIME (http://prime.inf.tu-dresden.de/) builds a prototype for an identity management system that gives the user the control over his personal data and its use for different applications e.g., e-commerce. The prototype to be build will make an appropriate design of the user side and possible server sides. This will need application providers to install this software on the server side and provide access to their services using identity management software.

Because a wide use of such architectures will probably take some more years we present measures from identity management to reach more pseudonymity in existing marketplace communities and the building up of trust to compensate the absence of expensive protection against unauthorized modification of information. Our goal is balancing trust in the community established and privacy requirements members have.

Privacy measures on the application layer, in this case marketplace communities assume that the underlying network layers already provide anonymity. Members of Internet communities can act anonymously by using anonymizing services. They have the choice between simple anonymous proxies (e.g., Anonymizer [1]) or more secure services like Web mixes [3] or Tor [16], both more or less based on Chaum's Mixes [5].

5   Trust and Reputation Systems

The critical point for trust within a marketplace community is whether within a trade seller's and buyer's expectation and behaviour regarding the exchange fit each other. Here we only consider reputation systems as a possibility to handle this trust. Every member involved in a trade in the role seller or buyer gets the possibility to give a rating to his trading partner. In the eBay community the member can choose between the discrete values 0, −1 or 1 as marks and add a comment depending on his satisfaction with the trade. A member's reputation is represented as a sum of the ratings given to him. By informing himself about another's member reputation before participating in a trade a member hopefully will get an indication about this member's future behaviour. According to the study in [10] there is an economical need for using reputation systems in Internet auctions. Their empirical result based on Pentium III as homogenous items with stable prices is that a seller's reputation affects the price bidders are willing to pay while the buyer's reputation does not. But this study does not address the use of reputations systems for non-homogenous items and users with varying expectations. A good reputation system collecting experiences from members should take several factors into consideration e.g., time of a trade, value of an item, reputation of the member rating another. Such a system should enable a user to enter his personal preferences and expectations regarding a trade and members whose reputation should be considered and whose not. But designing a reputation system is outside the scope of this paper, we would only like to give suggestions.

Certainly members may give unfair ratings in the positive or negative direction because they fear a possible revenge of the other member involved in the trade or want to take revenge themselves. This could be prevented by using a fair exchange of the reputation that should be given for a trade with eBay as trusted third party.

6   Privacy and Reputation Systems

In the context of person-to-person marketplaces privacy mostly is not addressed. Experience has shown that many users do not worry about trust in other members but about privacy of their own personal data they worry even less. In the U.S. the Federal Trade Commission offers guidelines to users of Internet auctions [8] concerning trust management but does not address privacy in this context.

Unfortunately the type of reputation systems used in common electronic marketplace communities like eBay allows to generate interest and behaviour profiles of pseudonyms, because the user who gave the rating and the respected sale is listed together with a member's reputation profile. For example time and frequency of participation as well as valuation of and interest in specific items can be collected for eBay pseudonyms that are person pseudonyms as already outlined in section 3. If the pseudonym becomes related to a real name, as it does for trading partners, the profile becomes related to the real name as well. This is true for trading partners who exchange item and reward directly because at least the seller necessarily has to know email and real address of the buyer.

Providers usually argue that these profiles of reputations are necessary to enhance trust in potential trading partners. But smart merchants also already use these data to generate user-specific advertising emails. Since 2001 EBay warns users about merchants offering products to email addresses they collected from bidders.

Our goal is to increase pseudonymity while maintaining the same level of trust provided by the reputation system. As already outlined briefly in [6] a pseudonym type that is restricted 'to only one per user per auction' should be used. Unlinkability between sales a member is involved as a `seller, prospect/buyer` can be reached by using role pseudonyms regarding to this roles. Using this type of pseudonym has the positive side effect that reputations for these roles are collected separately. This makes sense from the economical point of view as already outlined in Section 5 and even should increase the trust in the reputation system because members might be different trustworthy as `seller` than as `buyer/prospect`. Relationship and role-relationship pseudonyms cannot be used as `seller`.

Using transaction pseudonyms seems to be not sufficient because the trust reached by reputation collected under a pseudonym cannot be realized. To give members the possibility to use their reputation with different pseudonyms a similar mechanism than for convertible credentials could to be used [4]. The anonymity set in Internet marketplace is quite large, if a member is able to interact with pseudonyms difficult to link with his real identity. In reputation systems where the reputation is reflected by the numerical sum of ratings many members will have the same reputation and thus the anonymity set of one single member contains all members with the same reputation. If the reputation system allows users to give additional comments regarding their rating, the possibility for the formulation of comments has to be limited as well to guarantee an appropriate anonymity set. This gives members the possibility to determine the linkability of their actions within the community.

To guarantee a member's accountability for the provider his pseudonym must be linkable to the real name who has registered himself as this member and under this pseudonym.

7   Conclusion

In this paper, we analyzed the trust and privacy aspects in electronic marketplace communities. Especially we investigated the use of reputation systems to enhance trust in these communities. As shown by the example eBay unfortunately privacy is not addressed by their reputation system. We outlined how the use of other pseudonym types and the limitation of the possible ratings of a reputation system can increase privacy while maintaining the same level of trust in a marketplace community and with only little afford.

Note we only sketched a possible solution to balance privacy and trust in marketplace communities on the Internet. In future research the solution will be filled with a concrete implementation and analysis of the unlinkability provided in real-world situations with the use of different pseudoNM types.

In arbitrary electronic communities where most of the members will never meet personally trust and privacy issues are of great importance. Especially in communities that concentrate on self help members looking for help on the one hand usually want to remain anonymous while on the other hand they want to get help from trustworthy other members. These communities are not driven by the wish of economical benefit and have to be analyzed as well and even more carefully in future work.

References

1. The Anonymizer. http://www.anonymizer.com/
2. N. Asokan, Victor Shoup, and Michael Waidner. Asynchronous protocols for optimistic fair exchange. IEEE Symposium on Research in Security and Privacy, IEEE Computer Society Press, Los Alamitos, 86–99, 1998.
3. Oliver Berthold, Hannes Federrath, and Stefan Köpsell. Web mixes: A system for anonymous and unobservable internet access. Designing Privacy Enhancing Technologies. Proc. Workshop on Design Issues in Anonymity and Unobservability, LNCS 2009, Springer-Verlag, Heidelberg 2001, pp. 115–129.
4. David Chaum. Showing credentials without identification. signatures transferred between unconditionally unlinkable pseudonyms. EUROCRYPT '85, LNCS 219, Springer-Verlag, Heidelberg 1986, pp. 241–244.
5. David Chaum. Untraceable electronic mail, return addresses and digital pseudonyms. Communications of the ACM, 24(2), 1981, pp. 84–88.
6. Sebastian Clauî and Marit Köhntopp. Identity management and its support of multilateral security. Computer Networks.
7. Federal Trade Commission. Internet auction fraud targeted by law enforcers. available from http://www.ftc.gov/opa/2003/04/bidderbeware.htm, 2003.
8. Federal Trade Commission. Internet auctions: A guide for buyers and sellers. available from http://www.ftc.gov/bcp/conline/pubs/online/auctions.htm, 2003.
9. eBay. Annual report 2003. available from http://investor.ebay.com/annual.cfm, 2003.
10. Dan Houser and John Wooders. Reputation in auctions: Theory, and evidence from ebay. Feb. 2000, available at http://bpa.arizona.edu/ jwooders/ebay.pdf.
11. Harris Interactive. First major post-9/11 privacy survey finds consumers demanding companies do more to protect privacy. Rochester Feb. 2002, http://www.harrisinteractive.com/news/allnewsbydate.asp?NewsID=429.
12. Marit Köhntopp and Andreas Pfitzmann. Anonymity, unobservability, and pseudonymity – a proposal for terminology. Draft v0.12., June 2001.
13. Peter Kollock. The production of trust in online markets. Advances in Group Processes (Vol. 16), Greenwich, CT: JAI Press., 1999.
14. Andreas Pfitzmann. Technologies for multilateral security. G. Müller, K. Rannenberg (Eds.), Multilateral Security for Global Communication, Addison-Wesley, Reading, MA, 1999, pp. 85–91.
15. Pew Internet & American Life Project. Trust amd privacy online: why americans want to rewrite the rules. http://pewinternet.org/reports/loc.asp?Report=19, 2000-08-20.
16. Paul Syverson Roger Dingledine, Nick Mathewson. Tor: The second-generation onion router. available from http://freehaven.net/tor/tor-design.pdf, 2003.
17. Stuart G. Stubblebine and Paul F. Syverson. Fair on-line auctions without special trusted parties. 3rd International Conference on Financial Cryptography (FC '99), LNCS 1648, Springer-Verlag, Berlin 1999, 230–240.
18. Michael Waidner. Development of a secure electronic marketplace for Europe. ESORICS 96, LNCS 1146, Springer-Verlag Heidelberg, pp. 1–14.
19. Gritta Wolf and Andreas Pfitzmann. Properties of protection goals and their integration into a user interface. Computer Networks 32 (2000) 685 699.

Reducing Server Trust
in Private Proxy Auctions

Giovanni Di Crescenzo[1], Javier Herranz[2], and Germán Sáez[2]

[1] Telcordia Technologies, Piscataway, New Jersey, USA[*]
`giovanni@research.telcordia.com`
[2] Dept. Matemàtica Aplicada IV, Universitat Politècnica de Catalunya
C. Jordi Girona, 1-3, Mòdul C3, Campus Nord, 08034-Barcelona, Spain[**]
{`jherranz,german`}`@mat.upc.es`

Abstract. We investigate *proxy auctions*, an auction model which is proving very successful for on-line businesses (e.g., [9]), where a trusted server manages bids from clients by continuously updating the current price of the item and the currently winning bid as well as keeping private the winning client's maximum bid.

We propose techniques for reducing the trust in the server by defining and achieving a security property, called *server integrity*. Informally, this property protects clients from a novel and large class of attacks from a corrupted server by allowing them to verify the correctness of updates to the current price and the currently winning bid. Our new auction scheme achieves server integrity and satisfies two important properties that are not enjoyed by previous work in the literature: it has minimal interaction, and only requires a single trusted server.

While the privacy property of our scheme holds under a standard intractability assumption, the server integrity property holds unconditionally.

1 Introduction

The overwhelming expansion of the Internet is today being accompanied by a large increase of financial activities and transactions that are conducted on-line. An example of notable success is represented by on-line auctions. A few minutes navigation on the Internet allows to realize the existence of several sites offering easy to implement auctions as a way for anybody to sell items of any kind to the best bidder. Different are the types of auction that are being offered by these business, but one in particular is becoming very popular: proxy auctions.

In generic auctions a server is managing the selling of some item and receiving bids from clients, eventually choosing one of these bids according to some criteria.

In proxy auctions clients are invited to submit the maximum price they would like to pay for the item. While the client offering the maximum price

---

[*] Part of this work done while visiting UPC, Spain.
[**] Work partially supported by Spanish *Ministerio de Ciencia y Tecnología*, project TIC 2003-00866.

eventually wins, the price established for the purchasing is not necessarily the maximum offered price but it is just above the second maximum price offered. More precisely, the system acts as an electronic proxy that repeatedly places bids for the clients (up to the bidder's specified maximum price) to keep them ahead of other bidders. Therefore, a bidder can only be outbid if someone else enters a greater maximum price.

On one hand, proxy auctions seem very attractive, especially for Internet users, since they can submit their maximum bid and then not care about how the auction goes until the end of the auction itself. Instead, in a real-life (also called English-style) auction, users need to carefully listen how the auction goes and repeatedly submit bids to outbid other bidders.

On the other hand, proxy auctions put a significant amount of trust in servers. If servers are fully trusted then the auction winner and price is going to be fairly decided. However, if this is not the case, then both can be compromised. In the interest of maximizing the final selling price and therefore its commission fee, a server might both claim that one particular bidder outbid another one without this being the case, or decide to update the item price by an amount larger than what he is supposed to.

In this paper we present techniques for preventing these types of undesired behavior from corrupted servers in proxy auctions.

Our Model, Definition and Results. We consider a model composed of several clients who intend to purchase an item by participating in a proxy auction, and a server, taking care of operations such as setting starting and final date of the auction, and updating current price and currently winning bid.

We present a first formal definition of some basic security properties that one would expect in this type of auction. In particular, we define security against clients preventing other clients to win the auction, and privacy of the maximum price offered by the winning client. These properties are already achieved by many businesses on the Internet (e.g. [9]).

Most importantly, we focus on other security requirements not achieved by many businesses on the Internet, such as server-integrity. We formally define this property and propose a very simple and efficient auction scheme that achieves this property without compromising the above mentioned privacy property. We do not even compromise the main efficiency property of these schemes: that is, their round complexity. In fact, we believe one important property of our auction scheme is that it is non-interactive, in the sense that bidding requires a single message from client to server and updating current item value and currently winning bid also requires a single message from server to client. Another important property of our scheme is that it uses a single server to guarantee the correctness of the scheme, rather than many servers that cannot collude, as done previously in many works. Our investigation focused on enhancing the security of auction systems that are used in many business on the Internet. This should be contrasted with essentially all papers on auctions in the cryptographic literature that instead focus on designing elegant protocols with many interesting security properties but that unfortunately remain very far from protocols used in practice.

Crucial tools in the design of our auction scheme are new non-interactive perfect zero-knowledge proof systems (see, e.g. [3, 6]), which enlarge the class of languages that are known to have such systems. For instance, we show how to prove that a tuple of quadratic residues or non residues encrypts a value that is greater than a certain integer. We stress that these non-interactive zero-knowledge proofs are indeed quite efficient since they do not require any reduction of a problem instance to an instance of an arbitrary NP-complete problem. We also discuss known solutions for these proof systems that are even more efficient but however either require more rounds of interaction between the parties or assume the existence of a random oracle (currently known to be a false assumption).

Related Results. Several investigations have been done in the cryptographic literature on auctions (see, e.g., [7, 5, 15, 16, 11, 17]), mostly dealing with sealed-bid auctions. Some papers (see, e.g., [13, 1, 14]) dealt with proxy auctions, but all considered multi-server models to guarantee protocol correctness and required many rounds of interaction or assumed the existence of random oracles.

2   Definition of Secure Proxy Auctions

Setup: Parties, Items, Connectivity. The parties involved in a secure proxy auction are a server, denoted as S, and the clients, denoted as $C_1, C_2, \ldots, C_n$. The server is managing the auctioning of a single item (for simplicity) and the clients are allowed to send to the server bids they would like to pay in order to buy the item. Server must be connected with all clients by means of authenticated channels; but connection between any two clients is not necessary for the auction to properly function.

Basic Auction Mechanics. At some starting date sd the server S announces on a public site (e.g., a WWW site) the auctioning of the item, and also defines a starting price sp, a deadline date dd, and a minimal increment mi. The time of the auction goes then between sd and dd, where the following happens. First of all, the item is associated with publicly announced current price cp and currently winning bid cwb, where at time sd it holds that $cwb = cp = sp$.

Then, each client C_i can send to the server a message bid_i specifying the maximum price mp_i that C_i is willing to pay for the item. This is the bidding protocol.

After that, the price update protocol is executed: if $mp_i \geq cp + mi$ then the message bid_i is considered valid by the server, who checks if $mp_i \geq cwb + mi$. If so, then client C_i will hold the currently winning bid; that is, the value of cp is updated to $cwb + mi$, and cwb is set equal to mp_i. Otherwise, client C_i is sent a message by S saying that he has been outbid by another client, and the value cwb remains unchanged. At deadline time dd, the client who submitted cwb is declared winner of the auction and is supposed to buy the item at price cp.

We remark that each client would typically go through a registration phase with the server in order to be able to take part in the auction, possibly involving some exchange of personal information. We will assume that this phase is application-dependent and quite standard, and therefore we will only consider the auction phase from now on.

Note also that both the bidding and the price update protocols are non-interactive, in the sense that a single message is sent by one party to the other.

Requirements. Let m, n denote positive integers and k be a security parameter. We will denote by sd the starting date, by dd the deadline date, by $mi \in \{0,1\}^m$ the minimal increment, by $cp \in \{0,1\}^m$ the current price, and by $cwb \in \{0,1\}^m$ the currently winning bid. We also let ℓ denote the index in $\{1, \ldots, n\}$ such that mp_ℓ is the maximum among $mp_1, \ldots, mp_n$. (Here, the values n, ℓ are not fixed at the starting date, but only after the deadline date.) If we denote by Π_b the bidding protocol and by Π_{pu} the price update protocol, an execution of a proxy auction scheme, denoted as $\Pi \equiv (\Pi_b, \Pi_{pu})$, has the form of an iterated execution of protocol Π_b and protocol Π_{pu} between S and C_i, for some $i \in \{1, \ldots, n\}$.

Given these definitions, we require a secure proxy auction scheme $\Pi \equiv (\Pi_b, \Pi_{pu})$ to satisfy the following requirements:

Correctness. If S and all clients $C_1, \ldots, C_n$ honestly run all executions of protocols Π_b and Π_{pu}, then the probability that at the end of the auction scheme the client C_ℓ is declared winner is equal to 1.

Security against clients. If S honestly runs all executions of protocols Π_b and Π_{pu}, then for all algorithms $C'_1, \ldots, C'_{\ell-1}, C'_{\ell+1}, \ldots, C'_n$, the probability that at the end of the auction scheme Π the client C_ℓ is not declared winner is exponentially small (in k).

Privacy against clients. Let mp_i be the maximum price submitted using protocol Π_b from client C_i, at some time when the current price is cp, and before the current price is updated to cp'. Assume that the client C_i is outbid (resp., is not outbid and becomes the winner of the auction). For all probabilistic polynomial time algorithms $C'_1, \ldots, C'_{i-1}, C'_{i+1}, \ldots, C'_n$, trying to guess the value of mp_i, the probability that they succeed better than randomly choosing among all mi increments of interval $[cp, cp' - mi]$ (resp., $[cp, 1^m]$), is negligible.

Security against the server. There exists a probabilistic polynomial time algorithm J (for judge) such that for any probabilistic polynomial time algorithm S', if at some time during an execution of Π a client C_i submits during protocol Π_b a maximum price mp_i such that $mp_i \geq cwb + mi$ and the output of this protocol does not result in the current price to be updated to $cwb + mi$ and the currently winning bid to be updated to mp_i, then the probability that algorithm J, on input C_i's Π-view so far, does not return 1 is exponentially small in k.

Remark. The above definition captures a novel and large class of somewhat 'innocent-looking' (and therefore, more dangerous) attacks from a corrupted server. We do not consider but plan to study in future investigations more 'risky' (and therefore, less likely) attacks from a server, such as denial of service to a particular client, or coalitions server-client that will favor one client over another during the auction.

3   Server Integrity Proof Systems

Non-interactive zero-knowledge proof systems are techniques to prove in a single message from a prover to a verifier (sharing a random string) that a certain statement is true without revealing any additional information [4, 3].

In this section we present non-interactive zero-knowledge proof systems that will be used by the server of a proxy auction to prove that all updates during the execution of the auction are being performed according to the prescribed protocol. We present two solutions. The first solution uses known protocols in the literature, it has good efficiency properties but bases its security on the existence of random oracles. (Even if many papers in the literature propose protocols that can be proved secure assuming the existence of random oracles, current state of the art in Cryptography shows that random oracles cannot be constructed, and therefore such proofs can at most be considered heuristic arguments that cannot rule out successful attacks to the given protocol). The second solution is based on new non-interactive zero-knowledge proof systems, that avoid using random oracles, but are not as efficient. (In practice, an auction protocol does not require the greatest efficiency on the verification of such proofs as the event that any of these proofs is not accepting can be verified at any future time, it automatically disqualifies the server and makes the entire auction invalid.) We can plug in any of the two solutions in the scheme for secure proxy auctions that we later present in Section 4.

A First Solution. Let (KG, E, D) be an asymmetric encryption scheme, where KG is the key generation algorithm, E is the encryption algorithm and D is the decryption algorithm. Let c be a ciphertext for an integer message m, where $(pk, sk) = KG(1^n)$ and $c = E(pk, m)$. Then we define the language   GT $= \{(pk; c; t) \mid D(sk, pk, c) > t\}$, as the language of ciphertexts encrypting integers greater than a given integer t. There exist efficient constructions of asymmetric cryptosystems and of 3-round public-coin honest-verifier zero-knowledge proof systems for the associated language GT (see e.g. [12, 2]). These proof systems can be made non-interactive using the Fiat-Shamir heuristic of computing the verifier's public-coin message as the output of a hash on the input and the proof system's first message.

A Second Solution. This solution is based on new non-interactive perfect zero-knowledge proof systems for certain languages based on quadratic residuosity, thus enlarging the class of languages that are known to have such systems and perfectly-indistinguishable zaps (that is, 2-round public-coin witness-indistinguishable proof systems).

We start with some basic definitions and then define the language of interest.

Recall that for each integer x, the quadratic residuosity predicate of an integer $y \in Z_x^*$ can be defined as $\mathbb{Q}_x(y) = 0$ if y is a quadratic residue modulo x and 1 otherwise; for brevity we will call $\mathbb{Q}_x(y)$ the x-quadratic character of y. For integers $y_1, \ldots, y_m \in Z_x^*$, we then define $\mathbb{Q}_x(\boldsymbol{y})$ the x-quadratic character of $\boldsymbol{y}$, where $\boldsymbol{y} = (y_1, \ldots, y_m)$, as the positive integer whose binary representation is the m-tuple $b_1 \circ \cdots \circ b_m$, such that $b_i = \mathbb{Q}_x(y_i)$, for $i = 1, \ldots, m$. Also, by BL we denote the set of Blum integers (that is, integers products of two primes $\equiv 3 \bmod 4$). We can now define the language:

$$\mathrm{GT}_m = \{(x; y_1, \ldots, y_m; t) \mid x \in \mathrm{BL} \text{ and } \mathbb{Q}_x(y_1, \ldots, y_m) > t\}.$$

Theorem 1. The language GT_m has: 1) a non-interactive perfect zero-knowledge proof system ; 2) a 2-round perfect witness-indistinguishable proof system .

Proof. We only prove case 1) of Theorem 1 as case 2) follows by applying the techniques in [8] to the result in case 1). Since there exists a non-interactive perfect zero-knowledge proof system for language BL (see, e.g., [6]), the problem of presenting such a scheme for language GT_m is reduced to an analogous scheme for proving that $\mathbb{Q}_x(y_1, \ldots, y_m) > t$. Let $t_1 \circ \cdots \circ t_m$ be the binary representation of t, and let $b_1 \circ \cdots \circ b_m$ be the binary representation of $\mathbb{Q}_x(y_1, \ldots, y_m)$; in other words, $\mathbb{Q}_x(y_1, \ldots, y_m) = b_1 2^{m-1} + b_2 2^{m-2} + \ldots + b_{m-1} 2 + b_m$. Then the statement $\mathbb{Q}_x(y_1, \ldots, y_m) > t$ is equivalent to the following one: there exists $j \in \{1, \ldots, m\}$ such that $[b_j = 1]$ AND $[t_j = 0]$ AND $[\, b_i = t_i, \text{ for all } i = 1, \ldots, j-1\,]$.

A standard rewriting of this statement as a boolean formula over quadratic residuosity statements results in a formula which is currently not known to have a non-interactive perfect zero-knowledge proof system.

Instead, we rewrite the statement $\mathbb{Q}_x(y_1, \ldots, y_m) > t$ by noting that for exactly one out of the following $m + 1$ cases this statement is false: if for all $j = 0, \ldots, n$, it holds that $b_i = t_i$, for $i = 0, \ldots, j$, $b_{j+1} = 0$ and $t_{j+1} = 1$. Then we can rewrite the statement $\mathbb{Q}_x(y_1, \ldots, y_m) > t$ as an AND of $\psi_1, \ldots, \psi_{m+1}$, where, for $i = 1, \ldots, m$, it holds that $\overline{\psi_i} = t_i \wedge \overline{b_i} \wedge_{j=1}^{i-1} \overline{t_j \oplus b_j}$, and $\overline{\psi_{m+1}} = \wedge_{j=1}^{m} \overline{t_j \oplus b_j}$. By De Morgan's law, the ψ_i's can be rewritten as $\psi_i = b_i \vee \overline{t_i} \vee_{j=1}^{i-1} (t_j \oplus b_j)$, and $\psi_{m+1} = \vee_{j=1}^{m}(t_j \oplus b_j)$.

We note that each of the XOR substatements in the above ψ_i can be proved in non-interactive perfect zero-knowledge. For example, in order to prove that $\mathrm{XOR}(\mathbb{Q}_x(y_i), t_i)$, it is enough to prove a single quadratic residuosity statement; that is, $\mathbb{Q}_x((-1)^{1-t_i} y_i \bmod x) = 1$. Then each formula ψ_i can be seen as an OR of i quadratic non residuosity statement, which we know how to prove in non-interactive perfect zero-knowledge, and the AND of all formulae ψ_i can therefore be proved in non-interactive perfect zero-knowledge.

More formally, a non-interactive perfect zero-knowledge proof system (P,V) for GT_m is obtained as follows. Let (A,B) be the analogous protocol for language BL given in [6] and let (C,D) be the analogous protocol for language OR(QNR) given in [6]. Then, on input $(x, y_1, \ldots, y_m, t_1, \ldots, t_m)$, protocol (P,V) can be seen as the sequential and independent composition of proof systems:

(A,B) on input x; (C,D) on input $(x; y_1, (-1)^{1-t_1})$; and then, for $i = 2, \ldots, n$, proof system (C,D) on input $(x; y_i, (-1)^{1-t_i}, (-1)^{1-t_1} y_1, \ldots, (-1)^{1-t_{i-1}} y_{i-1})$.
□

4   A Proxy Auction Scheme with Server-Integrity

In this section we present a 1-server proxy auction scheme which enjoys the server-integrity property. Using any of the two variants of proof systems in Section 3, we obtain a different variant of a 1-server proxy auction scheme. One variant admits practical proofs of server integrity, but assumes the existence of random oracles. Another variant admits less efficient proofs of server integrity and is based on a standard cryptographic hardness assumption.

For concreteness of description, we continue with the latter variant. First of all we describe a proxy auction scheme based on quadratic characters of tuples of integers in Z_x^*, where x is a Blum integer. Then we show that the described scheme satisfies the requirements of the definition in Section 2. The basic ideas underlying the proxy auction scheme consist of the server proving non-interactively and using perfect zero-knowledge proofs that he is honestly running the price update protocol. In particular, there are two types of updates the server could be doing when receiving a new bid: updating the winner name and the item price. While updating the item price, the server considers the previously winning bid and the new bid, and reveals the decryption of the smaller one. This directly sets the current item price equal to the revealed bid plus a minimal increment. However, this also directly declares the currently winning client as either the previously winning client or the client who sent the latest bid. In order to prove that this decision was made correctly, the server will have to prove that one encryption of a bid is larger than the revealed smaller bid. All these proofs are required to be zero-knowledge so to preserve the privacy of the currently winning maximum price as it could be the auction winner's maximum price. Moreover, they are required to be non-interactive so not to increase the round-complexity of the auction scheme, which is, therefore, non-interactive. The realization of these ideas will make crucial use of the non-interactive perfect zero-knowledge proofs we have constructed in Section 3. (Note that we are not using non-interactive computational zero-knowledge proofs since those typically require expensive reductions of problem instances to arbitrary NP-complete instances.) Specifically, we will use the 2-round perfectly witness-indistinguishable (WI) version of these proofs so that we can avoid the assumption of a common reference string necessary for non-interactive zero-knowledge proofs. In this version, a client sends a random string $R = r_1 \circ \cdots \circ r_k$ to the server, that uses it to compute non-interactive zero-knowledge proofs using $r_i \oplus r$ as a reference string, for some random string r.

We divide the formal description into two phases: a setup phase and an auction phase.

Setup Phase. Both the server and all clients will refer to a public site, originally containing a common reference string σ, that is assumed to be uniformly distributed. The server S chooses a security parameter 1^k, a price parameter 1^m, a minimal increment $mi \in \{0,1\}^m$, a starting date sd, a deadline date dd, some item data id and a starting price sp. Then he sets current price $cp = sp$, currently winning bid $cwb = cp$. The server randomly chooses two $k/2$-bit prime numbers $p, q \equiv 3 \bmod 4$, and computes Blum integer $x = pq$. Moreover S randomly chooses a tuple $\boldsymbol{y} = (y_1, \ldots, y_m)$ such that the x-quadratic character of $\boldsymbol{y}$ is cp. The currently winning encrypted bid is set to $\boldsymbol{y} = (y_1, \ldots, y_m)$. Finally the server posts on the public site the tuple $(1^k, 1^m, sd, dd, id, cp, x, (y_1, \ldots, y_m))$, and keeps p, q, cwb secret.

Auction Phase. At any time between sd and dd a client C_i can decide to register to participate in the auction of item id. The details of this step are inessential for the rest of the scheme. Once registered, client C_i can run the bidding protocol Π_b to bid some maximum price $mp_i \in \{0,1\}^m$ she would be interested in paying for id. Protocol Π_b goes as follows:

1. C_i writes mp_i in binary, as $b_1 \circ \cdots \circ b_m$.
2. For $j = 1, \ldots, m$, C_i randomly chooses $r_j \in Z_x^*$ and computes $z_j = (-1)^{b_j} r_j^2$ mod x.
3. C_i generates a random string to be used by S for his zap proof;
4. C_i sends her encrypted bid $(R, z_1, \ldots, z_m)$ to S, in an authenticated way.

Digital signatures can be used to send the bid in an authenticated way. This avoids the possibility that a dishonest server claims that some client has sent a bid (for example, a very high one) that she has not really sent.

Upon receiving encrypted bid $(z_1, \ldots, z_m)$ from a client C_i, the server S runs protocol Π_{pu} to eventually update the current price cp, the currently winning bid cwb and the currently winning encrypted bid $\boldsymbol{y}$. Protocol Π_{pu} goes as follows:

1. Using p, q, server S computes the quadratic residuosity b_j of z_j, for $j = 1, \ldots, m$ (that is, the decryption of the encrypted bid $(z_1, \ldots, z_m)$).
2. Let mp_i be the integer whose binary expression is $b_1 \circ \cdots \circ b_m$.
3. If $mp_i < cp + mi$, then S sends the message "invalid" to the client, and the protocol stops.
4. If $mp_i \geq cwb + mi$ then:
   - S uses R to compute a perfectly WI proof π_1 that $\mathbb{Q}_x(\boldsymbol{y}) = cwb$;
   - S uses R to compute a perfectly WI proof π_2 that $\mathbb{Q}_x(\boldsymbol{z}) > cwb$;
   - S updates the current winning encrypted bid $\boldsymbol{y} = \boldsymbol{z}$, the current price $cp = cwb + mi$ and the current winning bid $cwb = mp_i$;
   - S posts π_1, π_2, the updated currently winning encrypted bid $\boldsymbol{y}$ and the current price cp on the public site.

   Else:
   - S uses R to compute a perfectly WI proof π_1 that $\mathbb{Q}_x(\boldsymbol{z}) = mp_i$;
   - S uses R to compute a perfectly WI proof π_2 that $\mathbb{Q}_x(\boldsymbol{y}) > mp_i$;
   - S updates the current price $cp = mp_i + mi$ and posts π_1, π_2, and cp on the public site.

Implementation Remarks: Proofs and Public Verifiability. In the above scheme, proof π_1 is simply an AND of quadratic residuosity statements and can be shown in non-interactive perfect zero-knowledge using, for instance, the protocol in [3]; furthermore, proof π_2 can be computed using our schemes in Section 3. We also remark that we have designed the scheme so that the server's honest behavior is publicly verifiable; that is, all parties can verify the correctness of the server's updates of both the current price and the currently winning encrypted bid. If this property is not required, minor modifications are needed; for instance, rather than posting all proofs, the server will send proofs only to the involved client in each bidding operation.

4.1   Properties of the Scheme

Theorem 2. The 1-server secure proxy auction scheme explained above satisfies the following properties:

1. the scheme is non-interactive;
2. the "privacy against clients" property holds under the assumption of the hardness of deciding quadratic residuosity modulo Blum integers;
3. the "security against clients" and the "security against server" properties hold unconditionally.

Proof. (Sketch). It is not hard to verify that the scheme is non-interactive, and that it satisfies the correctness and the security against server properties.

Privacy against clients. To guarantee this property we argue that a bidder who is never outbid by any other client can keep her maximum price "sufficiently" private (that is, private among all possible values of a bid that are greater than the final price of the auction item, that is required to be public by the auction rule.) It is clear from the development of the auction that the bidder's maximum price must be larger than the previously winning bid (or otherwise this client would have been outbid). However, we now show that no other information is revealed to the other clients about the value of this maximum price. First of all we note that each bidder only sends an encryption of her maximum value, without never revealing it in clear (and so is the server doing since she is never required to do so and she is assumed to be honest). Furthermore, the only other steps in the scheme that depend on this value are those from the server who must prove that this value is larger than some other maximum price that is submitted. Since this proof is perfect witness-indistinguishable, it leaves all possible values (greater than the current price) equally likely. Therefore, the only successful strategy to guess some information about the value of this maximum price is to break its encryption, which is infeasible assuming the intractability of deciding quadratic residuosity modulo Blum integers.

Security against server. In order to prove this property, we show that if the auction ends with a winner and at some point during the auction, the server did not follow its price update protocol, then a client can always show a proof of that to some judge. Specifically, assume that at some time a client is submitting a bid with her maximum price being the largest so far. There are two cheating scenarios that the server could use during its price update protocol after receiving this bid and we would like to show that our protocol prevents both of them.

A first cheating scenario is that, after a new bid, the server updates the price of the item to a price different from what stated in the auction rule. However, note that to be successful in this strategy, the server needs to either prove that the decryption of an encrypted bid is different from what sent from the associated client (which contradicts the soundness of proof π_1) or has to prove that the newly winning bid encrypts a larger value than the previous one when this is not the case (which contradicts the soundness of proof π_2).

A second cheating scenario is that, after a new bid, the server declares current winner the client that sent the smaller bid among the previously winning bid and the new one. However, note that to be successful in this strategy, the server needs to prove that the newly winning bid encrypts a larger value than the previous one when this is not the case (which contradicts the soundness of proof π_2).   □

References

1. M. Abe and K. Suzuki. $M + 1$-st Price Auction Using Homomorphic Encryption. *Proc. of Public Key Cryptography 2002*, Springer-Verlag, LNCS **2274**, pp. 115–224 (2002).
2. F. Boudot. Efficient Proofs that a Committed Number Lies in an Interval. *Proc. of Eurocrypt'00*, Springer-Verlag, LNCS **1807**, pp. 431–444 (2000).
3. M. Blum, A. De Santis, S. Micali and G. Persiano. Non-Interactive Zero-Knowledge. *SIAM Journal of Computing*, vol. **20**, no. **6**, pp. 1084–1118 (1991).
4. M. Blum, P. Feldman and S. Micali. Non-Interactive Zero-Knowledge and Applications. *Proc. of ACM Symposium STOC'88*, pp. 103–112 (1988).
5. C. Cachin. Efficient Private Bidding and Auctions with an Oblivious Third Party. *Proc. of the ACM Conference CCS'99*, pp. 120–127 (1999).
6. A. De Santis, G. Di Crescenzo and G. Persiano. The Knowledge Complexity of Quadratic Residuosity Languages. *Theoretical Computer Science*, vol. **132**, pp. 291–317 (1994).
7. G. Di Crescenzo. Private Selective Payment Protocols. *Proc. of Financial Cryptography 2000*, Springer-Verlag, LNCS **1962**, pp. 72–89 (2000).
8. C. Dwork and M. Naor. Zaps and Their Applications. *Proc. of FOCS'00*, pp. 283–293 (2000).
9. http://www.ebay.com/
10. S. Goldwasser, S. Micali and C. Rackoff. The Knowledge Complexity of Interactive Proof-Systems. *SIAM Journal on Computing*, vol. **18**, no. **1**, pp. 186–208 (1989).
11. M. Harkavy and D. Tygar. Electronic Auctions with Private Bids. *Proc. of 3rd USENIX Workshop on Electronic Commerce*, pp. 61–74 (1998).
12. H. Lipmaa. On Diophantine Complexity and Statistical Zero-Knowledge Arguments. *Proc. of Asiacrypt'03*, Springer-Verlag, LNCS **2894**, pp. 398–415 (2003).
13. H. Lipmaa, N. Asokan and V. Niemi. Secure Vickrey Auctions without Threshold Trust. *Proc. of Financial Cryptography 2002*, (LNCS 2357), pp. 87–101 (2002).
14. M. Naor, B. Pinkas and R. Sumner. Privacy preserving auctions and mechanism design. *Proc. of the ACM Conference on Electronic Commerce*, pp. 129–139 (1999).
15. K. Sako. An Auction Protocol Which Hides Bids of Losers. *Proc. of Public Key Cryptography 2000*, Springer-Verlag, LNCS **1751**, pp. 422–432 (2000).
16. K. Sakurai and S. Miyazaki. A Bulletin-Board based Digital Auction Scheme with Bidding Down Strategy. *Proc. of the International Workshop on Cryptographic Techniques and E-Commerce, CrypTEC'99*, City University of Hong Kong Press, pp. 180–187 (1999).
17. S. Stubblebine and P. Syverson. Fair On-line Auctions without Special Trusted Parties. *Proc. of Financial Cryptography 1999*, Springer-Verlag, LNCS **1648**, pp. 230–240 (1999).

Secure Ad-Hoc mBusiness: Enhancing WindowsCE Security*

Florina Alménarez, Daniel Díaz, and Andrés Marín

Telematic Engineering Department, Carlos III University of Madrid
Avda. Universidad, 30, 28911 Leganés, Madrid, Spain
{florina,dds,amarin}@it.uc3m.es

Abstract. Nowadays we can perform business transactions with remote servers interconnected to Internet using our personal devices. These transactions can also be possible without any infrastructure in pure ad-hoc networks. In both cases, interacting parts are often unknown, therefore, they require some mechanism to establish ad-hoc trust relationships and perform secure transactions. Operating systems for mobile platforms support secure communication and authentication, but this support is based on hierarchical PKI. For wireless communications, they use the (in)secure protocol WEP. This paper presents a WCE security enhanced architecture allowing secure transactions, mutual authentication, and access control based on dynamic management of the trusted certificate list. We have successfully implemented our own CSP to support the new certificate management and data ciphering.

1 Introduction

The mobile technology has motivated the deployment of new applications, services, and business models as well as the ad-hoc network presence, in order to adapt to highly dynamic situations, for instance, mobile customer service representatives carrying their mobile terminal for showing the catalogue, making orders, etc; payments from mobile phones, or e-wallets hosted in PDAs; and application download from Internet in our mobile phones. These business models that always include at least a mobile device are known as mobile Business (mBusiness). mBusiness transactions often involve limited devices connected to remote servers through Internet. However, it can also involve transactions between limited devices using ad-hoc networks for business-to-costumer (B2C) without Internet access as in emergencies, network failures, or simply when there is a lack of infrastructure. These transactions must be performed safely from anywhere, at anytime and with any device. For example, Paul, mobile customer service representative goes out to promote a new product. Paul visits his customers, but also he has found a new client, Marie. He uses his PDA for showing a new product. If Marie is interested in buying the new product, she must establish

* Thanks to UBISEC (IST STREP 506926) and EVERYWARE (MCyT N°2003-08995-C02-01) projects.

S. Katsikas, J. Lopez, and G. Pernul (Eds.): TrustBus 2004, LNCS 3184, pp. 90–99, 2004.

a trust relationship with Paul, exchanging personal information (certificates). Then, Marie can issue purchase orders to Paul. Eventually, when Paul's PDA has access to Internet, this information is synchronized with the enterprise's server.

Operating systems for mobile devices, such as Symbian OS and Windows CE (WCE), have support to establish secure communications using secure socket layer (SSL). SSL is based on conventional X.509 certificates (hierarchical PKI) for authentication of communicating parties. Trust models in PKI are generally hierarchical (usually top-down like in Visa SET [1], or PEM [2]), though practical approaches allow to mix hierarchies, keeping the trees manageable. Trust relationships require some kind of agreement between authorities; each party must implicitly trust the root CA (being a very sensitive point), or subordinate CAs to authenticate other entities. Establishing trust models across inter-domains with different root CAs becomes a problem of quite a degree. PKI models do not scale well, therefore, many works are being developed about these infrastructures [3].

In WCE-based devices, trust relationships are preconfigured by the manufacturer in a "static" trusted certificate list. It is unsuitable for ad hoc trust relationships between strangers because it always requires human intervention for trusting or administrators and lawyers for mapping policies; being incompatible with the nature of ad hoc networks where relationships are established dynamically in a spontaneous way. Thus, taking into account the WCE security lacks, we propose a WCE's security enhanced architecture in which the certificate trust list can be enlarged dynamically through a trust model independent of the security infrastructure. Trust plays an important role in the cooperation and interaction between real world entities; as Dasgupta states: "Trust is central to all transactions" [4]. To support the certificate management and data encrypt/decrypt we have developed a new Cryptographic Service Provider (CSP).

Other works related to WCE security have been developed in [5], [6], and [7].

Section 2 gives a brief explanation of the WCE's secure communication support. In section 3, we analyse the WCE's security lacks. In section 4, we present our Pervasive Trust Management (PTM) model to create dynamically certificate trust lists. Next, in section 5 we describe the implementation of our custom CSP and the tests performed. Finally, we summarise and mention our future research directions in section 6.

2   Secure Communications in Windows CE

In WCE .NET, the security between client and server applications is provided using SSL for integrity, confidentiality and authentication. SSL uses secure sockets to send and receive data over the communications links, relying on authentication and on CryptoAPI (CAPI) [8].

For authentication, X.509 certificates are used. The successful authentication depends on having certificates issued by trustworthy someone [9]. WCE maintains a SCHANNEL database of trusted CAs. When a secure connection is attempted by an application, WCE extracts the root certificate and checks the CA against the database. It then passes the results of that comparison and the root certificate to the application's callback function. The application is responsible for deciding whether or not to trust a particular certificate. When a certificate is rejected by returning an error, the socket connection is not completed.

SCHANNEL database depends directly on the security support provider (SSP) and is the bridge between secure sockets and CAPI as shown the Fig. 2. SSP includes other authentication methods supported through the SSP Interface (SSPI). Once the user is authenticated, its identity serves for granting access rights using user list.

CAPI provides data encryption/decryption and services to verify certificates. CAPI works with a number of Cryptographic Service Providers (CSPs) that perform the cryptographic functions and key storage. These functions are the basis of the security service architecture in Windows platforms.

On the other hand, for wireless communications (ad-hoc networks), WCE supports Wired Equivalent Privacy (WEP) [10] which is an 802.11's optional encryption standard. WEP encrypts data by using static symmetric keys (40 and 128 bit keys), this fact together with the relatively short initial vectors make WEP vulnerable. Furthermore, WEP is intended only for enterprise deployments, therefore, it does not support mutual authentication, and it requires authentication methods to be customized by plugging them in.

2.1   CryptoAPI

WCE supports CAPI 2.0 as well as Windows NT, 2000, and 2003. The low level secure operations are provided by CSPs. The CSP's implementation uses an Independent Software Vendor (ISV) model. Using this ISV model, developers can use more than one CSP to increase security and strength of the ciphers since several providers implement different public key algorithms, symmetric ciphers and hash algorithms or upgrade the existing ones incrementing the key length.

CSPs do not serve CAPI functions directly, it serves another API known as CryptoSPI that is managed by the operating system as shown Fig. 1. Applications can perform cryptographic operations through CAPI; then, the operating system selects the suitable CSP according to the operations required by the application. These CSPs can be implemented in software, hardware or both. Hardware smartcard implementations provide the

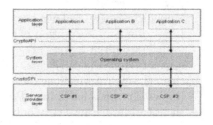

Fig. 1. CrytoAPI.

most secure key management, but a limited number of keys can be stored and the key generation is slow. WCE implements software CSP, Microsoft Enhanced Cryptographic Provider (MECP).

Certificate Stores CAPI provides API functions for managing certificates, "certificate stores", and for working with them "certificate revocation lists (CRLs)" and "certificate trust lists (CTLs)" within those stores. Certificate stores are served by different providers: system registry, disk file, and memory. These providers always support a predefined storage depending on the intended use of the certificates that holds. Certificates for trusted CA are generally kept in the "Root store", which is persisted to a registry sub key. Certificates that do not need to be kept are temporarily stored in memory. Besides, each user has a personal "My store" where user's certificates are stored. My store can be at many physical locations (i.e. the registry on a local or remote computer, a disk file, a database, directory service, or a smart card). Certificates in My store need a private key. Private keys are generated and stored in key containers by CSPs.

3   Security Analysis

WCE-based devices security infrastructure is not enough to guarantee secure communications, mutual authentication and access control between autonomous devices. They can act as secure clients, but they cannot act as secure peers.

3.1   Secure Communications and Authentication

As we mentioned above, WCE provides secure communications and authentication based on traditional hierarchical PKI. SCHANNEL database is "static" and can be updated using CAPI. But, WCE only supports a CAPI's capabilities subset, that is, encoding/decoding certificates. Tools to manage CTLs and CRLs, low-level messaging functions, and simplified messaging functions are not supported. Therefore, the user could not manage its CTL; this fact implies that if a device A forms an ad-hoc network with another device B for authenticating and communicating safely themselves, it is required that:

- A's certificate issuer CA and B's certificate issuer CA are trustworthy, that is, the CA's certificates must be stored in the CTL of each device. Generally these certificates are not issued by typical preconfigured CAs such as Verisign, Thawte, Entrust.net, or Cybertrust.
- If not, human intervention is required: to install the CA's certificate (DER format) from the web, to accept the CA's certificate every time that devices interact (since the certificates are temporarily stored in memory), or to copy them through ActiveSync.
- Implementations for limited WCE-based devices do not support mutual authentication, because they only have SSL client-side.

Likewise, security in wireless ad-hoc networks is not enough since it uses a (in)secure protocol to encrypt/decrypt data, is based on symmetric cryptography, and the authentication methods require additional implementation.

3.2   Access Control

Access control mechanisms are offered by the server applications. For limiting the access to services and data and granting certain permissions, WCE uses access control lists (ACLs) called UserList. To do this, it is necessary to set the UserList value for each of the servers that are currently running.

For dynamic and open environments, the use of ACLs is unsuitable because it requires manual configuration for each user. Thus, whenever a mobile customer service representative knows a new client, he must setup the new client and assign permissions.

3.3 Conclusions

For overcoming the lacks of security mentioned above, we propose a WCE security enhanced architecture (as shown Fig. 2), including the modules into dotted lines: a module for dynamic management of certificates (Trust Manager) minimizing the human intervention, another module for managing certificate stores (CertManager Extension), and a CSP (UC3M CSP) to support the new management. TrustManager implements the trust management model explained in the next section, and the conversion of PKCS#12 format certificates to DER format in order to install them automatically (a program called crtimprt has been developed for converting certificates [7]). On the other hand, CAPI must also be extended in two ways: first, we extend a Microsoft certificate store provider to create our own certificate store by using callbacks certificate manager functions (CertManager Extension). The second way is implementing our own CSP (UC3M CSP).

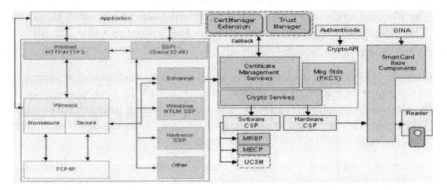

Fig. 2. Windows CE Security Enhanced Architecture.

In addition, the trust management model is used as basis for authorisation. We have defined trust-based access control (TrustAC) using the trust degree associated to the user to assign privileges. TrustAC have been tested in a Pocket PC using the XACML standard [11].

4 Dynamic Trusted Certificate List Management

Trust between devices could be based on a single CA or on multiple CAs of different trust domains. Current PKIs models make difficult to implement such inter-domains relationships. Our model, Pervasive Trust Management (PTM) model overcomes these challenges. PTM assumes that all devices have certain autonomy to manage its own security similar to Pretty Good Privacy (PGP) [12]. These devices act on behalf of a physical body such as persons, organizations, etc. If there are established trust relationships among CAs these would be used; but a device can also create its own trust relationships. That is, our model is compatible with PKI but it allows higher dynamicity and new trust relations can be established also in ad-hoc mode. So, each device handles its protected certificates list with trust values associated with them.

4.1   Pervasive Trust Management Model Architecture

Our architecture clearly shows that in a specific context, the devices (or entities) establish trust relationships (Fig. 3). For the first time, devices do not have evidence of past experiences to establish a trust value. In order to establish an initial value, we have two information sources: previous knowledge (direct) or recommendation (indirect).

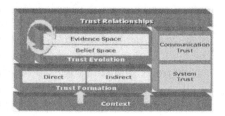

Fig. 3. PTM Architecture.

Direct. Previous knowledge is given by the entity's nature or past interactions in the physical world, without requesting information to a trusted third party (TTP). Then, we assign an initial value as the ignorance value, for instance, which is increased by the user manually or with additional information.

Indirect. When there are two unknown entities (to each other) willing to interact, some trust knowledge is needed, that is, a TTP by both of them. In that case, the trusted entity (B) may be able to recommend another entity (C) to (A) through either a recommended trust value or a certificate. Both mechanisms are called "recommendations" and require a trust value:

- When A is provided with a recommended trust value given by B (R_B), R_B would be the trust value. This trust value is exchanged using a recommendation protocol defined by the authors in [13].
- When the recommendation is given by a certificate issued by the recommender B, R_B is 1.

The trust value (R_B) is weighed by our trust degree on the recommender B, to calculate the C's trust degree $(R(A,C) = R_B.R(A,B))$. However, we will often have more than one recommendation, then we will compute the trust degree as the average of all recommendations (R_{B_i}) weighed by the trust degree of the recommender $(R(A,B_i))$:

$$R(A,C) = \frac{1}{n}\sum_{i=1}^{n} R_{B_i}.R(A,B_i) \qquad (1)$$

We make a weighted average (WA) of the recommendations (eq. 1) because the recommender's trust degree is important for evaluating the reliability of the sources; unlike the belief combination model proposed by Dempster-Shafer [14] and the consensus operator (CO) by Jøsang [15] which assume equally reliable sources. We believe in the recommendations as long as we trust the entity. In addition, WA is simpler than others recommendation combination mechanisms being more suitable for limited devices. Finally, we have compared our results (using the well known example of Zadeh [15]) with the original Dempster's rule (DR) and CO. The comparison proves that WA and CO have same results when the uncertainty is 0 and that WA gives almost the same result as CO and DR when there is uncertainty. The main difference between WA and CO, when there is uncertainty, is that in our model the uncertainty is a negative factor representing incomplete knowledge about some entity. These results are showed in [16], but it is also stated that WA (or WAO) is not associative, but we argue that it can be computed by an algorithm that ensures its associativiness. The algorithm stores: i as the number of opinions that have been computed, and $R_{i-1}(A,C)$ as the latest result.

Once we have an initial trust value, this initial value is our belief forming a belief space similar to the Jøsang's model [17]. But our belief can change according to the entity's behaviour along the time providing feedback about entity's performance during the interaction. We define the behaviour as our evidence space, which modifies our belief.

Belief Space. Our belief about another entity is the result from either the previous knowledge about it or the evidences obtained. The belief is described as a set of propositions (fuzzy logic) expressing the ownership degree of an entity to the set of trustworthy entities.

Evidence Space. It is formed by past and current experiences as shown eq. 2. The experiences are facts in the entity's knowledge base. These experiences allow us to measure the entity's behaviour according to its actions[1]. Actions can be positive (right actions) or negative. However, we assume that all negative actions are not the same, for this reason because we distinguish between wrong actions (bad actions that do not cause any damage or cause mild damages) and malicious actions (attacks). To calculate the value of the actions (V_a), each action has an associated weight applying fuzzy logic. The weight is rewarded or penalized according to the past behaviour and the security level (m).

When a new action is performed, V_a is recalculated, reflecting the present behaviour of the entity. The new trust value will take it into account and modify the current trust value ($R(A,C)_{previous}$):

$$R(A,C)_{new} = \begin{cases} V_a.\beta + R(A,C)_{previous}.(1-\beta) & V_a > 0 \\ 0 & \text{else} \end{cases} \qquad (2)$$

Where β is a configurable parameter to give weight to the present with respect to the past. Therefore, β equal 0 means we will never change our opinion, and

---

[1] Action modelling is beyond the scope of this paper.

β equal 1 means that we do not have any memories and we are only interested in the present. Neither β equal 0 nor β equal 1 are good options, it should exist an equilibrium between the past and the present.

5   CSP Implementation

We have developed our own CSP that implements well known cryptographic algorithms. We plan to use this CSP as the basis for including a Trust Manager in WCE security architecture. We also plan to include more algorithms in future versions of the CSP. In the actual version we have implemented: RSA for public key operations, RC2 and RC4 for symmetric ciphers, and MD5 and SHA as hashing algorithms.

RSA encryption supports keys of at least 512 bits key length and with the upper limit of 1024 bits (in compliance with the smart cards we have used). RC2 and RC4 fixed key size is 128 bits. The CSP support direct RSA encryption with PKCS#1 version 1.5 padding by default. The default cipher mode for RC2 is CBC. The CSP uses OpenSSL algorithms implementation. Once the CSP is completely tested (section 5.1), it is necessary to get the signed CSP dll by Microsoft because unless you get this signature the system does not allow the CSP to run. Moreover the operating system checks the signature of all the dlls called by the CSP, so sometimes a monolithic approach will be suitable for CSP developing as Microsoft recommends.

Communication with a CSP starts with the acquisition of a context through CAPI. In our CSP, every context acquired is linked to a key container handled by the CSP. Our CSP allows the acquisition of an unlimited number of context and keys, which are stored in memory. We have considered memory storage because this has been developed as a general structure allowing future developers to move to a practical design maintaining the general structure and developing only the storing routines such as file system storage or Smartcard storage using JavaCard technology [18] or USB token storing. We have also developed the file system storage of the keys.

Our CSP provides an object that supports the context operations. The context operations are performed using a container, a linked list of symmetric keys, the signature and exchange RSA keys, and a linked list of hash objects.

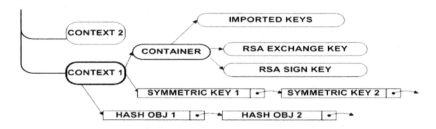

Fig. 4. UC3M CSP.

5.1   Testing a CSP

There are two ways to test CSPs depending on the platform. In a Windows 98 platform, the developer can use `cspsign` (CSP SDK) utility to sign the CSP with a debug signature. A custom CSP (compiled with debug flag) can thus be tested. In Windows 2000, XP and WCE platforms, users must use a kernel debugger as unique way to test a CSP. In addition, in WCE is required the Platform Builder. `cspsign` does not work in these platforms. Initially, the tests in windows 2000 were performed using kernel debugging, since our CSP had not been signed by Microsoft yet. Nevertheless, after having our CSP signed by Microsoft, it performs exactly the same as it did when tested with the kernel debugger. The results to the tests where exactly the same in both cases.

In addition of getting the CSP signed by Microsoft, it is necessary to write a setup program that registers the CSP creating the appropriate registry entries. These entries need to be written under the `HKEY_LOCAL_MACHINE \ Software \ Microsoft \ Cryptography \ Defaults \ Provider`. Under that key setup program it should be written a new entry with the name of the CSP. Under this registry entry some values as `Image Path` (path of the dll), `Type` (type of CSP) and `Signature` (Microsoft's digital signature) should also be written.

These procedures are standards. CSP can also include two functions as dll entry point: `DllRegisterServer` and `DllUnregisterServer`, which implement the required setup routines and are called with the Windows command `regsvr32`.

As we said before the CSP signature is copied in the registry. When `SigInFile` is specified in the registry, the operating system searches dll resources to find the signature rather than reading it from the registry.

6   Conclusions and Future Work

In this paper, we introduced the importance of using pure ad-hoc networks for B2C models in mBusiness. mBusiness involves mobile devices, therefore, we have analysed the WCE-based devices security lacks for performing secure business transactions. Our work has two important contributions. The first is the introduction of a dynamic certificate management model based on trust, PTM, to support secure sockets. PTM is totally decentralized making use of the autonomy and cooperable behaviour of the devices. In addition, it provides more granularity to define trust levels and can be used to establish access control permissions instead of using UserLists. The second important contribution is the successful implementation of our own CSP for supporting the new certificate management and data ciphering/deciphering.

Nowadays, we are implementing PTM in WCE-based devices (i.e. a Pocket PC 2003). Likewise, we are going to test our CSP in WCE. In addition, we are implementing some improvements in our CSP, for example, persistent storage in a smart card.

These works are the continuation of previous works of the group: Acero PKI (based on OpenSSL and servlets) and the JCCM (an open `PKCS#11` for Java Card) [18]. PTM has been proposed to provide a secure service discovery protocol for ad hoc networks [19].

Acknowledgments

The authors thank Carlos García and Celeste Campo for their comments and help. This work is being developed in the Pervasive Laboratory (PerLab) Group.

References

1. Visa, MasterCard: Secure electronic transaction SET (1999)
2. Kent, S.: Privacy enhancement for internet electronic mail (1993)
3. Dawson, E., Lopez, J., Montenegro, J.A., Okamoto, E.: BAAI: biometric authentication and authorization infrastructure. In: In IEEE International Conference on Information Technology (ITRE'03), IEEE Press (2003)
4. Marsh, S.P.: Formalising Trust as a Computational Concept. PhD thesis, University of Stirling (1994)
5. Ricci, L., McGinnes, L.: Embedded system security - designing secure system with windows CE. Embedded Computer System (2003) 1–33
6. et al., K.C.: Progress report on the penetration analysis of windows CE (2001)
7. Leeuw, J.D.: Pocket PC 2003 personal certificate import utility (2004)
8. Ash, M., Dasgupta, M.: Security features in windows CE .NET (2003)
9. Corporation, M.: Embedded operating system development (2002)
10. Fratto, M.: Tutorial: Wireless security. Network Computing (2001)
11. OASIS: extensible access control markup language (XACML) (2003)
12. Zimmermann, P.R.: The Official PGP User's Guide. MIT Press, Cambridge, MA, USA (95)
13. Almenárez, F., Marín, A., Campo, C., García, C.: Managing ad-hoc trust relationships in pervasive environments. In: Proceedings of the Workshop on Security and Privacy in Pervasive Computing SPPC 2004. (2004) http://www.vs.inf.ethz.ch/events/sppc04/program.html.
14. Shafer, G.: A mathematical Theory of Evidence. Princeton University Press (1976)
15. Jøsang, A.: The consensus operator for combinig beliefs. In: Artificial Intelligence Journal. Number 141/1-2 (2002) 157–170
16. Jøsang, A., Daniel, M., Vannoorenberghe, P.: Strategies for combining conflicting dogmatic beliefs. In: In the proceedings of the 6th International Conference on Information Fusion. (2003)
17. Jøsang, A.: An algebra for assessing trust in certification chains. In: Proceedings of the Network and Distributed Systems Security (NDSS'99) Symposium, The Internet Society. (1999)
18. Campo, C., Marín, A., García, A., Díaz, I., Breuer, P., Delgado, C., García., C.: JCCM: flexible certificates for smartcards with java card. In: Smart Card Programming and Security. Proceedings of the international Conference on Research in Smart Cards, E-Smart 2001, Springer-Verlag (2001)
19. Almenárez, F., Campo, C.: SPDP: a secure service discovery protocol for ad-hoc networks. In: In Workshop on Next Generation Networks - EUNICE 2003. (2003)

Role-Based Privilege Management
Using Attribute Certificates and Delegation

Gail-Joon Ahn, Dongwan Shin, and Longhua Zhang

University of North Carolina at Charlotte, Charlotte, NC 28232, USA
{gahn,doshin,lozhang}@uncc.edu

Abstract. The Internet provides tremendous connectivity and immense information sharing capability which the organizations can use for their competitive advantage. However, we still observe security challenges in Internet-based applications that demand a unified mechanism for both managing the authentication of users across enterprises and implementing business rules for determining user access to enterprise applications and their resources. These business rules are utilized for privilege management or authorization in a security context. In this paper, we design a role-based privilege management leveraging access control models and X.509 attribute certificate. We attempt to develop an easy-to-use, flexible, and interoperable authorization mechanism. Also, we demonstrate the feasibility of our architecture by providing the proof-of-concept prototype implementation using commercial off-the-shelf technologies.

1 Introduction

Many organizations have transited from their old and disparate business models based on ink and paper to a new, consolidated ones based on digital information on the Internet. The Internet is uniquely and strategically positioned to address the needs of a growing segment of population in a very cost-effective way. It provides tremendous connectivity and immense information sharing capability which the organizations can use for their competitive advantage. However, we still observe security challenges in Internet-based applications that demand a unified mechanism for both managing the authentication of users across enterprises and implementing business rules for determining user access to enterprise applications and their resources. These business rules are utilized for privilege management or authorization in a security context [13]. In this paper, we often use the term authorization and access control as an identical notion of privilege management. Authentication mechanisms have been practiced at considerable length and various authentication schemes such as SSL, LDAP-based, or secure cookies-based have been widely accepted. Unlike authentication mechanisms, authorization mechanisms which can conveniently enforce various business rules from different authorization domains among various applications still need to be investigated.

Role-based access control (RBAC) has been acclaimed and proven to be a simple, flexible, and convenient way of managing access control [6, 15]. This extremely simplifies management of privileges, reducing complexity and potential

S. Katsikas, J. Lopez, and G. Pernul (Eds.): TrustBus 2004, LNCS 3184, pp. 100–109, 2004.
© Springer-Verlag Berlin Heidelberg 2004

errors in directly assigning privileges to users. Another issue is to support such a simplified privilege management among distributed Internet-based enterprise applications. Privilege management infrastructure (PMI) [4, 5] has recently been introduced allowing us to establish the trustworthiness among different authorization domains as long as each of them keeps the meaning of attributes intact.

Our objective in this paper is to design a role-based privilege management leveraging RBAC features and X.509 attribute certificate in PMI. We attempt to develop an easy-to-use, flexible, and interoperable authorization mechanism. We also seek to address the issue of how to advocate selective information sharing in internet-based enterprise applications while minimizing the risks of unauthorized access.

The rest of this paper is organized as follows. Section 2 shows previous researches related to our work. Section 3gives an overview of background technologies. Section 4 describes our approach to designing a role-based privilege management with attribute certificates and delegation including system architecture and authorization policies. Implementation details are described in Section 5. Section 6 discusses lessons learned from our experiment and concludes the paper.

2   Related Works

Several researchers have been trying to accommodate RBAC features into large-scale systems of intranet or extranet focusing on various applications such as database systems, web servers, or web-based workflow systems. At the same time, delegation has been studied by a number of researchers as an important factor for secure distributed computing environment [7].

In the OSF/DCE environment [11], privilege attribute certificate (PAC) that a client can present to an application server for authorization was introduced. PAC provided by a DCE security server contains the principal and associated attribute lists, which are group memberships. This approach focused on the traditional group-based access control.

Similarly, Thompson et al. [18]   developed a certificate-based authorization system called Akenti for managing widely distributed resources. It was especially designed for system environments where resources have multiple stakeholders and each stakeholder wants to impose conditions for access. Their approach emphasized the policy-based access control in a distributed environment.

Also, several studies have been carried out to make use of RBAC features with the help of public-key certificates [1, 12]. Public-key certificates were used to contain attribute information such as role in their extension field. To add role information into public key certificates, however, may cause problems such as shortening of certificates' lifetime and complexity of their management [17].

In general, delegation is referred to as one active entity in a system delegates its authority to another entity to carry out some functions. In role-based systems, the delegated authorities are roles. The requirements related to role-based delegation have been identified in the literature [2, 8, 21]. A work closely related to ours is RBDM0 model proposed by Barka and Sandhu [2]. They developed a simple role-based delegation model. They explored some issues including revocation, delegation with hierarchical roles, partial delegation, and multi-step delegation. One limitation of RBDM0 is that this work does not address the relationships among each component of a delegation, which is a critical notion to the delegation model. A number of researchers have looked at the semantics of authorization, delegation, and revocation. Li et al. proposed a logic for authorizing delegation in large-scale, open, distributed systems [3, 10]. But in their logic, role-based concepts were not fully adopted; neither did they address revocation adequately.

3   Background Technologies

3.1   Role-Based Access Control

RBAC is an alternative policy to traditional mandatory access control (MAC) and discretionary access control (DAC). As MAC is used in the classical defense arena, the policy of access is based on the classification of objects such as top-secret level [14]. The main idea of DAC is that the owner of an object has discretionary authority over who else can access that object [9]. But RBAC policy is based on the role of the subjects and can specify security policy in a way that maps to an organization's structure. A general family of RBAC models called RBAC96 was defined by Sandhu et al [15]. Motivation and discussion about various design decisions made in developing this family of models is given in [15, 16]. Also, there are variations regarding distributed systems [20].

Figure 1(a) shows (regular) roles and permissions that regulate access to data and resources. Intuitively, a user is a human being or an autonomous agent, a role is a job function or job title within the organization with some associated semantics regarding the authority and responsibility conferred on a member of the role, and a permission is an approval of a particular mode of access to one or more objects in the system or some privilege to carry out specified actions. Roles are organized in a partial order $\geq$, so that if $x \geq y$ then role x inherits the permissions of role y. Members of x are also implicitly members of y. In such cases, we say x is senior to y. Each session relates one user to possibly many roles. The idea is that a user establishes a session and activates some subset of roles that he or she is a member of (directly or indirectly by means of the role hierarchy). A user may have multiple sessions open at the same time, each in a different window on the workstation screen for instance. Each session may have a different combination of active roles. The concept of a session equates to the traditional notation of a subject in access control. A subject is a unit of access control, and a user may have multiple subjects (or sessions) with different permissions active at the same time.

3.2   Privilege Management Infrastructure

PMI is based on the ITU-T Recommendation of directory systems specification [4], which introduced PKI in its earlier version. Public-key certificates are used in PKI while attribute certificates are a central notion of PMI. Public-key certificates are signed and issued by certification authority (CA), while attribute certificates are signed and issued by attribute authority (AA). PMI is to develop an infrastructure for access control management based on attribute certificate framework. Attribute certificates bind attributes to an entity. The types of attributes that can be bound are role, group, clearance, audit identity, and so on. Attribute certificates have a separate structure from that of public key certificates.

PMI consists of four models: general model, control model, delegation model, and roles model. General and control models are required, whereas roles and delegation models are optional. The general model provides the basic entities which recur in other models.

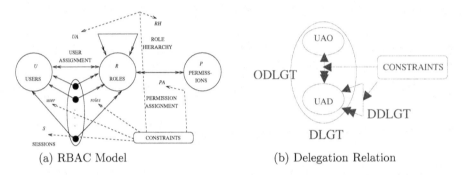

(a) RBAC Model   (b) Delegation Relation

Fig. 1. RBAC and Delegation.

4   Role-Based Privilege Management

4.1   Adopting Attribute Certificate

Our approach is based on basic entities in PMI. It consists of three foundation entities: the object, the privilege asserter, and the privilege verifier. The control model explains how access control is managed when privilege asserters request services on object. When the privilege asserter requests services by presenting his/her privileges, the privilege verifier makes access control decisions based upon the privilege presented, privilege policies, environmental variables, and object methods. PMI roles model also introduces two additional components: role assignment and role specification. Role assignment is to associate privilege asserters with roles, and its binding information is contained in attribute certificate called role assignment attribute certificate. The latter is to associate roles with privileges, and it can be contained in attribute certificate called role specification attribute certificate or locally configured at a privilege verifier's system. Our approach is based upon PMI roles model. Accordingly, two different attribute certificates are employed: role assignment attribute certificate (RAAC) and role specification attribute certificate (RSAC). The integrity of the bindings is guaranteed through digital signature in attribute certificate.

4.2   Constrained Role-Based Delegation

Zhang et al. [21] introduced RDM2000 (role delegation model 2000) for user-to-user delegation in role-based systems. Our work is based on RDM2000. It formalizes the relationship between two user assignments that form a delegation relation (DLGT), as shown in Figure 1(b). We first define a new relation called delegation relation (DLGT). It includes sets of three elements: original user assignments UAO, delegated user assignment UAD, and constraints. The motivation behind this relation is to address the relationships among different components involved in a delegation. In a user-to-user delegation, there are four components: a delegating user, a delegating role, a delegated user, and a delegated role. A delegation relation is one-to-many relationship on user assignments. It consists of original user delegation (ODLGT) and delegated user delegation (DDLGT). We assume each delegation relation may have a duration constraint associated with it. If the duration is not explicitly specified, we consider the delegation as permanent unless another user revokes it. The function $Duration$ returns the assigned duration-restriction constraint of a delegated user assignment. If there is no assigned duration, it returns a maximum value. Our delegation model has the following components and theses components are formalized from the above discussions.

- T is a set of duration-restricted constraint.
- DLGT $\subseteq$ UA $\times$ UA is one to many delegation relation. A delegation relation can be represented by $(u, r, u', r') \in$ DLGT, which means the delegating user u with role r delegated role r' to user u'.
- ODLGT $\subseteq$ UAO $\times$ UAD is an original user delegation relation.
- DDLGT $\subseteq$ UAD $\times$ UAD is a delegated user delegation relation.
- DLGT = ODLGT $\cup$ DDLGT.

In some cases, we may need to define whether or not each delegation can be further delegated and for how many times, or up to the maximum delegation depth. We introduce two types of delegation: single-step delegation and multi-step delegation. Single-step delegation does not allow the delegated role to be further delegated; multi-step delegation allows multiple delegations until it reaches the maximum delegation depth. The maximum delegation depth is a natural number defined to impose restriction on the delegation. Single-step delegation is a special case of multi-step delegation with maximum delegation depth equal to one.

   Also, we have an additional concept, delegation path (DP) that is an ordered list of user assignment relations generated through multi-step delegation. A delegation path always starts from an original user assignment. We use the following notation to represent a delegation path.

   $uao_0 \rightarrow uad_1 \rightarrow uad_i \rightarrow uad_n$

Delegation paths starting with the same original user assignment can further construct a delegation tree. A delegation tree (DT) expresses the delegation paths in a hierarchical structure. Each node in the tree refers to a user assignment and each edge to a delegation relation. The layer of a user assignment in the tree is referred as the delegation depth. The function Prior maps one delegated user assignment to the delegating user assignment; function Path returns the path of a delegated user assignment; and function Depth returns the depth of the delegation path.

Constraints are an important aspect of RBAC and can lay out higher-level organizational policies. In theory, the effects of constraints can be achieved by establishing procedures and sedulous actions of security administrators [6]. Constraints are enforced by a set of integrity rules that provide management and regulators with the confidence that critical security policies are uniformly and consistently enforced. In the framework, when a user delegates a role, all context constraints that are assigned to the user and anchored to the delegated role are delegated as well.

Rule-Based Policy Specification Language. We also define policies that allow regular users to delegate their roles. It also specifies the policies regarding which delegated roles can be revoked. A rule-based language is adopted to specify and enforce these policies. It is a declarative language in which binds logic with rules. The advantage is that it is entirely declarative so it is easier for security administrator to define policies.

A rule takes the form:

$H \leftarrow F1\&F2\&\ldots\&Fn$

where H, F1, F2,..., Fn are Boolean functions.

There are three sets of rules in the framework: basic authorization rules specify organizational delegation and revocation policies; authorization derivation rules enforce these policies in collaborative information systems; and integrity rules specify and enforce role-based constraints. For example, a user-user delegation authorization rule forms as follows:

$can\_delegate(r, cr, n) \leftarrow$.

where r, cr, and n are elements of roles, prerequisite conditions, and maximum delegation depths respectively.

This is the basic user-to-user delegation authorization rule. It means that a member of the role r (or a member of any role that is senior to r) can assign a user whose current membership satisfies prerequisite condition cr to role r (or a role that is junior to r) without exceeding the maximum delegation depth n.

Constraints Specification. In order to represent role-based privilege management constraints, we define rules that are extremely suited for constraints specification as well as enforcement. We articulate several constraints and specify them using a rule-based language introduced in [21].

A **static separation of duty (SSOD): incompatible roles assignment constraint** states that no common user can be assigned to conflicting roles in the incompatible role set $ira = \{r_1, r_2, \ldots\}$. This constraint can be represented as:

$cannot\_assign(u, r) \leftarrow$
  $senior(r, one\_element(ira))\&$
  $member\_of(u, one\_element(all\_other(ira, one\_element(ira)))).$
   where $u \in U$, $r \in R$, and $ira \in \mathrm{IRA}$.
The rule says if r equals one element of a set of the incompatible role assignments ira, and a user u is already member of another role other than r in the incompatible role set, then u cannot be assigned role r.

An **incompatible users constraint** states that two conflicting users in the incompatible user set $iu=\{u1, u2, ...\}$ cannot be assigned to the same role. This constraint can be represented as:
$cannot\_assign(u, r) \leftarrow$
  $equals(u', one\_element(all\_other(iu, u)))\&$
  $member\_of(u', r).$

An **incompatible permissions constraint** states that two conflicting permissions in the incompatible user set $ip=\{p1, p2, ...\}$ cannot be assigned to the same role. This constraint can be represented as:
$cannot\_assignp(r, p) \leftarrow$
  $equals(p', one\_element(all\_other(ip, p)))\&$
  $in(p', permissions\_role(r)).$

A **role cardinality constraint** states that a role can have a maximum number N of user members. This constraint can be represented as:
$cannot\_assign(u, r) \leftarrow$
  $greater\_than(cardi(r), maxcardi(r) - 1).$

A **user cardinality constraint** states that a user can be member of a maximum number N of roles. This constraint can be represented as:
$cannot\_assign(u, r) \leftarrow$
  $greater\_than(cardi(u), maxcardi(u) - 1).$
We have demonstrated how different constraints can be specified using rules.

5   Implementation Details

Our implementation leverages role-based delegation features and X.509 attribute certificate. We attempt to implement the proof-of-concept prototype implementation of our architecture. An overview of the preliminary architecture is shown in Figure 2.

It consists of a number of services and management agents together with the objects to be managed. The enforcement agents are based on a combination of roles and rules for specifying and interpreting policies. Since delegation and revocation services are only part of a security infrastructure, we choose a modular approach to our architecture that allows the delegation and revocation services to work with current and future authentication and access control services. The

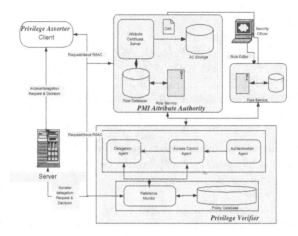

Fig. 2. Operational architecture for role-based EAM.

modularity enables future enhancements of our approach. The role service is provided by a role server and a role server maintains RBAC database and provides user credentials, role memberships, associated permissions, and delegation relations of the system. The rule service is provided by a rule server, which manages delegation and revocation rules. These rules are always associated with a role, which specifies the role that can be delegated. They are implemented as authorization policies that authorize requests from users. The rule editor is developed to simplify the management of these rules. As a portion of an integrated RBAC administration platform to manage various components, the rule editor is used to view, create, edit, and delete delegation and revocation rules. The delegation agent is an administrative infrastructure, which authorizes delegation and revocation requests from users by applying derivation authorization rules and processes delegation and revocation transactions on behalf of users. We implement these components as the delegation/revocation service: users' delegation/revocation requests are interpreted, authorized, and processed by the service; it creates RDM2000 elements based upon users' requests and maintains the integrity of the database by checking and enforcing consistency rules. The core of this service is a rule engine. We implemented the rule inference engine by extending SWI-Prolog [19] using its C++ interface. The rule engine has three functional units: a pre-processor, an inference engine, and a post-processor.

In Figure 2, three components are identified for managing attribute certificates: privilege asserter, privilege verifier, and PMI attribute authority as we described in Section 4. A privilege asserter is developed by using ActiveX control, named attribute certificate manager. The manager enables a user to import downloaded BER-encoded RAACs into Windows registry. Internet Information Server (Version 5.0) is used as a privilege verifier. An HTTP raw data filter, called AC filter, was developed using Microsoft ISAPI (Internet Server API) technology. An attribute certificate server was developed to generate R A A C s and R SAC s. The programming library, called AC SDK, was built for supporting the functionality related to the generation of the attribute certificates. Netscape Directory Service 5.0 was used for both a role database and an AC storage. We also developed an application working as an access control policy server. This application has been developed in C++. An engine for making access control decisions is a major component in this application.

6   Conclusion and Future Works

Authentication mechanisms have been practiced at considerable length and various authentication schemes have been widely accepted. Unlike authentication mechanisms, privilege management which can conveniently enforce various business rules from different authorization domains among various applications still need to be investigated. In this paper, we have discussed issues of privilege management. We also attempted to utilize an existing delegation framework and attribute certificates in PMI. In addition, we demonstrated the feasibility of our architecture through a proof-of-concept implementation. We believe that this work would lead Internet-based applications to consider privilege management as a core component in their design and deployment.

Acknowledgements

This work was partially supported at the Laboratory of Information of Integration, Security and Privacy at the University of North Carolina at Charlotte by the grants from National Science Foundation (NSF-IIS-0242393) and Department of Energy Early Career Principal Investigator Award (DE-FG02-03ER25565).

References

1. G. Ahn, R. Sandhu, M. Kang, and J. Park. "Injecting RBAC to secure a Web-based workflow system," In *Proceedings of 5th ACM Workshop on Role-Based Access Control.* Berlin, Germany, July 2000.
2. E. Barka and R. Sandhu. Framework for role-based delegation model. In *Proceedings of 23rd National Information Systems Security Conference*, pages 101–114, Baltimore, MD, October 16-19 2000.
3. E. Bertino, E. Ferrari and V. Atluri. The specification and enforcement of authorization constraints in workflow management systems. *ACM Transactions on Information and System Security*, Vol.2 No.1, p.65-104, Feb. 1999
4. ITU-T Recommendation X.509. Information Technology: Open Systems Interconnection - The Directory: Public-Key And Attribute Certificate Frameworks, 2000. ISO/IEC 9594-8:2001.
5. S. Farrell and R. Housley. An Internet Attribute Certificate Profile for Authorization, PKIX Working Group, June 2001.

6. D. Ferraiolo, J. Cugini, and D.R Kuhn. "Role Based Access Control: Features and Motivations," In *Annual Computer Security Applications Conference*, IEEE Computer Society Press, 1995.

7. M. Gasser and E. McDermott. An Architecture for Practical Delegation a Distributed System. In *Proceedings of IEEE Computer Society Symposium on Research in Security and Privacy*, Oakland, CA, May 7-9,1990.

8. A. Hagstrom, S. Jajodia, F. P. Presicce, and D. Wijesekera. Revocations - a classification. In *Proc. 14th IEEE Computer Security Foundations Workshop*, pages 44–58, Nova Scotia, Canada, June 2001.

9. S. Jajodia, P. Samarati, V. Subrahmanian, and E. Bertino. A unified framework for enforcing multiple access control policies. In *Proceedings of the ACM SIGMOD international conference on management of data*, pages 474–485, 1997.

10. N. Li and B. N. Grosof. A practically implementation and tractable delegation logic. In *Proceedings of IEEE Symposium on Security and Privacy*, May 2000.

11. OSF DCE 1.0 Introduction to DCE, Open Software Foundation, Cambridge, MA, 1999.

12. J. Park, R. Sandhu, and G. Ahn. "Role-based Access Control on the Web," *ACM Transactions on Information and System Security*, 4(1), February 2001.

13. John Pescatore. Extranet Access Management Magic Quadrant, *Gartner Research Note (ID: M-13-6853)*, Gartner INC., May 2001.

14. R. S. Sandhu. Lattice-based access control models. *IEEE Computer*, 26(11):9–19, November 1993.

15. Ravi S. Sandhu, Edward J. Coyne, Hal L. Feinstein, and Charles E. Youman. Role-based access control models. *IEEE Computer*, 29(2):38–47, February 1996.

16. R. Sandhu. Rationale for the RBAC96 family of access control models. In *Proceedings of the 1st ACM Workshop on Role-Based Access Control*. ACM, 1997.

17. D. Shin, Gail-J. Ahn, and S. Cho. Role-based EAM Using X.509 Attribute Certificate. In *Proceedings of Sixteenth Annual IFIP WG 11.3 Working Conference on Data and Application Security*, King's College, University of Cambridge, UK July 29-31, 2002.

18. M. Thompson, W. Johnston, S. Mudumbai, G. Hoo, K. Jackson, and A. Essiari. "Certificate-based Access Control for Widely Distributed Resources," In *Proceedings of the 8th USENIX Security Symposium*, Washington, D.C., August 1999.

19. Wielemaker. "J. SWI-Prolog," http://www.swi.psy.uva.nl/projects/SWI-Prolog/

20. N. Yialelis, E. Lupu, and M. Sloman. Role-based security for distributed object systems. In *Proceedings of the IEEE Fifth Workshops on Enabling Technology: Infrastructure for collaborative enterprise*. IEEE, 1996.

21. L. Zhang, Gail-J. Ahn and B. Chu. A Rule-Based Framework for Role-Based Delegation and Revocation. *ACM Transactions on Information and System Security*, Vol.6, No.3, August 2003.

Consent as a Threat. A Critical Approach to Privacy Negotiation in e-Commerce Practices

A. Daniel Oliver-Lalana

University of Zaragoza, Faculty of Law, Ciudad Universitaria, 50009 Zaragoza, Spain
prodatos@unizar.es

Abstract. Although e-commerce systems are increasingly concerned with data protection, they follow a property-based approach to privacy which leads to privacy negotiation and bargaining upon the base of the data subjects' consent. After considering the technological and regulative strategies of protecting consumer privacy, this paper discusses the shortcomings of that approach and claims that, as long as a general privacy culture has not yet evolved in the (web) society, it might collide with the notion of data protection as a fundamental right.

1 Introduction

The relation between data protection and e-commerce is usually approached in terms of conflict. On the one hand, emphasis is laid on the rise of little brothers collecting and misusing personal information, whilst, on the other, data protection law is often taken to undermine the development of commercial and informational exchanges. A number of factors might be highlighted which make it difficult to find a balance between these two poles. Firstly, the infrastructure of the web society, and thus of e-commerce systems, is based on the massive processing of personal data. As the expansion of online profiling techniques has shown, the classic *the more, the better* view dominates personal information practices of e-businesses, which take advantage of the technological infrastructures in order to collect and process huge amounts of personal information, frequently in a way invisible to data subjects [8]. Furthermore, online privacy becomes a hardly achievable target because of regulatory differences and lacks [2], which are typical for Internet-related law. As a result, even in countries with strong data protection laws, these remain largely ineffective when applied to virtual environments, where the whole privacy issue is perceived as a non-tariff barrier hampering the growth of e-commerce. It appears that any balance is deemed to disappoint any of the involved parties: companies, customers or privacy advocates. Nonetheless, new approaches are sought for which are able to introduce elements of personal data protection in e-commerce without collapsing it. They may be classified into technology-based and law-based regulative strategies. Both of them may in turn be used by different theoretical models.

2 Technological Strategies

The well-known significance of technical infrastructures for regulatory purposes has been successfully pointed out by Lessig, who claims that the *code* of the cyberspace is

S. Katsikas, J. Lopez, and G. Pernul (Eds.): TrustBus 2004, LNCS 3184, pp. 110–119, 2004.

built into its software and hardware [17]. These are also expected to play a paramount role in our context. Since the Internet exists, a wide range of technical measures have emerged which eliminate or reduce the need for personal data, or prevent its unnecessary and undesired processing, without losing the functionality of the information systems [5, 20]. They are referred to under the broad concept of privacy enhancing technologies (PETs). The question now is whether, and to what extent, these technologies can be fruitfully applied in e-commerce. If privacy protection can be achieved at the technological level, there will be a lesser damage or no damage at all for e-commerce systems. Three major solutions can be underlined in this direction.

The first one has been promoted by the web industry, which has attempted to modify the architecture of the Internet and its underlying *code* by developing the so-called Platform for Privacy Preferences (P3P). This protocol offers a means for exchanging machine-readable information about both websites privacy practices and users' choices on the collection and use of personal data. Being part of the *code*, this platform seems to be an optimal way to bring the colliding drives of privacy and e-commerce together. A striking evidence for this is that it has been promptly implemented by the most popular websites [1]. But, it shows important limits as concerns online privacy protection. In special, P3P cannot assure on its own that websites abide by their privacy policies, neither that these offer enough privacy guarantees. The storage and disclosure of personal information are even facilitated for online activities that do not require it, such as simply visiting a site. Moreover, provided that the P3P scenario does not base on strong data protection standards, as they are laid down in the European Union directives, the European Council 108 Convention or the OECD privacy guidelines, it remains asymmetric in favor of companies.

A second strategy would be to offer e-commerce technological tools and devices with built-in data protection utilities. In this regard, some experiences have been set going in the field of intelligent software agents [3], which are becoming more and more popular in e-commerce. They are software programs, at times coupled with dedicated hardware, which complete tasks autonomously on behalf of their users. For this purpose agents contain detailed informative profiles, which are the basis for the actions they perform: searching for information, matching it with personal profiles and making transactions on the web. There exist in the data protection community a widespread reluctance to use them, because they handle large amounts of personal data, sometimes of sensitive character, without privacy protection measures, let alone the fear that they conceal spyware or E.T. software. Many customers may also be hesitant to reveal information about their lives to electronic entities that might expose it inappropriately as they crawl across the web [12]. The challenge would be then to design privacy incorporated software agents that minimize the processing of personal information or keep it anonymous where possible. In contrast to P3P, these agents embed higher privacy standards and could be backed by some official certification system. However, as they usually compare prices, many websites may be willing to block them, which can be taken to endanger the functionality of e-commerce. A third solution has been developed in the marketplace to surmount this problem.

Nowadays specialized service providers offer privacy protection and personal information brokering services that help consumers to maximize the value of their data. These brokers have become widely known as infomediaries [12]. By combining profiling and privacy tools, this business model renders useful functions for both companies and consumers partaking in it. While vendors and direct marketers obtain accurate and high quality information on clients, consumers are given the option either to share their personal data in exchange for certain benefits or to remain anonymous in electronic interactions. The idea lying behind this model is that, being personal information a valuable resource for electronic companies, these should only process and profile it upon the basis of consent. To a certain degree, infomediaries are a sophisticated application of permission marketing approaches [10] and are, in the last analysis, the natural way to translate data protection concerns into the economic language of e-commerce: privacy rights are reformulated in terms of negotiable goods, and intermediate persons provide for technical and organisational tools to speed up the bargaining process. All in all, it is a nice and market-ready strategy of data protection.

I will turn back later to this economically-tinged version of privacy. For now it suffices to make two comments on the technical solutions. In the first place, they imply some kind of privacy negotiation, which is mainly carried out at the technological level. Their guiding target is to confine the privacy aspects of virtual interactions to software and hardware, and thereby liberate customers from the cumbersome self-management of their personal information. Secondly, none of them is able by itself to introduce a proper data protection level in e-commerce practices. No doubt that it must be welcomed that privacy is being integrated into the technological infrastructure of e-commerce, as well as being taken up by many companies as a business case. Anyhow, any technology-based solution must be always supported by a regulatory and enforceable framework, and by no means should be expected to replace it. This leads us to the second group of strategies.

3   Regulative Strategies

Let us dwell on the two inherent limits to technological models of privacy. First, these cannot assure that e-businesses, as data controllers, comply with strong privacy laws where these are applicable. Only courts and special agencies are entrusted to do this. The second limit is that technology itself does not suffice to maintain privacy protections in borderless and interconnected environments, or at least does not provide protections which can be deemed adequate in the light of strong privacy laws (such as the European ones). What must be the morphology of data protection regulation in the field of e-commerce in order to attain this twofold goal? I shall tackle this point by differentiating two intertwined strategies: self-regulation and interface or hinge law. The former is the most efficacious way to bring strong privacy standards closer to e-commerce, but it presupposes a shared data protection culture. In order to extend strong privacy models in global frameworks, hybrid or mixed forms of regulation are needed which are able to combine elements of diverging privacy cultures.

3.1   Self-regulation

Privacy law is usually regarded as an external constraint to e-commerce, as it forbids common business practices of information processing, obligates firms to set up special cautions concerning personal data and increases transaction costs altogether. Its very existence is deemed a non tariff barrier to the freedom of trade and commerce. Since businesses tend naturally to disregard data protection law, direct attempts to introduce it into e-commerce can easily fail, as it is solely backed by legal sanctions. A different steering model, known as self-regulation or reflexive law [22], has evolved in the last decades and has proved much more successful for governing social areas with their own rules and well-established practices, such as the Internet as a whole and, more concretely, the field of e-commerce. The key idea is that laws cannot be imposed from outside, but must be acknowledged by those agents operating in the social field which they are expected to regulate.

In a proper sense, self-regulation does not equate to any social or private standard, but rather implies some sort of legal control. Through reflexive or self-regulative norms, the state provides the statutory basis for social groups to create substantive rules and norms in a self-regulative process, that is, regulates social self-regulation. The aim is to structure social systems by providing procedures in which they can regulate themselves and on certain occasions by establishing minimum compulsory legal contents and requirements. In either case, private regulative schemes are supposed not to express merely the interests of single enterprises, associations or sectors – as it may happen if regulation is by and large left to the private sector, which sometimes is unduly defined as self-regulation – but convey a certain social legitimacy and consensus. The European data protection directive has resorted to this strategy to facilitate the introduction of privacy in particular social fields (see Article 27) [25]. Thanks to the openness of statutory legislation to private forms of regulation, a strong privacy protection model can be combined with regulative instruments which are generated and thus accepted by the social agents operating in the field of e-commerce.

This approach entails several advantages. It offers an added value by adapting basic and general legislative requirements to the specific concepts, needs and issues of e-commerce. This contributes to that data protection law is no longer perceived as a strange, but as an integrated element in the e-commerce system and as an additional aspect of the firm-client relationship, which ultimately opens much better chances of compliance. Self-regulation may even strengthen privacy protection by filling legislative gaps, as it happened in Spain with children data and invisible data processing. In a nutshell, privacy is likely to have a much more accepted and hence efficacious impact through reflexive law. Besides, official privacy protection will profit from it in another sense. As self-regulative instruments use to entail alternative and even on-line dispute resolution schemes, they can also absorb jurisdictional risks and litigation. This is of great significance because the expansion of e-commerce leads to an unstoppable increase of complaints and litigation which otherwise would overload the official data protection system. All in all, self-regulation, provided that it is backed by strong privacy laws, is the best way to introduce privacy in e-commerce environments. Yet the next challenge is to protect consumer privacy in an interconnected, borderless world. Further regulative strategies must be developed for this purpose.

3.2 Hinge-Law

It is a matter of course that online data protection cannot be achieved without data protection in – and from – the United States and several Asian countries [5, 14]. In particular, the overwhelming dominance of U.S. based companies on the Internet makes it impossible to assure a strong level of data protection in Europe, or elsewhere, unless they assume certain privacy standards. As these, however, are still largely neglected within their legal culture, the need arises of making two different cultural and legal traditions compatible with each other. This can be achieved through new forms of regulation (self-regulation) which can work out in a global environment by merging contradicting legal frameworks. Such hybrid institutions are taken to be the seed of the forthcoming regulation models for the knowledge society, and are even considered as the only way in which state law can be able to cope with Internet-related regulation problems [11]. Through this sort of hinge-law (*Scharnierrecht*), legal interfaces are created which preserve the autonomy of national or regional regulative systems, making them at the same time compatible with the global and decentralized organization of the Internet [7, 14].

As concerns the intersection between data protection and e-commerce, this role is to be played by the Safe Harbor Agreement, which aims to conciliate two opposite approaches to privacy regulation, namely the European strong and state law model, on the one side, and the U.S. model, largely based on private norms and policies under little or lacking official control (improperly called self-regulation), on the other [7]. This is not a surface opposition, but is firmly rooted in both legal cultures. Data protection is approached in Europe as a fundamental right prevailing *prima facie* over economic interests, whereas in the United States it is rather a mere commercial issue, so that the companies claim ownership over customer information and tend to deal with it just as they do with any other company asset. It belongs to the spirit of Safe Harbor to harmonize these approaches without outstanding damages in either model. European states attempt to provide their consumers with a pragmatic level of data protection, but not at any rate. In a non-traumatic way, i.e. through self-regulation, this agreement is ultimately expected to export strong data protection standards to the United States, where domestic law and weak self-regulation leave much to desire as far as privacy protection is concerned. By now, this attempt has partly failed. It is obvious that substantive rules are not as strong as those laid down in the European directives: the Safe Harbor principles are vaguely formulated and are accompanied by too many exceptions. Yet this could be a fair price to pay for a better privacy protection. The major problem is that even this reduced privacy standards lack a reliable enforcement system. As I cannot discuss at length the limited safety of Safe Harbor [7, 24], let me confine myself to unfold the theoretical conflict that lies behind.

4 The Property-Model of Privacy

The theoretical model that suits e-commerce best is the conception of privacy as a negotiable property. In fact, technological and regulative data protection strategies for e-commerce are often associated to a certain conception about the availability of privacy rights. Leading scholars have pointed out that the conception of privacy as a property is anchored in the base of market societies and is a functional requirement for e-commerce systems to survive. And it is even good for privacy protection. If people are accorded a property right over their data, those companies willing to process them are forced to negotiate an adequate price or convenience before collecting or using them [17]. This way, the market will protect individuals to the extent to which they valuate their privacy. In this view, the right to data protection is taken to be a simple right of consumers, whereby they might negotiate over it without restrictions. By today, the goal of companies is precisely to acquire ownership rights over personal data, as "the winners and losers of this new era will be determined by who has rights to on-line customer profiles" [12].

It will be objected, mostly by Europeans, that this property model is incompatible with the notion of privacy as a fundamental right of every citizen. Basic rights, it is argued, are not any kind of negotiable stuff. They cannot be subordinated to economic preferences and monetary valuations, since this would cast serious doubts on the normative force of constitutional guarantees [13]. Privacy should not become a costly commodity, so that individuals are forced to take great efforts to buy back their personal data or to face the consequences of having sold it [9]. In strong models of privacy it cannot be accepted that there are no restrictions to the availability of privacy rights, as these are of basic character. Yet this objection can be defeated with pragmatic as well as with legal arguments. As to the former ones, we are not discussing whether we should live in a world in which personal data are collected, used and sold: we already live in such a world and need workable solutions rather than ideal aspirations [17]. At least, negotiation over privacy may work out, and this is better than nothing when it comes to protect (European) consumers on the Internet. In addition to that, it must be stressed that there are no absolute rights, and even basic rights may give priority, under certain circumstances, to other legally-protected goods and interests, both collective and private, such as the market economy or the freedoms of trade and information. In this respect, prominent European scholars hold that it would be both possible and desirable to avoid the increasing number of legal regulations in the private sector by conceiving privacy as a property-like position that can operate within market processes [15]. The fundamental character of data protection rights would not be an obstacle for this, as both the market operations and the property rights are an essential part of democratic societies. Therefore legislation should be limited to provide for those conditions under which disposition rights over privacy can fairly be negotiated according to the market rules. As mentioned, this approach fit at best into the e-commerce system, and can be easily integrated into technological and self-regulative strategies. But its main strength is above all that it is respectful with, and even enhances, the basic legal principle governing all strong data protection models: the principle of consent, which can be taken to imply the claim to freely negotiate over one's privacy in the market.

In the end, e-commerce and data protection seem to flow together. It is undeniable that privacy always increases companies' costs, but the benefit of taking it seriously will over-compensate them. Companies would be ready to concern themselves with privacy if they realize that this is a competitive advantage in the marketplace. Their goal seems to be simple: use privacy to win and keep customers, which is today's emerging business issue [5]. Actually, privacy is not that expensive. Data protection laws have set on e-businesses two kinds of duties, which affect, on the one hand, the company relationships with actual or potential clients (information, consent, transparency, access and removal rights...) and, on the other, the internal organization of the company as for the management of personal information (security measures, relationships with the official agencies...). It can be argued that, even if the latter group of duties does lead to a considerable increase of costs, this is not only due to data protection laws, but would be also partly provoked by the market needs. Anyway, what seems clear is that the former duties are not a significant cost for companies, as they are mainly of informative nature. As a result, privacy laws cannot be longer considered to hamper the commercial practices of personal information processing. After ten years of data protection directive European companies are doing essentially the same as they did when no legislation was in force. Of course, they have to inform clients about several issues, and often they have to ask for consent for processing their personal data. Once this twofold requirement has been met, companies are legitimated to do almost everything with those data. And this is precisely because they are collected and used upon the basis of the informed consent of data subjects. It has been noted that European legislation has entitled citizens to verify their data or find out whether they are being electronically processed, but that is all: almost any processing may be legitimated by consent and must only comply with accuracy and updating requirements, which does not assure control [16]. Under the property model, and apart from the initial organizational costs, data protection law is not that harmful to e-businesses, and does not interfere with their practices of personal information processing. Quite on the contrary, as there will be an incentive for customers if they know that companies abide by legal standards, data protection can be a beneficial factor for the e-commerce system. As the privacy outcry is becoming more and more present, a clear tendency emerges to take it as a business case. Let us not forget that costumers do belong to this system as well, and that trust is a crucial – but scarce – element for its development. Even the mere compliance with privacy legislation can be used for the sake of increasing consumers trust. In this regard, many seals and other symbolic indicators of compliance do not add any value to the legal standards, but are just intended to neutralize the psychological barriers blocking the expansion of e-commerce.

In spite of all this, one should not overestimate the importance that privacy has to consumers. Up to a point, the level of privacy protection offered by companies has no direct relation to its sales rate. This seemingly contradiction is due the lacking data protection culture among citizens. In Spain, for instance, only 14 per cent of Internet users feel worried about personal data processing when it comes to enter electronic transactions [21]. This fact serves to illustrate why, even if the property-approach implies a certain improvement of privacy protection in countries with no privacy laws, it entails outstanding risks for the European strong data protection model.

5   The Fundamental-Right-Model of Data Protection

Can a basic right be negotiated without ceasing to be a basic right and without any significant decrease in the protection that citizens obtain through it? Under current conditions, should privacy be an available right? I think that the answer must be negative, as there good reasons to maintain that consent is not an unlimited legitimating mechanism for personal data processing and thus that the property model cannot be accepted without more ado.

In recent years the right to data protection has been widely acknowledged as a basic or fundamental right (Article 8 of European Convention for the Protection of Human Rights and Article 8 of the Charter of Fundamental Rights of the European Union). Several consequences must be drawn from this. Basic rights are not only subjective or personal rights, but entail an unavailable dimension since they belong to the objective conditions of any democratic society. This is also the case of data protection. Let me recall now the two main arguments that have been put forward to justify the property model. On the one hand, there are no absolute rights, and even basic rights be constrained by other private or collective interests. On the other, it belongs to the essential core of privacy that citizens must have control over their personal information, whereby this control also covers their choices about privacy provided that they are based on consent. Any model that denies this shall be reproached to be concealing a paternalistic ideology, a top-down attitude to information which is opposed to real notions of community, responsibility and citizenship [16]. Both arguments must be taken seriously, as they make it difficult to justify the imposition of restrictions on the availability of privacy. Still in the following I will argue that the property model underlies three weaknesses. The first one is that it gives a misleading interpretation of consent and overlooks that consent cannot be taken to legitimate a complete loss of control over one's personal information. The second weak point is a wrong appreciation of the factual circumstances in which privacy negotiation is carried out. This provokes in turn a third mistake which affects the assessment of the value of the colliding goods, say, data protection and market economy.

Inside the normative content of privacy there exist two diverging forces: the data subject's consent, which implies the power of *disposition* of personal data, and the possibility of *control* over personal data, which is recognised as the core element of data protection. In the field of e-commerce, it is often the case that these two forces collide. In most online transactions, giving consent to personal data processing leads to loosing any possibility of control over them. The idea of privacy consent might become a sly joke: consumers are forced to accept the contract clauses because otherwise they undergo the opportunity for business [9]. If the necessary information is provided, the company may be legally entitled to disclose our data to many other companies, no matter where they are located, and for a wide range of purposes which have been broadly formulated (privacy clauses are often drafted in a misleading manner enabling companies to process personal information without restrictions). By this, consumers give up their control rights factually, despite of that they are not legally allowed to do it. Under these conditions, the consent cannot be taken to override automatically the possibility of control over one's personal information, as the property approach seems to accept.

Any balance between privacy and commercial freedom or market economy must take into account the factual circumstances in which privacy is to be protected. One of them is the lacking or at least reduced data protection culture. Property approaches seem to resort to the idea of consumer sovereignty. But, for consumers to be sovereign, they should be aware of the significance of their personal information, from both the economic and the social and axiological dimension. In this is correct, the prerequisite for technological and regulative strategies, as well as for accepting the property model, would be a psycho-sociological condition: consumers should be aware of the implications and consequences of giving away their data. And this is seldom the case, as the data protection culture has not yet evolved. Privacy still points in the direction of the individual, rather than the social, and steers the discussion towards personal, individual preferences. Being biased towards the individual market it is hard, if not impossible, to make visible its value as social good [23]. Moreover, there is still an abyss between the theoretical concern about data protection and its practical relevance for citizens or consumers. In real life, consumers are ready and happy to loose the control over their data in exchange for any beneficial client-card of the supermarket [16, 18]. Whenever discounts or conveniences are offered, it does not really matter that their personal data are stored, analysed, sold and even exported abroad. Without awareness of all what entails, consumers cannot be said to give their consent freely. If consent must be always informed consent, any consent given without such awareness cannot be properly regarded as consent. As usually interpreted by the property model, thus, the idea of consent might undermine the strong model of data protection.

Thirdly, the normative import of privacy protection and that of the healthy market cannot be unduly equated. I still wonder what arguments can be brought forward to hold that property and market should always prevail, under the aforementioned circumstances, over the possibility of controlling one's personal information. When assessing the importance of the colliding goods, privacy and market, we should bear in mind that privacy is not a basic right among others, but it is rather *the* fundamental right upon which the information society should be normatively constructed. Being a constitutive element of citizens' freedom, it is not only a personal right, but also a transversal basic right which reflects the communicative content of basic rights altogether [19]. That is why it operates as a criterion for political legitimacy, affecting both the public sector and the private companies and organisations (horizontal impact of basic rights). In this regard, one of its major tasks is to equilibrate real informative unbalances between companies and citizens. The property model cannot render this function, as it remains tied to the market. However, if this task is given up, the law of the information society might be running the risk of loosing its legitimacy.

6 Data Protection and the Forthcoming Society

I concede that such a strong conception of privacy is probably too strong, unworkable and therefore deemed to conflict with current e-commerce trends. As it happens with environmental protection, it requires that both citizens and companies take not only the monetary value of personal information into account, but also its social and axiological import. And this, by now, is almost an illusion. One should better be content with those trends, since they point to a worldwide improvement of privacy protection. I am deeply convinced, nevertheless, that it is necessary to keep on holding strong normative visions, in particular when the discussion is about the legal model which fits better into the interconnected society. Let us not forget that the arguments about privacy models are, ultimately, arguments about the information society in which we want to live.

References

1. Adkinson, W, Eisenach, J., Lenard, T.: Privacy Online: A Report on the Information Practices and Policies of Commercial Websites, Washington, PFF (2002)
2. Banisar, D., Davies, S.: Global Trends in Privacy Protection. An International Survey of Privacy, Data Protection and Surveillance Laws and Developments, The John Marshall Journal of Computer & Information Law XVIII no 1 (1999) 1-111
3. Borking, J.: Proposal for building a privacy guardian for the electronic age, Registrariekamer, Den Haag (2000)
4. Borking, J. Raab, Ch.: Laws, PETs and Other Technologies for Privacy Protection, The Journal of Information, Law and Technology 1 no 1 (2001)
5. Cavoukian, A., Hamilton, T.J.: The Privacy Payoff. How Successful Business Build Customer Trust, McGraw-Hill and Ryerson, Toronto (2002)
6. Challis, W.S., Cavoukian, A.: The Case for a US Privacy Commissioner: A Canadian Commissioner's Perspective, The John Marshall Journal of Computer & Information Law, vol. XIX no 1 (2000) 1-36
7. Farell, H.: Hybrid Institutions and the Law: Outlaw Arrangements or Interface Solutions, Zeitschrift für Rechtssoziologie 23 (2002) 25-40

8. Federal Trade Commission, On-line Profiling: A Report to Congress (2000)
9. Garfinkel, S.: Database Nation: The Death of Privacy in the 21st Century, O'Reilly and Associates, Cambridge (2000)
10. Godin, S.: Permission Marketing, Simon and Schuster, New York (1999)
11. Goldsmith, J.: Unilateral Regulation of the Internet: A Modest Defense, European Journal of International Law 11 No. 1 (2000), 135-48
12. Hagel, J, Singer, M.: Net Worth: Shaping Markets When Customers Make the Rules, Harvard Business School Press, Cambridge (1999)
13. Heydebrand, W.: From Globalization of Law to Law under Globalization, in: Nelken, D., Feest, J. (eds.), Adapting Legal Cultures, Hart Publishing, Oxford Portland (2001) 117-140
14. Holznagel B., Werle, R.: Sectors and Strategies of Global Communication Regulation, Zeitschrift für Rechtsoziologie 23 (2002) 3-24
15. Kilian, W.: Rekonzeptualisierung des Datenschutzrechts durch Technisierung und Selbstregulierung?, in: Freundesgabe für A. Büllesbach, J.F. Steinkopf Druck, Stuttgart (2001) 151-160
16. Leith, Ph.: Confidentiality, Privacy and E-Government: Clarifying the Notion of Public Space in: Galindo, F., Traunmüller, R. (eds.), E-Government: Legal, Technical and Pedagogical Aspects, University of Zaragoza and IFIP, Zaragoza (2003) 105-122
17. Lessig, L.: Code and Other Laws of Cyberspace, Basic Books, New York (1999)
18. Lyon, D.: The Electronic Eye: The Rise of Surveillance Society, Minneapolis, University of Minnesota Press (1994)
19. Roßnagel, A., Pfitzmann, A., Garstka, H.: Modernisierung des Datenschutzrechts: Gutachten im Auftrag des Bundesministers des Innern (2002)
20. Schartum, D.W.: Privacy Enhancing Employment of ICT: Empowering and Assisting Data Subjects», International Review of Law, Computers and Technology 1 no 2 (2001), 157-170
21. Spanish E-commerce Association: Survey on B2B e-commerce (2003), at www.aece.org
22. Teubner, G: Substantive and Reflexive Elements in Modern Law, Law and Society Review 17 no 2 (1983) 239-85
23. Viseu, A., Clement, A., Aspinall, J.: Situating Privacy Online: Complex Perceptions and Everyday Practice, University of Toronto, Toronto (2003)
24. European Working Party on Data Protection, Working Document on Functioning of the Safe Harbor Agreement (2002)
25. European Working Party on Data Protection: Opinion 3/2003 on the European Code of conduct of FEDMA for the use of personal data in direct marketing

Dealing with Privacy Obligations:
Important Aspects and Technical Approaches

Marco Casassa Mont

Hewlett-Packard Laboratories, Filton Road, Stoke Gifford
BS34 8BF Bristol, UK
`marco.casassa-mont@hp.com`

Abstract. The management and enforcement of privacy obligations is a challenging task: it involves legal, organizational, behavioral and technical aspects. This area is relevant for enterprises and government agencies that deal with personal identity information. Privacy and data protection laws already regulate some of the related aspects. Technical work has been done for the management of obligations subordinated to authorization aspects and simple data retention obligations: however, dealing with ongoing and long-term aspects of obligations is still a green field and open to research. This paper explores and analyses the explicit management of privacy obligations for identity information. It focuses on technical aspects even if the problem cannot be solved only by deploying technological solutions. Mechanisms are required to represent, manage, monitor and enforce obligation policies in complex and heterogeneous environments. Our research is work in progress: we illustrate some of our technical work and investigations in this space.

1 Introduction

In the last decade a lot of work has been done in the area of privacy, in particular from a legal and legislative perspective. This includes European Community data protection privacy laws, various US privacy laws (HIPAA, COPPA, GLB, FRC, etc.) and more specific national privacy initiatives. An overview of these initiatives can be found at [1]. Various guidelines are also available on the protection of privacy and flows of personal data, including OECD guidelines [2] that describe concepts such as collection limitation, data quality and purpose specification principles.

Privacy policies are a suitable tool to represent and describe privacy laws, guidelines and privacy statements. They, at the very base, express rights, permissions and obligations.

Privacy policies are formulated and stated in a wide variety of contexts including the e-commerce, financial, health care and government sectors. For example, in e-commerce and web sites, privacy policies describe the rights of users about their personal information, the permissions given to service providers and service providers' obligations. These policies let consumers know about web sites' privacy practices: consumers can then decide whether or not these practices are acceptable, when

S. Katsikas, J. Lopez, and G. Pernul (Eds.): TrustBus 2004, LNCS 3184, pp. 120–131, 2004.

to opt-in or opt-out and who to do business to. Examples of guidelines for formulating online privacy policies can be found at [3].

If on one hand the expression of privacy statements via policies is a significant advancement in communicating privacy rights, permissions and obligations, on the other hand, are quite often difficult to understand: they take a long time to read and can change without notice. Privacy policies might also be hard to enforce via IT solutions. The enforcement of privacy rights, permissions and obligations related to confidential and personal data requires the mapping of these concepts into rules, constraints and access control, the meaning of which must be unambiguous so that it can be deployed and enforced by software solutions.

In many cases the full enforcement of privacy policies cannot be achieved only via technological approaches but it still requires that the entities involved in the management of confidential and personal data follows best practices and good behaviours. However, being able to automate aspects of the enforcement of privacy policies and reduce the involved costs is of primary importance and interest for enterprises, web sites, e-commerce and financial organisations that more and more recognise that dealing correctly and honestly with privacy matters can have a beneficial return in terms of branding, trust and business.

Advancements in this direction have already been made when dealing with the (technological) enforcement of privacy permissions. Extended access control and authorization mechanisms have been built to check privacy permissions against users' rights, the purpose of the confidential information (that needs to be accessed) and the declared intents. More details are provided in the related work section.

On the other hand, we argue that the management and enforcement of privacy obligations, as first class citizens, is still a green field and open to research. The events that trigger the fulfilment of privacy obligations can be completely orthogonal to the ones that are relevant for privacy permissions. Privacy obligations can have ongoing aspects that need to be monitored and satisfied. In this paper we analyse some of the related issues and describe possible technical approaches to move towards a more explicit management and enforcement of privacy obligations.

2 Privacy Obligations

It is hard to classify privacy obligations in a manner which is satisfactory for all environments. Different types of privacy obligations have been defined for financial institutions, health-care, enterprises and e-commerce: they have different interpretations, implications and enforcement requirements depending on the context and the legislative framework where they are applied.

The description of responsibilities and commitments dictated by privacy obligations can range from being very abstract to very specific. Privacy obligations can be very abstract. An example is: "Every financial institution has an affirmative and continuing obligation to respect customer privacy and protect the security and confidentiality of customer information" - Gramm-Leach-Bliley Act (1999).

Other privacy obligations can dictate more refined responsibilities given specific contexts, for example with respect to disclosure of personal information. Obligations can be expressed in terms of notice requirements, opt-out options, limits on reuse of information and information sharing for marketing purposes.

At the other extreme, privacy obligations can dictate very specific requirements. This is the case where data retention has to be enforced for a long period of time or data is temporarily stored by organisations: privacy obligations can require that personal data must be deleted after a predefined number of years, e.g. 30 years, (long-term commitment) or in a few days if user's consent is not granted (short-term commitment) or their account is closed.

Privacy obligations can have "ongoing" and long-term commitments for organisations or might apply only for a short period of time and be transient.

When dealing with privacy obligations, different aspects need to be kept in account:

1. **The timeframe (period of validity) that applies for obligations:** it could be for a short or a long period of time;
2. **The situations/events that trigger the need to fulfil obligations:** it could be triggered by a specific event or be ongoing, for example dictated by law. Events include deadlines, specific transactions/interactions and contextual changes;
3. **The enforceability of obligations:** an obligation can be technically enforceable or its implementation can only happen as the result of guidelines, human behaviours and best practices;
4. **The target of an obligation and the implications:** for example the target can be confidential data, personal profiles, medical or criminal data, etc. In case of long term privacy obligations, data has to ensure its survivability and longevity;
5. **The entities that are responsible for enforcing obligations** and criteria specifying their accountability;
6. **Exception or special cases that applies for obligations.**

The topic related to "privacy obligations" is complex and exploring all the possible implications and involved aspects goes far beyond the purpose of this paper. In this paper we specifically focus on enforceable privacy obligations related to personal and confidential data for enterprises and business organisations.

3   Important Issues and Requirements

The following important issues and related requirements need to be considered when dealing with the management and enforcement of privacy obligations:

1. **Modelling and representation of privacy obligations:** aspects of privacy obligations need to be modelled, including representing which data is affected by the obligation, the events and conditions that trigger the fulfilment of an obligation, actions to be carried on, who is responsible and accountable for their enforcement;

2. **Association of obligations to data:** the association of privacy obligations to the targeted confidential data must be strong i.e. not easy to be broken. This aspect is particularly challenging in dynamic environments where confidential data can be processed, moved around or sent to other parties. Breaking the association of data to their associated privacy obligations is, on its own, a violation of these obligations;

3. **Mapping obligations into enforceable actions:** when possible, actions must be expressed in a way that can be programmatically enforced. Otherwise they should trigger related processes and workflows (involving the human intervention) and clearly state responsibilities;

4. **Compliance of refined obligations to high-level policies:** refined privacy obligations are usually an interpretation and adaptation of high-level policies to specific contexts. High-level policies can change and, as a consequence, refined policies need to be modified. This mapping process should be managed explicitly and tools built to spot potential inconsistencies and dependencies;

5. **Tracking the evolutions of obligation policies:** as obligation policies can be carried on over long periods of time, they are subject to changes. An important issue is related to the tracking of these changes, for accountability reasons and to deal with the evolution of the contexts and frameworks where these obligations apply. This introduce requirements in terms of dealing with versioning of obligation policies and context tracking;

6. **Dealing with long-term obligation aspects:** the fact that obligation policies might require long-term commitments has implications on the longevity and survivability of related processes and the involved data. Events and conditions related to obligations need to be monitored over long period of time. Solutions need to be built in a way that can be easily extended and modified over time. The format of stored data needs to evolve to take into account technological advancements. Openness and flexibility are two important requirements;

7. **Accountability management:** as anticipated above, the explicit management of accountability is fundamental to ensure that the enforcement of privacy obligations is carried on with clear responsibilities of the involved parties. Responsibilities should be explicitly defined and communicated. This introduces requirements in terms of auditing, tracking of obligations and their monitoring;

8. **Monitoring obligations:** it is important that the fulfilment of obligations is monitored and checked against expected situations and behaviours. Despite all the good intents and enforcement mechanisms, it can always happen that the fulfilment of obligations is omitted. Monitoring mechanisms must be orthogonal to the enforcement mechanisms. Monitoring tasks need to be aware of the set of "active" privacy obligations and access evidence about the enforcement of obligations, such as audit logs. In case of discovery of overdue obligations they should trigger their enforcement and create awareness about the encountered problems;

9. **User involvement:** at the very base, privacy policies and obligations are defined and enforced to preserve user's rights on their personal data. It is important that these rights are well understandable by users. Users should also have visibility of which obligations an organisation has with them and potentially monitor their ful-

filment. This introduces requirements of transparency about organisational practices, along with the provision of tools that allow users to monitor and directly manage privacy obligations;

10. **Complexity and cost of instrumenting applications and services:** last but not least, an important issue is related to the impact that the enforcement and monitoring of obligation policies has on the involved applications and services, both in terms of their instrumentation and costs. As long as possible, a privacy obligation framework should be deployed in a way that requires a minimum impact on applications and services.

Dealing with the management and enforcement of privacy obligations can be reasonably easy when the events that trigger them are well defined and simple to capture. For example, a web transaction between a user and a service provider might require the access or the disclosure of user's confidential data to third parties: in this context, obligations might dictate the need for notifying users or requesting their authorization.

More complex is, for example, the case of privacy obligations for ongoing and long-term obligations, triggered by the occurrence of events and conditions unrelated to any transaction, interaction or time. Some of these events might not be so easy to intercept or the software cannot be instrumented to deal with them. Solutions might need to be deployed and kept running for long periods of time to fulfil these obligations.

4   Addressed Problems

In this paper we address the problem of dealing with an explicit management of privacy obligations, including ongoing and long-term privacy obligations. This implies dealing with the explicit monitoring, enforcement, and tracking of privacy obligations. Related to this we also want to address the problem of dealing with the strong association of privacy obligations to data, enforce accountability and provide more transparency to users.

Work has already been done to deal with some of these issues, in particular related to the representation of privacy policies (and obligations), their enforcement in transactional and interaction-driven contexts and the management of simple long-term aspects of obligations in particular for data retention. In many cases, though, obligation policies are considered as second-class entities the enforcement of which is subordinated to other aspects of privacy policies, such as permissions and access control.

We believe that a more explicit and comprehensive approach to privacy obligations is required, where they are considered and managed as "first-class citizens".

5   Technical Details

This section provides technical details about the approaches and solutions under exploration to address the problems stated in section 4.

Fig. 1 shows a high-level architecture of a system providing an explicit management of privacy obligations.

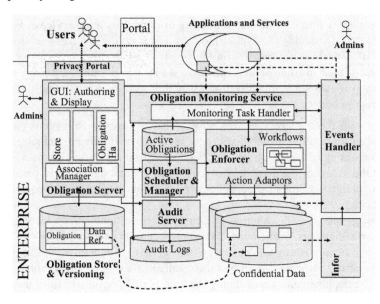

Fig. 1. High-level architecture of an obligation management system.

The obligation management system consists of:

1. **Obligation Server:** it is the component that deals with the authoring, management and storage of obligations. It allows the management of the association of privacy obligations to confidential data and their tracking and versioning. Administrators and users can access, review and manage privacy obligations of their competence. It pushes active obligations, i.e. valid obligations, to the "obligation scheduler & manager" and relevant events to the event handler for their monitoring. One or more obligation servers can be deployed (and synchronised), depending on needs;

2. **Obligation Store and Versioning:** it is the data repository storing obligations and their mapping to confidential data. Multiple versions of obligations are also stored in this system;

3. **Obligation Scheduler and Manager:** it is the component that is aware of which obligations are currently active, their ongoing deadlines and relevant events. When events/conditions trigger the fulfilment of one or more obligations, this component activate the correspondent "workflow processes" of the "obligation enforcer" that will deal with the enforcement of the obligation.

4. **Obligation Enforcer:** at its core it is a workflow system containing workflow processes describing how to enforce one or more obligations. The enforcement can be automatic and/or could require human intervention, depending on the nature of the obligation. It is configurable via "action adaptor" plug-ins, specialised in per-

forming specific actions dictated by obligations (deletion of data, transformation/obfuscation of data, e-mail notification, etc.);

5. **Events Handler:** it is the component in charge of monitoring and detecting relevant events for privacy obligations. These events are defined and pushed by the obligation server. The detection of events can happen via instrumented application/services. They can also be directly generated by users, administrators, the "obligation monitoring service" and the information tracker;

6. **Obligation Monitoring Service:** it is the component, orthogonal to the scheduling and enforcement systems that monitors active obligations and if they have been enforced (by analysing and checking for effects of the involved actions);

7. **Information Tracker:** it is a component that focuses on intercepting events generated by data repositories, databases and file systems containing confidential data and providing this information to the event handler. It is aware of the location of confidential data (as described by the obligation policies) and checks for movements and changes happening to this data;

8. **Audit Server:** it audits the relevant events and information generated by the overall system components and involved applications/services.

In our model, privacy obligations describe relevant events/conditions, actions, target (i.e. related confidential data) and accountable entities. A simple XML-based example of privacy obligation is shown in Fig. 2.

```
<Obligation Policy>
 <id: 21435 version: 1.0>
 <Obligation trigger descriptor>
   <type: event>
   <subtype: time-based event>
   <parameters>
     <relevant time: DD/MM/YYYY>
   </parameters>
 </Obligation trigger descriptor>
 <Target>
  <Data Owner> refXYZ </Data Owner>
   <Data Locators>
    <data locator> "select ... from ...where ..." </data locator>
    <data locator> X:\\filesyst1\sub1\sub2\*.doc </data locator>
   </Data Locators>
  </Target>
 <Enforcement>
 <Actions>
   <action> Workflow.delete_data_process </action>
   <action> Workflow.notify_process </action>
 </Actions>
 </Enforcement>
 <Responsibilities>
    <Responsible> Roles.Obligation_Manager_DataCenter1 </Responsible>
 </Responsibilities>
</Obligation Policy>
```

Fig. 2. A simple XML-based example of privacy obligation.

The content of this privacy obligation is self-explicative. It is about the deletion of confidential data at a specific point of time. The policy contains a reference to the actions to be enforced (in the example they are two workflow processes for deleting data and notifying relevant entities) and the entities responsible for this obligation.

The privacy obligation policy also contains information about the "targeted data" and specifies the association to this data along with the owner(s). In the example the obligation refers to data stored both in a relational database (accessible via an SQL query) and in a file system. Other mapping mechanisms can be used.

If the system is deployed in a stable and well-controlled environment, managing the association of data to obligations can be handled via a mixture of automation mechanisms and manual intervention (of administrators and users). Issues arise when the overall environment is dynamic and data can be moved around. In this case, despite all the efforts of handling events and tracking movements, the association of data to obligations policies can be broken or be left in an inconsistent state.

To address this issue we are exploring a variant of the architecture shown in Fig. 1, where stronger mechanisms are introduces to manage the association of obligations to data. Fig. 3 shows the additional components.

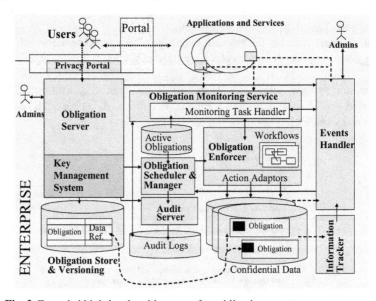

Fig. 3. Extended high-level architecture of an obligation management system.

Confidential data is obfuscated and strongly associated to privacy obligations by using cryptographic techniques. A key management system is introduced to deal with this task. For example a symmetric key is generated by the key management system and used to obfuscate data. An envelope (e.g. based on PKCS#7) is created: it contains (at least) the hash value of the obligation policy along with the symmetric key. This envelope is encrypted with the public key [3] associated to the key management system.

The triple consisting of <obligation policy, encrypted envelope, obfuscated data> is stored as a replacement of the original data. The obligation policy must contain a reference to the competent Obligation Server but it could omit the reference to confidential data, as the policy is now directly associated to this data.

In this way, the encrypted confidential data can be moved around and transmitted to other parties without any strict control. The receiving party has to interact with the Obligation Server to decrypt the data: this allows the system to track and audit where the data is, check for relevant obligations and update its obligation store. The basic principles and additional details on how this approach can be implemented are described in [9].

The technical approach described in Fig. 1 is almost transparent to applications and services that are affected by privacy obligations: the system needs (in most of the cases) only to be aware of relevant events. The second approach, in Fig. 3, on one hand introduces more control and accountability; on the other hand, applications and services might need to be modified in order to handle encrypted data and the associated process. Data repositories might need to change the way they store information, to accommodate encrypted data. We are currently exploring how a hybrid solution can be used to accommodate different needs and requirements and the overall implications on the underlying environment.

6 Discussion

The system described in this paper centralises the storage of privacy obligations along with their management. It can support the management of versions of privacy obligations over time and enable the tracking of their changes for auditing and accountability reasons. We are exploring how these aspects can be distributed to avoid potential bottlenecks and central points of failure, without compromising the overall security of the system.

The obligation scheduler coupled with the event handler allows for the management of short and long-term obligations. The monitoring system provides an additional mechanism for spotting enforcement omissions thanks to the fact it can understand the effects of actions dictated by privacy obligations (such as deletion and manipulation of data, notifications, etc.). Information logged by the audit server is used during these monitoring tasks.

Our system explicitly focuses on the management and enforcement of obligations: this does not imply that it has to happen independently by other privacy aspects, such as permissions. It should be considered as a sub-system of a more comprehensive privacy management framework. Similarly, the representation of obligations is part of the wider task of representing privacy policies.

Even if the system enables automation when dealing with privacy obligations, it also allows the human intervention in a variety of contexts. Administrators and users can intervene during the enforcement of obligations, if required (for example to explicitly authorise actions). Administrators and users can access and manage the privacy obligations of their competence in a monitored and audited way: this increases the transparency of the enterprise's privacy practices and the involvement of the interested parties.

We assume that the enterprise is willing to be compliant with privacy policies and, more specifically, privacy obligations. However the system must be deployed by keeping in mind good security practices, especially for the platforms that will host our system components. As most of the system components are critical, they require to be secured accordingly. Additional assurance and accountability can be added by hardening the audit server and involving trusted third parties in the monitoring of the enforcement of obligation policies.

When dealing with long-term obligations it is also important to ensure the reliability, survivability and longevity of the platforms running our system components and the involved data (including the representation of privacy obligation). Work has already been done in this space, including [15,16,17,18,19], and can be leveraged.

7 Related Work

Relevant work in the space of privacy management for enterprises is described in [4,5,6,7]. An Enterprise Privacy Architecture is introduced and described in [7], encompassing a policy management system, a privacy enforcement system and an audit console. Paper [6] introduces more architectural details along with an interpretation of the concept of privacy obligations. This concept is framed in the context of privacy rules defined for authorization purposes. This approach is further refined and described in the Enterprise Privacy Authorization Language (EPAL) specification [8].

The above work makes important advancements in exploring and addressing the problem of privacy management in enterprises. Our main comments are on the suggested approach to handle privacy obligations i.e. consider the authorization and access control perspective as the key driver for the representation, management and enforcement of obligations. This approach is definitely pragmatic and can be leveraged by current access control mechanisms available within enterprises. However it has still to be fully demonstrated that privacy obligations can be managed at their best only from an authorization-based perspective. Privacy obligations can include aspects that are not really driven by authorization, especially when the set of events that triggers these obligations is extended, to include, for example, dealing with the deletion of confidential data at a specific date/event, periodically providing notifications to users about stored confidential data, dealing with ongoing requests dictated by users or laws.

We believe that modularity and separation of concerns are important aspects. In particular, the representation, management and enforcement of privacy rights, obligations and permissions should be addressed without imposing any specific or dominant perspective. In our approach obligation policies are first-class citizens with their explicit management. However the proposed system can be considered as a subsystem of a more comprehensive policy management framework. Even if our architecture has high-level commonalities with the architecture described in [4,5,6,7] we further refine the concept of obligations, we introduce the concept of obligation versioning and tracking. We further split the enforcement mechanisms in two parts by including a scheduling mechanisms and an obligation enforcer where the obligations actions are carried out by flexible workflow processes that allows automation but also people involvement.

Approaches to deal with (privacy) obligations have already been implemented in products, in particular for data retention [10] and in a variety of document management systems. Nevertheless, these approaches are very specific, focused on particular domains and handle simple obligation policies. Our work wants to push the barrier even further to create an obligation management framework that can be leveraged in multiple contexts, for different purposes.

A lot of work has been done in representing privacy policies, including obligations such as [8,11,12]. Work describing the monitoring of obligations in policy management is described in [12]. Relevant work on mechanisms to associate policies to data is described in [4,5,6,7,9,14]. Each mechanism has pros and cons in terms of the implications for existing enterprise applications, services and data repositories. We can leverage aspects of this work, in particular [9] to provide a stronger association of obligation policies to confidential data.

8   Current and Future Work

We are in the process of developing a prototype of the system components described in this paper. Components, when possible, will be implemented as web services and deployed within an enterprise scenario: different types of confidential data and repositories will be considered. Obligation policies will be represented by using an XML format to allow future extensions.

Our work and research is definitely in progress: technical aspects needs to be further refined and investigated especially the ones related to the life-cycle management of privacy obligations and events. The overall implications for the involved enterprise applications and services have to be fully understood. One of the reasons of developing our prototype is to make advancements in these areas by experimenting and refining our concepts.

Tools and mechanisms to address the compliance of refined obligations to high-level policies are also under investigation.

9   Conclusions

The management of privacy obligation is important for enterprises and organisations to preserve their reputation and brand, be compliant with legislation and customers' requirements and increase business opportunities.

In this paper we describe important issues that need to be kept into account when dealing with privacy obligations. In our vision obligation policies (as well as for other privacy aspects, including rights and permissions) need to be considered as first-class citizens in privacy management frameworks.

We introduce a technical approach to deal with the explicit management of privacy obligations, on an ongoing basis, including long-term privacy obligations. We provide a high-level description of system components dealing with the monitoring, enforcement, and tracking of privacy obligations. Related to this we also address the problem of dealing with the strong association of privacy obligations to data, accountability management and users involvement. Our research and work is in progress. A prototype will soon be developed to test and refine our ideas.

References

1. Laurant, C., Privacy International: Privacy and Human Rights 2003: an International Survey of Privacy Laws and Developments, Electronic Privacy Information Center (EPIC), Privacy International. http://www.privacyinternational.org/survey/phr2003/ (2003)
2. OECD: OECD Guidelines on the Protection of Privacy and Transborder Flows of Personal Data. http://www1.oecd.org/publications/e-book/9302011E.PDF (1980)
3. Online Privacy Alliance: Guidelines for Online Privacy Policies. http://www.privacyalliance.org/, Online Privacy Alliance (2004)
4. Karjoth, G., Schunter, M.: A Privacy Policy Model for Enterprises. IBM Research, Zurich. 15th IEEE Computer Foundations Workshop (2002)
5. Karjoth, G., Schunter, M., Waidner, M.: Platform for Enterprise Privacy Practices: Privacy-enabled Management of Customer Data. 2nd Workshop on Privacy Enhancing Technologies, Lecture Notes in Computer Science, Springer Verlang (2002)
6. Schunter, M., Ashley, P.: The Platform for Enterprise Privacy Practices. IBM Zurich Research Laboratory, 2002
7. Karjoth, G., Schunter, M., Waidner, M.: Privacy-enabled Services for Enterprises. IBM Zurich Research Laboratory, TrustBus 2002 (2002)
8. IBM: The Enterprise Privacy Authorization Language (EPAL), EPAL 1.1 specification. http://www.zurich.ibm.com/security/enterprise-privacy/epal/, IBM (2004)
9. Casassa Mont, M., Pearson, S., Bramhall, P.: Towards Accountable Management of Privacy and Identity Information, ESORICS 2003, 2003
10. IBM: IBM Tivoli Storage Manager for Data Retention (2004)
11. Bettini, C., Jajodia, S., Sean Wang, X., Wijesekera, D.: Obligation Monitoring in Policy Management (2002)
12. Damianou, N., Dulay, N., Lupu, E., Sloman, M.: The Ponder Policy Specification Language (2001)
13. Housley, R, Ford, W., Polk, W., Solo, D.: RFC2459: Internet X.509 Public Key Infrastructure Certificate and CRL profile. IETF (1999)
14. Agrawal, R., Kiernan, J., Srikant, R., Xu, Y.: Hippocratic Databases. IBM Almaden Research Center (2002)
15. Anderson, R. J.: The Eternity Service. Proc. PRAGO-CRYPT 96, CTU Publishing House, Prague (1996)
16. Ellison, R.J., Fisher, D.A., Linger, R.C., Lipson, H.F., Longstaff, T.A., Mead, N.R.: Survivability: Protecting your Critical Systems. Proceeding of the International Conference of Requirements Engineering (1998)
17. Kubiatowicz, J., Bibdel, D., Chen, Y., Czerwinski, S., Eaton, P., Geels D., Gummadi, R., Rhea, D., Weatherspoon, H., Weimer, W., Wells, C., Zao, B.: OceanStore: An Architecture for Global Scale Persistent Storage. University of California, Berkeley, ASPLOS 2000 (2000)
18. Neumann, P.G.: Practical Architectures for Survivable Systems and Networks. SRI International, Army Research Lab (1999)
19. Wylie, J.J., Bigrigg, M. W., Strunk, J. D., Ganger, G. R., Kiliccote, H., Khosia, P.K.: Survivable Information Storage Systems. IEEE Computer (2000)

Offer Privacy in Mobile Agents Using Conditionally Anonymous Digital Signatures

Ming Yao, Matt Henricksen, Ernest Foo, and Ed Dawson

Information Security Research Centre
Queensland University of Technology
Brisbane, QLD, 4000, Australia
{m.yao,m.henricksen,e.foo,e.dawson}@qut.edu.au

Abstract. For a shopping mobile agent that collects offers from vendors' servers on behalf of its owner, offer privacy is an important property. In this paper, we propose a protocol using a "conditionally anonymous digital signature scheme" to achieve offer privacy based on a fair blind signature. The proposed scheme provides a method for a server to sign its offer without revealing any information about its identity to any other server or the originator. When a server's identity needs to be revealed, the offer privacy can be reversed, with the assistance of the e-market authority.

1 Introduction

Mobile agents are autonomous software entities that move code, data and state to remote hosts. We consider a scenario where a mobile agent is ordered to search for the best price of a specific product [4]. The agent migrates to multiple servers, collects price quotes and is free to choose its next move dynamically based on the data it acquired from its journey. The agent finally returns to the buyer with the offers of all the vendors. Using the agent data, the buyer chooses the best offer.

"Offer privacy" is one of the major security concerns with respect to this scenario. Assume n servers will be included in the agent's itinerary. Yao et. al [5] defined "offer privacy" in mobile agent systems as follows: If a mobile agent visits a sequence of servers S_1, S_2, ..., S_n, none of the identities of the *honest* servers traversed by an agent can be traced from the contents of the offers o_1, o_2, ..., o_n. Yao et. al [5] also stressed that offer privacy should be revokable. In this paper, we use a trusted third party as the mediator to disclose the identity of an intended server.

"Offer privacy" can be attained by hiding the identity of the server, and its relationship to the data. However, an "offer privacy" mobile agent system is more vulnerable to offer integrity threats: since the ownership of the offer is obscured, attackers are provided fewer deterrents to replace, modify or delete the offers from the agent.

Note that the "offer privacy" is different to a server's privacy in that the "offer privacy" concentrates on breaking the link between the offer and the server,

S. Katsikas, J. Lopez, and G. Pernul (Eds.): TrustBus 2004, LNCS 3184, pp. 132–141, 2004.

whereas the server's privacy focuses on anonymity of the server itself without considering the correspondence with its offer. With the "offer privacy", a server's identity may be known to others, however nobody can link the identity with a particular offer.

Contribution. In this paper, we propose a "chained signatures with conditional anonymity" protocol using a "conditionally anonymous digital signature scheme" to achieve offer privacy for mobile agent systems. Mechanisms are also designed to enable revokable offer privacy. The "conditionally anonymous digital signature scheme" utilises an "anonymous public-key certificate" where the identity of the public key's owner is hidden, but, the authenticity and the validity of the public key is still verifiable by others. Offer integrity is also provided by a chaining relationship.

Organisation. The rest of the paper is organised as follows: Section 2 describes the proposed "conditionally anonymous digital signature scheme". A new protocol using the "conditionally anonymous digital signature scheme" is demonstrated in Sect. 3 to achieve the "offer privacy" property. We analyse this scheme in terms of security in Sect. 4. Section 5 concludes the paper.

For ease of reading, the notation used in the paper is listed in Table 1. (An extended version of this paper is available upon request from the authors.)

Table 1. Notation used in this paper ($0 \leq i \leq n$ unless i is indicated).

Model Notation	Meaning
$\prod$	An agent's code.
S_0	ID of the originator.
$S_i, 1 \leq i \leq n$	ID of server i.
o_0	A secret possessed by S_0 to identify the agent instance on return. It can be regarded as a dummy offer and is known only to the originator.
$o_i, 1 \leq i \leq n$	An offer (a partial result) from S_i.
εo_i	An encrypted offer of server S_i
O_i	An encapsulated offer (cryptographically protected o_i) from S_i. It is an element of the append-only container carried by the agent.

Cryptographic Notation	Meaning
r_0, r_{EG}, r_i	Random numbers generated by S_0, e-market gateway and S_i.
$\mathbb{Z}_q$	The integers modulo q is the set of integers $\{0, 1, \cdots, q-1\}$.
$E_{y_0}(m)$	A message m asymmetrically encrypted with the public key of S_0. The encryption scheme is probabilistic such as ElGamal scheme [2].
$H(m)$	A one-way collision-free hash function.
(sk_i, pk_i)	A pair of anonymous private/public keys of S_i.
$Sig_{sk_i}(m_i)$	A signature of S_i on the message m_i with anonymous private key sk_i. The signature is sent to the receiver with m_i.
$Ver_{pk_i}(s_i, m_i) =$ true or false	Verification of the signature s_i on the message m_i. It is true when $Sig_{sk_i}(m_i) = s_i$; false otherwise.

2   A Conditionally Anonymous Digital Signature Scheme

This section introduces a new "conditionally anonymous digital signature". The basic idea is to anonymise a pair of public/private keys to generate digital signatures, so the signature gives no information about the signer, yet is still verifiable.

2.1   The Anonymous Public-Key Certificate Generation

An "anonymous public-key certificate" contains two parts: data and a signature, which are different from these of a regular public-key certificate: The data part includes a public key and the associate owner's pseudonym , instead of the owner's identifier; the signature is a blind signature, instead of a regular digital signature, generated on the data part by an authority.

To generate a traceable "anonymous certificate", a fair blind signature proposed by Stadler et. al [3] is utilised to allow the sender of a blind signature to be traceable under certain conditions.

Let A be a sender who has a key pair (sk_A, pk_A) to be blindly signed by a signer B, where sk_A is the secret key of A and pk_A is the corresponding public key. A judge J has a signature scheme producing a signature $Sig_J(m)$ on a message m, so that everybody can verify messages signed by the judge. The other system parameters are:
- a group G of prime order q, for which it is hard to compute discrete logarithms, and a publicly known element $g \in G$.
- the signer's public key $y_B = g^{x_B}$, where x_B is the signer's private key.

Applying Pseudonyms.
To acquire pseudonyms from the judge, the following steps need to be taken by the sender A and the judge J.

1. After mutual identity authentication, the judge randomly selects a bit string σ and forms a pseudonym $P_A = I_A + \sigma \pmod{q}$, where I_A is the sender A's identity.
2. Next the judge selects a number $\rho \in \mathbb{Z}_q$ at random and computes $\tilde{P}_A = P_A{}^\rho$.
3. The judge computes $Sig_J(P_A||0)$ and $Sig_J(\tilde{P}_A||1)$.
4. The judge sends $\{P_A, Sig_J(P_A||0)\}$ and $\{\rho, Sig_J(\tilde{P}_A||1)\}$ to the sender A.
5. The sender A validates the judge's signatures $Sig_J(P_A||0)$ and $Sig_J(\tilde{P}_A||1)$. A can also verify whether $\tilde{P}_A$ is correctly constructed in $Sig_J(\tilde{P}_A||1)$ by checking $\tilde{P}_A \overset{?}{=} P_A^\rho$.

The pseudonyms of the sender A are $(\tilde{P}_A, P_A)$. Note that bits 0 and 1 appended to the pseudonyms are to prevent a dishonest server from swapping the two pseudonyms.

Obtaining Blind Signature on the Public Key.
Following the "signature generation protocol" described in [3], the sender A can request the signer B to blindly sign pk_A with the aforementioned pseudonyms.

Let $\beta, \gamma \in \mathbb{Z}q$. The resulting signature on pk_A is the 6-tuple $(\tilde{P}_A, Sig_J(\tilde{P}_A||1)$, $\tilde{z}, \tilde{t}_1, \tilde{t}_2, \tilde{s})$, where $\tilde{z} = (P_A{}^{x_B})^\rho$ and x_B is the private key of B, $\tilde{t}_1 = (g^r)^\beta g^\gamma$ and $\tilde{t}_2 = (P_A^r)^{\rho\beta}\tilde{P}_A^\gamma$, and $\tilde{s} = \beta(r + cx) + \gamma \pmod{q}$. It can be verified by first verifying $Sig_J(\tilde{P}_A||1)$ and by checking whether $g^{\tilde{s}} \overset{?}{=} \tilde{t}_1 y_B^{\tilde{c}}$, and $\tilde{P}_A{}^{\tilde{s}} \overset{?}{=} \tilde{t}_2 \tilde{z}^{\tilde{c}}$, where y_B is the public key of B, and $\tilde{c} = H(pk_A||\tilde{P}_A||\tilde{t}_1||\tilde{t}_2)$. In the rest of the paper, we denote this process as $\mathtt{VERIFY}_{y_B}()$. If B is an authority, the resulting blind signature on pk_A is referred to as an anonymous public-key certificate, denoted as $\hat{Cert}_A$. Hence, $\hat{Cert}_A = \{pk_A, (\tilde{P}_A, Sig_J(\tilde{P}_A||1), \tilde{z}, \tilde{t}_1, \tilde{t}_2, \tilde{s})\}$ consists of the public key pk_A and the corresponding blind signature from B.

Note that the pseudonym included in $\hat{Cert}_A$ is one of the pseudonyms generated during the blind signature generation. There is no extra pseudonym needed.

2.2   Conditionally Anonymous Digital Signatures

Using "anonymous public-key certificate", a new "conditionally anonymous digital signature" is proposed. The key pair (sk_A, pk_A) of A can be used to generate or verify a "conditionally anonymous digital signature", using the same algorithm for a regular digital signature. The only difference occurs when the authenticity of the public key pk_A is verified by the anonymous public-key certificate $\hat{Cert}_A$ instead of a regular public key certificate [2]. In the rest of the paper, we refer to the key pair (sk_A, pk_A) as an "anonymous key pair", sk_A and pk_A as an "anonymous private and public keys" respectively.

Conditionally Anonymous Digital Signature Verification
Let $Sig_{sk_A}()$ denote the conditionally anonymous signature by A. B denotes the issuer of anonymous public-key certificate (i.e., the blind signature signer in Sect. 2.1). To verify $Sig_{sk_A}()$, the verifier first obtains the anonymous public-key certificate $\hat{Cert}_A$ and B's public key y_B. The verifier checks the signature on $\hat{Cert}_A$ using y_B. If the verification is successful, the verifier accepts that $\hat{Cert}_A$ is a valid certificate. The verifier then uses pk_A to validate $Sig_{sk_A}()$ by computing $Ver_{pk_A}(s, m) \overset{?}{=} true$ where Ver indicates a signature verification algorithm. It is true when $Sig_{sk_A}(m) = s$; otherwise false.

Anonymity Revocation
A suspect signer (i.e., the blind signature sender in Sect. 2.1) of a conditionally anonymous signature can be traced from its anonymous public-key certificate. The signature verifier sends the pseudonym and the corresponding signature $(\tilde{P}_A, Sig_J(\tilde{P}_A||1))$ to the judge. The judge checks its own signature and accepts $\tilde{P}_A$ if the verification succeeds. The judge then searches for the corresponding P_A and recovers I_A from P_A.

Aside from the "anonymity" of the signer, a "conditionally anonymous digital signature" shares the other properties that a regular digital signature possesses such as data integrity and signer non-repudiation, and can also be publicly verified by using the certificate attached to the anonymous key pair.

3 Using "Conditionally Anonymous Digital Signatures" to Provide Offer Privacy

In this section, we propose a new "chained signatures with conditional anonymity" protocol to demonstrate how to use the "conditionally anonymous digital signature" scheme. The protocol can be implemented in an e-market environment where the e-market authorities play the role of the judge to grant the pseudonyms and the "anonymous public-key certificates" issuer.

3.1 Overview of the Proposed Protocol

In general, the system model of shopping agents is as follows: the agent executes on a server, and collects from it a signed offer. The offer is signed using the server's anonymous private key, which can be verified by the corresponding anonymous public key. The hash chaining mechanism linking the previous server's offer and the next server's pseudonym is embedded in the signed offer. Any illegal manipulation of the chain, including deletion or insertion of elements, will invalidate the link for all members dependent on the altered element [1].

Participants and an Electronic Market
The participants in our protocol include: (1) a buyer (the originator), (2) a number of vendors' servers, and (3) authorities, including a judge J for generating pseudonyms, revoking the anonymity of the certificate when needed, and an issuer B of anonymous public-key certificates.

Note that all mobile agents enter and leave through an "e-market gateway", which ensures that none of the participant servers is visible to the originator.

Chaining Relationship and Data Integrity
Yao et. al [5] discussed that a chaining relationship can be used to provide integrity to the elements in the "chain". The general form of a chaining relationship is $h_j = H(O_{j-1}, I_{j+1})$ where O_{j-1} is the offer made by the previous server S_{j-1} and I_{j+1} is the identity of its next server S_{j+1}. Each entry of the chain depends on some of the previous and succeeding members, therefore, any illegitimate change in O_{j-1} and/or I_{j+1} will invalidate the chaining relationship.

In our new scheme, we adapt the idea of a chaining relationship; however we use pseudonyms instead of servers' identities. The pseudonyms are contained in the anonymous public-key certificates through which they can be verified.

3.2 Chained Signatures with Conditional Anonymity

We now employ the "conditional anonymous digital signatures" in mobile agent applications. A server can sign a message anonymously with respect to its public key, which is validated by the anonymous public key certificate.

Registration. Before the "conditional anonymous digital signatures" protocol execution, each participant server has to ensure it has acquired the pseudonyms and the anonymous public key certificate for the signing key pair.

The registration stage is only needed for new participant servers and the registered servers whose pseudonyms and/or anonymous public key certificates are revealed or compromised.

Upon completion of registration, the agent starts to travel from server to server, collecting intermediate results.

Entering e-Market. In order to retain consistency within the chaining relationship, the originator and e-market gateway, although not active participants in our scheme, need to generate dummy offers. The dummy offers can be signed using regular signatures. Consequently there are two signature schemes coexisting in our framework.

In the following, we assume that the public keys of the originator, e-market gateway, the judge and the anonymous certificates' issuer are published beforehand and available to all the servers.

Let us assume the agent will visit n servers. $(\hat{Cert}_i, sk_i, pk_i)$ denote S_i's anonymous public-key certificate, anonymous private key and anonymous public key respectively. $\hat{Cert}_i$ contains one of S_i's pseudonyms, $\tilde{P}_i$. $\text{VERIFY}_{y_B}(\hat{Cert}_i)$ denotes the verification of the anonymous public-key certificate $\hat{Cert}_i$.

At the Originator (S_0) and the e-Market Gateway (EG). Figure 1 and 2 illustrate the protocol at S_0 and EG. Random numbers r_0 and r_{EG} are chosen for use in probabilistic encryption. In Fig. 2, upon receiving the agent and its data, the e-market gateway retrieves the originator's public key y_0 and verifies the signature on O_0. If the verification is successful, the e-market gateway looks into the agent's (the buyer's) requests and searches for the potential service providers. The e-market gateway, providing directory services to the buyers, can randomly select a server S_1 from the candidates to be the first visited server. Note, before the e-market gateway dispatches the agent, it needs to request S_1's pseudonym.

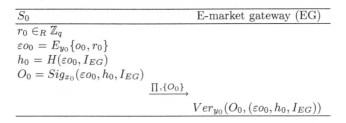

Fig. 1. Chained Signatures with Conditional Anonymity Scheme: $S_0 \rightarrow$ E-market gateway (EG).

Within e-Market. From S_1 onwards, each server S_i performs the steps in Fig. 3. The agent exits from the e-market gateway upon the completion of the task. Hence the last server S_n will send the agent to the e-market gateway. S_n includes I_{EG} in its encapsulated offer O_n instead of a pseudonym.

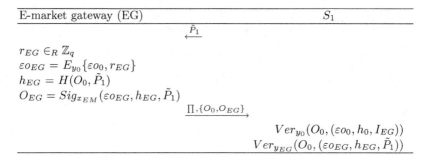

Fig. 2. Chained Signatures with Conditional Anonymity Scheme: E-market gateway (EG) $\rightarrow S_1$.

Verification. Any intermediate server can verify the offers already collected by the agent, by checking whether the chain is valid at O_i, and abort the agent's itinerary if necessary.

When the agent arrives at server S_{i+1} ($0 \leq i < n$), carrying a set of previously collected encapsulated offers $\{O_0, O_{EG}, O_1, \cdots, O_i\}$, S_{i+1} can conduct verification as follows:

Step 1. Validate hash chaining at S_i. S_{i+1} first extracts $\tilde{P}_{i+1}$ from the chain and checks whether it is its pseudonym. S_{i+1} then obtains O_{i-1} and h_i from the chain. S_{i+1} computes $h_i' = H(O_{i-1}, \tilde{P}_{i+1})$ and checks if $h_i' \overset{?}{=} h_i$. The valid hash chain proves that no illegal modification, insertion or deletion has occurred at S_n, as we have discussed above.

To check the correctness of the other pseudonyms, say $\tilde{P}_j$ ($1 \leq j \leq i$), S_{i+1} needs to check the correspondence of $\tilde{P}_j$ in O_{j-1} (or $\tilde{P}_1$ in O_{EG}) and $\tilde{P}_j'$ of $\hat{Cert}_j$ in O_j. If $\tilde{P}_j = \tilde{P}_j'$, S_{i+1} ensures that S_{j-1} is committed to release the agent to travel to S_j due to the signer's non-repudiation in its anonymous digital signature. If S_{j-1}'s anonymously signed offer O_{j-1} contains $\tilde{P}_j$, which is bound to the next server's signature O_j (i.e, a commitment of S_j), S_{i-1} cannot deny the fact that it has sent the agent to S_j.

Step 2. Validate the conditionally anonymous digital signature O_i. S_{i+1} extracts $\hat{Cert}_i$ from the data chain. Following the same steps in Sect. 2.1, S_{i+1} uses $\hat{Cert}_i$ to check the authenticity and validity of pk_i, which is then used to validate O_i, if no violation is detected.

Step 3. As such S_{i+1} keeps tracing backwards through the offers and validating each offer until O_0. If S_{i+1} can successfully verify the signature on O_0 using the originator's public key and check the validity of h_0, S_{i+1} then ensures that the agent is genuinely sent by the originator.

If no integrity violation is detected, the agent continues its execution; otherwise, aborts its computation early.

Return to the Originator. After the agent has finished its journey, it returns to the e-market gateway with the collected data $\{O_0, O_{EG}, O_1, O_2, \cdots, O_n\}$.

S_i $(1 \leq i \leq n)$	S_{i+1} $(1 \leq i \leq n)$

$$\overset{\tilde{P}_{i+1}}{\longleftarrow}$$

$r_i \in_R \mathbb{Z}_q$
$\varepsilon o_i = E_{y_0}\{o_i, r_i\}$

$h_1 = H(O_{EG}, \tilde{P}_2)$
$h_i = H(O_{i-1}, \tilde{P}_{i+1})$ $(1 < i < n)$
$h_n = H(O_{i-1}, I_{EG})$

$O_i = Sig_{sk_i}(E_{y_0}\{o_i, r_i\}, \hat{Cert}_i,$
$h_i, \tilde{P}_{i+1})$ $(1 \leq i < n)$
$O_n = Sig_{sk_i}(E_{y_0}\{o_i, r_i\}, \hat{Cert}_i,$
$h_i, I_{EG})$

$$\overset{\Pi, \{O_0, O_{EG}, O_1, ..., O_i\}}{\longrightarrow}$$

$$Ver_{y_0}(O_0, (\varepsilon o_0, h_0, I_{EG}))$$
$$Ver_{y_{EG}}(O_0, (\varepsilon o_{EG}, h_{EG}, \tilde{P}_1))$$
$$\text{VERIFY}_{y_B}(\hat{Cert}_{A_j})\ (1 \leq j \leq i)$$
$$Ver_{sk_j}(O_j)\ (1 \leq j \leq i)$$

Fig. 3. Chained Signatures with Conditional Anonymity Scheme: $S_i \rightarrow S_{i+1}$ $(1 \leq i \leq n)$.

The e-market gateway sends the agent and its data back to the originator via a secure channel.

Choose Winner. The originator first conducts a verification process by repeating steps 1−3 of the ***Verification*** stage above. The originator also decrypts o_0 and r_0 from the first node $E_{y_0}\{o_0, r_0\}$ in the chain. The originator checks the integrity of o_0. This is to check whether the instance of the returned agent is the same as that of the originator sent at the beginning of the protocol.

If an offer O_j is an invalid signature, the originator will send it to the trusted third party for further investigation(see "**Dispute**").

If the originator succeeds in verification, it obtains and decrypts each of $\{\varepsilon o_1, \cdots, \varepsilon o_n\}$ to gain the entire list of offers $\{o_1, o_2, ...o_n\}$.

The originator is able to select the best offer. However the originator does not know the real identity of the winning server S_k. To reveal the winner's identity, the originator sends O_k with the entire collected data to the judge (J).

Winner Announcement. The judge first verifies $Sig_J(\tilde{P}_k||1)$. If the verification is successful, the judge believes that S_k is a registered legitimate server. Thereafter the judge searches its database to retrieve the corresponding identity I_k.

J then contacts the originator (the buyer). I_k can be sent to the originator in an encrypted form using the originator's public key and signed by J.

After the winner is revealed, J publishes all the collected data $\{O_0, O_{EG}, O_1, O_2, \cdots, O_n\}$ by the agent, allowing victim servers to complain.

Dispute. If a visited server S_c discovers its offer is not in the published list, it can request an investigation and sends J the received string of agent-provided data $\{O_0, O_{EG}, O_1, \ldots O_{c-1}\}$. J checks whether O_{c-1} contains S_c's pseudonym. If O_{c-1} indeed includes $\tilde{P}_c$, S_{c-1} is the suspect malicious server as the conditional anonymous digital signature is non-repudiable. Following the steps that we have demonstrated in **Winner Announcement** stage, J reveals the identity of the bogus server.

4   Security Analysis

The proposed scheme provides "offer privacy" to the visited servers. The scheme can prevent some known attacks such as deletion, insertion and modification attacks [1, 4].

4.1   Offer Privacy

Assuming that the fair blind signature scheme is secure, given an anonymous public key pk_i and a corresponding anonymous public-key certificate $\hat{Cert_i}$, without the assistance of the judge, one can not determine the identity of $\hat{Cert_i}$'s holder, S_i.

In our proposed protocol, both originator and servers possess some knowledge regarding the offers, the identities and the pseudonyms of previous/next servers respectively. However, it is impossible for either to determine the ownership of an offer. We reason this as follows:

1. Any server S_i may know the identities and the pseudonyms of S_{i-1} and S_{i+1}. However, it has no knowledge of o_{i-1} and o_{i+1} (probabilistically encrypted).

2. The originator cannot determine the signers of all the offers $o_1, \ldots, o_n$ from the conditional anonymous digital signatures. Knowing all the offers is not sufficient to determine the ownerships of the offers.

Due to the arguments above, "offer privacy" is achieved in our proposed scheme, whereby nobody can determine who made a particular offer without the assistance of the judge.

4.2   Defense Against Some Known Attacks

The "conditionally anonymous digital signature scheme" and the "chained signatures with conditional anonymity" prevent some known attacks that have been commonly noted in the literature [1, 4].

Modification, Insertion, Deletion Attacks. The new protocol includes a chaining relationship and can defend these attacks. Any of these attacks can be detected during the "Verification" stage (see Sect. 3.2).

Truncation Attack. Assume the victim server is S_v. The proposed digital signature scheme can defend against the "truncation attack" because the encapsulated offer O_{v-1} contains the pseudonym $\tilde{P}_v$ of the next server S_v, which can verified through the anonymous public-key certificate. The proposed digital signature scheme is signer non-repudiable, so S_{v-1} cannot deny the fact that it has sent the agent to S_v. Note that this attack can only be discovered after all the collected encapsulated offers are published.

Colluding Servers Attack. Since the proposed new scheme provides non-repudiation of the signer, nobody can forge a conditional anonymous digital signature without knowing the private key. Hence even if two servers collude, they cannot modify the offers between them without making valid signatures. If the colluding servers delete or insert node(s) between them, the chaining relationship will be invalid at the colluding servers.

Defence against other attacks and performance analysis are described in the extended paper.

5   Conclusion

We have proposed a new scheme to provide "offer privacy" to servers that participate in a transaction. The idea of the new scheme is to anonymise the owner of signing keys using the fair blind signature scheme. The result of the anonymisation is a pair of certified keys, which will be used to generate digital signatures on the offers. The new digital signature scheme also possesses the property of reversible anonymity. Hence the owner can be revealed with assistance of a judge, for example, when a dispute takes place. The new scheme also adopts a chaining relationship to prevent some known attacks and therefore provides data integrity.

Future improvements include investigating security mechanisms to enable the "truncation attack" to be discovered during the protocol execution.

References

1. Karjoth, G., Asokan, N., Gülcü, C.: Protecting the Computation Results of Free-Roaming Agents. In: Rothermel, K., Hohl, F.. (eds.): Proceedings of the 2nd International Workshop on Mobile Agents (MA '98). Lecture Notes in Computer Science, Vol. 1477. Springer-Verlag, Berlin Heidelberg New York (1998) 195–207.
2. Menezes, A., Oorschot, P. van, Vanstone, S.: Handbook of Applied Cryptography. CRC Press Inc. (1996)
3. Stadler, M., Piveteau, J.-M., Camenisch, J.: Fair blind signatures. In: Guillou, L. C., Quisquater, J.-J.. (eds): Advances in Cryptology — EUROCRYPT '95. Lecture Notes in Computer Science, Vol. 921. Springer-Verlag, Berlin Heidelberg New York (1995) 209–219.
4. Yao, M., Foo, E., Peng, K., Dawson, E.: An Improved Forward Integrity Protocol for Mobile Agents. Proceeding of the 4th International Workshop on Information Security Applications (WISA 2003), Jeju Island, Korea. Springer-Verlag, Berlin Heidelberg (2003) 272–285
5. Yao, M., Henricksen, M., Maitland, G., Foo, E., Dawson, E.: A mobile agent system providing offer privacy. To apprear in Proceeding of the 9th Australian Conference on Information Security and Privacy (ACISP 2004), Sydney, Australia. LNCS. Springer-Verlag, Berlin Heidelberg (2004).

Privacy Preserving Data Generation
for Database Application Performance Testing*

Yongge Wang, Xintao Wu, and Yuliang Zheng

UNC Charlotte, USA
{yonwang,xwu,yzheng}@uncc.edu

Abstract. Synthetic data plays an important role in software testing. In this paper, we initiate the study of synthetic data generation models for the purpose of application software performance testing. In particular, we will discuss models for protecting privacy in synthetic data generations. Within this model, we investigate the feasibility and techniques for privacy preserving synthetic database generation that can be used for database application performance testing. The methodologies that we will present will be useful for general privacy preserving software performance testing.

1 Introduction

Functionality and performance testing is essential for software application development. Currently, two approaches dominate software application testing. With the first approach, application developers carry out their tests on their own local *development* synthetic data sets. Obviously this approach can not fulfill the requirements of all the testing phases if the synthetic data sets are of small size or do not reflect the real data sets. In particular, the performance could be significantly different if the synthetic data is not similar to the production databases. With the second approach, new applications are tested over *live production* databases. This approach cannot be applied in most situations due to the high risks of disclosure and incorrect updating of confidential information.

Recently, Wu, Wang, and Zheng [11] have proposed a general framework for privacy preserving database application testing by generating *synthetic* data sets based on some a-priori knowledge about the current *production* data sets. The generated data sets will be used to help software vendors to arrive at a close estimate of the performance of a software application. In this paper, we investigate the tradeoff of privacy preserving and performance preserving in detail. We also present an approach on privacy preserving data generation based on the generation location model. Specifically, our contributions include: (1) A model for quantifying the privacy leakage and application performance metric difference in the synthetic data set; (2) Some infeasibility results for privacy preserving synthetic data generation; (3) A heuristic approach for privacy preserving synthetic data generation within our model.

The current state of the art is that there has been little work dedicated to application software testing that achieves both goals: privacy preserving and performance

---

* This research was supported by USA National Science Foundation Grant CCR-0310974.

S. Katsikas, J. Lopez, and G. Pernul (Eds.): TrustBus 2004, LNCS 3184, pp. 142–151, 2004.

preserving. One related research area is the privacy preserving statistical databases [1, 6] which has developed methods to prevent the disclosure of confidential individual data while satisfying requests for aggregate information. Though the experience in statistical database research are useful for the study of privacy preserving application software testing, it does not consider the performance preserving issues. Furthermore, most statistical database literatures considered two types of indirect confidential information leakage : re-identification disclosure and prediction disclosure. The statistical information or some rules/patterns about the production database are also considered as the confidential information.

Also related to our research is private information retrieval and privacy preserving data mining. The theoretical work of private information retrieval [4, 8] enables users to obtain information from databases while keeping their queries secret from the database managers. The objective of privacy-preserving data mining (e.g., distortion based approach [2, 7]) is to prevent the disclosure of confidential individual values while preserving general patterns and rules. There have been some prior investigations into data generation [3, 9], however, the current data generation tools are built either for testing data mining algorithms or for assessing the performance of database management systems, rather than testing database applications. In addition, they lack the required flexibility to produce more realistic data needed for software testing and do not take into consideration privacy issues.

The organization of the paper is as follows. In Section 2, we present the general location model which we will use to describe the distribution of the underlying data set. In Section 3, we give a formal definition for the model of privacy preserving synthetic data generator. Section 4 briefly describes a heuristic approach to privacy preserving synthetic data generators. Section 5 concludes the paper.

2   The General Location Model

Let $A_1, A_2, \cdots, A_p$ denote a set of categorical attributes and $Z_1, Z_2, \cdots, Z_q$ a set of numerical ones in a table with n entries. Suppose A_j takes possible domain values $1, 2, \cdots, d_j$, the categorical data $\mathbf{W}$ can be summarized by a contingency table with total number of cells equal to $D = \prod_{j=1}^{p} d_j$. let $\mathbf{x} = \{x_d : d = 1, 2, \cdots, D\}$ denote the number of entries in each cell. Clearly $\sum_{d=1}^{D} x_d = n$.

The general location model [10] is defined in terms of the marginal distribution of $\mathbf{A}$ and the conditional distribution of $\mathbf{Z}$ given $\mathbf{A}$. The former is described by a multinomial distribution on the cell counts $\mathbf{x}$,

$$\mathbf{x} \mid \pi \sim M(n, \pi) = \frac{n!}{x_1! \cdots x_D!} \pi_1^{x_1} \cdots \pi_D^{x_D}$$

where $\pi = \{\pi_d : d = 1, 2, \cdots, D\}$ is an array of cell probabilities corresponding to $\mathbf{x}$. Given $\mathbf{A}$, the rows $z_1^T, z_2^T, \cdots, z_n^T$ of $\mathbf{Z}$ are then modeled as conditionally multivariate normal. We assume that

$$z_i \mid \mu_i = E_d, \mu_d, \Sigma \sim N(\mu_d, \Sigma)$$

is independent for $i = 1, 2, \cdots, n$, where μ_d is a q-vector means corresponding to cell d, and Σ is a $q \times q$ covariance matrix. The parameters of the generation location model can be written as $\theta = (\pi, \mu, \Sigma)$, where $\mu = (\mu_1, \mu_2, \cdots, \mu_D)^T$ is a $D \times q$ matrix of means. The maximum likelihood estimates of θ is as follows:

$$\hat{\pi}_d = \frac{x_d}{n}, \quad \hat{\mu}_d^T = x_d^{-1} \sum_{i \in B_d} z_i^T, \quad \text{and} \quad \hat{\Sigma} = \frac{1}{n} \sum_{d=1}^{D} \sum_{i \in B_d} (z_i - \hat{\mu}_d)(z_i - \hat{\mu}_d)^T \quad (1)$$

where $B_d = \{i : \mu_i = E_d\}$ is the set of all tuples belonging to cell d.

Table 1. An Example of ACCOUNT Database.

AccountID	ZipCode	Categorical			Numerical	
		Background	Age	Gender	Balance	Interest
1	10001	Asia	20	M	10k	20.5
2	10001	Asia	30	F	15k	80
.	.	.	.	.	.	.
m	10001	British	25	M	80k	320

In this paper, we view the database as a multi-dimensional table with categorical attributes and numerical attributes and model it by using the *general location model*. Table 1 shows an example ACCOUNT database with m tuples where the categorical attributes part (e.g., *ZipCode, Background, Age*) can be modeled by multinomial distribution while the numerical attributes part (e.g., *Balance and Interest*) can be modeled as conditionally multivariate normal distribution.

3 (γ, τ)-Privacy Preserving Synthetic Data Generator

Notation. N is the set of natural numbers and R is the set of real numbers. $\Sigma = \{0, 1\}$ is the binary alphabet, Σ^* is the set of (finite) binary strings and Σ^n is the set of binary strings of length n. The length of a string x is denoted by $|x|$. For strings $x, y \in \Sigma^*$, xy is the concatenation of x and y. For a string $x \in \Sigma^*$ and an integer number $n \geq 0$, $x[0..n]$ denotes the initial segment of length $n + 1$ of x ($x[0..n] = x$ if $|x| \leq n + 1$) and $x[i]$ denotes the ith bit of x, i.e., $x[0..n] = x[0] \cdots x[n]$.

3.1   Definition

A database application software package $\mathcal{F}$ that needs to be tested can be regarded as a Turing machine defined on binary strings. Its input can be divided into two parts, the database part x (with size of MBs or GBs) and the test case input y (with a relatively small size). The test case input y could be a simple SQL command or a script file such as a collection of SQL commands. Private information in a database x could be defined as a Turing computable function $\tau(x, i)$ where i is the index of the private information. In another word, the private information in a database x is a sequence of binary strings: $\tau(x, 1), \tau(x, 2), \tau(x, 3), \ldots, \tau(x, m)$.

Example 1 *Consider the following confidential information: "The average balance range of term deposits from Asian people in a specific zip code area". We translate this property to a binary string. For a 90-bit binary string z, let $z[0..19]$ represent the zip code, $z[20..29]$ represent the background of the people (e.g., 0000000001 for Asia, 0000000002 for British, etc.), $z[30..59]$ and $z[60..89]$ represent the term deposit average balance lower bound and upper bound respectively for the people from $z[20..29]$ background and $z[0..19]$ zip code area. The above private information could be indexed as the first private information by letting $\tau(x, 1) = z$ if and only if the people from $z[20..29]$ background and $z[0..19]$ zip code area have average balance of term deposit in the interval $[z[30..59], z[60..89]]$.*

Output of the performance testing for $\mathcal{F}$ can be measured by a metric function $T_{\mathcal{F}}$. In particular, $T_{\mathcal{F}}$ can be regarded as a mapping from $\Sigma^* \times \Sigma^*$ to N. The metric function $T_{\mathcal{F}}(x, y)$ could represent the time used by the software package $\mathcal{F}$ when running on database x with input test case y. The goal of the synthetic data generation is to produce a synthetic data set x' from the production data set x such that metric function outputs $T_{\mathcal{F}}(x, y)$ and $T_{\mathcal{F}}(x', y)$ are approximately the same for most input test cases y. At the same time the synthetic data x' should contain no private information. Our above discussion can be formalized as in the following definition.

Definition 1. *Let $\gamma : \Sigma^* \times \Sigma^* \to N$ be a function denoting the acceptable metric difference for the testing purpose, $\tau : \Sigma^* \times N \to \Sigma^*$ be a Turing computable privacy function, $\mathcal{F} : \Sigma^* \times \Sigma^* \to \Sigma^*$ be a Turing machine denoting the software package, and $T_{\mathcal{F}} : \Sigma^* \times \Sigma^* \to N$ be a metric function defined for $\mathcal{F}$. We say that a probabilistic Turing machine $\mathcal{G} : \Sigma^* \to \Sigma^*$ is a (γ, τ)-privacy preserving synthetic data generator for $\mathcal{F}$ if the following conditions are satisfied:*

1. *For all $x \in \Sigma^*$, $|\mathcal{G}(x)| = |x|$.*
2. *(Performance similarity) $|T_{\mathcal{F}}(x, y) - T_{\mathcal{F}}(\mathcal{G}(x), y)| \leq \gamma(x, y)$ with overwhelming probability, where the probability is taken over all possible values for x, y, and internal coin tosses of $\mathcal{F}$ and $\mathcal{G}$.*
3. *(Privacy preserving) Let $\delta(\cdot) : N \to R$ be the acceptable level function of privacy leakage which is generally a negligible function. For each database x and each i, we have*

$$\sum_w |\text{Prob}[\tau(x, i) = w | \mathcal{G}(x), \text{priorK}] - \text{Prob}[\tau(x, i) = w | \text{priorK}]| \leq \delta(i),$$

where the sum is over all potential output w of $\tau(x, i)$, and priorK is the prior knowledge that is known to the software tester before the testing.

Remarks:

- In definition 1, we assume that all functions and Turing machines are defined for all inputs. In practice, there is no guarantee that a program will halt in finite many steps on all inputs. For these scenarios, we assume that when a Turing machine does not halt in expected time (which should be large enough) on an input, then it will halt and output a default result.

- In the item 1, the requirement $|\mathcal{G}(x)| = |x|$ is only for the convenience of our analysis. In practice, the generated synthetic data set may have different (but approximately same) size than the original data set.
- In the item 3, the prior knowledge could include the schema definition of the database x and other prior knowledge about x.
- From the definition, it is straightforward to see that a privacy preserving synthetic data generator must be one-way. Otherwise one can compute x from $\mathcal{G}(x)$ and then compute the value of $\tau(x, i)$, violating condition 3 of Definition 1.

In section 1, we briefly described researches on privacy leakage in related areas such as statistical database and privacy preserving data mining. We observed that existing definitions for privacy leakage are not sufficient for our research. Our definition of privacy leakage is closely related to the statistical indistinguishability concept in cryptographic research . It is straightforward to check that our definition covers both straight (upward) privacy breach and inverse (downward) privacy breach defined in [7]. However, our definition is more general as it also covers the collective privacy breaches: for each individual event, the observable probability difference is small, but, collectively, the sum of these observable probability differences are large enough. This kind of collective privacy breaches could be important for many applications.

3.2   Infeasibility

In the following, we first show that, for given conditions, a (γ, τ)-privacy preserving synthetic data generator for $\mathcal{F}$ does not necessarily exist.

Statement 1 (γ, τ)-*privacy preserving synthetic data generator for $\mathcal{F}$ does not necessarily exist if the Turing machine $\mathcal{F}$'s running time depends on some bits of the input and these bits are indeed the private information identified by τ.*

Example 2 *Assume that, according to prior knowledge, the first bit $x[0]$ of the database x is uniformly distributed over Σ, $\mathcal{T}_{\mathcal{F}}$ is the time complexity of $\mathcal{F}$,*

$$\mathcal{T}_{\mathcal{F}}(0z, y) = 4 \cdot \max\{\gamma(0z, y), \gamma(1z, y)\},$$
$$\mathcal{T}_{\mathcal{F}}(1z, y) = 2 \cdot \max\{\gamma(0z, y), \gamma(1z, y)\},$$
$$\tau(x, 1) = x[0],$$

and $\mathcal{G}$ is a (γ, τ)-privacy preserving synthetic data generator for $\mathcal{F}$. Then in order to satisfy the condition 2 of Definition 1, we must have $\mathcal{G}(x)[0] = x[0]$ for almost all x. Otherwise, for $x = bz$,

$$|\mathcal{T}_{\mathcal{F}}(bz, y) - \mathcal{T}_{\mathcal{F}}(\mathcal{G}(bz), y)| = 2 \cdot \max\{\gamma(0z, y), \gamma(1z, y)\} \geq 2\gamma(bz, y) > \gamma(bz, y)$$

for any $b \in \Sigma$ and $z \in \Sigma^*$. Then for $w = \mathcal{G}(x)[0]$, we have

$$\text{Prob}[\tau(x, 1) = w | \mathcal{G}(x), \text{priorK}] - \text{Prob}[\tau(x, 1) = w | \text{priorK}] = 1 - \frac{1}{2} = \frac{1}{2}.$$

Thus the privacy leakage is larger than (or equal to) a non negligible value $\frac{1}{2}$ and the condition 3 of Definition 1 is not satisfied. This is a contradiction, which shows that no (γ, τ)-privacy preserving synthetic data generator for $\mathcal{F}$ exists.

Statement 2 *Even if there is no* conflict *between τ and the running time of $\mathcal{F}$, (γ, τ)-privacy preserving synthetic data generator for $\mathcal{F}$ may still not exist if the Turing machine $\mathcal{F}$ has some conflict with the performance requirement $\gamma(x, y)$.*

Example 3 *For any binary string $x \in \Sigma^*$, let int_x denote the positive integer whose binary representation is x. Assume that $\mathcal{T}_{\mathcal{F}}$ is the time complexity of $\mathcal{F}$ with the property that*

$$\mathcal{T}_{\mathcal{F}}(x, y) = 2 \cdot int_x \cdot \max\{\gamma(z, y) : |z| = |x|\},$$

$\tau(x, i)$ is a non-trivial privacy function (that is, a function whose output values depend on input values), and $\mathcal{G}$ is a (γ, τ)-privacy preserving synthetic data generator for $\mathcal{F}$. As we have noted in the previous paragraph, $\mathcal{G}$ should be one-way, thus $\mathcal{G}(x) \neq x$ for almost all x. Then

$$
\begin{aligned}
|\mathcal{T}_{\mathcal{F}}(x, y) - \mathcal{T}_{\mathcal{F}}(\mathcal{G}(x), y)| &= 2 \cdot |int_x - int_{\mathcal{G}(x)}| \cdot \max\{\gamma(z, y) : |z| = |x|\} \\
&\geq 2 \cdot \max\{\gamma(z, y) : |z| = |x|\} \\
&> \gamma(x, y)
\end{aligned}
$$

for almost all $x \in \Sigma^*$.

The above two statements essentially show that if the Turing machine $\mathcal{F}$ is a "distinguisher" of some privacy bits or a "distinguisher" of the input strings, then privacy preserving synthetic data generator does not exist. On the other hand, if the Turing machine $\mathcal{F}$ has approximately same metrics on all inputs of the same length, then any random mapping serves as the privacy preserving synthetic data generator for $\mathcal{F}$. That is, if $|\mathcal{T}_{\mathcal{F}}(x_1, y) - \mathcal{T}_{\mathcal{F}}(x_2, y)| \leq \gamma(x_1, y)$ for all x_1 and x_2, then any length-preserving random mapping is a (γ, τ)-privacy preserving synthetic data generator for $\mathcal{F}$. In this paper, we will concentrate on Turing machine $\mathcal{F}$ which do not go to the two extremes that we have just mentioned.

3.3   Problem Formulation

Problem 1. Given a private property τ, and $\delta(i)$, find a synthetic database x' to minimize

$$\sum_y |\mathcal{T}_{\mathcal{F}}(x, y) - \mathcal{T}_{\mathcal{F}}(x', y)| \cdot \text{Prob}[y]$$

subject to $\sum_w \big| \text{Prob}[\tau(x, i) = w | x', \text{priorK}] - \text{Prob}[\tau(x, i) = w | \text{priorK}] \big| \leq \delta(i)$.

Problem 2. Given acceptable performance metric $\gamma(x, y)$, and private property τ, find synthetic database x' to minimize

$$\sum_i \sum_w \big| \text{Prob}[\tau(x, i) = w | x', \text{priorK}] - \text{Prob}[\tau(x, i) = w | \text{priorK}] \big|$$

subject to $|\mathcal{T}_{\mathcal{F}}(x, y) - \mathcal{T}_{\mathcal{F}}(x', y)| \leq \gamma(x, y)$ for almost all y.

The two problems are related to each other. In the remaining part of this paper, we will focus on Problem 1. One should note that the subject condition in Problem 1 is generally not a linear inequality and the distribution of y is not uniform (i.e., $\text{Prob}[y]$ is not a constant). Thus the Problem 1 is not a linear programming problem and heuristic methods are needed to solve this problem.

4   Constructing (γ, τ)-Privacy Preserving Data Generator

It is clear that the distribution of underlying data affects the execution time of workload. Our intuition is that, for database applications, if two databases x and x' are approximately the same from a statistical viewpoint, then the performance of the application on the two databases should also be approximately the same. For example, the approximate joint distribution on $Zip, Background, Balance$ from Table 1 would satisfy the performance requirements of workload (Q1 and Q2).

Q1: INSERT INTO ACCOUNT VALUES ()
Q2: SELECT * FROM ACCOUNT WHERE ZipCode = z AND Background = b

In this paper, we assume that file organizations, sorted fields, and index structures of the production database x are not private information and the synthetic data generator will use these information to build the synthetic database $\mathcal{G}(x)$ in the same way that x has been built. However, the joint distribution may contain sensitive information about private properties. In the next subsection, we will present an heuristic algorithm to derive approximate joint distribution based on the general location model and to check whether it contains confidential information.

4.1   A Greedy Algorithm

We view the database as a multi-dimensional table with categorical attributes and numerical attributes and model it by using the *general location model*. We also assume the general location model itself is not confidential information and only the parameters of the general location model are confidential. We can see from Equation 1 that the maximum likelihood estimates of $\theta = (\pi, \mu, \Sigma)$ can be fully derived from statistics (e.g., the frequencies of tuples which satisfy some conditions of categorical attributes, the mean and variance values of tuples which belong to same cell). Those statistics are not completely contained in database catalog[1]. However, it is straightforward to derive those statistics by imposing various queries if we are allowed to access the original data.

It is worth pointing out that we do not need to build the general location model at the finest level as those statistics are with very high complexity which is exponential to the size of contingency table and many statistics do not have effects on a given workload performance. Hence an approximate and condensed general location model on the subsets of attributes is sufficient for performance testing. Here the condensed model is derived from a condensed contingency table which is formed by a subset of categorical attributes (even with coarser domain values) which can be identified by SQLs in workload.

For the reason of convenience, we use $\mathcal{DB}^0_{\mathcal{F},x}$ to denote all the information (e.g., the distribution, rules and the priori knowledge priorK) needed to build database x to satisfy the condition 2 of Definition 1. We call the distribution $\mathcal{DB}^0_{\mathcal{F},x}$ the *performance characteristic* of a database x for the application $\mathcal{F}$. The heuristic method for solving the problem 1 could be given as follows.

---

[1] In current commercial database datalog, only simple statistics (e.g., mean, max, min etc.) of each single column are collected.

- Step 1. Extract $\mathcal{DB}^0_{\mathcal{F},x}$ from the real database x based on workload and construct the estimated performance error function $\gamma(x,y)$.
- Step 2. Specify a list of confidential information $\tau(x,i)$ and an acceptable privacy leakage level $\delta(i)$ for each privacy indexed by i.
- Step 3. Check whether the performance characteristic $\mathcal{DB}^0_{\mathcal{F},x}$ leaks any privacy information defined in $\tau(x,i)$ in a non-acceptable level (that is, larger than $\delta(i)$) according to Definition 1 (see section 4.2).
- Step 4. If the privacy leakage is not acceptable, repeat the following until $\mathcal{DB}'_{\mathcal{F},x}$ leaks privacy information about $\tau(x,i)$ in the acceptable level defined by δ.
  - Step 4.1. The analyzer constructs a new characteristic $\mathcal{DB}'_{\mathcal{F},x}$ by perturbing θ as $\theta' = (\pi + \delta_\pi, \mu + \delta_\mu, \Sigma + \delta_\Sigma)$.
  - Step 4.2. The performance analyzer constructs a new estimated performance error function $\gamma'(x,y)$ according to the new distribution $\mathcal{DB}'_{\mathcal{F},x}$. This is generally larger than the previous $\gamma(x,y)$.
- Step 5. A synthetic data generator generates a synthetic data set using the distribution $\mathcal{DB}'_{\mathcal{F},x}$.

During Steps 1 and 4.2, we statistically test whether the generated data x' using $\mathcal{DB}'_{\mathcal{F},x}$ has the same distribution with original data (assuming a sample is given). As there is no test statistics which can be directly used for the general location model, we decompose the general location model to two parts and use χ^2 test for multinomial distribution and Kolmogorov-Smirnov test [5] for multivariate normal distributions of each cell.

4.2   Privacy Analyzer

In this section, we will address techniques to decide whether there are private information leakage in $\mathcal{DB}^0_{\mathcal{F},x}$ and, if the answer is yes, how to construct a new distribution $\mathcal{DB}'_{\mathcal{F},x}$ that contains no confidential information. Without loss of generality, we assume that the function τ is defined only for the first index. We write this confidential information as $\tau(x) = \tau(x,1)$ for short. In the following, we give some examples to illustrate how to decide whether there is information leakage about $\tau(x)$ in a distribution $\mathcal{DB}^0_{\mathcal{F},x}$.

Example 4 *Let l and m be two integers such that $n = l \times m$. For a database x, let $X[i] = x[il] \ldots x[il + l - 1]$ for $0 \le i \le m - 1$. In practice, $X[0], \cdots, X[m-1]$ may correspond only to one column of a table. For the reason of simplicity, in this example, we assume that the database has one table which has one column $X[0], \cdots, X[m-1]$. Assume that the following conditions hold:*

1. *According to priorK, $X[0], \ldots, X[m-1]$ follow a normal distribution $N(\mu, \sigma)$ and μ is uniformly distributed over $100 \le \mu \le 500$;*
2. *$\tau(x) = \dfrac{\sum_{i=0}^{m-1} X[i]}{m}$; and*
3. *according to $\mathcal{DB}^0_{\mathcal{F},x}$, $X[0], \ldots, X[m-1]$ follow the normal distribution $N(\mu_0, \sigma_0)$.*

Then

$$\left| \text{Prob}[\tau(x) = \mu_0 | \mathcal{DB}^0_{\mathcal{F},x}] - \text{Prob}[\tau(x) = \mu_0 | \text{priorK}] \right| \\ = \left| (1 - \varepsilon) - \frac{1}{400} \right| = \frac{399}{400} - \varepsilon \tag{2}$$

for some small ε. Obviously $\mathcal{DB}^0_{\mathcal{F},x}$ leaks significant information about $\tau(x)$. Thus we need to modify the performance characteristic $\mathcal{DB}^0_{\mathcal{F},x}$. One potential solution is to pick a random value v, and use a new distribution $N(\mu_0 + v, \sigma_0)$. This may have further impact on the application performance and we need to re-compute the new performance error function $\gamma(x, y)$ for this new distribution. If we choose $|v| \le t$, then for any $\mu_0 + v - t \le w \le \mu_0 + v + t$,

$$\left| \mathrm{Prob}[\tau(x) = w | \mathcal{DB}'_{\mathcal{F},x}] - \mathrm{Prob}[\tau(x) = w | \mathrm{priorK}] \right| \\ = \left| \left(\tfrac{1}{2t} - \varepsilon \right) - \tfrac{1}{400} \right| = \tfrac{1}{2t} - \tfrac{1}{400} - \varepsilon \tag{3}$$

for some small ε. When t is large enough, the value in equation (3) is small enough so that the sum on all w is less than the pre-specified value δ [2].

The example in the previous paragraph shows a heuristic method to modify the performance characteristic to meet the privacy requirements. We close this section by giving a formula for evaluating $\mathrm{Prob}[\tau(x) = w | \mathcal{DB}'_{\mathcal{F},x}]$ for the new distribution $\mathcal{DB}'_{\mathcal{F},x}$, where w is any given string. Note that this computation is necessary for checking whether the information leakage is acceptable.

Let DBco denote the conversion method, that is used to convert $\mathcal{DB}^0_{\mathcal{F},x}$ to $\mathcal{DB}'_{\mathcal{F},x}$, together with the prior knowledge. Then one can evaluate the probabilities of possible values $\mathcal{DB}$ of $\mathcal{DB}^0_{\mathcal{F},x}$ given $\mathcal{DB}'_{\mathcal{F},x}$. Using Bayes formula, one can compute the posterior probabilities:

$$\mathrm{Prob}[\mathcal{DB} | \mathcal{DB}'_{\mathcal{F},x}, \mathrm{DBco}] = \frac{\mathrm{Prob}[\mathcal{DB}] \cdot \mathrm{Prob}[\mathcal{DB}'_{\mathcal{F},x} | \mathcal{DB}, \mathrm{DBco}]}{\mathrm{Prob}[\mathcal{DB}'_{\mathcal{F},x} | \mathrm{DBco}]}$$

Note that the probabilities $\mathrm{Prob}[\mathcal{DB}]$ of possible values $\mathcal{DB}$ of $\mathcal{DB}^0_{\mathcal{F},x}$ can be easily computed when the distribution of the general location model's parameters, $\theta = (\pi, \mu, \Sigma)$, are given (e.g., we can assume θ has a uniform distribution over a specified range $[\theta_l, \theta_u]$). The probability $\mathrm{Prob}[\mathcal{DB}'_{\mathcal{F},x} | \mathrm{DBco}]$ can be computed using the formula:

$$\mathrm{Prob}[\mathcal{DB}'_{\mathcal{F},x} | \mathrm{DBco}] = \sum_{\mathcal{DB}} \mathrm{Prob}[\mathcal{DB}] \cdot \mathrm{Prob}[\mathcal{DB}'_{\mathcal{F},x} | \mathcal{DB}, \mathrm{DBco}]$$

Thus the posterior probability $\mathrm{Prob}[\tau(x) = w | \mathcal{DB}'_{\mathcal{F},x}]$ could be computed as:

$$\mathrm{Prob}[\tau(x) = w | \mathcal{DB}'_{\mathcal{F},x}] = \sum_{x', \mathcal{DB}} \left(\mathrm{Prob}[\mathcal{DB} | \mathcal{DB}'_{\mathcal{F},x}] \cdot \mathrm{Prob}[x' | \mathcal{DB}] \cdot \mathrm{Prob}[\tau(x) = w | x'] \right),$$

where we omitted the prior knowledge DBco from the formula.

5   Conclusion

We studied the problem of generating synthetic data for database application performance testing while preserving privacy. We presented a model for quantifying the pri-

---

[2] Note that the computation in the equation (3) is only for illustration purpose and is not exact. At the end of this section, we will give exact evaluation formulae for the computation of posterior probability.

vacy leakage and application performance metric difference by using the general location model. Our infeasibility results show the strict privacy preserving synthetic data generator does not necessarily exist when the application workload is a "distinguisher" of some privacy properties or a "distinguisher" of the input strings. A heuristic method was given for the relaxed problem, i.e., to construct the generator which satisfies performance requirements as many as possible while preserving all the privacy properties.

Analysis in this paper shows that it is a challenging problem to design efficient privacy preserving synthetic data generators. One open problem is to study complexity issues. Another topic for future work is to extend our approach to multiple tables and integrate with a-priori rules and constraints in databases.

References

1. N. R. Adam and J. C. Wortman. Security-control methods for statistical databases. *ACM Computing Surveys*, 21(4):515–556, Dec 1989.
2. R. Agrawal and R. Srikant. Privacy-preserving data mining. In *Proc. ACM SIGMOD International Conference on Management of Data*, pages 439–450. Dallas, Texas, May 2000.
3. D. Chays, Y. Deng, P. Frankl, S. Dan, F. Vokolos, and E. Weyuker. Agenda: a test generator for relational database applications. Technical report, TR-CIS-2002-04, Polytechnic University, 2002.
4. B. Chor, O. Goldreich, E. Kushilevitz, and M. Sudan. Private information retrieval. In *Proc. of FOCS*, 1995.
5. R.B. Dagostino and M.A. Stephens. *Goodness-of-fit Techniques*. New York Dekker, 1986.
6. I. Dinur and K. Nissim. Revealing information while preserving privacy. In *Proc. 22nd Symposium on Principles of Database Systems*, pages 202–210, 2003.
7. A. Evfimievski, J. Gehrke, and R. Srikant. Limiting privacy breaches in privacy preserving data mining. In *Proc. 22nd Symp. on Principles of Database Systems*, pages 211–222, 2003.
8. Y. Gertner, Y. Ishai, E. Kushilevitz, and T. Malkin. Protecting data privacy in private information retrieval schemes. *JCSS*, 60(3):592–629, 2000.
9. Quest. http://www.quest.com/datafactory.
10. J.L. Schafer. *Analysis of Incomplete Multivariate Data*. Chapman Hall, 1997.
11. X. Wu, Y. Wang, and Y. Zheng. Privacy preserving database application testing. In *Proc. ACM Workshop on Privacy in Electronic Society*, pages 118–128, 2003.

An Efficient Mixnet-Based Voting Scheme Providing Receipt-Freeness*

Riza Aditya[1], Byoungcheon Lee[1,2], Colin Boyd[1], and Ed Dawson[1]

[1] Information Security Research Centre
Queensland University of Technology
GPO BOX 2434, Brisbane, QLD, 4001, Australia
{r.aditya,b6.lee,c.boyd,e.dawson}@qut.edu.au
[2] Joongbu University
101 Daebak-Ro, Chuboo-Meon, Kumsan-Gun, Chungnam, 312-702, Korea
sultan@joongbu.ac.kr

Abstract. Receipt-freeness is an essential security property in electronic voting to prevent vote buying, selling or coercion. In this paper, we propose an efficient mixnet-based receipt-free voting scheme by modifying a voting scheme of Lee *et al*. The receipt-freeness property is obtained through the randomization service given by a trusted administrator, and assuming that two-way untappable channel is used between voters and the administrator. The efficiency is improved by employing a more efficient mixnet, which is a modification of Golle *et al*.'s optimistic mixnet. In the proposed scheme, the administrator provides both randomization (ballot re-encryption) and mixing service in the voting stage. Afterward, the ballots are mixed using the proposed efficient mixnet. Our mixnet-based voting scheme offers receipt-freeness in an efficient manner.

Keywords: Electronic voting, receipt-freeness, mixnet, re-encryption, randomization, designated-verifier re-encryption proof.

1 Introduction

Voting is often related to political and financial gain, and cheating is an inherent threat to voting. Thus, security aspects in voting must also be thoroughly considered. This results in extensive security requirements for e-voting.

- **Privacy:** Normally, the vote is encrypted prior to submission, where the ballot is in the form of an encrypted vote. Voter-vote relationship must be kept private, to ensure that voters express their true opinion without fear of being intimidated.
- **Eligibility:** Only authorized voters are allowed to vote, preventing fraudulent votes from being counted in the tally stage.
- **Prevention of double voting:** This ensures that all voters are allowed to vote only once, such that each voter has equal power in deciding the outcome of the voting.

---

* Project funded by ARC Linkage International fellowship 2003, Grant No: LX0346868.

S. Katsikas, J. Lopez, and G. Pernul (Eds.): TrustBus 2004, LNCS 3184, pp. 152–161, 2004.

- **Fairness:** No partial tally is revealed before the end of the voting period, to enforce privacy and ensure that all candidates are given a fair chance during the voting period.
- **Receipt-freeness:** Introduced by Benaloh and Tuinstra [4], voters must neither be able to obtain nor construct a receipt which can prove the content of their vote to a third party. This is to prevent vote selling/buying, ensuring that voters are not used as a proxy to cast votes.
- **Robustness:** The system must be able to tolerate certain faulty conditions by managing some disruptions.
- **Verifiability:** Correct voting processes must be verifiable to prevent incorrect voting result.

Secret-ballot e-voting schemes typically employ either mixnet or homomorphic encryption to provide voters privacy. Our proposed scheme employs mixnet since it offers more flexibility on the ballot structure as opposed to employing homomorphic encryption, e.g. in preferential voting [3].

To provide receipt-freeness, many schemes normally employ a trusted authority to randomize the ballot prior to vote submission stage. Many of the schemes are oriented toward homomorphic encryption approach since accumulation of votes is obtained by decrypting combination of the ballots, where individual ballots are never decrypted. Providing receipt-freeness in mixnet-based voting schemes is more problematic since all ballots are decrypted individually for tallying, and a voter can prove the content of his ballot using his knowledge of the random value used to construct his ballot (encrypt his vote).

Obtaining both receipt-freeness and efficiency, both the receipt-free mixnet-based voting scheme of Lee et al. [9] and the optimistic mixnet scheme of Golle et al. [8] are modified, and then combined as follows:

- the administrator provides both the re-encryption service (by the tamper-resistant hardware randomizer in [9]) and mixing service (by the first mix server in [8]) together,
- the administrator is trusted not to collude with the mix servers to reveal voter-vote relationship, and
- the communication channel between the administrator and the voter is untappable.

The remainder of the paper is organized as follows. Section 2 provides more background and motivation to our proposed scheme. Reviews of the mixnet-based voting scheme in [9] and the optimistic mixnet scheme in [8] are provided in more detail. Section 3 describes the modification made to the optimistic mixnet scheme to provide receipt-freeness and cancel known attacks to it. Section 4 presents our proposed efficient mixnet-based receipt-free voting scheme using the proposed efficient mixnet. Section 5 analyses the security and efficiency of the proposed scheme. Section 6 is a conclusion.

2   Related Work

Based on the verification of mixing, mixnet schemes are classified into verifiable mixnet and optimistic mixnet. **Verifiable mixnets** [1, 7] offer robustness at the cost of efficiency. Proof of correct mixing is accurate and requires more computation and bandwidth compared with optimistic mixing. **Optimistic mixnets** [5, 8] offer efficiency at the cost of robustness. Proof of correct mixing is quite simple, though less accurate, compared with the verifiable ones. Confidence of correct mixing provided by optimistic mixing is less than that offered by verifiable mixnet schemes. However, it is much more efficient.

Schemes using verifiable mixnet can be made more efficient by employing an optimistic mixnet. We recall a mixnet-based receipt-free voting scheme in the following subsection, and recall an optimistic mixnet scheme in the subsection afterward.

2.1   Mixnet-Based Receipt-Free Voting Scheme by Lee *et al.*

The mixnet-based receipt-free voting scheme by Lee et al. [9] focuses on removing user-chosen randomness in ballots to provide receipt-freeness. This is achieved as ballots are randomized by a third party. In their scheme, a tamper-resistant hardware device named tamper-resistant randomizer (TRR) is used to act as the third party randomizer and also provide untappable channel. Correct re-encryption by the randomizer is verifiable by the use of designated verifier re-encryption proof (DVRP). The re-encrypted ballots are anonymized by the mixnet, and the outputs of the mixnet are individually decrypted by a quorum of decryption authorities.

The voting stage consists of four sub-stages. First, each voter prepares a first ballot by encrypting his vote. The ballot is then sent to TRR for randomization. Second, the TRR randomizes the first ballot with re-encryption to produce a final ballot. Third, the TRR also produces a Designated Verifier Re-encryption Proof (DVRP) to prove the correctness of re-encryption to the voter. The final ballot and the DVRP are then sent to the voter. Finally, the voter checks the DVRP, then signs and subm its the final ballot if the check is accepted.

As the scheme employs verifiable mixnet, efficiency improvement is possible by alternatively using an optimistic mixnet.

2.2   Optimistic Mixnet by Golle *et al.*

Golle et al. [8] proposed a very efficient mixnet scheme using the optimistic approach. Correct mixing is proved by using the proof of product (POP), proving that the product of input messages is preserved in the product of the output messages. The proof of product exploits the homomorphic property of the underlying ElGamal encryption scheme. However, a checksum is required to verify the integrity of the messages. Also, the inputs are required to be encrypted twice, named double enveloping, to support backup mixing.

Double enveloping protects the anonymity of the original sender from a relation attack by a dishonest server. When the input message is encrypted only once, a dishonest server can modify its output by multiplying two inputs b_i and $b_{i'}$ and outputs the re-encryptions of $b_i b_{i'}$ and 1, where $i \neq i'$. This attack passes the proof of product test. By observing the attacked (combined) plaintext output after decryption, the related ciphertexts can be identified. Double encryption is used to prevent such attack, so that when the first mixing for the outer encryption is found to be incorrect, the inner encrypted messages are recovered by the decryption authorities and mixed again using a more robust, heavy-weight verifiable mixnet.

Based on the scheme by Pedersen [10], a threshold version of ElGamal cryptosystem is employed with properly generated parameters as in [10], private key x, and public key $(g, y = g^x)$. Several decryption authorities share the private key x using Shamir's (t, m) secret sharing scheme [11]. A message v is encrypted with a random value r using an encryption function E and the public key y as $E_y(v, r) = (\alpha = g^r, \beta = vy^r)$. A collision-resistant hash function H is used to produce the hash checksum as $h = H(\alpha, \beta)$. The double encrypted ciphertext is then produced with different random values r_1 and r_2 as $E_y(\alpha, r_1), E_y(\beta, r_2)$ and the hash checksum is also encrypted with a random value r_3 as $E_y(h, r_3)$. For n messages $(i = 1, \ldots, n)$, inputs to the mixnet is a triple of the form $(E_y(\alpha_i, r_{i,1}), E_y(\beta_i, r_{i,2}), E_y(h_i, r_{i,3}))$, where $h_i = H(\alpha_i, \beta_i)$.

The mixnet scheme is a basic re-encryption mixnet, where each mix server receives inputs (α_i, β_i, h_i), re-encrypts them by selecting different random values $r'_{i,1}, r'_{i,2}, r'_{i,3}$ and compute $(\alpha'_i, \beta'_i, h'_i)$, and outputs them in a random order. Afterward, the mix server proves the preservation of product of messages in the mixing (proof of product) by proving:

$$\prod \alpha_i = \prod \alpha'_i \ \wedge \ \prod \beta_i = \prod \beta'_i \ \wedge \ \prod h_i = \prod h'_i \tag{1}$$

Computational complexity (in terms of modular exponentiations) using this technique is independent of n, the number of messages.

After the mixing is finished, each output is decrypted using threshold decryption by a quorum of decryption authorities. The final output of the mixnet are triplets in the form of $(\alpha'_{\pi(i)}, \beta'_{\pi(i)}, h'_{\pi(i)})$, where $\pi(i)$ represents the result of total permutation of i. The integrity of each result is also verified by checking:

$$h'_{\pi(i)} = H(\alpha'_{\pi(i)}, \beta'_{\pi(i)}) \text{ for } i = 1, \ldots, n \tag{2}$$

Recent research revealing possible attacks on this mixnet scheme include the paper by Abe and Imai [2] and Wikström [12].

3   Proposed Efficient Mixnet Scheme

To provide the required receipt-freeness property in the proposed voting scheme and to eliminate attacks as in [2, 12], we apply the following modifications to the scheme by Golle et al. [8].

- The hash checksum is removed to invalidate the relation attacks as in [2, 12].
- Single encryption is used instead of double encryption to prevent a sender from using the inner encryption of the double enveloping as a receipt.
- We only check that $\prod v_i = \prod v_i'$ in the proof of product, where v_i and v_i' are messages before and after the mixing.

Threshold version of ElGamal cryptosystem is employed as in Section 2.2. The two primes are p and $q|p - 1$, the secret key is x, and the public key is $(g, y = g^x)$. Assume that there are n voters V_i where $i = 1, \ldots, n$. Each voter V_i interacts with the administrator to generate a ciphertext (α_i, β_i) for his vote v_i (will be detailed in Section 4). These ciphertexts are input to the mixnet.

The proposed mixnet protocol works as follows:

1. Re-encrypt and randomly permute the ordering of messages:
   Each mix-server receives n input ciphertexts (α_i, β_i). Choosing random values $r_i \in_R \mathbb{Z}_q$, the ciphertexts are re-encrypted as $(\alpha_i', \beta_i') = (\alpha_i g^{r_i}, \beta_i y^{r_i})$. The mix-server then outputs the re-encrypted ciphertexts in a random order $(\alpha_{\pi(i)}', \beta_{\pi(i)}')$, where $\pi(i)$ is a random permutation of i.
2. Prove preservation of products (individual mix server verification):
   Each mix-server proves the following equation in zero knowledge.

$$\log_g \frac{\prod_{i=1}^n \alpha_i'}{\prod_{i=1}^n \alpha_i} = \log_h \frac{\prod_{i=1}^n \beta_i'}{\prod_{i=1}^n \beta_i} \tag{3}$$

The correctness of the mixing is verifiable by anyone as g, y, and input (α_i, β_i) and output ballots (α_i', β_i') are made public. This zero-knowledge proof requires 2 exponentiations for proving and 6 exponentiations for verification using the Chaum-Pedersen protocol [6].

If the mixnet is highly trusted, a variation named global verification can be used. This verification technique takes a more optimistic approach as the preservation of product is verified, not by the mix servers in each mixing stage, but by the decryption authorities after all mixings are finished. The decryption authorities decrypt the product of the first input ballots to the mixnet and the product of the last output ballots from the mixnet, and check the equality of these two values.

Individual mix server verification offers early detection of error in the mixing. Thus, mixing can be aborted and done by other mix servers. This verification technique is preferable as it provides a correctness check on each mix server. Using global verification, each mix server is not required to produce any proof. Thus, mixing process can be performed more efficiently, however errors will only be detected when the proof of products are decrypted.

Our proposed mixnet scheme uses a single encryption removing the use of double encryption and hash checksum (3 encryptions). Thus attacks [2, 12] on the original mixnet scheme [8] are not applicable to our scheme, while efficiency is improved three times.

4 Proposed Voting Scheme

Our efficient mixnet-based receipt-free voting protocol uses the proposed optimistic mixnet as described in Section 3. The parameters p, q, g, y are made public, while x is kept secret. Each voter registers to a registration authority and obtains a public-private key pair through an already established key distribution mechanism such as Public Key Infrastructure (PKI). The voting protocol consists of the following three stages:

Stage 1. Voting
Voting stage is an interactive protocol between the voters and the administrator through an untappable channel. During the actual voting period, votes are cast by the voters, published by the administrator and approved by the voters.

1. Vote casting (using two-way untappable channel):
   Each voter V_i chooses and encrypts his vote v_i as $(\alpha_i, \beta_i) = E_y(v_i, r_i)$, where r_i is a random value chosen by the voter. The encrypted vote (α_i, β_i) is then sent to the administrator with voter's signature. The administrator checks the eligibility of the voter and the validity of voter's signature.
2. Ballot publishing:
   After the voting period finishes, the administrator re-encrypts each ballot using a new random value τ_i as $(\alpha_i', \beta_i') = (\alpha_i g^{\tau_i}, \beta_i h^{\tau_i})$ [1], and posts the re-encrypted vote (α_i', β_i') in a random order on the bulletin board.
3. DVRP (using two-way untappable channel):
   The administrator provides each voter with a DVRP which proves the correctness of the re-encryption. Using DVRP, the administrator proves personally to the voter that he knows either the random value τ_i or the private key of the voter x_i (public key of voter is $y_i = g^{x_i}$) as the following:
   (a) The prover selects random values of $k, r, t \in_R \mathbb{Z}_q$.
   (b) The prover computes commitments of $(a, b) = (g^k, y^k)$ and $d = g^r y_i^t$.
   (c) The prover computes the challenge using a one-way collision-resistant hash function H as $c = H(a, b, d, \alpha_i', \beta_i')$.
   (d) The prover then calculates the response $u = k - \tau_i(c + r)$.
   (e) The prover sends (c, r, t, u) to V
   (f) The verifier checks:

   $$c \overset{?}{=} H(g^u(\alpha_i'/\alpha_i)^{c+r}, y^u(\beta_i'/\beta_i)^{c+r}, g^r y_i^t, \alpha_i', \beta_i') \tag{4}$$

4. Approval:
   Each voter checks the validity of the DVRP (Equation 4) and posts an approval message with his signature on the bulletin board if the DVRP is accepted, and refutes otherwise. The approval message format can be pre-agreed in the system such that it is fresh but not include any personal information which can be used as a receipt. For example, voters can sign the hash value of all the published ballots.

---

[1] The re-encryption exploits the homomorphic property of ElGamal cryptosystem. In the re-encryption, the random value r of the original ciphertext is changed by τ to be $r + \tau$. Thus, the re-encrypted ciphertext will still decrypt to v.

Stage 2. Mixing
The input ballots are re-encrypted and outputted in a random order by the mix servers using the proposed efficient mixnet described in Section 3. Depending on the confidence level of the voting process, an individual mix server verification or a global verification can be employed.

Stage 3. Tally
During this stage, votes are tabulated by the talliers and the result is published on the bulletin board.

1. The output of the mix-network are individually decrypted by a quorum of talliers using threshold decryption. The threshold decryption is publicly verifiable as each tallier proves that his decryption share is correct.
2. The voting result is published by the talliers on the bulletin board.

If an invalid vote (not in pre-determined format) is found after decryption, the particular output can be traced back to identify the entity who had invalidated it. This can either be a mix-server, the administrator or the voter.

Trace-Back Protocol:

1. The last mix-server is required to reveal the i-th input corresponding to the $\pi(i)$-th invalid output, and prove the correctness of his re-encryption by revealing his random number. This process is repeated to all mix-servers in the reverse order of mixing until an invalid mixing is found.
2. If mixing was found to be correct, the administrator is required to reveal the corresponding input and output re-encryption, and prove the re-encryption by revealing the random number.
3. If the re-encryption by the administrator was found to be correct, the voter is identified to submit the invalid vote.

5   Analysis

5.1   Security

Our proposed voting scheme is based on known building blocks whose security properties are already known. This section discusses the security of our mixnet scheme and the overall security of our mixnet-based voting protocol. We analyse our proposed scheme based on the security requirements in Section 1.

- **Privacy:** The ballots are randomized and mixed first by the administrator and then by the mix servers. If at least one of these entities remains honest, privacy of voters is kept. A threat in privacy can occur when a specific invalid ballot is traced back to the voter. If the invalid ballot is traced back only to the mix servers, privacy is kept since we assume that the administrator does not disclose the voter-vote relationship.
- **Eligibility:** The list of eligible voters are made public and only authenticated voters are allowed to participate.

- **Prevention of double voting:** Voters can vote only once since they participate in voting with their signature. Any misbehaviour by the administrator, for example, deletion or addition of ballot, is prevented, since voter's approval is required to be a valid ballot.
- **Fairness:** Since we assume the threshold trust for the talliers, no partial tally is revealed. This guarantees the fairness of voting.
- **Receipt-freeness:** Since voter's ballot is randomized additionally by the administrator, a voter loses his knowledge of the randomness of the encrypted ballot and cannot construct any receipt. Also the voter cannot transfer the DVRP of the administrator to any third party, since it is a personal proof and the voter can open it in any way using his private key. Since a two-way untappable channel is used between the voter and the administrator, a buyer cannot observe the communication between the voter and administrator during the voting stage.
- **Robustness:** Using individual mix server verification, backup mixing is possible when an invalid mixing in the proof of product is detected.
- **Verifiability:** In the voting stage a voter can personally verify the correctness of administrator's randomization by checking the DVRP. Correct mixing operation is publicly verifiable as anyone can observe and verify the equality of the product of input and output ballots. The tally stage is publicly verifiable.

A corrupt mix server can disrupt the voting by invalidating some ballots when he mixes the ballots. For example, a mix server takes two messages c_i and c_j, with $i \neq j$, and produces two output messages which are re-encryptions of 1 and $c_i c_j$. As the product of messages is still preserved, the proof of correct mixing is accepted, but recovered messages are invalid. However, the cheating mix-server will be identified using the trace-back protocol and be punished. When a trace-back occurs to a specific mix server in the middle of the mix servers, the voter-vote relationship will not be revealed. When an invalid ballot is traced back to the first mix server, the administrator will know the voter-vote relationship. Thus, we assume that the administrator is a reputable entity and does not disclose his knowledge when a trace-back occurs. The mix servers can easily perform this invalidation attack, but they cannot obtain any useful information unless they can collude with the administrator, while their identity can be easily found through a public trace-back protocol. Compared to the current manual paper-based voting, although our scheme may not offer improvement for anonymity control, it provides better protection against fraudulent votes.

5.2   Efficiency

Compared with Golle et al.'s scheme, our voting scheme is more efficient both in computational (number of exponentiations) and communication (message size in bits) complexity as shown in Table 1. The efficiency mainly comes from the fact that our scheme uses single encryption, while the scheme by Golle et al. [8] uses three encryptions for the double enveloping.

Table 1. Comparison of computational and communication efficiency of our scheme against Golle *et al.*'s scheme, where n is the number of voters.

Computational efficiency			Proposed	Golle *et al.* [8]
Voting	Voter	Encrypt	2	8
		Verify (DVRP)	6	N/A
	Admin	Re-encrypt	2	N/A
		Prove (DVRP)	4	N/A
Mixing	Mixer	Re-encrypt	$2n$	$6n$
		Prove	2	6
	Public	Verify	6	18
Communication efficiency			Proposed	Golle *et al.* [8]
Voting	Voter	Encrypt	$2|p|$	$6|p|$
	Admin	Proof (DVRP)	$4|q|$	N/A
Mixing	Mixer	Re-encryption	$2n|p|$	$6n|p|$
		Proof	$2|p| + |q|$	$6|p| + 3|q|$

In the voting stage, our scheme requires each voter to encrypt the vote once (2 modular exponentiations), submit it to the administrator, and later verify DVRP from the administrator (6 modular exponentiations). The scheme by Golle et al. [8] requires each voter to perform double encryption (8 modular exponentiations). We do not compare the cost for digital signature, since it is an essential operation and requires the same cost.

In the mixing stage, our scheme requires three times less computation compared with the scheme by Golle et al. [8], since our scheme uses single encryption while [8] uses three encryptions for the double enveloping. In terms of proof of product (POP), our scheme requires three times less computation, if we use the individual mix server verification. If we use the global verification (Section 3), our scheme is much more efficient, since only the initial input product and final output product are decrypted by a quorum of decryption authorities and compared.

In the tally stage, our scheme only requires one threshold decryption for each ballot, where the scheme by Golle et al. [8] requires four threshold decryption.

Ballot size in our scheme is $2|p|$ bits as we use single ElGamal encryption, and the DVRP by the administrator is $4|q|$ bits. Ballot size in the scheme by Golle et al. [8] is $6|p|$ bits as they use double encryption. In the mixing stage, our scheme requires three times less bandwidth compared with the scheme by Golle et al. [8]. However, in the voting stage our scheme requires interactive communication between voters and the administrator since voters have to cast ballot first and approve it later.

6   Conclusion

An efficient mixnet-based voting scheme providing receipt-freeness has been presented. We successfully combined two mixnet-based voting schemes by Lee et al. [9] and Golle et al. [8] to provide both efficient mixing and receipt-freeness together. In our scheme, the administrator provides both randomization service and mixing service together in the voting stage. Our proposed optimistic mixnet is more light-weight because single encryption is used. Although it is more optimistic and invalidation attack by mix servers is possible, public traceback procedure discourages any misbehaviour by the administrator or the mix servers. Because of its efficiency, the proposed voting scheme can be preferred in practical real world election applications such as political elections in which the administrator is considered to be a reputable entity and a timely tally is required. Moreover this mixnet-based voting scheme can offer more flexibility on the ballot structure, such as preferential voting.

Two major problems of our scheme are the trust assumption on the administrator and the possibility of invalidation attack by mix servers, although any misbehaviour causing invalidation can be traced back easily. Our future work will be focused on solving these problems.

References

1. Masayuki Abe. Mix-networks on permutations networks. In *Advances in Cryptology – ASIACRYPT 99*, pages 258–273, 1999.
2. Masayuki Abe and Hideki Imai. Flaws in some robust optimistic mix-nets. In *Advances in Cryptology – ACISP 03*, pages 39–50, 2003.
3. Riza Aditya, Colin Boyd, Ed Dawson, and Kapali Viswanathan. Secure e-voting for preferential elections. In *Second International Conference, EGOV 2003*, pages 246–249, 2003.
4. Josh Benaloh and Dwight Tuinstra. Receipt-free secret-ballot elections. In *Proceedings of the Twenty-Sixth Annual ACM Symposium on the Theory of Computing*, pages 544–553, 1994.
5. Dan Boneh and Philippe Golle. Almost entirely correct mixing with applications to voting. In *9th ACM Conference on Computer and Communications Security – CCS 02*, pages 68–77, 2002.
6. David Chaum and Torben Pryds Pedersen. Wallet databases with observers. In *Advances in Cryptology – CRYPTO 92*, pages 89–105, 1993.
7. Jun Furukawa and Kazue Sako. An efficient scheme for proving a shuffle. In *Advances in Cryptology – CRYPTO 01*, pages 368–387, 2001.
8. Philippe Golle, Sheng Zhong, Dan Boneh, Markus Jakobsson, and Ari Juels. Optimistic mixing for exit-polls. In *Advances in Cryptology – ASIACRYPT 02*, pages 451–465, 2002.
9. Byoungcheon Lee, Colin Boyd, Ed Dawson, Kwangjo Kim, Jeongmo Yang, and Seungjae Yoo. Providing receipt-freeness in mixnet-based voting protocols. In *Information Security and Cryptology – ICISC 03*, pages 245–258, 2004.
10. Torben P. Pedersen. A threshold cryptosystem without a trusted party (extended abstract). In *Advances in Cryptology – EUROCRYPT 91*, pages 522–526, 1991.
11. Adi Shamir. How to share a secret. *Communications of the ACM*, 22(11):612–613, November 1979.
12. Douglas Wikström. How to break, fix and optimize "optimistic mix for exit-polls". Technical report, Swedish Institute of Computer Science, 2002. Available from http://www.sics.se/libindex.htlm, last accessed 08 October 2003.

Trust in Public Administration e-Transactions: e-Voting in the UK

Alexandros Xenakis and Ann Macintosh

International Teledemocracy Center
Napier University
10, Colinton Rd., Edinburgh, EH10 5DT
a.xenakis@napier.ac.uk

Abstract. This paper explores the issue of trust in information and communication technologies (ICT) mediated public administration transactional environments. This is particularly important in the case of the e-electoral process since it is necessary to maintain the existing level of citizen trust for current electoral arrangements, in the newly introduced e-voting processes. In our analysis we adopt a process stage approach of e-elections. We identify the different agents involved in the e-electoral process so as to indicate who generate trust and to whom they convey their trust during the evolution of the process. We then describe agent responsibilities for each of the process stages in order to indicate the issues on which some agents trust others. Thus we indicate why trust was needed to support the deployment of electronic voting. Finally, based on our analysis we describe cases where "inherited trust" was indirectly conveyed between agents.

1 Introduction

The introduction of information and communication technologies (ICT) in the service of traditionally delivered public administration, has re-engineered the transactional environment for many of the government owned and delivered processes [20]. The gradual deployment of electronic government initiatives has provided researchers with the opportunity to explore how the agents involved in the delivery of ICT mediated public administration processes alter and adjust their transactional behavior. Within this greater discussion one of the aspects explored has been focused on the issue of trust, surrounding and supporting the delivery of the re-designed processes. In the UK, the recent e-voting pilots, undertaken in 2002 and 2003 [2], [3], have provided yet another example of ICT deployment in the service of government provided democratic processes. This paper explores the different aspects of trust as identified in the case of the UK e-voting pilots and aims to demonstrate the generic role of the trust factor in the successful implementation of similar future initiatives.

2 Trust in e-Government and e-Voting Processes

Different approaches have been followed in order to develop trust in the newly introduced e-government systems. From a user perspective it has been claimed that build-

S. Katsikas, J. Lopez, and G. Pernul (Eds.): TrustBus 2004, LNCS 3184, pp. 162–171, 2004.

ing trust in the system can be achieved through increased efficiency, increased transparency and the overall transformation of the e-service in relation to the traditionally offered service [14]. Interactivity of the new systems has also been suggested in the literature as a factor facilitating the development of user trust in e-government systems [22]. McKay-Hubbard and Macintosh [10] in their analysis suggest models of trust, which could allow a PA to modify processes and address issues of internal cooperation in a targeted, trust focused manner, thus facilitating a reasonably smooth transition to an e-service environment. It has also been suggested that the use of ICT to support public services, will accordingly restore public trust in the overall system of government [13]. On the contrary, it has been empirically proven that distrustful citizens will not increase their trust irrespective of the medium of interaction [16].

This last argument is further proven by the experience gained in the UK e-voting pilots. The positive effect that the introduction of e-voting technologies might have on declining voter turnout has always been one of the strategic targets for deploying the pilots however to this date no relation, neither positive or negative, has been established between the two [2], [3]. However trust in the new transactional environment is related to the existing trust in the process this serves. The Caltech-MIT [1] Voting Technology Project, in their report quote: "People do not use things in which they have no confidence. Losing confidence in elections means loosing confidence in our system of government."(p. 42), while the ICAVM report (The UK Independent Commission on Alternative Voting Methods) [9] accordingly argues that: "One thing is for certain: public confidence in democratic elections takes decades to develop and far less time to destroy" (p. 6). Despite the predominant role of the electorate's trust in the use of e-voting processes, in our analysis of the UK pilots we also identified organizational [7] aspects of trust which were developed between the agents involved in their delivery, and assumed a vital role for the successful completion of the pilots.

3 Pilot Description and Research Methodology

In the UK, following the Government's aim to put "robust systems in place for an e-enabled General Election after 2006" (p47) [8], 16 e-voting pilots took place in May 2002 [17] and 20 more in May 2003 [4], on a Local Authority level. These were in all cases legally binding elections. The different e-voting technologies piloted involved electronic counting schemes combined with traditional paper ballots, touch-screen voting kiosks both in supervised (polling station) and unsupervised locations, internet voting, interactive voice response (IVR) landline telephone voting and SMS text message voting in 2002. Digital television voting and smart card technology for partial voter identification were additionally introduced in 2003. Several local authorities (4 in 2002 and 13 in 2003) offered these technologies as alternative channels of voting, therefore providing a multiple channel e-voting process. In the pilots where two or more channels of voting were offered simultaneously an electronic on-line version of the electoral register was developed and used to provide the necessary voter identification infrastructure. The use of the on-line electronic register at polling stations enabled voters to cast their vote at any polling station of their convenience within the pilot wards.

The research presented in this paper forms part of a doctoral programme concerned with the identification of the emerging constraints in re-designing the electoral process in relation to information and communication technologies. After completing an extensive literature review of the issues involved in the implementation of electronic voting, we have proceeded to the analysis of the detailed evaluation reports of the 2002 and 2003 UK e-voting pilots, provided by the Electoral Commission. Additionally, observations and interviews were undertaken in one of the 2003 pilot Local Authorities (PA), which also provided us directly with further research data. Four semi-structured interviews were held, three of which are relevant to the scope of this paper. These include the PA's Returning Officer who has the legal responsibility for the conduct of elections in his/her area, the PA's e-voting manager who had the managerial responsibility for the overall voting process and production of the final result and the commercial supplier's management executive who had the task of co-ordinating all technical systems providers for that pilot.

In our analysis we adopt a process stage approach of e-elections. We identify the different agents involved in the e-electoral process so as to indicate who generate trust and to whom they convey their trust during the evolution of the process. We then describe the responsibilities of each agent for each of the process stages in order to indicate the issues on which some agents trust some others. Thus we indicate why trust was needed to support the deployment of the pilots. The stage approach also provides an indication as to when this trust is needed during the different stages of the overall e-electoral process. We identify fourteen distinct trust flows among agents, which we indicate as they appear in each stage.

Then, using the SmartGov trust framework [19], we allocate each trust flow to one of the four models that the framework provides. The SmartGov framework, originally distinguishes between an internal and an external model of trust. Internal trust relationships develop between service providers (i.e. for the case of e-voting all agents exempt citizens and those seeking elections), while external trust relationships derive from service users (i.e. citizens and those seeking election) and are oriented towards those providing the service. Each model is then further analyzed according to the mode of trust it fosters, with two possible modes, latent or situational trust. Latent trust exists over a long period of time, it may be based on written procedures and it is accepted as a given. Situational trust has a relatively short time frame, is negotiated in the present time between agents directly, and is specific to the context of the relationship. The combination of the two original models of trust with the two suggested modes of trust provides four different trust models: a) Internal latent trust, b) Internal situational trust, c) External latent trust and d) External situational trust.

The framework relates each model to bases of trust. Each of the above models could be knowledge, institutional, cultural or identification based [18], [11]. Thus, by allocating information flows identified in the e-voting process to the above models, we can trace through the framework, the bases of each trust flow. Finally, based on our analysis we discuss cases where "inherited trust" was indirectly conveyed between agents.

4   Agents

Fairweather and Rogerson [6] suggest seven main agents involved in the deployment of electronic elections: central government, local government, those seeking election, minority groups, citizens as voters, suppliers of technological elements and systems developers. For the purpose of this paper however we need to further define the different groups of agents included in each of the above high-level categories. In the UK pilots, central government was represented by more than one organisation. The pilots were funded and procured by the ODPM (Office of the Deputy Prime Minister), legally approved by the Westminster Parliament and evaluated by the Electoral Commission. Public authorities (PA) were involved with more than one of their internal departments. In all cases these included the office of the Returning Officer who is legally responsible for the outcome of any election within his/her area [21] and the electoral office holding the administrative responsibility for conducting elections in the same area. Occasionally, these would be further assisted by other departments such as IT, or the e-government department, however this would depend on the project management approach adopted in each of the pilots.

Those seeking election should also be considered separately. Candidates should be differentiated from political parties since they may hold a different opinion on the adoption of common policy with regard to the introduction of electronic voting. Furthermore candidates should also be divided among those who are running for re-election and those seeking election. The main difference between them is that the first have the power to stop an e-voting pilot from happening, therefore their trust in the proposed innovation assumes higher significance. We consider that minority groups on a trust level, should not be differentiated from the rest of the electorate. Minority groups are usually ethnic minority or groups of disabled voters. Although special provisions must be made so as to avoid social exclusion phenomena, and possibly, dedicated mediums could be used to secure trust building in these groups, the trust building arguments themselves would remain the same as for the rest of the electorate. Citizens as voters however should be considered as three distinct groups: non-voters (not voting at all), voters (opting to vote the traditional way providing it is still offered) and e-voters (those trusting the piloted e-voting technologies to cast their ballot).

Suppliers of technological elements and system developers should also be considered in the same category with regard to the issue of trust as system developers were just one of the internal departments involved in delivering the expected performance of e-voting systems. However commercial suppliers of e-voting solutions were further divided into co-operating partners, infrastructure providers and sub-contracted partners. Co-operating partners (i.e. e-voting technology providers) and infrastructure providers (i.e. ISP, database administrators) formed collaborative consortia in order to deliver a complete e-voting pilot. Each of these providers could sub-contract further external partners so as to secure the delivery of their contractual obligations to the ODPM and their service to the PA.

All these different agents according to their roles and responsibilities in the process stages of the e-electoral process were either asked to trust other agents or in turn receive trust flows. The next section demonstrates how this trust circulated around the process of the e-voting pilots creating a chain of coherence and holding the process together, therefore enabling its realisation.

5 Trust Flows per Process Stage

Xenakis and Macintosh [23], suggest eleven different stages of the e-electoral process. In our analysis we do not address two of these stages, the election campaign and candidate nomination stage, as we consider the trust involved in these stages to be political trust, which is not related to the trust flows generated to support the deployment of the pilots. However we consider that voters verifying the correct casting of their ballot should be considered as a different stage from the numerical verification of ballots cast against the marked copy of the register. We therefore introduce a new stage in the process, the confirmation stage, meaning that voters receive confirmation for the correct casting of their ballot, which is also in line with the system requirements set by the ODPM for the 2003 pilots [15]. We therefore base our analysis on the following ten process stages which are consecutive with the exception of the general administration stage which is spread all along its successive stages: Procurement (e-voting pilot procurement), General Administration, Registration (voter registration), Authentication (voter), Casting the vote, Confirmation of correct casting of the vote, Verification (numerical audit of voters per votes cast), Counting (of paper and e-ballots), Tabulation and Declaration (of result).

Procurement: In all of the UK pilots, there was considerable trust and good faith developed between the above-mentioned agents, for the e-voting pilots to take place. Before and during the pilot procurement stage the ODPM was responsible to create an accredited list of e-voting technology suppliers who were approved and therefore trusted by the central government to provide their products and services for the deployment of the pilots. This is the first trust flow in the process (**TF1**) from the ODPM to the commercial suppliers. As this trust was developed through the supplier accreditation procedure and was contract based, it is an example of the internal latent model of trust. This trust flow was un-officially extended to cover the sub-contracted suppliers of the accredited partners, thus this was a case of inherited trust from the ODPM to the sub-contracted suppliers. Suppliers also had to trust the central government, as developing the e-voting applications had started a long time before actually being given a contract by the ODPM. Therefore this second information flow from the commercial suppliers to the ODPM (**TF2**) is an example of the internal situational model of trust. During the procurement stage consortia of suppliers had promotional contacts with PAs. Trust bonds between preferred suppliers and PA officials were then formed. PAs applied to the ODPM, suggesting their preferred commercial supplier but it remained at the discretion of the ODPM to combine PAs with commercial suppliers. After the PA applications had been submitted, the ODPM had to examine them and according to their scope, approve or reject them. Approved PAs would then be attributed commercial suppliers and the ODPM contracted the services and products of the suppliers on behalf of PAs. However due to the limited time scale followed, PAs and commercial suppliers had to initiate some project stages for the deployment of the pilots prior to the official legislation being passed by the Parliament and the sign-off of suppliers' contracts [3]. As a result suppliers were committed to system development and customisation prior to being awarded a contract by the ODPM, which served as a proof of the supplier commitment towards the PAs. The trust flow (**TF3**) from the PAs to the commercial suppliers is also an example of the internal situational trust model. In such cases TF3 was developed directly between the two agents.

In all the interviews undertaken with PA officials it was emphasized that their confidence, in order to undertake the pilots, was based on their trust towards the commercial suppliers of the e-voting systems. It should be noted that interviews were held with a pilot PA, which was matched with its preferred supplier. In all cases however,

PAs had to trust the technology providers so as to provide the service promised, as they were not able to control how the service was provided or if it was provided the way it should be, not having the technical expertise to do so. In order to cover that lack, technology providers had to be chosen for the PA by the ODPM. Therefore PAs trusted the ODPM (**TF4**) through an internal latent model of trust and in an indirect way local authorities inherited the trust of the central government towards the chosen technology providers. There was however one case of a PA which refused to go ahead with the pilot although it had been approved by the ODPM, because the PA was matched by the ODPM with a commercial supplier other than its preferred commercial supplier. With this decision the PA demonstrated that the trust formatted during the procurement stage (TF3) with its preferred commercial supplier was stronger than the trust existing towards the central government organization (TF4). Finally during the procurement stage political support for the deployment of the pilots had to be gained on a local authority level. Elected councilors and political parties were asked to trust the local authority staff (**TF5**), to properly run the pilots and accept the final results. At the same time however they were asked to indirectly extend their trust to the ODPM (**TF6**) and the commercial suppliers (**TF7**) directly contracted by the ODPM to deliver the pilots. As elected councilors and parties are considered as agents served by the e-voting process and are not involved in its delivery, these were examples of external situational models of trust, which did not pre-exist in the traditional voting process and were generated for the purpose of the e-voting pilots.

General Administration: In the general administration stage, those immediately influenced by the outcome of the electoral process, i.e. citizens (**TF8**) and those seeking election (**TF9**), trust the Returning Officer (RO) and PA staff, to provide for all the requirements of an election, in a manner that will produce a valid, undisputed result. These are examples of external yet latent models of trust as they are based on pre-existing trust flows. However in the case of e-voting, since the provision of voting technology is outsourced to commercial IT suppliers, PAs have to trust suppliers (TF3) that they will deliver on their contractual obligations (towards the ODPM). Therefore the trust conveyed to the PA on this matter is in turn inherited to suppliers of e-voting technologies to the extent that PAs trust (or are obliged to trust) them. Therefore two new trust flows are indirectly generated form citizens (**TF10**) and those seeking election (**TF11**) towards commercial suppliers for the duration of the pilots, therefore both trust flows follow the external situational trust model.

Registration: In the voter registration process those seeking election trust the PA that only eligible voters are included in the formation of the electoral register (TF9). In turn due to the process followed for voter registration in the UK (home occupant/s registration as opposed to personal registration), there is a considerable amount of trust from the PAs to the citizens during this stage. This pre-existing, in the traditional voting process, trust flow (**TF12**), is an example of the external latent trust model. The issue of the electoral register is however generic to the whole of electoral process rather than just the e-electoral process [5]. Moreover the voter registration process has yet to be served by ICTs in the UK.

Authentication: Voter authentication in the UK also involves trust in order to be achieved. In the traditional process voters are not obliged to produce any kind of personal identification token in order to ask for a ballot at a polling station. Voters only have to be registered and state their name and address to the polling official. Therefore an inherent amount of trust is already built in the voting process with PAs trusting this form of "verbal declaration of identity" from the voter (TF12), and those seeking election trusting that PA staff (TF9) to follow the commonly accepted identification process. Similarly citizens-voters trust the PA (TF8) to follow the process in order to exclude the possibility of double voting from malicious voters. When it comes to e-voting these trust flows are further supplemented by the trust of PAs towards to e-voting technology suppliers (TF3), that the electronic authentication tokens produced are valid when distributed to voters and consumed after their first use. The authentication process is no longer controlled by the PA, thus all trust conveyed to the PA on this matter is automatically inherited to commercial suppliers.

Casting the Vote: When a voter casts a ballot, one trusts the PA to be provided with correct ballot paper, a private environment to make one's choice, to maintain the secrecy of one's choice, and safeguard the ballot until it has been counted. In the case of e-voting each of these four reasons generating voter trust towards the PA is accordingly affected. PAs have no way of securing that voters will be presented with correct ballot paper other than trusting that e-voting system performance will be maintained by the commercial suppliers to the promised standards (TF3). The same applies in the matter of keeping the voters' choice secret. Although voter data and cast ballot data are stored separately to maintain voter anonymity, in the UK there is a legal requirement that ballot can be back-traced to voters for judicial verification of the election [21]. Therefore the technical means are available to allow such a process to happen. Mercuri and Neumann [12] refer to the matter of personnel integrity in relation to the security of e-voting processes, a breach of which could lead to the disclosure of cast ballot secrecy. Similarly the PA has no means to safeguard the e-ballots cast until they are counted. E-ballots are stored within the e-voting systems and yet again PAs have to trust system suppliers and convey the existing trust flows on the matter by other agents. In the matter of privacy nevertheless the trust flow is inverted. While in traditional voting PAs have to provide voters with a private environment to cast a ballot, in remote unsupervised voting it is PAs that have to trust voters to cast their e-ballot in privacy. As voters are in possession of their remote voting credentials, they are in control of the level of privacy that they require to cast a ballot providing that they own the technical means to do so. PAs therefore trust that each individual voter (TF12) will make legal use of one's voting credentials and will not use voting credentials belonging to other voters (i.e. the credentials of the previous occupier of a house, or incorrectly delivered credentials) even with their consent (i.e. family voting or vote trading).

Confirmation of Correct Casting of the Vote: In the traditional voting process there is no need for this process stage as voters are certain that they cast the correct ballot the moment they receive it, mark it and physically insert it in the ballot box. Yet as all the previous steps lack their physical aspect voters must receive a confirmation that their ballot has been digitally stored once cast. E-voters therefore directly trust the voting technology suppliers to have correctly stored the e-ballot cast when they receive the relevant confirmation produced by the e-voting system once the e-ballot has been stored. This newly generated trust flow (**TF13**) is the first to be directly conveyed from e-voters to commercial suppliers and falls under the external situational trust model.

Verification and Counting: In the UK traditional voting process, at the close of polls, the verification and counting of the paper ballots takes place in dedicated counting locations. Both these process stages are transparent and open to scrutiny. Trust of all interested agents (citizens-TF8 and those seeking election-TF9) in the outcome of these two PA delivered process stages is gained through transparency and external audit. In the case of e-ballots these two stages are digitally provided. As a result PAs (TF3) as well as citizens (TF13) and those seeking election **(TF14)** have to directly trust commercial suppliers to provide accurate verification and counting of the e-ballots. This last trust flow also falls under the external situational trust model, as it is similar to TF13.

Tabulation and Declaration (of Result): Finally the stages of tabulating and declaring the result of the e-election remain with the PA so the existing trust from citizens and those seeking election remains with the PA as is the case for the traditional process (TF8, TF9). It should be noted however that since the tabulation and declaration of results are based on the results produced in the two previous stages (verification and counting), trust in these last two stages is also directly oriented from the interested agents to commercial suppliers (TF13 and TF14 trust flows). From the description of trust flows between agents we have identified that trust flows can be direct or inherited. In the following section we discuss the matter of inherited trust.

6 Inherited Trust

In all the process stages previously described we have identified several cases of indirect "inherited" trust. Trust flows in the e-voting process are mostly founded on the pre-existing trust flows in the traditional voting process. Additionally trust flows can occur between two or more agents who interact directly in the e-voting process. However, due to the multiplicity of the agents involved and the re-design of the voting process through the use of ICTs, trust flows conveyed towards a specific agent in some cases inevitably are redirected to different agents than the one originally intended. This happens in two main cases. Firstly when trust oriented towards the PAs is redirected towards commercial suppliers, as PAs are partially substituted by suppliers in the transition from the traditional to the e-voting process. Secondly when trust oriented towards directly contracted suppliers is redirected towards their sub-contractors who are not directly related nor interact with the rest of the agents involved in the e-voting process, nevertheless the sub-contractor's role is necessary for the completion of the e-electoral process. In both cases however the trust flows swift from one agent to another following the delegation of responsibilities from one agent to another, due to the re-design of the process. Thus as PAs lose control of some process stages, which they traditionally delivered, due to the use of e-voting technologies, they redirect the trust they previously received by the agents interested in the result of the electoral process to commercial suppliers who assume control of these process stages in the new e-voting process. Nevertheless, when it comes to the case of indirectly sub-contracted providers, the trust flows that directly contracted providers receive form the remaining agents is "silently" conveyed to the their sub-contractors. This form of inherited trust that sub-contactors receive is therefore imposed to the agents who originally provide it. As a result, citizens and those seeking election trust one commercial agent for the delivery of a process, when in reality this process is delivered by a sub-contracted agent, the existence of whom they may even ignore.

7 Conclusions

Citizen trust could be supported by the introduction of explicit understandable security procedures. Procedural security is related to agent responsibilities and their role in the voting process. Therefore it is more easily perceived by non technical experts as it originates from the security administrative processes which surround the traditional voting process. Whatever measures used to support the introduction of electronic voting, trust can primarily be achieved through transparency. The use of open source software to allow public scrutiny of the source code used and the extended role of the media for public monitoring purposes could improve the level of transparency and create the basis for more trust oriented towards electronic voting. However issues of commercial confidence have been used to encounter the previous arguments. We therefore suggest that transparency could be gradually introduced as a trust building measure in three stages. First allow transparent observation to trusted experts. On a second stage, to allow scrutiny undertaken by representatives of all the interested parties involved and finally, allow open scrutiny by the general public, as is the case in traditional UK elections. If transparency is put in place then there will be no need to "technically" generate agent trust. Finally one should always keep in mind that elections are more of a decision making process than an administrative one. The emphasis on the process is relevant to the importance of the result it produces. Therefore the public trust needed to accept the new e-voting technologies should be considered in relation to the context and scope of the election served.

References

1. CalTech MIT (2001). Voting: What is, What Could Be, Report of the CalTech MIT Voting Technology Project.
2. Electoral Commission (2002), Modernizing Elections A Strategic Evaluation of the 2002 Electoral Pilot Schemes 2002
3. Electoral Commission. (2003). The shape of elections to come: A strategic evaluation of the 2003 electoral pilot schemes, July 2003
4. Electoral Commission. (2003a) Local electoral pilot schemes 2003, Briefing, April 2003
5. Electoral Commission (2003b), The electoral registration process, Report and Recommendations, June 2003
6. Fairweather, B. & Rogerson, S. (2002.) Technical Options Report, De Montfort University, Leicester.
7. Gilbert. J., T.L.-P. Tang, (1998) eds. An Examination of Organizational Trust Antecedents. Public Personnel Management. Vol. 27. 1998. 321-338.

8. HM Government. (2002) In the Service of Democracy - a consultation paper on a policy for electronic democracy. Published by the Office of the e-Envoy, Cabinet Office.
9. ICAMV (2002). Independent Commission on Alternative Voting Methods Elections on the 21st Century: from paper ballot to e-voting. Electoral Reform Society.
10. McKay-Hubbard, A. and Macintosh, A. (2003) Models of Trust for Knowledge-Based Government Services. In proceedings of DEXA, E-GOV 2003, Springer.
11. McKnight, D.H. and L. Cummings (1998), Initial Trust Formation in New Organizational Relationships. Academy of Management Review, 1998. 23(3): p. 473-490.
12. Mercuri, R., Neumann, P., (2003) Verification of electronic balloting systems, in Secure Electronic Voting, Gritzalis, D., Ed., Kluwer Academic Publishers
13. Moon, M. J., (2003). "Can IT help government to restore public trust?: Declining public trust And potential prospects of IT in the public sector", Proceedings of the 36th Annual Hawaii International Conference on System Sciences (HICSS 2003)
14. Northrup, T., and Thorson, S. (2003). "The Web of Governance and Democratic Accountability." Proceedings of the 36th Annual Hawaii International Conference on System Sciences (HICSS 2003)
15. ODPM (2002) Electoral Modernization Pilots, Statement of requirements
16. Parent, M., Vandebeek, C.A., Gemino, A.C., (2004) "Building citizen trust through e-government", Proceedings of the 37th Annual Hawaii International Conference on System Sciences (HICSS 2004)
17. Pratchett, L. (2002) " The implementation of electronic voting in the UK " LGA Publications, the Local Government Association
18. Shapiro, D., B. Sheppard, and L. Cheraskin, (1992) Business on a Handshake. Negotiation Journal, 1992. 8: p. 365-377.
19. SmartGov (2004), A Governmental Knowledge Based Platform for Public Sector On-line Services, IST-2001-35399, Deliverable D71: A Framework for e-government services, available at: www.smartgov-project.org (as surveyed March 2004).
20. Taylor, J.A., Snellen I.Th.M. and Zuurmond, A. (1997). Beyond BPR in Public Administration: an institutional transformation in an information age, IOS Press.
21. Watt, B. (2002). Implementing Electronic Voting, A report addressing the legal issues by the implementation of electronic voting, University of Essex.
22. Welch, E. and Hinnant., C., (2003). "Internet Use, Transparency and Interactivity Effects on Trust in Government." Proceedings of the 36th Annual Hawaii International Conference on System Sciences (HICSS 2003) Ed. Ralph H., Sprague, Jr.
23. Xenakis, A. & Macintosh, A. (2003). A Taxonomy of Legal Accountabilities in the UK e-voting pilots. In proceedings of DEXA, E-GOV 2003, Springer.

An Unbalanced Protocol
for Group Key Exchange[*]

Javier Herranz and Jorge L. Villar

Dept. Matemàtica Aplicada IV, Universitat Politècnica de Catalunya
C. Jordi Girona, 1-3, Mòdul C3, Campus Nord, 08034-Barcelona, Spain
{jherranz,jvillar}@mat.upc.es

Abstract. In a group key exchange protocol, a group of players must compute a common secret key by using only public channels. There are many proposed protocols for group key exchange, and all of them are balanced or symmetric: all the players must perform the same amount of computation in the protocol.

We propose an unbalanced group key exchange scheme: two of the players perform most of the computations of the protocol. This scheme can be useful in situations where players do not all have the same computational and communication resources. The security of the protocol is based on the Decisional Diffie-Hellman Assumption.

1 Introduction

There are many situations where a set of users must share a common secret key (also known as session key). For example, if they want to use symmetric-key cryptography for encryption and authentication of their communication, in order to construct secure channels in a public network like the Internet.

Diffie and Hellman introduced the idea of key exchange protocols in [7], where they considered the case with only two users. Later, many works have deal with this scenario and with the more general one, which considers n users (see [8, 1, 5, 10, 4, 9], for example). Most of the resulting protocols require a number of rounds of communication which is $O(n)$; however, the protocol of Burmester and Desmedt [5], whose security has been formally proved in [9], requires only 3 rounds. Other protocols requiring a constant number of rounds have been recently proposed in [2, 3].

With respect to the security of this kind of protocols, it is necessary to deal with an external adversary. In this way, it is possible to provide privacy and mutual authentication among honest players. Otherwise, if the adversary is allowed to corrupt any of the players in a group, he can trivially obtain the resulting session key. Therefore, the goal is to prove that an external adversary is not able to obtain any information about the session key; that is, he cannot distinguish the resulting key from a random value.

---

[*] This work was partially supported by Spanish *Ministerio de Ciencia y Tecnología* under project TIC 2003-00866.

S. Katsikas, J. Lopez, and G. Pernul (Eds.): TrustBus 2004, LNCS 3184, pp. 172–180, 2004.

We can consider two types of external adversary. A passive adversary only sees all the information that is made public during an execution of the protocol but does not take part in it. On the other hand, an active adversary can also initiate sessions, inject fake messages on the channels, etc.

Most of the key exchange protocols that have been proposed until now are in some sense symmetric, or balanced (an exception is [2]): all the players of the group play the same role in the generation of the session keys. In this work we propose a new unbalanced key exchange scheme. Therefore, our scheme could be considered in situations where members of a group do not all have the same computational resources. It requires, as the one in [2] does, a constant number of rounds of communication. With respect to the operations that players must perform, two of them must compute $O(n)$ exponentiations, while the rest of players must compute only 2 exponentiations. The total number of computations is comparable with the most efficient balanced proposals. The number of bits that must be broadcast during the protocol are also distributed in an unbalanced way.

The security of our basic protocol against a passive adversary can be proved in the standard model, assuming the Decisional Diffie-Hellman Assumption. By applying a compiler proposed in [9], which transforms any key exchange protocol secure against a passive adversary to an authenticated protocol secure against an active adversary, we could automatically obtain a protocol achieving the highest level of security in the standard model. Note that the other known unbalanced key exchange protocol [2] is proved to be secure in the random oracle model.

The rest of the work is organized as follows. In Section 2 we informally explain the basic ideas behind group key exchange and the required properties, we recall the Decisional Diffie-Hellman Assumption and we review the protocol proposed by Burmester and Desmedt, which is considered as the most efficient one for group key exchange. Then, in Section 3, we proposed our unbalanced scheme, we discuss its efficiency and we prove its security against a passive adversary. The work is concluded in Section 4.

2 Preliminaries

2.1 Group Key Exchange Protocols

In a group key exchange protocol, n players must obtain a common secret key K, by employing only a public network. The efficiency of these schemes is evaluated according to the required number of rounds of communication and the computations performed by each player in each execution of the protocol.

The two basic properties that a group key exchange scheme must satisfy are correctness and secrecy. Correctness means that, if all the players behave honestly in the execution of the protocol, then they obtain the same secret common key.

Secrecy is defined by considering an external adversary who tries to distinguish between the secret key resulting from a specific execution Π^* of the protocol and a random value. A passive adversary is allowed to know the secret session keys obtained in other executions of the protocol, different from Π^*. An active adversary can also force the players to initiate a specific execution of the protocol, can inject its own messages in the network, etc.

Usually, a necessary condition to achieve secrecy against an active adversary is to consider a public key infrastructure (PKI) and to require players to sign all the messages that they send to the network.

2.2   The Decisional Diffie-Hellman Assumption

Let us recall the Decisional Diffie-Hellman (DDH) Assumption. Let p and q be large prime numbers such that q divides $p - 1$. Consider an element g with order q in $\mathbb{Z}_p^*$. We denote $\mathcal{G} = \langle g \rangle \subset \mathbb{Z}_p^*$. We use the notation $a_1, \ldots, a_n \in_R A$ to mean that n elements $a_1, \ldots, a_n$ are chosen uniformly and independently in the set A.

Consider the two following distributions of probability:

$$\mathcal{D}_{DH} = (g^x, g^y, g^{xy}), \text{ where } x, y \in_R \mathbb{Z}_q ,$$

$$\mathcal{D}_{rand} = (g^x, g^y, g^r), \text{ where } x, y, r \in_R \mathbb{Z}_q .$$

The triples which follow the distribution $\mathcal{D}_{DH}$ are called Diffie-Hellman triples. The DDH Assumption asserts that the two distributions $\mathcal{D}_{DH}$ and $\mathcal{D}_{rand}$ are computationally indistinguishable. A bit more formally:

Definition 1. (The Decisional Diffie-Hellman Assumption.) For any algorithm $\mathcal{A}$ running in polynomial time, we have that

$$| \Pr[\mathcal{A}(g^x, g^y, g^{xy}) = 1 \mid x, y \in_R \mathbb{Z}_q] \; - \; \Pr[\mathcal{A}(g^x, g^y, g^r) = 1 \mid x, y, r \in_R \mathbb{Z}_q] |$$

is a negligible function in the security parameter $k = \log_2 q$.

2.3   The Protocol of Burmester and Desmedt

In [5], Burmester and Desmedt proposed a protocol for group key exchange. In this section we review their protocol.

The set of players who want to obtain a group key is $\mathcal{P} = \{P_1, \ldots, P_n\}$. Let p and q be large prime numbers such that q divides $p - 1$. Consider an element g with order q in $\mathbb{Z}_p^*$. We denote $\ell = \log_2 p$ and $k = \log_2 q$.

First Round. Each player $P_i \in \mathcal{P}$ chooses at random $a_i \in \mathbb{Z}_q^*$ and broadcasts the value $A_i = g^{a_i}$. The cost of this modular exponentiation is $O(\ell^2 k)$ for each player, who broadcasts ℓ bits.

Second Round. Each player $P_i \in \mathcal{P}$ broadcasts $B_i = (A_{i+1}/A_{i-1})^{a_i}$. This computation has a cost of $O(\ell^2 k)$ basic operations for each player, who must broadcast again ℓ bits.

Key Computation Phase. The resulting key is $K = g^{a_1a_2+a_2a_3+\ldots+a_na_1}$. Each player P_i computes this key as:

$$K = (A_{i-1})^{na_i} \cdot B_i^{n-1} \cdot B_{i+1}^{n-2} \cdots B_{i-2}.$$

The key computation phase has a cost of $O\left(\ell^2(k + \sum_{i=1}^{n} \log_2 i)\right)$ for each player.

This protocol for group key exchange is probably the most efficient one: it requires two rounds of communication and a final phase for computing the key. Every user must compute three full-length modular exponentiations; the $n - 1$ remaining exponentiations that each player must compute are not full-length, because $n << q$ in practice. Besides these exponentiations, each player must multiply n values to compute the key.

With respect to communication efficiency, each player must broadcast 2ℓ bits, and so the total number of broadcast bits is $2n\ell$.

In [9], Katz and Yung proved the security of this protocol. First of all, they present a compiler that transforms any group key exchange protocol secure against a passive adversary into one that is secure against an active adversary who can control all the communications in the network. Then, they prove that the basic protocol of Burmester and Desmedt is secure against a passive adversary; that is, an adversary who obtains all the information which is broadcast in an execution of the protocol cannot distinguish between the resulting session key and a value taken at random from the session key space, assuming the Decisional Diffie-Hellman Assumption.

3 Our Proposal

The set of players is $\mathcal{P} = \{P_1, \ldots, P_n\}$. Let p and q be large prime numbers such that q divides $p - 1$. Consider an element g with order q in $\mathbb{Z}_p^*$. As before, we denote $\ell = \log_2 p$ and $k = \log_2 q$.

First Round. Each player $P_i \in \mathcal{P}$ chooses at random $a_i \in \mathbb{Z}_q^*$ and broadcasts the value $A_i = g^{a_i}$. The cost of this exponentiation is $O(\ell^2 k)$ for each player, who must broadcast ℓ bits.

Second Round. For $j = 3, 4, \ldots, n$, player P_1 computes and broadcasts the values $B_{1j} = g^{a_1a_j} = (A_j)^{a_1}$. These computations have a cost of $O((n-2)\ell^2 k)$ basic operations for player P_1, who must broadcast $(n-2)\ell$ bits.

Third Round. For $j = 3, 4, \ldots, n$, player P_2 computes and broadcasts the values $C_{12j} = g^{a_1a_2a_j} = (B_{1j})^{a_2}$. These computations have a cost of $O((n-2)\ell^2 k)$ basic operations for player P_2, who must broadcast $(n-2)\ell$ bits.

Key Computation Phase. The resulting key is $K = g^{a_1a_2}$. Each user can compute it with $O(\ell^2 k)$ basic operations, in the following way:

- Player P_1 computes $K = (A_2)^{a_1}$.
- Player P_2 computes $K = (A_1)^{a_2}$.
- For $j = 3, 4, \ldots, n$, player P_j computes $K = (C_{12j})^{a_j^{-1}}$.

It is easy to see that this protocol achieves the correctness property: if the players follow the steps of the protocol correctly, then they all obtain the same key $K = g^{a_1 a_2}$.

Another property that key exchange protocols must satisfy is that session keys should be uniformly distributed in the session key space. Note that our scheme satisfies this condition, and that no player can impose the value of the session key, if all of them behave honestly, and messages in each round are all broadcast at the same time (that is, we do not consider rushing scenarios).

3.1 Efficiency of the Protocol

The total number of bits that must be broadcast in an execution of our protocol is $(3n-4)\ell$. This number is bigger than in the proposal by Burmester and Desmedt [5], but is unbalanced: players P_1 and P_2 must broadcast a large amount of bits (but they are assumed to be able to do it), whereas $P_3, \ldots, P_n$ broadcast half the bits that they would broadcast in an execution of the protocol by Burmester and Desmedt.

The basic protocol that we propose needs three rounds of communication, and a final key computation phase. Therefore, it requires one more round that the protocol explained in Section 2.3. In total, our protocol requires $4n - 4$ modular full-length exponentiations and the computation of $n - 2$ modular inversions. The total amount of computation that must be performed in an execution of our protocol is comparable to the one in the protocol of Burmester and Desmedt (see Section 2.3). The main difference is the way in which the computation is distributed among the players in the group.

In the protocol of [5], the computation is perfectly distributed among all the players: they do exactly the same number of operations. On the other hand, in our protocol, there are two players who perform each one n exponentiations, where the rest of $n-2$ players compute each one 2 exponentiations and 1 modular inversion.

This unbalanced distribution of both communication and computational efforts makes sense in a situation where players of the group do not all have the same resources. In this case, only the two most powerful players will perform n exponentiations and broadcast $(n - 1)\ell$ bits each, whereas the majority $(n - 2)$ of the players will compute only 2 exponentiations and broadcast ℓ bits.

3.2 Secrecy of the Protocol

In this section we prove that out protocol is secure against a passive adversary who sees all the broadcast information of the protocol, but cannot corrupt any player in the network. Then, by applying the compiler constructed by Katz and

Yung in [9], which adds one more round of communication, we would obtain an authenticated protocol, secure against an active adversary.

The view of a passive adversary after one execution of our protocol consists of $\{g^{a_i}\}_{1 \leq i \leq n}$, $\{g^{a_1 a_j}\}_{3 \leq j \leq n}$ and $\{g^{a_1 a_2 a_j}\}_{3 \leq j \leq n}$. The protocol will achieve the secrecy property if the adversary cannot distinguish, from this view, between the resulting key $g^{a_1 a_2}$ and a random value g^r. In other words, the protocol is secure if the two following distributions $\mathcal{D}_1$ and $\mathcal{D}_4$ are indistinguishable:

$$\mathcal{D}_1 = \left(g^{a_1}, g^{a_2}, \{g^{a_j}\}_{3 \leq j \leq n}, \{g^{a_1 a_j}\}_{3 \leq j \leq n}, \{g^{a_1 a_2 a_j}\}_{3 \leq j \leq n}, g^{a_1 a_2} \right),$$

where $a_1, \ldots, a_n \in_R \mathbb{Z}_q$.

$$\mathcal{D}_4 = \left(g^{a_1}, g^{a_2}, \{g^{a_j}\}_{3 \leq j \leq n}, \{g^{a_1 a_j}\}_{3 \leq j \leq n}, \{g^{a_1 a_2 a_j}\}_{3 \leq j \leq n}, g^{r} \right),$$

where $a_1, \ldots, a_n, r \in_R \mathbb{Z}_q$.

Theorem 1. Assuming the DDH Assumption, the distributions $\mathcal{D}_1$ and $\mathcal{D}_4$ are computationally indistinguishable (we denote this fact as $\mathcal{D}_1 \approx \mathcal{D}_4$).

Proof. We define the two following distributions $\mathcal{D}_2$ and $\mathcal{D}_3$:

$$\mathcal{D}_2 = \left(g^{a_1}, g^{a_2}, \{g^{a_j}\}_{3 \leq j \leq n}, \{g^{a_1 a_j}\}_{3 \leq j \leq n}, \{g^{r a_j}\}_{3 \leq j \leq n}, g^{r} \right),$$

where $a_1, \ldots, a_n, r \in_R \mathbb{Z}_q$.

$$\mathcal{D}_3 = \left(g^{a_1}, g^{a_2}, \{g^{a_j}\}_{3 \leq j \leq n}, \{g^{a_1 a_j}\}_{3 \leq j \leq n}, \{g^{s a_j}\}_{3 \leq j \leq n}, g^{r} \right),$$

where $a_1, \ldots, a_n, s, r \in_R \mathbb{Z}_q$.

We are going to prove $\mathcal{D}_1 \approx \mathcal{D}_2 \approx \mathcal{D}_3 \approx \mathcal{D}_4$, and this fact directly implies $\mathcal{D}_1 \approx \mathcal{D}_4$.

$\mathcal{D}_1 \approx \mathcal{D}_2$. In effect, we prove that if there exists an algorithm $\mathcal{F}_{12}$ that distinguishes between the distributions $\mathcal{D}_1$ and $\mathcal{D}_2$, then $\mathcal{F}_{12}$ can be used to solve the Decisional Diffie-Hellman problem (which consists of deciding if a given triple in $\mathcal{G}^3$ is a Diffie-Hellman triple or not).

Let (X, Y, Z) be an input for the DDH problem. We choose uniform and independent random values $a_3, a_4, \ldots, a_n \in \mathbb{Z}_q$, and we define the following distribution:

$$\delta_{12} = \left(X, Y, \{g^{a_j}\}_{3 \leq j \leq n}, \{X^{a_j}\}_{3 \leq j \leq n}, \{Z^{a_j}\}_{3 \leq j \leq n}, Z \right).$$

If (X, Y, Z) is a Diffie-Hellman triple, then $\delta_{12} = \mathcal{D}_1$. If, on the other hand, (X, Y, Z) is a random triple in $\mathcal{G}^3$, then $\delta_{12} = \mathcal{D}_2$. Therefore, by running $\mathcal{F}_{12}$ on input δ_{12}, we could solve the DDH Problem on input (X, Y, Z).

$\mathcal{D}_2 \approx \mathcal{D}_3$. Again, if there exists an algorithm $\mathcal{F}_{23}$ that distinguishes $\mathcal{D}_2$ from $\mathcal{D}_3$, then $\mathcal{F}_{23}$ can be used to distinguish Diffie-Hellman triples.

Let (X, Y, Z) be an input for the DDH problem. We choose uniform and independent random values $a_1, a_2, b_4, b_5, \ldots, b_n \in \mathbb{Z}_q$, and we execute $\mathcal{F}_{23}$ on input the following distribution:

$$\delta_{23} = \left(g^{a_1}, g^{a_2}, \{X, X^{b_4}, \ldots, X^{b_n}\}, \{X^{a_1}, X^{b_4 a_1}, \ldots, X^{b_n a_1}\}, \right.$$
$$\left. \{Z, Z^{b_4}, \ldots, Z^{b_n}\}, Y \right).$$

It is not difficult to see that, if (X, Y, Z) is a Diffie-Hellman triple, then the distribution δ_{23} is exactly equal to $\mathcal{D}_2$. Otherwise, if (X, Y, Z) is a random triple in $\mathcal{G}^3$, then $\delta_{23} = \mathcal{D}_3$. Thus, $\mathcal{F}_{23}$ could solve the DDH Problem on input (X, Y, Z).

$\mathcal{D}_3 \approx \mathcal{D}_4$. We repeat the same argument: if there exists an algorithm $\mathcal{F}_{34}$ that distinguishes $\mathcal{D}_3$ from $\mathcal{D}_4$, then we can use it to distinguish Diffie-Hellman triples.

Let (X, Y, Z) be an input for the DDH problem. We choose uniform and independent random values $a_3, a_4, \ldots, a_n, r \in \mathbb{Z}_q$, and we execute $\mathcal{F}_{34}$ taking as input the distribution:

$$\delta_{34} = \left(X, Y, \{g^{a_j}\}_{3 \leq j \leq n}, \{X^{a_j}\}_{3 \leq j \leq n}, \{Z^{a_j}\}_{3 \leq j \leq n}, g^r \right).$$

If (X, Y, Z) is a Diffie-Hellman triple, then $\delta_{34} = \mathcal{D}_4$. If (X, Y, Z) is a random triple in $\mathcal{G}^3$, then $\delta_{34} = \mathcal{D}_3$. Therefore, $\mathcal{F}_{34}$ could distinguish $\mathcal{D}_{DH}$ and $\mathcal{D}_{rand}$, contradicting in this way the DDH Assumption.   □

3.3 What if Some Player Is Dishonest?

As we have stated before, a basic requirement that our protocol satisfies is that all the players obtain the same secret key, if they follow the protocol correctly. However, player P_2 can cheat without being detected.

In effect, players $P_3, \ldots, P_n$ cannot cheat, essentially because their role is limited to compute the secret key. On the other hand, P_1 cannot cheat without being detected, because any player P_j, for $j = 3, \ldots, n$, can verify the correctness of the value B_{1j} by checking that $B_{1j} = A_1^{a_j}$.

But nobody can verify the validity of the values C_{12j} broadcast by P_2 (otherwise, the Decisional Diffie-Hellman could be solved). Then, player P_2 could for example broadcast a false value C_{12j}^*, for some player P_j, whereas the rest of values could be valid. In this way, all the players would obtain the same secret key, except P_j.

To avoid this situation and provide our protocol with a kind of robustness against dishonest behaviors of the players, we could add to our scheme some extra steps. In the second round, every player P_j verifies that $B_{1j} = A_1^{a_j}$, for $j = 3, \ldots, n$. Then, in the third round, player P_2 must use a non-interactive zero-knowledge proof of knowledge to show, for $j = 3, \ldots, n$, that the discrete logarithm of $C_{12,j}$ with respect to the base B_{1j} is the same than the discrete logarithm of A_2 with respect to the base g (see [6], for example). If P_1 or P_2 are detected to be cheating, the protocol stops and the dishonest player is rejected.

This robust version has the disadvantage that the efficiency of the resulting scheme decreases. Furthermore, the use of this kind of non-interactive proofs of knowledge implies that the scheme can achieve the security requirements only in the random oracle model.

Note, however, that the same problem appears in other key exchange protocols, for example in the proposal by Burmester and Desmedt [5], explained in Section 2.3. In effect, any player P_i can cheat in the second round of this protocol and broadcast, instead of the correct value $B_i = (A_{i+1}/A_{i-1})^{a_i} = g^{a_{i+1}a_i - a_i a_{i-1}}$, a false value $B'_i = g^{\alpha'_i}$, where $\alpha'_i \neq a_{i+1}a_i - a_i a_{i-1}$. Later, in the key computation phase, each player would obtain a different session key. Therefore, to prevent this situation it would be necessary to force players to prove that their values B_i are consistent with the values broadcast in the first round. This can be done, as we have said before, by using non-interactive zero-knowledge proofs of knowledge to show that the discrete logarithm of B_i with respect to the base A_{i+1}/A_{i-1} is the same than the discrete logarithm of A_i with respect to g.

3.4   Adding Contributory Property

A desirable property for group key exchange protocols is that of being contributory: all the players must contribute to the final value of the session key. The protocol that we present in Section 3 is not contributory, because only P_1 and P_2 contribute to the value of the key. In particular, if these two players collude, they can bias the distribution of the session key.

We can solve this point by imposing the final session key to be

$$K' = g^{a_1 a_2 + a_3 + a_4 + \ldots + a_n}$$

instead of $K = g^{a_1 a_2}$. The new key K' can be easily computed by every player, multiplying K with $\prod_{3 \leq j \leq n} A_j$, which can be computed from information that is public from the first round of the protocol. Note that the secrecy property for this new key can be proved in the same way as in Section 3.2.

4   Conclusion

In this work we propose an unbalanced group key exchange protocol, suitable for situations where the players who want to establish a common secret have different computational resources. With respect to the other known unbalanced protocol [2], our proposal achieves the security requirements in the standard model, not in the random oracle model. Furthermore, the proposal of [2] does not achieve forward secrecy against active adversaries, whereas we can apply the general compiler proposed in [9] to our basic protocol and achieve forward secrecy, which means that corruption of players by the adversary (obtaining their long-term private keys and their current session-state) does not compromise the secrecy of the common secret keys obtained in the past sessions.

By including some extra steps to our basic protocol, we can add robustness in order to detect possible dishonest behaviors of the players. This situation is not usually considered in the rest of proposals of key exchange schemes. However, this addition implies the assumption of the random oracle model for proving security.

In our model we do not consider rushing adversaries, who can take profit if messages from different users are not broadcast exactly at the same time in each round of communication. This kind of adversaries has been considered in [3]. It would be desirable to modify our scheme in order to achieve security also against rushing adversaries; this remains as an interesting open problem.

Acknowledgments

The authors wish to acknowledge the anonymous referees for their interesting comments about the contributory property of group key exchange protocols.

References

1. M. Bellare and P. Rogaway. Entity authentication and key distribution. *Proceedings of Crypto'93*, LNCS **773**, Springer-Verlag, pp. 232–249 (1993).
2. C. Boyd and J.M. González-Nieto. Round-optimal contributory conference key agreement. *Proceedings of PKC'03*, LNCS **2567**, Springer-Verlag, pp. 161–174 (2003).
3. E. Bresson and D. Catalano. Constant round authenticated group key agreement via distributed computation. *Proceedings of PKC'04*, LNCS **2947**, Springer-Verlag, pp. 115–129 (2004).
4. E. Bresson, O. Chevassut and D. Pointcheval. Dynamic group Diffie-Hellman key exchange under standard assumptions. *Proceedings of Eurocrypt'02*, LNCS **2332**, Springer-Verlag, pp. 321–336 (2002).
5. M. Burmester, Y.G. Desmedt. A secure and efficient conference key distribution system. *Proceedings of Eurocrypt'94*, LNCS **950**, Springer-Verlag, pp. 275–286 (1994).
6. D. Chaum and T.P. Pedersen. Wallet databases with observers. *Proceedings of Crypto'92*, LNCS **740**, Springer-Verlag, pp. 89–105 (1992).
7. W. Diffie and M.E. Hellman. New directions in cryptography. *IEEE Transactions on Information Theory*, Vol. **22** (6), pp. 644–654 (1976).
8. I. Ingemarsson, D.T. Tang and C.K. Wong. A conference key distribution system. *IEEE Transactions on Information Theory*, Vol. **28** (5), pp. 714–720 (1982).
9. J. Katz and M. Yung. Scalable protocols for authenticated group key exchange. *Proceedings of Crypto'03*, LNCS **2729**, Springer-Verlag, pp. 110–125 (2003).
10. M. Steiner, G. Tsudik and M. Waidner. Key agreement in dynamic peer group. *IEEE Transactions on Parallel and Distributed Systems*, Vol. **11** (8), pp. 769–780 (2000).

Certified E-Mail with Temporal Authentication: An Improved Optimistic Protocol

Clemente Galdi[1] and Raffaella Giordano[2]

[1] Computer Technology Institute and
Dept. of Computer Eng. and Informatics
University of Patras - 26500, Rio, Greece
clegal@ceid.upatras.gr
[2] Italsime s.r.l.
Via Cinthia, 25 Parco S. Paolo
80126, Napoli, Italy
giordano.r@italsime.it

Abstract. In this paper we present a protocol for Certified E-Mail that ensures temporal authentication. We first slightly modify a previously known three-message optimistic protocol in order to obtain a building block that meets some properties. We then extend this basic protocol enhancing it with the temporal authentication by adding a single message, improving the message complexity of known protocols. The fairness of the protocol is ensured by an off-line Trusted third party that joins the protocol only in case one of the players misbehaves. In order to guarantee temporal authentication we assume the existance of an on-line time stamping server.

1 Introduction

One of the most known and used features provided by the Internet is the e-mail. This service allows users to exchange information in a quick and cheap way. Unfortunately the basic email protocol does not provide any security neither in terms of privacy of the information nor in terms of message integrity. This problem makes the use of electronic mail impossible whenever the information to be sent is, in some way, official or confidential.

Certified email protocols basically provide the following property: user Bob receives an email message from user Alice if and only if the latter receives a receipt for this communication, i.e., a proof that the message has been delivered to the recipient. The receipt is such that the recipient cannot deny to have received the message. Along with this property, many certified email protocols provide other features like confidentiality of the message, proof of integrity and so forth.

Temporal authentication is, in some cases, a strict requirement, e.g., patent submission. Enhancing email systems with temporal authentication could simplify such kind of applications by reducing them to the simple operation of sending an email.

S. Katsikas, J. Lopez, and G. Pernul (Eds.): TrustBus 2004, LNCS 3184, pp. 181–190, 2004.

The problem of certified email can be seen as an instance of the fair exchange problem in which two parties A and B want to exchange two objects O_A and O_B such that A receives O_B if and only if B receives O_A.

Fair Exchange protocols can be essentially classified as on-line (or in-line) and off-line (or optimistic) protocols. In the first class, a Trusted Third Party (TTP for short) has a central role in the protocol in the sense that each exchange involves the TTP. In the optimistic protocols, the TTP comes into play only if the players misbehave while, in the other cases, the users run the protocols by themselves.

It is clear the latter class of protocols has a number of advantages with respect to the former one. In-line protocols are usually simpler than optimistic ones but have the drawback that the TTP could become a bottlneck for the system. On the other hand, optimistic protocols do not provide accountability since whenever the players behave properly, the TTP does not even know a pair of players exchanged messages.

1.1   Certified Email Protocol Properties

The need of specific solutions to the problem of certified email is due to the fact that this class of protocols should satisfy a set of properties that are not usually an issue in "general" fair exchange protocols. We list some of the properties that a certified email protocol should satisfy.

Fairness: The protocol should be fair in the sense that neither Alice nor Bob should be able to obtain an advantage on the other player. In other words, either Bob receives the message and Alice the corresponding receipt or none of them receives useful information.

Non-repudiation of origin: Alice should not be able to deny the fact that she sent the message. This means that Bob, at the end of the protocol, should have enough information to prove the sender's identity.

Non-repudiation of receipt: Bob should not be able to deny the fact that he received the message. Alice should get a receipt for the message that can be used as a proof in a court of law.

Authenticity: The players should be guaranteed of their reciprocal identity.

Integrity: The parties should not be able to corrupt the message and/or its receipt, e.g., Alice should not be able to obtain a receipt for a message different from the one received by Bob and vice versa.

Confidentiality: The protocol should be such that only Alice and Bob will be able to read the content of the message. Notice that this property also holds for the TTP in the sense that he should not be able to infer useful information about the message.

Timeliness: The protocol terminates within a finite and known a priori time.

Temporal Authentication: Some applications, e.g., patent submission, require the possibility to verify the time at which the message was sent. The timestamp should be observable by the players and should be ensured by a trusted authority.

Sending Receipt: Since certified email protocols are interactive protocols that may involve human interaction, it could be desirable that the sender obtains an evidence of the fact that he started the process of sending a certified email. Notice that this receipt may not contain any information generated by the recipient, e.g., it is produced by a third authority.

1.2   Related Work

A number of approaches have been used in order to solve the problem of fair exchange. Early solutions consisted of protocols implementing a gradual exchange of information [6]. The drawback of this approach is that the protocols in this class usually require high communication overhead or round complexity. A second class of protocols uses an on-line third party in order to guarantee the fairness of the exchange[1, 13]. Since the TTP becomes crucial in the protocols' execution, it may also become a bottleneck for the whole system. As pointed out in [1], most of the commercial systems providing a certified email service [10, 11], implement protocols that belong to this class. The idea of optimistic protocols was first introduced in [3]. In this setting efficient fair exchange protocols have been presented in [2, 3, 5].

A hybrid model for certified email has been proposed in [4] starting from the idea of semi-trusted third party introduced in [8]. Among the optimistic protocols we recall three-message protocol presented in [12] specifically designed for certified email. The same protocol has been modified in [4] in order to ensure timeliness.

As far as we know, the only paper that specifically addresses the problem of ensuring temporal authentication is [7][1]. We elaborate along this line of research and we present an improved protocol that reduces the number of messages exchanged by the players.

1.3   Our Contribution

In this paper we present a four-message optimistic protocol that guarantees temporal authentication. Since the protocol uses an on-line trusted Time Stamping Server (TSS for short), the protocol is essentially optimal[2] with respect to message complexity. Notice that, although the TSS is on-line, the protocol is still optimistic since the TTP comes into play only when the players misbehave.

We first start by presenting a modified version of the protocols presented in [12]. This protocol, presented in Section 3 has essentially the same structure of the one presented in [12] but it's messages have been modified in order to guarantee timeliness and message verifiability.

Starting from this protocol, we present the first optimistic protocol for certified email that consists of four-messages that ensures timestamping of the messages. We then obtain an optimistic protocol that ensures all the properties

---

[1] Also [4] uses timestamps within the messages. In this case timestamps are only used to prevent reply attacks and not as a mean of time certification.

[2] Informally, the optimality w.r.t. message complexity follows by the fact that two messages are required in order to send a request to and obtain a feedback form the TSS and two messages are needed to exchange information between sender and receiver.

listed in Section 1.1 and that uses five messages, improving on the previous result presented in [7].

2   Definitions and Notations

We identify four different entities. Through the paper we will refer to Alice as the message sender while the message receiver will be called Bob. The trusted third party will be called either TTP or Ted. The fourth entity is the Time Stamping Server, which we call either TSS or Sam. The TSS is responsible for maintaining the timestamp of the messages during the execution of the protocol. Both Sam and Ted are assumed to be trusted, i.e., they will collude neither with Alice nor with Bob. Furthermore we assume the network connection between any party and either the TTP or the TSS is reliable, i.e., a message will always reach the intended receiver within a finite known a priori time bound, but insecure, i.e., all the users can read and or write on the channel. We make no assumption on the communication channel between the parties Alice and Bob. A message sent from Alice to Bob can be modified, delayed arbitrarily or not delivered at all. This assumption reflects the behaviour of the most email delivery systems that try to deliver an email as soon as the user tries to send it. In case this operation is not successfull, the system queues the email and retries regularly for a fixed number of times.

We assume each player has a pair public key/private key and that the public key is known to all the other players, or, alternatively, can be obtained in an authenticated way by each player. We also assume each player has a pair signing key/verification key (that we do not require to be different from the previous pair). Also in this case, the verification key is known to the other players.

Each message m is associated to the message subject we will denote by m_{subj}.

We will denote by $PK_X(m)$ the encryption of the message m using the public key of the player X, where $X \in \{A(lice), B(ob), T(ed), S(am)\}$. Similarly, we denote by $Sig_X(m)$ the signature of player X on message m. We assume the signature of a player X on a message m is publicly verifiable, i.e., there exists a public verification algorithm that, given as input the message m, the signature $Sig_X(m)$ and the public information, e.g., X's verification key, outputs true if and only if $Sig_X(m)$ was obtained using the signing algorithm with inputs X's signing key and the message m.

It is well known that, in order to consider an encryption scheme secure, the encryption algorithm must be randomized [9]. We will denote by $\overline{PK}_X(m, r)$ the encryption of the message m, obtained by using the public key of the player X and random string r. We assume that the encryption scheme used takes as input the random string that will be used for the encryption. We stress that, once the variables, X, m and r are fixed, the algorithm is deterministic.

We will denote by $m : X \to Y$ the event "player X sends the message m to player Y". Finally, we denote by $\langle x, y \rangle$ the concatenarion of strings x and y and by $h(\cdot)$ a collision resistant one-way hash function.

3   Basic Protocol

The protocol consists of three messages exchanged between Alice and Bob. It is obtained by slightly modifying the protocol presented in [12] in order to guarantee timeliness and message verifiability. The key idea is that Alice uses an electronic envelope to lock the message. She then appends the subject of the message to the envelope and sends this message to Bob. At this point Bob signs the received string and sends the signature back to the Alice. Finally, Alice verifies the received signature and sends the original message to Bob along with some information that allow him to verify the compliance of the message with the information received in the first round of communication.

It is clear that the core of the protocol is the specification of the content of the first message Alice sends to Bob. It must be the case that the "envelope" must be verifiable, i.e., Bob should be able to verify, at the end of the protocol, that the receipt sent to Alice corresponds to the received message. At the same time it must reveal no information about the actual content of the message. Furthermore, it must contain the minimum information required by the TTP for verifying the identities of the sender and recipient of the message. Finally the first message must guarantee the confidentiality of the message with respect to the TTP. Notice that, in case Alice maliciously stops the protocol, the first message is the only information Bob can send to Ted in order to recover the message. Figure 1 formally describes the protocol.

Protocol Cert-E(m_{subj}, m)

1. Alice computes:
   $msg = \langle m_{subj}, m \rangle$
   $env = \langle ID_A, ID_B, PK_B(\langle m_{subj}, h(\langle m, r \rangle) \rangle), \overline{PK}_T(PK_B(msg), r) \rangle$
   $m_1 = \langle env, Sig_A(env) \rangle$
   m_1: Alice $\longrightarrow$ Bob.
2. Bob computes:
   $m_2 = Sig_B(m_1)$
   m_2: Bob $\longrightarrow$ Alice
3. Alice verifies the Bob's signature and computes
   $m_3 = \langle \langle PK_B(msg), r \rangle, Sig_A(\langle PK_B(msg), r \rangle) \rangle$
   m_3: Alice $\longrightarrow$ Bob.

Fig. 1. Basic Protocol

The envelope computed by Alice is basically composed by the players' identities and two parts. The first part contains information that can be read (only) by Bob as soon as he receives the message m_1. This information will be used to verify that the message received corresponds to the one for which the receipt has been sent. The second part of env consists of the actual content of the email encrypted using Ted's public key. This ensures that Bob has no "useful" information about the content of the email in case he stops the protocol after the receipt of the first message.

Bob first verifies Alice's signature contained in m_1 and then signs the hash of the message m_1 and sends the result to Alice. The message m_2 constitutes the message receipt for m.

After the signature verification, Alice sends to Bob the message $\langle m_{subj}, m \rangle$ encrypted using Bob's public key along with the random string r that Alice used to encrypt the same information using Ted's public key. At this point Bob can verify that the receipt sent to Alice corresponds to the received message. Bob extracts m_{subj} and m from m_3 and verifies that (a) m_{subj} received in the first message matches the one received in m_3; (b) the hash of $\langle m, r \rangle$ received in m_3 corresponds to the one received in m_1 and (c) the second part of env is the encryption of $PK_B(\langle m_{subj}, m \rangle)$ using Ted's public key with random string r.

It is clear that, if Alice and Bob behave correctly, at the end of the protocol Bob will receive the message m and Alice will receive the corresponding receipt.

3.1   Recovery Procedures

Recovery procedures are started by one of the players either when the other player misbehaves, i.e., by sending a message containing wrong information, or by not sending any message at all. Notice that the second case can be seen like a misbehaviour of one of the players but we need to specifically take it into account in order to ensure timeliness. In case the player P misbehaves on the message m_i, we say the P failed on m_i.

Alice's Failures. It is reasonable to assume that Alice never fails on m_1 in the sense that she never sends a "random string" to Bob. Although this assumption seems to be strong, it is justified by the fact that Bob can detect such behaviour immediately, when extracting m_{subj}, or as soon as he receives m_3.

Let us assume that Alice does not maliciously fail on m_1. In case Alice fails on message m_3, Bob will send to Ted the messages m_1 and m_2. Ted verifies (a) the identities of the sender and recipient of the message, (b) Alice's signature on env and (c) Bob's signature m_2 on m_1, computes $enc = PK_B(\langle m_{subj}, m \rangle)$ from m_1 and sends send enc to Bob and m_2 to Alice.

Alice could maliciously constructs m_1 and m_3 in a way that the information contained in m_1 and m_3 do not match, but she will fail on m_3 since Bob verifies both the value of $h(\langle m, r \rangle)$ and the correct encryption in the second part of env. In this case Bob can obtain the message for which he issued a receipt by contacting the TTP. Furthermore, since messages m_1 and m_3 are signed by Alice, he also has a proof of Alice's misbehaviour. We stress that in any case Bob will receive the message for which he issued a receipt.

Bob's Failures. Bob can only fail on message m_2. In this case Alice will send the message m_1 to Ted that will forward it to Bob. If Bob fails to reply, Ted sends to Alice a special message $rej = \langle \langle REJ, m_1 \rangle, Sig_T(\langle REJ, m_1 \rangle) \rangle$.

In case Bob properly replies with m_2, Ted forwards m_2 to Alice. Notice that this case can happen if Bob undergoes a temporary fault. From this point on, the protocol proceeds normally, i.e., Alice will send m_3 to Bob.

3.2   Protocol Analysis

In this section we will discuss the properties of the presented protocol. In particular, Cert-E ensures all the properties listed in Section 1.1 but the sending receipt and the time authentication.

We first notice that the protocol is optimistic since, in the case in which the players follow the protocol, the TTP does not come into play.

The protocol fairness is ensured since, whichever is the players' behaviour, either they both receive the correct information or they do not receive any "useful" information. Notice that, since Ted is trusted, he will never reveal to Bob any information if he does not provide a receipt for the message m_1. On the other hand, when Bob sends the receipt to Alice, he already holds an encrypted version of the message that can be decrypted by the TTP in case Alice misbehaves. Similarly, Alice cannot claim Bob's failure but she needs to involve Ted in the protocol's execution.

The first message sent by Alice to Bob contains all the information needed by Bob to identify the message "content" and the sender's information. Since the message is signed by Alice, Bob can verify her signature. This will ensure the non-repudiation of origin. Similarly, Bob's signature of message m_1 and the assumption that the TTP is always available and trusted ensures the non-repudiation of receipt.

The authenticity of the messages is ensured by the assumption that each player obtained an authenticated copy of the public key of each other entity in the system.

The protocol's integrity from Alice point of view is based on the security of the signing algorithm used by Bob. From Bob's point of view, the integrity of the protocol is guaranteed by Alice's impossibility to find a collision for the value $h(\langle m, r \rangle)$ sent in message m_1.

It is clear that the confidentiality of the message m with respect to the TTP and to players that have a read access to the (insecure) communication channel is guaranteed by the fact that all the messages are encrypted using Bob's public key.

To ensure timeliness we allow the players to execute recovery procedures in case of timeouts. In particular, let π the time needed by each player to process a message and λ be an upper bound on the time needed by a message to reach the TSS/TTP. We consider a message sent by Alice (resp. Bob), to Bob (resp. Alice) to be lost after λ time units.

Given these bounds, it is hard to see that the protocol terminates after at most $4\pi + 10\lambda$ time units, by properly setting timeouts.

4   Ensuring Timestamping and Sending Receipt

In this section we will present two extensions of the basic protocol presented in the previous section. The first extension allows the users to obtain a time certification of the message. The protocol presented consists of four messages exchanged among the players Alice, Bob and Sam. We further modify the protocol in order to provide the sender with the sending receipt.

As stated in Section 1.2, as far as we know, the only paper that specifically addresses the property of temporal authentication is [7]. The protocol proceeds as follows. Alice requires to the TSS a timestamp for a message m. The TSS sends to Alice the required information. This constitutes the only involvement of the TSS in the protocol, i.e, the TSS does not communicate with Bob at all. After the receipt of the timestamp Alice exchanges messages with Bob with the first message containing the timestamping sent by the TSS to Alice. The problem with this protocol is that Alice could maliciously delay sending the first message to Bob so to make either the message useless or forcing Bob to reject the message. Notice that, from a theoretical point of view, this is not an issue since either Alice sends the messages within the known a priori time bounds or she cannot claim a valid receipt. On the other hand, from a practical point of view, a wrong setup of the parameters could make possible the attack described above for the "urgent" messages.

Consider for example the case in which Alice has to send to Bob the message "You should come here before January 1st or I will get your money". It is clear that Alice can obtain a timestamp for this message before January 1st and send the message after this date. If Bob accepts the message, Alice will get a receipt for the message timestamped before, January 1st but the message is useless for Bob. Furthermore, Bob cannot prove to have received the message after the date contained in the timestamp while Alice can prove that she sent the message at the proper time. We stress that this case can arise in the case in which the user interaction is required, or, in other words, when a user has to wait a long time before invoking a recovery procedure because of a timeout.

Ensuring TimeStamping. The key idea to overcome the problem above is to allow Sam to communicate with Bob. Since Sam has to send a message, namely the timestamp associated to m, we do not add any overhead if we ask Sam to send a message to Bob instead of sending back the timestamp to Alice.

Informally, the protocol is the following: Alice sends the message m_1 to Sam. The TSS computes the timestamp $t(m_1)$ associated to the received message, signs the pair $\langle m_1, t(m_1) \rangle$ and sends the message $m_2 = \langle \langle m_1, t(m_1) \rangle, Sig_S(\langle m_1, t(m_1) \rangle) \rangle$ to Bob. This message has essentially the same information of message m_1 in Cert-E along with the timestamp. From this point on, the protocol continues as Cert-E. In this case, Alice cannot delay the delivery of the first message to Bob. This ensures that the timestamp contained in the messages exchanged by the user is the actual time at which Alice started the process. On the other hand, Bob could try to delay the sending the receipt to Alice of at most π time units, but this does not affect the validity of the receipt received by Alice. A more detailed description of this protocol is reported in Figure 2.

Notice that we need to modify the recovery procedure in case of Bob's failure since Alice should, in this case, obtain a receipt that contains the temporal authentication. In case Bob fails to contact Alice, she will ask the TSS to recover the timestamp for the message m_1. Sam will recover $t(m_1)$ from his database,

Protocol Time-Cert-E(m_{subj}, m)

1. Alice computes:
   $msg = \langle m_{subj}, m \rangle$
   $env = \langle ID_A, ID_B, PK_B(\langle m_{subj}, h(\langle m, r \rangle) \rangle), \overline{PK}_T(PK_B(msg), r) \rangle$
   $m_1 = (env, Sig_A(env))$
   m_1: Alice $\longrightarrow$ Sam.
2. Sam computes:
   Timestamp $t(m_1)$ associated to m_1
   $m_2 = \langle \langle m_1, t(m_1) \rangle, Sig_S(\langle m_1, t(m_1) \rangle) \rangle$
   m_2: Sam $\rightarrow$ Bob
3. Bob computes:
   $m_3 = \langle m_2, Sig_B(m_2) \rangle$
   m_3: Bob $\longrightarrow$ Alice
4. Alice verifies the Bob's signature and computes
   $m_4 = \langle \langle PK_B(msg), r \rangle, Sig_A(\langle PK_B(msg), r \rangle \rangle$
   m_4: Alice $\longrightarrow$ Bob.

Fig. 2. Certified E-Mail with Timestamping

construct the message, $m_s = \langle m_1, t(m_1) \rangle$ and he will send to Ted $\langle m_s, t(m_s) \rangle$, i.e., by adding a new timestamp to the message. Ted verifies that the distance between $t(m_1)$ and $t(m_s)$ is no greater than $5\lambda + 3\pi - 1$ [3]. In this case he starts the recovery procedure described in the previous section. If Bob fails to reply, Ted sends to Alice a special message $rej = \langle \langle REJ, m_t \rangle, Sig_T(\langle REJ, m_t \rangle) \rangle$. In case Bob properly replies with m_3, Ted forwards m_3 to Alice that will send m_4 to Bob. By using the same arguments discussed above, it is not hard to see that the protocol Time-Cert-E satisfies all the properties that Cert-E meets. Let us analyze the temporal authentication property. Since the TSS is trusted and reliable, Alice's first message will be properly timestamped and (timely) delivered to Bob. On the other hand, if Bob fails on message m_3, Alice will contact Ted to resolve the dispute.

Obtaining Sending Receipt. As described in Section 1.1, the sending receipt constitutes an evidence that the sender of the message started the process of sending a certified email. In the case in which the values of λ and π, i.e., the time a message needs to travel along the network and the time needed by a player to process a message respectively, are small, the sender's receipt seems to be useless. In the real world there are some cases in which such a receipt is particularly important. As an example we can consider the case in which the user herself has to accept the incoming message, possibly after reading the subject. In this case, to ensure timeliness, the value of π should be large enough, e.g., three days, to guarantee the user is able to read the email and accept or reject the message.

---

[3] This valus is computed as follows: Alice times out after $3\lambda + 2\pi$ time units; after this amount of time she contacts the TSS (λ) that will generate the message to send to Ted in π time units; finally the message reaches Ted after, at most λ time units.

In order to obtain a sender's receipt it is sufficient that the TSS sends a copy of the message m_2 to Alice too. Since the TSS is trusted, this will indeed constitute a proof that Alice started the protocol. Notice that, m_2 by itself does not constitute a proof that Bob failed since such a proof is only provided by Ted.

Acknowledgements

The authors want to thank Carlo Blundo and Pino Persiano for helpful discussion and comments on an early version of this paper and the anonymous referees for helpful comments on the presentation of the paper.

References

1. M. Abadi, N. Glew, B. Horne, and B. Pinkas, "Certified Email with a Light On-Line Trusted Third Party: Design and Implementation" Proceedings of the Eleventh International World Wide Web Conference (May 2002), 387-395.
2. N. Asokan, Matthias Schunter, Michael Waidner, "Optimistic Protocols for Fair Exchange" Proc. of 4th ACM Conference on Computer and Communications Security, pp. 7-17, 1997.
3. N. Asokan, Victor Shoup, Michael Waidner, "Asynchronous Protocols for Optimistic Fair Exchange" Proceedings of the IEEE Symposium on Research in Security and Privacy pp. 86–99, 1998.
4. G. Ateniese, B. de Medeiros and M. T. Goodrich, "TRICERT: Distributed Certified E-mail Schemes", ISOC 2001 Network and Distributed System Security Symposium (NDSS'01).
5. F. Bao, R.H. Deng, W. Mao. "Efficient and Practical Fair Exchange with Off-line TTP", Proceedings of the IEEE Symposium on Research in Security and Privacy, 1998.
6. M. Ben-Or, O. Goldreich, S. Micali and R.L. Rivest, "A fair protocol for signing contracts", IEEE Transactions on Information Theory, 36(1):40–46, January 1990.
7. C. Blundo, S. Cimato, R. De Prisco, "Certified Email: Design and Implementation of a New Optimistic Protocol", in Proceedings of 8th IEEE Symposium on Computers and Communications (ISCC 03), pp 828-833.
8. M. Franklin and M. Reiter, "Fair exchange with a semi-trusted third party", in Proc. ACM Conference on Computer and Communication Security, 1997.
9. S. Goldwasser and S. Micali, "Probabilistic Encryption," Journal of Computer and System Sciences vol. 28(2), pp. 270-299, 1984.
10. http://certifiedmail.com/
11. http://izymail.com/
12. S. Micali, "Certified e-mail with invisible post offices", Invited presentation at RSA '97 conference.
13. J. Zhou and D. Gollmann, "Certified electronic mail". Proceedings Computer Security–ESORICS'96, pages 160-171. Springer-Verlag, 1996.

Efficient Password-Based Group Key Exchange

Su Mi Lee*, Jung Yeon Hwang, and Dong Hoon Lee

Center for Information Security Technologies(CIST)
Korea University, 1, 5-Ka, Anam-dong, Sungbuk-ku, Seoul, 136-701, Korea
{smlee,videmot}@cist.korea.ac.kr, donghlee@korea.ac.kr

Abstract. Password-based authenticated group key exchange (denoted by PGKE) provides n parties holding a common human-memorable password with secure group communication. Most PGKE protocols proposed so far are inefficient since they require $O(n)$ communication rounds where n is the number of group members. In the paper, we propose the first 2-round PGKE protocol with 3-exponentiations required per user and prove its security in the random oracle model and the ideal cipher model under the intractability of the decision Diffie-Hellman problem and computation Diffie-Hellman problem. The proposed protocol also provides forward secrecy.

1 Introduction

To communicate securely over an insecure public network, it is essential that secret keys (session keys) are exchanged securely. A group key exchange protocol allows users of a group to agree on a session key while achieving implicit authentication which simply ensures secrecy of session keys against an adversary passively eavesdropping on the protocol executions and also sending messages of its choice to the various parties. Recently, secure and efficient group key exchange protocols have received much attention with increasing applicability in various collaborative and distributive group settings such as multicast communication, audio-video conference, multiplayer game, etc.

Password-based group key exchange (PGKE) protocols are designed to provide parties communicating over an insecure channel and sharing only a human-memorable password with a session key, which maybe subsequently be used to achieve several cryptographic goals such as confidentiality or integrity. However, a password is a string such as a natural language phrase that people recognize easily and is derived from a relatively small space. This makes a password-based protocol susceptible to dictionary attacks where an adversary records the traffic and tries candidate passwords until the correct one is found. Therefore, it is important to make the protocol derive a strong shared group key from a weak shared password.

---

* This work was supported by grant No. $R01 - 2001 - 000 - 00537 - 0$ from the Korea Science & Engineering Foundation.

S. Katsikas, J. Lopez, and G. Pernul (Eds.): TrustBus 2004, LNCS 3184, pp. 191–199, 2004.

1.1   Related Works and Our Contributions

Related W ork. Since a password-based 2-party KE protocol has been suggested by Bellovin and Merritt [6], many related works have been studied to share a key between two parties without PKI. Specially, Bellare et al. [3] have suggested a formal model for password-based 2-party KE and proved the security of the proposed protocol in the ideal cipher model. Boyko, et al. [8] have also suggested a password-based 2-party KE protocol and proved its security in the random oracle model using multi-party simulatability technique. Katz, et al. [13] and Goldreich and Lindell [12] have suggested 2-party KE protocols and proved security in the standard model.

To share a group key when a group shares a password, in [1], Asokan et al. proposed a group key exchange protocol with forward secrecy based on the group key exchange protocol of Becker and Wille [2]. Their protocol requires $O(n)$ rounds and $O(n)$ exponentiations per user, where n is the number of participants. The security proof of the protocol was not provided. Bresson et al. [10] have suggested the first provably-secure password based group Diffie-Hellman key exchange with forward secrecy and proved its security in the random oracle model and the ideal cipher model. However the proposed protocol requires a linear number of communication rounds.

Our Contributions. In addition to provable security, the recent researches in PGKE have concentrated on the efficiency which is related to the costs of communication and computation. Especially the number of rounds may be of critical concern in practical environment where the number of group members are quite large and a group is dynamic. As noted in [9], even in the case of a group where only few members have a slow network connection, the efficiency of the protocol with n rounds for a group of n members can be severely degraded. Furthermore, it is clear that a scheme with n rounds is not scalable. In the paper, we propose a 2-round PGKE protocol, to which the group key exchange protocol in [15] is extended. We first provide a formal proof of the protocol in [15]. No proof of security for the scheme has previously appeared. We then provide the proof of the proposed PGKE protocol under the computational Diffie-Hellman assumption and the decision Diffie-Hellman assumption. The protocol requires only 3-exponentiations per group member. Furthermore, the protocol provides forward secrecy in the sense that the exposure of a password does not compromise the security of previous group session key. In Sectoin 2, we provide cryptographic assumptions to be used to prove the security of the proposed scheme. Section 3 defines a security model in which the proposed scheme is proved. Section 4 reviews Lee et al.'s group key exchange (GKE) protocol in [15] on which our PGKE is based and prove the security under the decisional DH assumption. We then present a scalable PGKE protocol and prove the security of the proposed PGKE protocol in Section 5.

2   Assumptions

We will prove the security of our scheme under the computational Diffie-Hellman assumption and the decision Diffie-Hellman assumption.

Decisional Diffie-Hellman (DDH) Assumption. The DDH problem is defined as follows: Given a group G, a generator g of G, and two elements g^a and $g^b \in G$, where a and b are unknown, distinguish g^{ab} from a random value. An algorithm $\mathcal{A}$ running in time t is said to solve the DDH problem with the an advantage $\mathsf{Adv}_G^{\mathsf{DDH}}(t)$ of ϵ if:

$$|\Pr[a, b \leftarrow \mathbb{Z}_q : \mathcal{A}(g, g^a, g^b, g^{ab}) = 1]$$
$$- \Pr[a, b, r \leftarrow \mathbb{Z}_q : \mathcal{A}(g, g^a, g^b, g^r) = 1]| \geq \epsilon.$$

We say the DDH assumption holds in G if no probabilistic polynomial time (*ppt*) algorithm $\mathcal{A}$ can solve the DDH problem with non-negligible advantage.

Computation Diffie-Hellman (CDH) Assumption. The CDH problem is defined as follows: Given a group G, a generator g of G, and two elements g^a and $g^b \in G$, where a and b are unknown, compute g^{ab}. An algorithm $\mathcal{A}$ running in time t is said to solve the CDH problem with the an advantage $\mathsf{Adv}_G^{\mathsf{CDH}}(t)$ of ϵ if:

$$|\Pr[a, b \leftarrow \mathbb{Z}_q : \mathcal{A}(g, g^a, g^b) = g^{ab}]| \geq \epsilon.$$

We say the CDH assumption holds in G if no *ppt* algorithm $\mathcal{A}$ can solve the CDH problem with non-negligible advantage.

3   The Model

We assume that members of the group are honest and adversaries are not in the group. Our model described in this section is based on that of Bresson et al. [11] which follows the model by Bellare and Rogaway [4, 5].

3.1   Security Model

Participants and Initialization. We assume for simplicity a fixed non-empty set of users $\mathcal{U} = \{U_1, \ldots, U_n\}$, where the number of users is polynomial in the security parameter. We also assume that all users share a common password pw obtained at the start of the protocol using a password generation algorithm $\mathcal{PG}(1^k)$ which outputs pw uniformly distributed from a finite set on input a security parameter 1^k. In the model we allow each user U_i to execute the protocol many times with different users.

Adversarial Model. The adversary $\mathcal{A}$ is a probabilistic polynomial time machine that controls all communications and can make queries to any instance. An oracle Π_i^s denotes the s-th instance of a group key exchange protocol of U_i. The list of queries that $\mathcal{A}$ can make is as follows:

- Execute($\mathcal{U}$): This query models passive attacks. $\mathcal{A}$ gets back the protocol flows of an honest execution between the participants in $\mathcal{U}$.
- Send($\Pi_i^s, \mathcal{M}$): This query allows the adversary to make the principal U_i run the protocol normally. This sends message $\mathcal{M}$ to Π_i^s and returns the reply generated by Π_i^s.

· Reveal(Π_i^s): This query is to model the adversary's ability to find a group key. If a group key $\mathcal{SK}_{\Pi_i^s}$ has previously been accepted by Π_i^s then it is returned to the adversary.
· Corrupt(U_i): This query is to model the attacks revealing the long-term secret pw. This outputs the secret password pw but does not outputs any internal data of U_i.
· Test(Π_i^s): This query models the semantic security of a group key. This query is allowed only once by the adversary $\mathcal{A}$, and is only available to $\mathcal{A}$ if Π_i^s is *fresh*. A random bit b is chosen; if $b = 1$, then the group key is returned to $\mathcal{A}$ while if $b = 0$, then a random string is returned from the same distribution as the group key.

In our model we consider two types of adversaries. A passive adversary is given access to Execute, Reveal, Corrupt, and Test oracles, while an active adversary is additionally given access to Send oracle. Execute oracle can be simulated by calling to Send oracle repeatedly. But Execute oracle is essential to distinguish on-line dictionary attacks from off-line dictionary attacks.

3.2   Security Notions

Partnering. Let sid_i^s be the concatenation of all (broadcast) messages that oracle Π_i^s has sent and received. The messages can be ordered according to the sender's identity. Let partner ID pid_i^s for Π_i^s be the identities of the participants in the group with which Π_i^s intends to establish a group key, including U_i itself. We say Π_i^s and Π_j^s are partnered if $pid_i^s = pid_j^s$ and $sid_i^s = sid_j^s$.

Freshness. We say an oracle Π_i^s is fresh (or hold a fresh key $\mathcal{SK}$) if:

- Π_i^s has accepted a group key $\mathcal{SK} \neq$ NULL and neither Π_i^s nor its partners have been asked for Reveal query, and
- No Corrupt query has been asked before a query of the form Send($\Pi_i^s, *$).

Definition of Security. We define the security of the protocol by the following game between the adversary and an infinite set of oracles Π_i^s for $U_i \in \mathcal{U}$ and $s \in \mathbb{N}$

1. In the initialization phase, run password generation algorithm $\mathcal{PG}(1^k)$ to set the value pw of the password.
2. Initialize any oracle Π_i^s with $\mathcal{SK}$=NULL.
3. Run adversary $\mathcal{A}$ and answer queries made by $\mathcal{A}$.
4. At some stage during the execution Test query is performed by the adversary to a *fresh* oracle. The adversary may continue to make other queries and eventually outputs its guess b' for the bit b involved in Test query and terminates.

The advantage of the adversary $\mathcal{A}$ in this game is measured by the ability of the adversary that distinguishes a group key from a random string. We define Guess to be the event that $\mathcal{A}$ correctly guesses the bit b used by Test oracle in answering this query. The advantage of an adversary $\mathcal{A}$ attacking a protocol $\mathcal{P}$ is defined as $Adv_{\mathcal{P},\mathcal{A}}(k) = |2 \cdot Pr[Guess] - 1|$. We say a protocol $\mathcal{P}$ is a *secure* PGKE scheme if the following two properties are satisfied:

- Correctness: In the presence of an active adversary partner oracles accept the same key.
- Indistinguishability: For every *ppt* active adversary $\mathcal{A}$, $Adv_{\mathcal{P},\mathcal{A}}^{PGKE}(k)$ is negligible.

Forward Secrecy. Forward secrecy is modeled by Corrupt query which allows an adversary to learn the value of long term keys. Forward secrecy means that an adversary does not learn any information about previously established group key when a long term key is compromised. We denote PGKE-fs advantage by $Adv_{\mathcal{P}}^{PGKE-fs}(t, q_{ex}, q_s)$ to be the maximal advantage of any active adversary attacking forward secure PGKE protocol $\mathcal{P}$, running in time t and making q_{ex} calls to Execute oracle and q_s calls to Send oracle.

Authentication. In this paper, we focus on an authenticated group key exchange with implicit authentication; A key exchange protocol is said to provide implicit key authentication if participants are assured that no other users except partners can possibly learn the value of a particular secret key [7].

4   Lee et al.'s Group Key Exchange Protocol

Before we construct a scalable password-based group key exchange protocol in Section 5 we recall a group key exchange protocol proposed by Lee et al. [15]. No proof of security for the protocol has previously appeared. In this part, we briefly review Lee et al.'s protocol for the static membership and prove the security under the DDH assumption.

We assume that $\{U_1,...,U_n\}$ are n parties who wish to share a group key. Indices are subjects to module n, i.e. if $i=j \bmod n$ then $U_i=U_j$. ID_i denotes U_i's identity and the identities are arranged in the lexicograhic order and the parties can know the identity of the sender of the broadcasted message. In the following description the arithmetic is in a finite cyclic group $G=<g>$ of order q, where g is a generator of G and q is a prime number, and $\mathcal{H} : \{0,1\}^* \rightarrow \{0,1\}^k$ and $h : \{0,1\}^* \rightarrow \{0,1\}^l$ are public collision-resistant hash functions. To enable a concrete security analysis, we define $Adv_{\mathcal{P}}^{GKE-fs}(t,1)$ to be the maximum advantage of any passive adversary attacking GKE protocol $\mathcal{P}$, running in time t and making single Execute query.

[Lee et al.'s GKE Protocol]

1. Each U_i selects a random number $x_i \in_R \mathbb{Z}_q^*$ and sends $ID_i||g^{x_i}$ to U_{i-1} and U_{i+1}.
2. Upon receiving the message $ID_{i-1}||g^{x_{i-1}}$ and $ID_{i+1}||g^{x_{i+1}}$ from the neighbor parties U_{i-1} and U_{i+1}, U_i broadcasts a message $w_i=h(g^{x_{i-1}x_i}) \oplus h(g^{x_i x_{i+1}})$.
3. Each user U_i computes $h(g^{x_{j-1}x_j})$ $(1 \le j \le n)$ sequentially and $\mathcal{SK}$ as follows:

$$h(g^{x_{j-1}x_j})=w_j \oplus h(g^{x_j x_{j+1}}) =h(g^{x_{j-1}x_j}) \oplus h(g^{x_j x_{j+1}}) \oplus h(g^{x_j x_{j+1}}),$$
$$\mathcal{SK} = \mathcal{H}(h(g^{x_1 x_2})||\cdots||h(g^{x_{n-1}x_n})||h(g^{x_n x_1}))$$

Theorem 1. Lee et al.'s protocol is a secure GKE one achieving forward secrecy under the DDH assumption for G. Namely,

$$Adv_{\mathcal{P}}^{GKA-fs}(t,1) \leq 2|U|Adv_G^{DDH}(t).$$

We can prove $Theorem1$ in two steps. First we show that the computational distance between the real transcript of $\mathcal{P}$ and the randomized transcript of the real one is negligible. Second, in randomized transcript, we show that the variables related to the shared value in the first round are independent of the randomized transcript. The security analysis is similar to that Katz et al.[14]. For space limitation we omit the proof. The proof of $Theorem1$ will appear in the full version.

5   Our Password-Based Group Key Exchange Protocol

In this section we present a scalable password-based authenticated group key exchange protocol based on Lee et al.'s GKE protocol. We denote this protocol by $\mathcal{P}'$ for convenience. Our protocol $\mathcal{P}'$ uses a cipher $\mathcal{E} \colon \Gamma \times G \longrightarrow C$, where Γ is a password set of size N. In the security analysis the cipher is considered as an ideal cipher. Many concrete constructions to instantiate such an ideal cipher are presented [3].

We assume that all users secretly share a common password pw uniformly chosen from a password set Γ in advance. All users $U_1,...,U_n$ are arranged in a lexicographic order. To share a group session key, the legitimate users execute the following steps.

1. Each user U_i selects a random number $x_i \in_R \mathbb{Z}_q^*$ and sends a message $ID_i||$ $\mathcal{E}_{pw}(g^{x_i})$ to all group users participating in the execution of the protocol.
2. Upon receiving $ID_j|| \mathcal{E}_{pw}(g^{x_j})$, each user U_i computes $w_i = h(g^{x_{i-1}x_i}) \oplus h(g^{x_i x_{i+1}})$ and broadcasts a message $ID_i||w_i$.
3. Upon receiving $ID_j||w_j$ $(i \neq j)$, each user U_i computes $h(g^{x_{j-1}x_j})$ $(1 \leq j \leq n)$ sequentially and a group session key $\mathcal{SK}$ as follows:

$$h(g^{x_{j-1}x_j}) = w_j \oplus h(g^{x_j x_{j+1}}) = h(g^{x_{j-1}x_j}) \oplus h(g^{x_j x_{j+1}}) \oplus h(g^{x_j x_{j+1}}),$$
$$\mathcal{SK} = \mathcal{H}(h(g^{x_1 x_2})|| \cdots ||h(g^{x_{n-1}x_n})||h(g^{x_n x_1})).$$

The following theorem is proved under the assumption that an adversary $\mathcal{A}$ uses only one Execute query. The proof under an adversary asking several Execute queries will appear in the full version.

Theorem 2. The protocol $\mathcal{P}'$ is a secure password-based authenticated group key exchange protocol achieving forward secrecy under the DDH and CDH assumptions for G. That is,

$$Adv_{\mathcal{P}'}^{PGKE-fs}(t,q_{ex},q_s) \leq q_T \cdot Adv_{\mathcal{P}}^{GKE-fs}(t,1) + \frac{n \cdot q_h}{2} Adv_G^{CDH}(t)$$

$$\Leftrightarrow Adv_{\mathcal{P}'}^{PGKE-fs}(t,q_{ex},q_s) \leq 2q_T n \cdot Adv_G^{DDH}(t) + \frac{n \cdot q_h}{2} Adv_G^{CDH}(t)$$

where $q_T = q_{ex} + q_s$ denotes the total number of Execute and Send queries and q_h denotes the number of Hash query made by $\mathcal{A}'$.

Proof. Let $\mathcal{A}'$ be an active adversary attacking the protocol $\mathcal{P}'$. To consider forward secrecy, $\mathcal{A}'$ is allowed to issue a Corrupt query to obtain a long-term key pw. $\mathcal{A}'$ can get an advantage by attacking the authentication part, i.e. finding the password, or the protocol itself without finding the password. In this proof we construct a passive adversary $\mathcal{A}$ attacking protocol $\mathcal{P}$ using the active adversary $\mathcal{A}'$.

Initial Setup. The adversary $\mathcal{A}$ chooses pw and a guess $\alpha \in [1, q_T]$ such that the α-th Send/Excute query of $\mathcal{A}'$ activates the instance to which $\mathcal{A}'$ will ask its Test query. $\mathcal{A}$ simulates the oracle queries of $\mathcal{A}'$ as described below.

Execute Queries. If Execute queries is not the α-th Send/Execute query of $\mathcal{A}'$ then $\mathcal{A}$ simply generates a transcript of an execution of $\mathcal{P}'$ and returns this to $\mathcal{A}'$. If an Execute query is the α-th Send/Execute query of $\mathcal{A}'$ then $\mathcal{A}$ requests the same query (Execute($U_1, \cdots, U_n$)) to its own Execute Oracle and receives a transcript T of an execution of $\mathcal{P}$. Next $\mathcal{A}$ executes a transcript of an execution of $\mathcal{P}'$ using a password pw.

Send Queries. For Π_U^s, we define $\mathcal{U}_U^s = U\|U_1\|\cdots\|U_n$. If Send query (Send($\Pi_U^s, *$)) is not the α-th Send/Execute query of $\mathcal{A}'$, then $\mathcal{A}$ looks in Q_{list} for an entry of the form $(\mathcal{U}_U^s, c)$. We consider two cases:

- If such an entry exists and $c = 1$ then $\mathcal{A}$ has already queried its Execute oracle and received a transcript T of an execution of $\mathcal{P}$ from Execute Oracle. In this case, $\mathcal{A}$ finds the suitable message $(U\|w)$ in T. If this query is for the second flow of $\mathcal{P}'$, then $\mathcal{A}$ just gives $(U\|w)$ to $\mathcal{A}'$. But, if this query is for the first flow of $\mathcal{P}'$, then $\mathcal{A}$ computes $(U\|\mathcal{E}_{pw}(w))$ and returns it to $\mathcal{A}'$. $\mathcal{A}$ can do this computation since pw was chosen by itself.
- If no such entry exists, $\mathcal{A}$ adds $(\mathcal{U}_U^s, 0)$ to Q_{list}. In this case or if the entry exists and $c = 0$, then $\mathcal{A}$ simulates the corresponding actions of this instance. The returned value can be computed as in the other case.

If a Send Query is the α-th Send/Execute query of $\mathcal{A}'$, then $\mathcal{A}$ proceeds as follows:

- If a Corrupt query has been previously asked by $\mathcal{A}'$, then $\mathcal{A}$ aborts since the guess α of $\mathcal{A}$ is incorrect and the correspond instance is not fresh.
- If an instance (Π_U^s) is fresh, then $\mathcal{A}$ looks in Q_{list} for an entry the form $(\mathcal{U}_U^s, c)$. If such an entry does not exist, $\mathcal{A}$ adds $(\mathcal{U}_U^s, 1)$ in Q_{list}. Then $\mathcal{A}$ queries Execute($\mathcal{U}_U^s$) to obtain a transcript T and finds the appropriate message $(U\|w)$ in T. If this query is for the second flow of $\mathcal{P}'$, then $\mathcal{A}$ just gives $(U\|w)$ to $\mathcal{A}'$. But, if this query is for the first flow of $\mathcal{P}'$, then $\mathcal{A}$ computes $(U\|\mathcal{E}_{pw}(w))$ and returns it to $\mathcal{A}'$. $\mathcal{A}$ can do this computation since pw was chosen by itself.

Corrupt Queries. When $\mathcal{A}'$ requests Corrupt(U), $\mathcal{A}$ returns a password pw.

Reveal Queries. When $\mathcal{A}'$ queries Reveal(Π_U^s) for the terminated instance $\mathcal{U}_U^s$ which must exist in Q_{list}, $\mathcal{A}$ finds the entry $(\mathcal{U}_U^s, c)$ in Q_{list}. If $c = 1$ then $\mathcal{A}$

aborts since a guess α is incorrect. Otherwise, $\mathcal{A}$ simulates this instance itself and computes the suitable group key $\mathcal{SK}$ of the session. $\mathcal{A}$ returns $\mathcal{SK}$ to $\mathcal{A}'$.

Test Queries. When $\mathcal{A}'$ queries $\mathsf{Test}(\Pi_U^s)$ for the terminated instance $\mathcal{U}_U^s$ which must exist in Q_{list}, $\mathcal{A}$ finds the entry $(\mathcal{U}_U^s, c)$ in Q_{list}. If $c = 1$ then $\mathcal{A}$ asks its Test query to its Test Oracle and forwards the resulting answer to $\mathcal{A}'$. Otherwise, the guess α is incorrect and hence aborts.

Let Good denote the event that $\mathcal{A}$ guesses correctly α and $Succ_{pw}$ denote the event that $\mathcal{A}'$ succeeds in the dictionary attack. If Good and $\overline{Succ_{pw}}$ occur, then the above simulation succeeds.

$$
\begin{aligned}
|2Pr_A[Guess] - 1| &= |2Pr_{A'}[Guess \wedge Good \wedge \neg Succ_{pw}] + 2Pr_{A'}[\neg Good \vee Succ_{pw}] - 1| \\
&= |\frac{2}{q_T} \cdot Pr_{A'}[Guess \wedge \neg Succ_{pw}] + 2Pr_{A'}[Succ_{pw}] \\
&\qquad\qquad + 2Pr_{A'}[\neg Good|\neg Succ_{pw}]Pr_{A'}[\neg Succ_{pw}] - 1| \\
&\geq |\frac{2}{q_T} \cdot Pr_{A'}[Guess] - \frac{2}{q_T} \cdot Pr_{A'}[Guess \wedge Succ_{pw}] \\
&\qquad\qquad + Pr_{A'}[Succ_{pw}] + \frac{q_T - 1}{q_T}(1 - Pr_{A'}[Succ_{pw}]) - 1| \\
&\geq \frac{1}{q_T}|2Pr_{A'}[Guess] - 1| - \frac{1}{q_T}|2Pr_{A'}[Guess \wedge Succ_{pw}] - Pr_{A'}[Succ_{pw}]| \\
&= \frac{1}{q_T}|2Pr_{A'}[Guess] - 1| - \frac{1}{q_T}|Pr_{A'}[Succ_{pw}]|
\end{aligned}
$$

By proving the following claim, we can obtains the results in the theorem.

Claim. Let the hash function h be a random oracle. Let q_h and q_s be the number of *Hash* queries and *Send* queries, respectively. Let $\mathcal{A}'$ be an adversary mounting dictionary attacks and let an advantage of the $\mathcal{A}'$ be Π. Then there exists an adversary $\mathcal{B}$ that can solve the CDH problem. This implies that $\Pi \leq \frac{n \cdot q_h}{2} Adv_G^{CDH}(t)$.

For space limitation we omit the proof. The proof of *Claim* will appear in the full version.

References

1. N. Asokan and P. Ginzboorg. *Key Agreement in Ad-hoc Networks*, In Proc. of the Journal of Computer Communications, 23(17):pages 1627-1637, 2000.
2. K. Becker and U.Wille. *Communication Complexity of Group Key Distribution*, In Proc. of the 5th ACM confernce on Computer and Communications Security, pages 1-6, 1998.
3. M. Bellare, D. Pointcheval, and P. Rogaway. *Authenticated key exchange secure against dictionary attacks*, In Proc. of Eurocrypt '00, LNCS 1807, pages 139-155. Springer-Verlag, 2000.
4. M. Bellare and P. Rogaway. *Entity authentication and key distribution*, In Proc. of Crypto '93, LNCS 773, pages 232-249, Springer-Verlag, 1993.
5. M. Bellare and P. Rogaway. *Provably secure session key distribution-the three party case*, In Proc. of the 27th ACM Symposium on the Theory of Computing, 1995.
6. S. Bellovin and M.Merritt. *Encrypted Key Exchange: Password-Based Protocols Secure against Dictionary Attacks*, In Proc. of the Symposium on Security and Privacy, pages 72-84. IEEE, 1992.

7. S. Blake-Wilson and A. Meneses. *Authencicated Diffe-Hellman Key Agreement Protocols*, In Proc. of SAC'99, LNCS 1556, pages 339-361. Springer-Verlag, 1999.
8. V. Boyko, P. MacKenzie, and S. Patel. *Provably Secure Password-Authenticated Key Exchange Using Diffie-Hellman*, In Proc. of Eurocrypt '01, LNCS 1807, pages 156-171, Springer-Verlag, 2001.
9. E. Bresson and D. Catalano. *Constant Round Authenticated Group key Agreement via Distributed Computation*, In Proc. of PKC 2004, LNCS 2947, pages 115-128. Springer-Verlag, 2004.
10. E. Bresson, O. Chevassut, and D. Pointcheval. *Group Diffie-Hellman Key Exchange Secure Against Dictionary Attacks*, In Proc. of Asiacrypt '02, LNCS 2501, pages 497-514, Springer-Verlag, 2002.
11. E. Bresson, O. Chevassut, D. Pointcheval, and J.-J. Quisquater. *Provably Authenticated Group Diffie-Hellman Key Exchange*, In Proc. of the 8th ACM conference on Computer and Communications Security, pages 255 - 264, 2001.
12. O. Goldreich and Y. Lindell. *Session-Key Generation using Human Passwords Only*, In Proc. of Crypto '01, LNCS 2139, pages 408-432. Springer-Verlag, 2001. 5Springer-Verlag, pp.36 − 49, 1996.
13. J. Katz, R. Ostrovsky, and M. Yung. *Efficient Password-Authenticated Key Exchange using Human-Memorable Passwords*, In Proc. of Eurocrypt '01, LNCS 2045, pages 475-494, Springer-Verlag, 2001.
14. J. Katz and M. Yung. *Scalable Protocol for Authenticated Group Key Exchange*, In Proc. of Eurocrypt '03, LNCS 2729, pages 110-125, Springer-Verlag, 2003.
15. S. M. Lee, H. J. Kim, D. H. Lee, J. I. Lim and C. S. Park. *Scalable Gruop Key Management with Minimally Trusted Third Party*, In 4th International Workshop on Information Security Applications, pp. 575–583, Aug 2003.

Optimality in Asynchronous Contract Signing Protocols

Josep Lluís Ferrer-Gomila, Magdalena Payeras-Capellà,
and Llorenç Huguet-Rotger

Departament de Ciències Matemàtiques i Informàtica, Universitat de les Illes Balears
Carretera de Valldemossa km 7.5, Palma de Mallorca 07122, Spain
{dijjfg,mpayeras,dmilhr0}@uib.es

Abstract. Garay et alter [9] prove that for the multi-party contract signing with n participants, at least n rounds are necessary. To date, the best solution is Baum-Waidner's scheme [6], with $t+2$ rounds (where t is the number of dishonest signatories, so with $t=n-1$, the number of rounds is $n+1$). Here, we propose an optimal solution with exactly n rounds. On the other hand, Pfitzmann et alter [10] state that "there is no asynchronous optimistic contract signing scheme with three messages in the optimistic case". However, it seems that Ferrer et alter [7] invalidate the previous theorem with a counterexample, presenting an asynchronous protocol with only three messages. In this paper, we clarify this apparent contradiction.

1 Introduction

Practical solutions for contract signing require of the existence and possible involvement of a trusted third party (TTP). To obtain efficiency, three objectives are usually pursued:

1. To reduce the involvement of the TTP.
2. To reduce the number of messages to be exchanged.
3. That the possible implication of the TTP does not require expensive operations, neither the storage of high volume of information.

The first objective has been achieved in some proposals. They are the optimistic solutions [1, 2, 8, 12]: the TTP are not involved in every protocol run. Regarding the number of messages to be exchanged, Pfitzmann et alter, in [10], demonstrate that in this kind of solutions, for the two-party version, more than 3 messages are necessary. On the other hand, [7] proposes an optimistic solution with only three messages, but doesn't explain if this way the theorem is invalidated. In section three we will explain that both visions are compatible.

Much attention has been devoted to the two-party contract signing problem. Nevertheless, we need a multi-party version when more than two signatories have to be involved in the same contract signing process, and every party wants to be bound to the contract if *all* parties are bound at the end of the exchange, because nobody wants a partially signed contract. A few solutions [3-9] have been presented, and some of them are not very efficient. Theorem 3 of [9] states: "Any complete and fair optimistic contract-signing protocol with n participants requires at least n rounds in an optimistic run". Here we present a protocol with exactly n rounds for n participants,

S. Katsikas, J. Lopez, and G. Pernul (Eds.): TrustBus 2004, LNCS 3184, pp. 200–208, 2004.
© Springer-Verlag Berlin Heidelberg 2004

which is the optimal solution. The best previous solution was that proposed by Baum-Waidner et alter in [6].

Protocols for contract signing (two-party or multi-party) have to provide evidence to parties to prove, at the end of the exchange, if the contract is signed and the terms of the contract. Some additional properties have to be achieved in optimistic protocols [2, 12]:

- Effectiveness: if parties behave correctly the TTP will not be involved;
- Fairness: no party will be in advantageous situation at any stage of a protocol run;
- Timeliness: parties can decide when to finish a protocol run;
- Non-repudiation: parties can not deny their actions;
- Verifiability of the third party: if the TTP misbehaves, all damaged parties will be able to prove it.

The presented protocol achieves the previous requirements.

2 Multi-party Proposal

Theorem 3 of [9] states: "Any complete and fair optimistic contract-signing protocol with n participants requires at least n rounds in an optimistic run". To date the best solution is Baum-Waidner's protocol [6] with $n+1$ rounds. Next, we present an asynchronous contract signing protocol for n parties, with exactly n rounds: the optimal solution. Parties agree the text of the contract, constitute an ordered ring to exchange messages, etc., before starting the execution of the contract signing protocol. The *exchange* sub-protocol is as follows:

1.1	$A_1 \to A_2$:	$m_{1,1} = sig_{A1}(C_1)$
1.2	$A_2 \to A_3$:	$m_{1,1}, m_{1,2} = sig_{A2}(C_1)$
...	... ...	... ...
1.n	$A_n \to A_1$:	$m_{1,2}, ..., m_{1,n} = sig_{An}(C_1)$
2.1	$A_1 \to A_2$:	$m_{1,3}, ..., m_{1,n}, m_{2,1} = sig_{A1}(C_2)$
2.2	$A_2 \to A_3$:	$m_{1,4}, ..., m_{1,n}, m_{2,1}, m_{2,2} = sig_{A2}(C_2)$
...	... ...	... ...
2.n	$A_n \to A_1$:	$m_{2,2}, ..., m_{2,n} = sig_{An}(C_2)$
...	... ...	... ...
n.1	$A_1 \to A_2$:	$m_{n-1,3}, ..., m_{n-1,n}, m_{n,1} = sig_{A1}(C_n)$
n.2	$A_2 \to A_3$:	$m_{n-1,4}, ..., m_{n-1,n}, m_{n,1}, m_{n,2} = sig_{A2}(C_n)$
...	... ...	... ...
n.(n-1)	$A_{n-1} \to A_n$:	$m_{n,1}, m_{n,2}, ..., m_{n,n-1} = sig_{An-1}(C_n)$

In every round the sender signs a message $C_i = (id, C, i)$, where id is the unique identifier for this contract, C is the text of the contract, and i is the round number. Observe that each signatory retransmits all the information corresponding to the previous round; consequently, every participant gets all the information without broadcasting. This way our proposal will be better than Baum-Waidner's protocol, regarding the number of messages to be exchanged. If no party stops before the end of the protocol, the exchange will be fair and without TTP's involvement. Therefore, the protocol meets the *effectiveness* requirement.

At any time (*timeliness* requirement) a party can contact T, sending $resolve_{r, i}$ (round r, signatory i) that contains all the information received until that point. If this is the first time T is asked about this contract (i.e., *id*) then T initializes two boolean variables *signed* := false and *aborted* := false, and two sets *con* := 0 and *abort_set* := 0. The variables *signed* and *aborted* indicate T's current decision, *signed* or *aborted*. On the other hand, *con* is the set of all indices of signatories that contacted T, and *abort_set* is the set of all *aborted*-messages sent by T. Processing a request cannot be interrupted, i.e., it cannot happen that T processes two different requests concurrently (relating the same protocol run). T has to follow sequentially the following rules, checking the conditions until a rule is applicable, in each case.

- **Rule T0:** T accepts only one request from each A_i. All other requests are ignored.

    If $i \in con$ **then**
    $\quad\quad$ T ignores $resolve_{r, i}$.

- **Rule T1:** If T receives a request from $r = 1$, $i \neq n$ and has not yet decided *signed* then T sends an *abort* to the requester, if this requester is not signatory n.

    If $i \notin con$ and *signed* = false and $r = 1$ and $i \neq n$ **then**
    $\quad\quad$ T sets $aborted_{1, i}$:= $sig_T(C, 1, i, aborted)$
    $\quad\quad$ T sets *abort_set* := *abort_set* $\cup$ $\{aborted_{1, i}\}$
    $\quad\quad$ T sets *con* := *con* $\cup$ $\{i\}$
    $\quad\quad$ T sets *aborted* := true
    $\quad\quad$ T sends $aborted_{1, i}$ to A_i.

- **Rule T2:** If T receives a request from signatory n ($i = n$) and has not yet decided *aborted* then T sends a *signed* to the requester.

    If $i \notin con$ and *aborted* = false and $i = n$ **then**
    $\quad\quad$ T sets $signed_{r, n}$:= $sig_T(C, r, n, signed)$
    $\quad\quad$ T sets *signed* := true
    $\quad\quad$ T sets *con* := *con* $\cup$ $\{n\}$
    $\quad\quad$ T sends $signed_{r, n}$ to A_n.

- **Rule T3:** If T receives a request from round $r > 1$, $i \neq n$ and has not yet decided *aborted* then T sends a *signed* to the requester. A decision *signed* is always preserved.

    If $i \notin con$ and *aborted* = false and $r > 1$, $i \neq n$ **then**
    $\quad\quad$ T sets $signed_{r, i}$:= $sig_T(C, r, i, signed)$
    $\quad\quad$ T sets *signed* := true
    $\quad\quad$ T sets *con* := *con* $\cup$ $\{i\}$
    $\quad\quad$ T sends $signed_{r, i}$ to A_i.

- **Rule T4:** If T receives a request from round $r = 1$ and has already decided *signed* then T sends a *signed* to the requester.

  If $i \notin con$ and *signed* = true and $r = 1$ **then**
  > T sets $signed_{1, i} := \text{sig}_T(C, 1, i, signed)$
  > T sets $con := con \cup \{i\}$
  > T sends $signed_{1, i}$ to A_i.

- **Rule T5:** If T receives a request and has decided *aborted* then T checks whether all previous requests came from dishonest signatories, using *Lemma* 1 and *Lemma* 2. If this is the case, it changes the decision to *signed*, otherwise T sticks to *aborted*.

  If $i \notin con$ and *aborted* = true and ($\forall aborted_{s, k} \in abort\_set$ we have $s < r-1$)
  and ($\forall aborted_{r-1, k} \in abort\_set$ we have $k < i$) **then**
  > T sets $signed_{r, i} := \text{sig}_T(C, r, i, signed)$
  > T sets *signed* := true
  > T sets *aborted* := false
  > T sets $con := con \cup \{i\}$
  > T sends $signed_{r, i}$ to A_i

      else
  > T sets $aborted_{r, i} := \text{sig}_T(C, r, i, aborted)$
  > T sets $abort\_set := abort\_set \cup \{aborted_{r, i}\}$
  > T sets $con := con \cup \{i\}$
  > T sends $aborted_{r, i}$ to A_i.

Lemma 1. If T receives $resolve_{r, i}$ and finds $aborted_{s, k} \in abort\_set$ for an $s \leq r-2$ then A_k is dishonest.

Proof. Assume T finds $aborted_{s, k} \in abort\_set$ with $s \leq r-2$. Since $s \geq 1$ we have $r \geq 3$, and therefore $resolve_{r, i}$ includes all information until round $r-1$. In consequence A_k participated in round $r-1$, and since $r-1 > s$ this means that A_k was still active after having sent $resolve_{s, k}$ to T. As a result, A_k is dishonest.

Lemma 2. If T receives $resolve_{r, i}$ and finds $aborted_{r-1, k} \in abort\_set$ for a value $k < i$ then A_k is dishonest.

Proof. Assume T finds $aborted_{r-1, k} \in abort\_set$ with $k < i$. $Resolve_{r, i}$ includes all information until round $r-1$, and information of round r until signatory $i-1$. Since $i > k$ therefore A_k participated in round r, and this means that A_k was still active after having sent $resolve_{r-1, k}$ to T. As a result, A_k is dishonest.

Theorem 1. If T is trusted, the presented multi-party contract signing scheme is fair.

Proof. Assume a party A_i can prove that the contract is *aborted*, and another party A_k can prove that the contract is *signed*.

- If A_i can prove that the contract is *aborted*, it means that A_k cannot prove that the contract have been *signed* with T's intervention. For that reason, A_k has received all messages in the *exchange* sub-protocol.
- Consequently, signatories with $j < k$ have also received all messages in the *exchange* sub-protocol. Therefore, we have $i > k$.
- As a consequence, A_i had received, at least, messages until round n-1, and she alleged that she had not received last message, and T sent her $aborted_{n-1,\,i}$.
- According T's rules this means that there is some signatory A_j that received $aborted_{n-2,\,j}$.
- Inductively, some signatory A_p received $aborted_{1,\,p}$. Therefore, n-1 signatories contacted with T (from round 1 to round n-1). Since n-1 signatories have contacted T and $i > k$, therefore $k = 1$.
- On the other hand, for *Lemma 1*, *Lemma 2* and T's rules, signatory n cannot abort in round 1, therefore signatory n-1 contacted T in round 1, signatory n-2 in round 2, and so on, until signatory 2, that contacted T in round n-2. In consequence, no signatory contacted T in round n-1.
- This contradicts our assumption.

3   Contract Signing Between Two Parties

We have adapted the notation used in [10] (Pfitzmann et alter protocol, PSW) to our proposal. A_1 and A_2 are the signatories, while V is called verifier and T is the third party. C is the contract text they want to sign, and *id* is the common unique transaction identifier, which will be used to distinguish information from different protocol runs. The protocols are based on the digital signature scheme [11], where $sig_X(m)$ denotes X's signature under message m. It is assumed tacitly that sequence numbers, names of participants and the *id* are included into all signed messages, and that the signatures contained in messages are verified upon receipt. Corrupted or unexpected messages have to be ignored. In the figures $X \rightarrow Y$: m denotes that X sends information m to Y.

3.1   Two-Party Version of the Multi-party Protocol of Section 2

The particularization of the multi-party protocol described in section 2 to two parties is very similar to [7] (protocol FPH). The *exchange* sub-protocol is as follows:

1. $A_1 \rightarrow A_2$: $m_{1,1} = sig_{A1}(C_1)$
2. $A_2 \rightarrow A_1$: $m_{1,2} = sig_{A2}(C_1)$
3. $A_1 \rightarrow A_2$: $m_{2,1} = sig_{A1}(C_2)$

The non-repudiation evidence for A_1 is $m_{1,2}$, and the non-repudiation evidence for A_2 is $m_{1,1}$ and $m_{2,1}$. A_1 and A_2 may initiate the *resolve* sub-protocol when they want. In order to *resolve* the exchange, T has to follow the next rules:

- **Rule T0:** T accepts only one request from each A_i. All other requests are ignored.

> **If** $i \in con$ **then**
> > T ignores $resolve_{r,i}$.

- **Rule T1:** If T receives a request from signatory $i = 1$, and has not yet decided *signed* then T sends an *abort* to the requester.

> **If** $1 \notin con$ and $signed = $ false and $i = 1$ **then**
> > T sets $aborted_{1,1} := sig_T(C, 1, 1, aborted)$
> > T sets $abort\_set := abort\_set \cup \{aborted_{1,1}\}$
> > T sets $con := con \cup \{1\}$
> > T sets $aborted :=$ true
> > T sends $aborted_{1,1}$ to A_1.

- **Rule T2:** If T receives a request from signatory $i = 2$ and has not yet decided *aborted* then T sends a *signed* to the requester.

> **If** $2 \notin con$ and $aborted = $ false and $i = 2$ **then**
> > T sets $signed_{1,2} := sig_T(C, 1, 2, signed)$
> > T sets $signed :=$ true
> > T sets $con := con \cup \{2\}$
> > T sends $signed_{1,2}$ to A_2.

- **Rule T3:** Does not apply.
- **Rule T4:** If T receives a request from signatory $i = 1$ and has already decided *signed* then T sends a *signed* to the requester.

> **If** $1 \notin con$ and $signed = $ true **then**
> > T sets $signed_{1,1} := sig_T(C, 1, 1, signed)$
> > T sets $con := con \cup \{1\}$
> > T sends $signed_{1,1}$ to A_1.

- **Rule T5:** If T receives a request from signatory $i = 2$ and has decided *aborted* then T sends an *abort* to the requester.

> **If** $2 \notin con$ and $aborted = $ true and $aborted_{1,2} \in abort\_set$ **then**
> > T sets $aborted_{1,2} := sig_T(C, 1, 2, aborted)$
> > T sets $abort\_set := abort\_set \cup \{aborted_{1,2}\}$
> > T sets $con := con \cup \{2\}$
> > T sends $aborted_{1,2}$ to A_2.

In [7] the authors prove that the protocol satisfies the desired requirements: effectiveness, fairness, non-repudiation, timeliness and verifiability of the TTP.

3.2 PSW Theorem

Theorem 2 of [10] states: "There is no asynchronous optimistic contract signing scheme with three messages in the optimistic case". To prove this Theorem, they use a Lemma indicating that the outcome of *abort* and *resolve* sub-protocols is determined only by inputs from the third party and the signatory starting the sub-protocol. In the proof of the theorem, we have to assume that T has not made a decision before involving the *id* in course.

If A_2 does not receive $m_{2,\,1}$, the third party has to decide locally that the contract is signed since A_1 may have obtained a valid contract $(m_{1,\,1}, m_{1,\,2})$. In consequence, A_2 may obtain a valid contract from the third party even if A_1 had only sent $m_{1,\,1}$.

Therefore, A_1 must be able to start *abort* with the third party after sending $m_{1,\,1}$, too. In this case, the third party is required to decide locally whether the contract is valid or not given only $m_{1,\,1}$ from A_1. If it now decides that the contract must be *aborted* based on $m_{1,\,1}$ only, an incorrect A_1 could make a contract invalid after a successful completion that not involve the third party (i.e., after sending $m_{2,\,1}$). If the third party decides *resolved* since A_2 may later *resolve*, then a valid contract could be obtained without A_2's participation.

The conclusion of the previous proof is that T can not decide on *resolved* for A_1 in the last case.

3.3 Discussing the Definition of Fairness

In the presented two-party protocol, assume A_1 is dishonest and sends the first message to A_2, *resolves* the contract with T, receives the second message from A_2, and stops. If A_2 contacts with T it will get an *abort* message, which *seems* inconsistent with the fact that A_1 already "has" a signed contract. However, A_2 can prove that A_1 is a cheating party, and for this reason, A_2 is not compelled to that contract. Therefore, it seems that the three-step asynchronous protocol is fair, even if A_1 tries to cheat using the described attack.

Let us assume A_2 needs to present a proof that A_1 signed the contract to another party V. V only needs to verify the signature of A_1, without contacting T to verify if A_1 *resolved* the contract and obtained an *aborted* message. If A_2 has first and third message (this last message from A_1 or from T) the contract is signed (A_1 cannot pretend that the contract is *aborted*).

Of course, A_1 can obtain *NR* evidence from A_2 and an *abort* message from T, while A_2 obtain *NR* evidence from A_1. She can do it, for instance, *resolving* after the end of the *exchange* sub-protocol. It seems that A_1 can affirm that the contract is signed or is not signed, depending on her usefulness. Nevertheless, A_2 possesses NR evidence that will prove that the contract is signed, and if A_1 tries to use the *abort* message, she will be proving she is a cheating party. As a conclusion, the protocol is fair and we have not made timing assumptions (the protocol is asynchronous, parties can contact with T when they want).

Let us assume now that A_1 needs to present a proof that A_2 signed the contract to another party V. V needs not only to verify the signature of A_2, but V has also to contact T (or A_2) and check if A_1 *resolved* the exchange *obtaining* an *abort* message. A_1 can have the second message from A_2, but she can also have an *abort* message obtained from T without sending the third message to A_2, and so the contract is not signed.

As a conclusion, V needs to verify with T or A_2 if the contract is signed or not. So, the protocol seems optimal (only three messages) and remains fair, optimistic and asynchronous.

The apparent contradiction between the theorem proved in [10] and the proposed protocol can be explained. The protocol described in [7] and the proposed protocol do not use the same concept of *fairness* than authors of [10]. In [10] a contract signing scheme is considered *fair* if it fulfills, among other requirements, the following one: "No surprises with Invalid Contracts: If a correct signatory, say A_1, output *aborted* then no correct verifier will output *signed*". The *verification* process is made between the verifier V and one of the signatories A_1 or A_2 (they restrict the model to two-party verification). In our protocol, a contract signing scheme is considered *fair* if parties can prove the actual state of the exchange in front of a verifier V, but considering that both, A_1 and A_2, have to provide their evidences to V. In fact, it is only necessary in one case.

With this definition of transferability, our protocol can be useful, but only in partial-transferable contracts. It means that the second signatory (A_2 can prove to V if the contract is signed (without contacting A_1, nor T). However, the first signatory (A_1) needs the collaboration of A_2 or T, in order to prove to V that the contract is signed. It means that the external verification in where a verifier contacts only with the first signatory are not possible. For A_1, the contract has to be private between her and A_2, and if she has problems then she will have to go in front of courts. Obviously, in this case, both parties have to be listened to. For this kind of contracts, our solution is better (optimal) than PSW scheme.

Finally, imagine a situation in where a user (second signatory of a contract) is going to ask for a loan and the signed contract will be part of the guarantee, but the first signatory does not need to prove anything to an external verifier: our protocol will be useful. However, if parties require the signature of a full-transferable contract (both signatories will want to prove to a verifier that a contract is signed, without contacting the other signatory or T), PSW scheme is better.

4   Conclusions

Pfitzmann et alter, in [10], state that "there is no asynchronous optimistic contract signing scheme with three messages in the optimistic case". On the other hand, it seems that [7] invalidates the previous theorem with a counterexample, presenting an asynchronous protocol with only three messages. In this paper, we clarify this apparent contradiction: both visions are possible with different definitions of *fairness*. Additionally, we propose a multi-party contract signing protocol with exactly n rounds: the optimal solution. Therefore, we improve Baum-Waidner's solution.

References

1. N. Asokan, M. Schunter and M. Waidner: "Optimistic protocols for fair exchange"; 4th ACM Conference on Computer and Communications Security, pp. 7-17, 1997.
2. N. Asokan, V. Shoup and M. Waidner: "Asynchronous Protocols for Optimistic Fair Exchange"; IEEE Symposium on Research in Security and Privacy, pp. 86-99, 1998.
3. N. Asokan, M. Schunter and M. Waidner: "Optimistic protocols for multi-party fair exchange"; Research Report RZ 2892 (#90840), IBM Research, 1996.
4. N. Asokan, B. Baum-Waidner, M. Schunter and M. Waidner: "Optimistic synchronous multi-party contract signing"; Research Report RZ 3089, IBM Research Division, 1998.
5. B. Baum-Waidner and M. Waidner: "Optimistic asynchronous multi-party contract signing"; Research Report RZ 3078, IBM Research Division, 1998.
6. B. Baum-Weidner and M. Waidner: "Round-optimal and abuse-free multi-party contract signing"; ICALP'2000, LNCS 1853, Springer Verlag, pp. 524-535, 2000.
7. J.L. Ferrer, M. Payeras and L. Huguet: "Efficient Optimistic N-Party Contract Signing Protocol"; ISC 2001, LNCS 2200, Springer Verlag, pp. 394-407, 2001.
8. J.A. Garay, M. Jakobsson and P. MacKenzie: "Abuse-Free Optimistic Contract Signing"; CRYPTO'99, LNCS 1666, Springer Verlag, pp. 449-466, 1999.
9. J.A. Garay and P. MacKenzie: "Abuse-Free Multi-party Contract Signing"; DISC'99, LNCS 1693, Springer Verlag, pp. 151-165, 1999.
10. B. Pfitzmann, M. Schunter and M. Waidner: "Optimal Efficiency of Optimistic Contract Signing"; PODC'98, pp. 113-122, 1998.
11. R. Rivest, A. Shamir and L. Adleman: "A Method for Obtaining Digital Signatures and Public Key Cryptosystems"; Communications of the ACM, 21, pp. 120-126, 1978.
12. J. Zhou, R. Deng and F. Bao: "Some Remarks on a Fair Exchange Protocol"; PKC 2000, LNCS 1751, Springer Verlag, pp. 46-57, 2000.

Development of Visible Anti-copy Patterns

JongWeon Kim[1], KyuTae Kim[2], JungSoo Lee[2,3], and JongUk Choi[1,2]

[1] College of Computer Software and Media Technology, Sangmyung University
7, Hongji-dong, Jongno-gu, Seoul, 110-743, Korea
{jwkim,juchoi}@smu.ac.kr
http://swc.smu.ac.kr/
[2] MarkAny Inc., 10F, Ssanglim Bldg., 151-11, Ssanglim-dong
Jung-gu, Seoul, 100-400, Korea
{jedam,jslee,juchoi}@markany.com
http://www.markany.com/
[3] Dept. of Electronics Eng., Hanyang University,
17, Haengdang-dong, Seongdong-gu, Seoul, 133-791, Korea

Abstract. Today, many governments try to implement e-government to provide one stop service through digitization of conventional document and providing public service through cyber systems. However, the last and the most difficult problem with the current e-government projects is that the government cannot provide on-line solution for issuing government certificates through cyber operations, because of the possible forgery and illegal modifications.

In this research, an algorithm of generating visible anti-copy patterns is suggested to issue government certificates or bank certificates in cyber space. In this scheme, people can print certificates at home or in office using ordinary printers. Visible anti-copy patterns provide a solution to distinguish copied documents from original ones through naked eyes. In order to generate visible anti-copy patterns, this research examines characteristics of digital image input and output devices. Different from traditional anti-forgery methods that need special equipment, visible anti-copy patterns developed in this research can be easily recognized with naked eyes whether the document is originally printed or it is copied or scanned and printed.

1 Introduction

Frauds using forged or altered documents are found even in records at the beginning of human history. In particular, the preciseness of forged and altered documents has been significantly enhanced with the development of digital image equipment, printers and computers and illegal papers produced in these ways are used in diverse unlawful acts. Some of such unlawful acts are providing forged IDs or driver licenses to illegal aliens and forging or modifying bank accounts for financial fraud. Damage caused by forged and altered documents has been increasing every year. In fiscal year 2002, the U.S. secret Service and international authorities seized $130million in counterfeit notes before they ever made it into circulation, thus preventing those

S. Katsikas, J. Lopez, and G. Pernul (Eds.): TrustBus 2004, LNCS 3184, pp. 209–218, 2004.
© Springer-Verlag Berlin Heidelberg 2004

counterfeit notes from being passed to victims [1]. As for technologies to prevent the forgery and alteration of valuable documents, physical and chemical methods have been developed including high-resolution printers (>4000 dpi) unavailable for common people, ink extremely sensitive to reproduction and holograms [2]. These technologies are frequently utilized in making bills and IDs but recently visual cryptography is drawing people's attention as a method of authenticating documents [2][3].

While various types of documents are generated using inexpensive printers with the development of the Internet, it is costly to use holograms or special types of ink in detecting altered and forged documents. Thus it is necessary to develop technologies of preventing alteration and forgery applicable to low-cost printers. Such technologies are CopySafe+TM paper, which is paper covered with silver foil, to prevent copying or scanning [4] and copy detection patterns to check whether a document is original or duplicate [5].

In authenticating the documents, watermarking and electronic signature have been frequently utilized until now. Watermarking technology is largely divided into analogue watermarking used in bills and digital watermarking used in protecting the copyright of multimedia contents [6]. Watermarking technologies for verifying integrity are fragile and semi-fragile watermarking. Fragile watermarking proves integrity as the forgery or the alteration of multimedia content breaks watermark on the corresponding part. Semi-fragile watermarking preserves watermark in normal acts such as compression but breaks it in forging or altering [7].

When digital watermarking technology is applied in preventing printed documents from being forged or altered, it is possible to use a solution that regards the processes of printing and scanning by semi-fragile watermarking as A/D conversion and D/A conversion respectively [4]. However, such a technique is inconvenient where a speedy verification is required because it has to rely on specific software or hardware for verification. In case of using high-resolution printer, a method of using micro letters is suggested to make it difficult to reproduce using scanners or other image processing devices, but it also requires an expensive special printer [8].

This study examined patterns that are distinguishable between the originals and duplicates with the naked eye while using inexpensive printers. For this purpose, it investigated the characteristics of copy machines and scanners and, based on the identified characteristics, developed patterns.

2   Visible Anti-copy Patterns

2.1   Copy Machines and Scanners

It is necessary to analyze the optical system of copy machines and scanners in order to create patterns for distinguishing duplicates from the originals. Copy machines and scanners are basically sampled imaging systems. Such systems are composed of an object, lens and CCD sensor or electrified drum. The sampled imaging system reflects a point of the object plane on a point of the image plane through the lens and, in the process, the point on the image is blurred by impulse response or psf (point spread function), which is a transfer function of the lens [9]. The process is repeated for a myriad of points on the object plane, and the image on the image plane is the sum of these points.

There are two important considerations here [9]. First, the process that the lens images the scene is linear and therefore superposition is held. The scene is accurately represented by the sum of individual points of light on the scene. In addition, the image is accurately represented by the sum of blurs resulting from the imaging of each individual point by the lens.

Second, it is assumed that the shape of optical blurs (namely, the shape of psf) does not depend on position within the field of view. In general this is not true for optical systems. Typically optical aberrations vary depending on position in the field of view. In an image, optical blurs are generally smaller at the center than at the edge. However, an image plane can generally be subdivided into regions, within each of which the optical blur is almost constant.

On this assumption, the brightness of an image $i_{mg}(x,y)$ in the sample image system can be expressed with the convolution of the brightness of the object $s_{cn}(x',y')$ as input and impulse response or psf $h(x,y)$ as Eq. (1).

$$i_{mg}(x,y) = \int_{-\infty}^{\infty}\int_{-\infty}^{\infty} h(x-x',y-y')s_{cn}(x',y')dx'dy' \tag{1}$$

Convolution can be expressed as a product in the frequency domain as in Eq. (2).

$$I_{mg}(\xi,\eta) = H(\xi,\eta)S_{cn}(\xi,\eta) \tag{2}$$

From Eq. (2), impulse response, namely, psf can be expressed as Eq. (3).

$$H(\xi,\eta) = \int_{-\infty}^{\infty}\int_{-\infty}^{\infty} h(x,y)e^{-j2\pi\xi x}e^{-j2\pi\eta y}\,dxdy \left/ \int_{-\infty}^{\infty} h(x,y)dxdy \right. \tag{3}$$

In the structure of copy machine, diffraction by the lens, the shape of the detector, sample-and-hold, monitor display spots and the eye blur the original target. This is simply interpreted as low pass filtering and the impulse response of the scanner produces a result like Figure 1 when it scans the original target. It is the key factor of pattern designs that, when scanned, the original target is blurred and violates its neighboring area, and as a result the boundary between the two areas crumbles away.

Fig. 1. Impulse response of a scanning system

2.2 Basic Concept of Visible Anti-copy Patterns

Low pass filtering in copy machines and scanners causes the blurring of boundaries in original patterns. In particular, it is impossible to align the original target with the detector or the CCD sensor. Thus original patterns become in misalignment with blurred patterns. Actually in a scanner, a line CCD sensor is used for 2D scanning, so it is impossible to align the object of scanning with the arrangement of line CCD. It may be possible to correct to some degree using image editing software but impossible to achieve resolution as high as the original object. Figure 2 shows misalignment on the assumption that line CCD scans the original object at a constant speed. As the figure shows, the original object is a straight line. If the line is in parallel with the direction of scanning, it may coincide with the scanned image for each pixel. Because it is impossible to align in parallel, however, discontinuous spots occur on the straight line in the scanned image as shown in Figure 2. This is the same in copy machines. Particularly in images scanned using the low pass filtering effect, boundaries are blurred and indistinguishable.

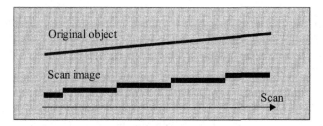

Fig. 2. Misalignment of line CCD

Figure 3 shows three vertical lines. The thickness of each line is a dot in 300 dpi and the space between two lines is also as big as a dot. When the three lines lie at the right angle to the direction of scanning, the result is the overlapping of low pass filtering effect as shown in Figure 1 with misalignment effect in Figure 2. Figure 3 (a) is the image of the original target that represent each pixel precisely, (b) is an image obtained by scanning the original target at 300dpi using a scanner (Canon Canoscan N670U) and (c) an image at 600dpi. Figure 3 (b) and (c) each have three images. In the first images, boundaries between the lines disappear because of the extreme effects of low pass filtering and misalignment. In the second and third images, boundaries between lines are distinguishable but are not so clear because of low pass filtering and misalignment.

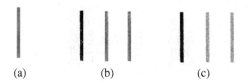

(a)   (b)   (c)

Fig. 3. Scanning effects (a) Original target (b) Scanned images (300dpi) (c) Scanned images (600dpi)

As discussed above, the low pass filtering and misalignment of scanners are factors that hinder the exact transfer of the original target. Using the characteristic, it is possible to create anti-copy patterns. Anti-copy patterns are basically divided into two groups, namely, delete patterns and survival patterns. Delete patterns are broken or lost when copied or scanned, and survival patterns are preserved when copied or scanned. When an anti-copy pattern $p_a(x,y)$ goes through a scanner or a copy machine with impulse response of $h_s(x,y)$, the resulting pattern is as follows. Here, $p_{ba}(x,y)$ is an anti-copy pattern created as a delete pattern and $p_{sa}(x,y)$ as a survival pattern.

$$p_b(x,y) = \int_{-\infty}^{\infty} \int_{-\infty}^{\infty} p_{ba}(x',y')h_s(x-x',y-y')dx'dy' \tag{4}$$

$$p_s(x,y) = \int_{-\infty}^{\infty} \int_{-\infty}^{\infty} p_{sa}(x',y')h_s(x-x',y-y')dx'dy' \tag{5}$$

In case we use the effect that delete patterns are broken, the outcome of Eq. (4) will be patterns that have gone through the process of low pass filtering, and in case we use the effect that delete patterns are lost, $p_b(x,y) = \phi(x,y) = 0$. When composing actual patterns, delete patterns and survival patterns are combined. Thus we can summarize as follows. Anti-copy patterns generated from Eq. (6) are transferred into patterns resulting from Eq. (7) and (8) by a scanner and a copy machine. Patterns resulting from Eq. (7) use the characteristic that anti-copy patterns break into delete patterns, and patterns resulting from Eq. (8) uses delete patterns in anti-copy patterns.

$$p_a(x,y) = p_{ba}(x,y) + p_{sa}(x,y) \tag{6}$$

$$\{p_b(x,y) + p_s(x,y)\} = \int_{-\infty}^{\infty} \int_{-\infty}^{\infty} p_a(x',y')h_s(x-x',y-y')dx'dy' \tag{7}$$

$$p_s(x,y) = \int_{-\infty}^{\infty} \int_{-\infty}^{\infty} p_a(x',y')h_s(x-x',y-y')dx'dy' \tag{8}$$

Anti-copy patterns created using delete patterns and survival patterns are largely divided into three types, which are expression type that expresses specific letters, delete type that removes specific letters and hybrid type that combines the two types. Another factor to consider in creating anti-copy patterns is the human visual system. The human visual system is highly affected by luminance in recognizing an object, particularly by contrast ration, the difference in luminance between the object and the background [10]. Because the effect of background is realized by the relative recognition of the human visual system, images may be viewed differently according to contrast [11].

What is more, the visual system can recognize difference between two objects only when the difference is larger than a specific level. Such a characteristic is explained with JND (just noticeable difference) [12]. JND is represented in percentage and, as shown in Eq. (9), it is measured by change from the original luminance. In general the human visual system is known to sense changes greater than 2% of JND. The value is of course not applicable at low or high intensity but is maintained constant at an appropriate range.

$$JND = \frac{\Delta I}{I} \times 100[\%] \qquad (9)$$

where, I is the intensity of the image, namely, the intensity of luminance and ΔI is the change of intensity.

3   Creating and Evaluating Visible Anti-copy Patterns

3.1   Creating Visible Anti-copy Patterns

Examples of broken patterns, delete patterns and survival patterns developed in this study are shown in Figure 4. Figure 4 (a) can be used in deleting letters when original patterns are copied or scanned and (b) in expressing letters as original patterns disappear as a result of copying or scanning. Pattern (c) is utilized in creating visible anti-copy patterns where letters are lost or expressed or anti-copy patterns where the two forms co-exist by being combined with pattern (b).

Because we have to use the effect of low pass filtering happening in a copy machine or a scanner in order to create Figure 4 (a), we use black lines or black dots. By giving spaces as large as a dot between black lines or black dots, we can induce the breaking of patterns by the effect of low pass filtering. A small pattern is created and the pattern is regularly disposed forming an image. For patterns to represent letters, spaces between black lines and between black dots are filled with black. The pattern in (b) is created only with black dots, in which gray level is determined by the percentage of area occupied by black dots in the entire image. If spaces between black dots are too narrow the effect achieved in the pattern of (a) is realized. Thus it is necessary to maintain spaces no smaller than 2 dots, and the lower gray level is the higher the effect of deletion is. Because the pattern in (c) has to survive scanning or copying, it uses patterns composed of 4 dots or black lines. In this case, it is possible to achieve gray level as in the pattern of (b) by adjusting spaces between dots or black lines, and to create visible anti-copy patterns by combining the two patterns. Theoretically if pattern (b) and pattern (c) are created with the same distribution of gray within a specific area, the two should be hardly distinguishable from each other, but the visual system recognizes differently according to pattern, so it is necessary to make a partial adjustment of the distribution of gray in the two patterns.

If basic patterns are created as Figure 4, using them are created visible anti-copy patterns as in Figure 5. Figure 5 (a) is an anti-copy pattern created only using Figure 4 (a). If it is created in the normal way the letters are readable but reproduction by a scanner or a copy machine destroys the background pattern other than the letters, which removes distinction between the letters and the background. Figure (b) and (c) are anti-copy patterns that express letters using delete patterns and survival patterns. In (b) survival patterns are used for the background and delete patterns for the letters so that the letters are manifested when copied or scanned. In (c), on the contrary, delete patterns are used for the background and survival patterns for the letters so that the letters are manifested when copied or scanned. Pattern (d) is a hybrid pattern created by deleting visually recognizable patterns in the letters using the fact that the manifested patterns in (c) are delete patterns of the background. Letters represented using the background disappear together with the background by scanning or copying and, as a result, letters composed of survival patterns are manifested.

(a) Broken pattern   (b) Delete pattern   (c) Survival pattern

Fig. 4. Three patterns for anti-copy pattern

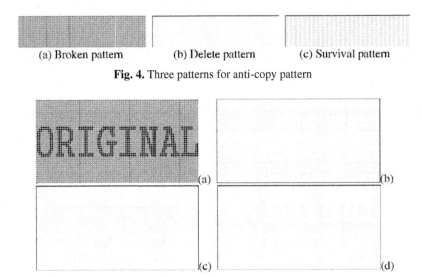

Fig. 5. Visible anti-copy patterns

3.2 Security of Visible Anti-copy Patterns

As explained in section 3.1, because anti-copy patterns are created by the regular disposition of a basic pattern, it is possible to reproduce visible anti-copy patterns if one knows information about the basic pattern. Thus it is necessary to take a measure to prevent the forgery of visible anti-copy patterns. In order to enhance the security of patterns such as Figure 4 (a) a random different pattern may be inserted into the arrangement of the basic pattern. A random different pattern is a slight variation of the basic pattern, which is inserted as a basic pattern in order defined based on a specific key generated from the document when the document is printed.

For the security of patterns created by the combination of delete patterns and survival patterns, this study applied the digital watermarking technology [13]. Survival patterns are difficult to change but delete patterns are not because they only need to adjust the distribution of gray. Thus this study uses the spread spectrum digital watermarking technology proposed by I. J. Cox [14]. Spread spectrum not only en-hances the security of watermark by creating watermark information as a random sequence of numbers with the characteristic of spread spectrum but also preserves watermark information throughout the whole frequency band. It is therefore possible to restore watermark information even if it is partially destroyed by an attack from outside. In addition, different random sequences of numbers may be created accord-ing to key value that generates the sequences, and errors in watermark detection may be minimized because created sequences of numbers are hardly correlated with one another.

Because delete patterns created using the digital watermarking technology cannot be reproduced without the key generating algorithm and digital watermarking algo-rithm, it is possible to enhance the security of visible anti-copy patterns. Although it is inconvenient to have to use a computer with a scanner in order to determine whether visible anti-copy patterns are forged or not, we can reduce the risk of forgery significantly using the digital watermarking technology.

3.3   Evaluation of the Visible Anti-copy Pattern

In order to evaluate the performance of visible anti-copy patterns developed in this study, we tested patterns generated in diverse printer environments. A total of 241 kinds of printers were tested. Table 1 shows tested printers by manufacturer.

Table 1. List of printers

Printer Manufacturer	Number of Models	No of Appropriate Model	No of Inappropriate Model	Remarks
HP	88	78	10	
Samsung	50	44	6	
Epson	27	27	0	
SindoRicoh	40	40	0	
Others	36	30	6	
Total	241	219	22	

As shown in Table 1, the reason for testing pattern outputs for diverse printers is that the type and condition of printers affect patterns printed out. Thus it is possible to set the optimal condition for each type of printer through output tests. Laser printers have an outstanding characteristic as they print out given patterns as they are, but inkjet printers occasionally make errors in printing patterns because of the blotting of ink.

Patterns in Figure 5 may be printed out differently. Patterns in Figure 6 are results obtained by copying them using SindoRicoh NT-4120.

In Figure 6 (a), the pattern was broken by copying and, as a result, the word 'ORIGINAL' disappeared. In (b) and (c), the word 'COPY' was manifested in-versely. In (d), the word 'ORIGINAL' disappeared and 'COPY' was manifested. Patterns in Figure 7 are the results of scanning with CanoScan N670U of cannon at 600dpi.

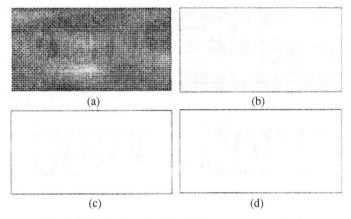

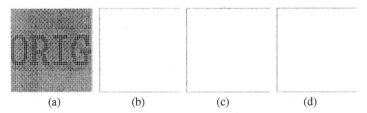

Fig. 6. Copied versions of the visible anti-copy pattern

Fig. 7. Scanned versions of the visible anti-copy pattern

4 Conclusions

This research examined visible anti-copy patterns with which we can distinguish between the originals and duplicates of printed documents with the naked eye. Because we can verify the integrity of output documents with the naked eye, visible anti-copy pattern is quite a convenient method. This kind of fast recognition through naked eyes is useful in implementing e-government project. Other implementation methods such as special printers, special inks and holograms generally require a huge amount of initial investment into infrastructure. Visible anti-copy patterns developed in this research can be widely used because they do not require special printers or equipment. They can be printed at ordinary printers of low performance and of low price. Also, many different patterns of anti-copy can be easily developed with minor modification. In particular, security of the technology is much enhanced using digital watermarking technology and the random patterns in order to prevent forgery.

In the evaluation of printers using the visible anti-copy patterns, this research confirmed that anti-copy technology could be safely applied to e-government implementation. In the experimentation, were used 241 kinds of printers, more than 10 types of copy machines and scanners, with varying types of anti-copy patterns. Because anti-copy patterns developed in this research are made in low-resolution printers, they may be forged using high-resolution scanners or digital copy machines. However, as digital watermarking is applied to security, the technology is considered highly usable in several areas such as online printing of official documents. The research team plans to develop more diverse patterns and to study further efficient patterns that are not affected by the feature of printers.

Acknowledgement

Solideo Gloria. The present work has been supported by the NRL (National Research Laboratory) Project in Korea (2000N-NL-01-C-286).

References

1. U.S. Secret Service on Currency Protection Fact Sheet, Counterfeit Deterrence, http://usembassy.state.gov/posts/in4/wwwhwn0514f.html
2. Q.B.Sun, P.R.Feng and R. Deng, "An Optical Watermarking Solution for Authenticating Printed Documents", International Conference on Information Technology ITCC-01, pp.65-70, 2001.
3. M. Naor and Benny Pinkas, "Visual Authentication and identification", Advances in Cryptology – CRYPTO '97, B. Kaliski Jr. Ed., Vol. 1294 of "Lecture Notes in Computer Science" Springer-Verlag, Berlin, pp.322-336, 1997.
4. George Phillips, "New digital anti-copy/scan and verification technologies", SPIE Vol.5310 Optical Security and Counterfeit Deterrence Techniques V, San Jose, 2004.
5. J. Picard, "Digital authentication with copy detection patterns", SPIE Vol.5310, Optical Security and Counterfeit Deterrence Techniques V, San Jose, 2004.
6. W. Bender, D Gruhl, N. Morimoto, and A. Lu, "Techniques for Data Hiding", IBM Systems Journal, Vol.25, pp.313-335, 1996.
7. C.-Y. Lin and S.-F. Chang, "Semi-Fragile Watermarking for Authenticating JPEG Visual Content", Proc. SPIE, Security and Watermarking of Multimedia Contents, San Jose, California, pp.140-151, January 2000.
8. http://www.sicc.com.sg/tradeser_index.html
9. H. Vollmerhausen and R. G. Driggers, Analysis of Sampled Imaging Systems, SPIE Press, Bellingham, WA, 2000.
10. P. G. J. Barten, Contrast Sensitivity of the Human Eye and its Effects on Image Quality, SPIE Press, Bellingham, WA, 1999.
11. http://web.mit.edu/persci/people/adelson/checkershadow_illusion.html
12. http://www.icaen.uiowa.edu/~aip/Lectures/eye_phys_lecture.pdf
13. I. J. Cox, M. L. Miller, and J. A. Bloom, Digital Watermarking, Academic Press, San Diego, CA, 2002.
14. I. J. Cox, J. Kilian, T. Leighton, and T. Shamoon, "Secure spread spectrum watermarking for multimedia" NEC Res. Insti., Princeton, NJ, Tech. Rep. 95-10, 1995

Holographic Image Watermarking for Secure Content

KyuTae Kim[1], JongWeon Kim[2], JungSoo Lee[1], and JongUk Choi[1,2]

[1] MarkAny Inc., 10F, Ssanglim Bldg., 151-11, Ssanglim-dong
Jung-gu, Seoul, 100-400, Korea
{jedam,jslee,juchoi}@markany.com
http://www.markany.com/

[2] College of Computer Software and Media Technology, Sangmyung University
7, Hongji-dong, Jongno-gu, Seoul, 110-743, Korea
{jwkim,juchoi}@smu.ac.kr
http://swc.smu.ac.kr/

Abstract. We propose a new watermarking scheme that can be used to embed multiple bits and also resilient to geometrical transforms such as scaling, rotation, and cropping, based on off-axis holographic watermark that allows multiple watermark recovery without original content(cover image). The holographic watermark is that Fourier transformed digital hologram is embedded into cover image in the spatial domain. The proposed method has not only increased robustness with a stronger embedding but also imperceptibility of the watermark in the evaluation process. To compare with the conventional scheme, the spread spectrum, we embedded and recovered maximum 1,024 bits that consist of binary number over PSNR(peak signal-to-noise ratio) 39dB. And also, we computed robustness with BER(bit-error rate) corresponding the above attacks.

1 Introduction

Practical watermarking schemes must make a trade-off between robustness from any kind of attacks and highly data payload with imperceptibility. General watermark attacks can be classified into JPEG compression and geometrical transformations such as rotation, scaling, and cropping. Spread spectrum schemes for watermarking purposes allow a low-energy signal to be embedded in each one of the frequency bands with a very low cross-correlation and is resistant to cropping, non-linear distortions of amplitude modulation and additive noise [1,2,3], but there are some drawbacks in synchronization. In this paper, it is not necessary to embed template to search synchronization during the watermark extraction process. The log-log mapping and log-polar map methods suggested to achieve scale and rotation invariance may not recover the watermark after a change of the aspect ratio. Furthermore, the overall robustness is not very good, since the watermark is embedded only in the amplitude of the Fourier transform [4,5,6]. The schemes of template matching and auto-correlation function can estimate the affined distortion applied to the image by comparing the configuration of the extracted peaks with their expected configuration

S. Katsikas, J. Lopez, and G. Pernul (Eds.): TrustBus 2004, LNCS 3184, pp. 219–231, 2004.

[7,8]. The limitation of the those methods is the complexity, since it has to compute several times Fourier transform in the translation recovery process.

In this paper we present a new approach that uses the digital hologram as the watermark. We call it the holographic watermark, which is resilient to geometrical transformations. Practical watermarking systems must make a trade-off between robustness and the competing requirements such as imperceptibility and information rate(payload). The proposed holographic watermark is satisfied with the above facts since hologram has redundancy and geometrical diffraction by nature. A hologram is recorded in interference pattern whose changing the rotation and the scale can make the diffracted light skew horizontally left or right with respect to the vertical axis. Since these two factors only alter the original position of the diffracted light, the proposed holographic watermark can recover the embedded data from geometrical transformations. And also the redundancy of the hologram can recover the original data from a partial hologram and then the holographic watermark is resilient to a cropping attack. In our simulations, we have made diffuse-type holographic watermark that is used in digital image processing by random phase modulation to reduce the strength of embedded data. To investigate the characteristics of the holographic watermark, we firstly compute the holographic watermark using a binary data stream and then embed it in 'lena' image with size of 256×256 pixels in the spatial domain. We analyze the holographic robustness to geometrical attacks using binary data of 90 bits and show recovery of embedded 1,024 bits binary data without bit error as the least image quality is 39dB.

2   Basics of Fourier Hologram

In 1948, D. Gabor proposed a novel lensless imaging process, which we know as holography [9]. Leith and Upatnieks suggested offset-reference hologram that solved twin image problem of Gabor's hologram [10]. Recording and reconstruction of the hologram is shown in Fig. 1. As shown in the Fig., the reference wave from a reference point is collimated by the Fourier lens and strikes the object wave from an object point. These two waves are superposed on recording medium and then recorded on intensity pattern of the resultant field, which is called hologram.

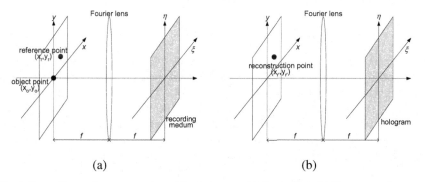

(a)   (b)

Fig. 1. Recording and reconstruction of the hologram (a) Recording, (b) Reconstruction

The hologram is added to object point's intensity pattern since each object point construct independent intensity pattern by above process. We used one object point like one bit data which number and coordinate effects energy level of embedding hologram pattern in this paper. The procedure of reconstruction from the hologram is shown in Fig. 1(b). We can recover embedding bit data using the Fourier transform of the product of the hologram and reference wave.

When the embedding bit data(object point) and reference point are denoted by $o(x_o, y_o)$ and $r(x_r, y_r)$ respectively, these can be superposed as Eq. (1) in recording medium,

$$U(\xi, \eta) = \int_{-\infty}^{\infty} \int_{-\infty}^{\infty} o(x - x_o, y - y_o) \exp[-j\frac{2\pi}{\lambda_1 f}(\xi x + \eta y)] d\xi \, d\eta$$

$$+ \int_{-\infty}^{\infty} \int_{-\infty}^{\infty} r(x - x_r, y - y_r) \exp[-j\frac{2\pi}{\lambda_1 f}(\xi x + \eta y)] d\xi \, d\eta \tag{1}$$

$$= O(\xi, \eta) \exp[-j\frac{2\pi}{\lambda_1 f}(\xi x_o + \eta y_o)] + R(\xi, \eta) \exp[-j\frac{2\pi}{\lambda_1 f}(\xi x_r + \eta y_r)],$$

where the first term is the Fourier transform of bit data, (x_o, y_o), and the second term is the Fourier transform of reference, (x_r, y_r). The parameters λ_1 and f indicate the wavelength and focal length of the recording process, respectively. The corresponding intensity distribution in the pattern between two waves of Eq. (1) is given by,

$$U_H(\xi, \eta) = |O(\xi, \eta)|^2 + |R(\xi, \eta)|^2$$

$$+ O(\xi, \eta)^* R(\xi, \eta) \exp[-j\frac{2\pi}{\lambda_1 f}(\xi x_r + \eta y_r) + j\frac{2\pi}{\lambda_1 f}(\xi x_o + \eta y_o)]$$

$$+ O(\xi, \eta) R(\xi, \eta)^* \exp[+j\frac{2\pi}{\lambda_1 f}(\xi x_r + \eta y_r) - j\frac{2\pi}{\lambda_1 f}(\xi x_o + \eta y_o)], \tag{2}$$

where * indicates the complex conjugate. This expression is called the hologram whose the intensity depends on both the amplitude and the phase of the integrated object points that are embedding bit rates. We have only used the third and fourth terms on the right hand side of Eq. (2) because the first and second terms result in no images in the reconstruction. When the reconstruction wave(point) is denoted by $(x_{r'}, y_{r'})$, the its complex wave can be written as,

$$U_R(\xi, \eta) = R'(\xi, \eta) \exp[-j\frac{2\pi}{\lambda_2 f'}(\xi x_{r'} + \eta y_{r'})], \tag{3}$$

where the parameters λ_2 and f' indicate the wavelength and focal length of the reconstruction process respectively. Two waves are reconstructed when hologram is multiplied with reconstruction wave by Eq. (3). These reconstructed waves are converging or diverging from points. It remains to determine the exact locations of these real or virtual points of convergence. If the wavelength and focal length of the reconstruction process are the same as recording, the reconstructed waves are given by,

$$U_1(\xi,\eta) = R'\,O^*\,R\,\exp[-j\frac{2\pi}{\lambda_1 f}(\xi x_r + \eta y_r) + j\frac{2\pi}{\lambda_1 f}(\xi x_0 + \eta y_o) - j\frac{2\pi}{\lambda_2 f}(\xi x_{r'} + \eta y_{r'})]$$

$$+R'\,O\,R^*\,\exp[+j\frac{2\pi}{\lambda_1 f}(\xi x_r + \eta y_r) - j\frac{2\pi}{\lambda_1 f}(\xi x_0 + \eta y_o) - j\frac{2\pi}{\lambda_2 f}(\xi x_{r'} + \eta y_{r'})] \qquad (4)$$

$$= R'\,O\,R^*\,\exp[-j\frac{2\pi}{\lambda_2 f}(\xi x_i + \eta y_i)],$$

where the coordinates (x_i, y_i) is the reconstructed bit data from the hologram. We conclude that the location x_i and y_i of the reconstructed bit data from the coefficients of the quadratic terms in x and y. Eq. (5) provides the fundamental relations that allow us to predict the locations of the reconstructed bit data,

$$\begin{cases} x_i = \mp x_0 \pm x_r + x_{r'} \\ y_i = \mp y_0 \pm y_r + y_{r'} \end{cases} \qquad (5)$$

where the upper set of signs applies for one bit data and the lower set of signs for the other in hologram. Two sets from Eq. (5) are reconstructed the virtual and real image which lie to the left and right of the hologram, respectively.

3 Principal of the Proposed Holographic Watermark

Now we describe application of the holographic watermark to conventional watermarking. As shown in above the hologram process, an embedded bit data is recorded in the Fourier hologram. This hologram is multiplied by weighting value α so that the holographic watermark cannot be recognized. The proposed holographic watermark can be realized by superposing the weighted hologram onto the content image in spatial domain. Watermarked image $w(x,y)$ can be expressed as follows.

$$w(x,y) = c(x,y) + \alpha H(\xi,\eta), \qquad (6)$$

where $c(x,y)$ and $H(\xi,\eta)$ indicate a content image and the holographic watermark. The proposed method does not need to embed multiple cross shapes by Gruhl and Bender or a calibration signal in the Fourier domain patented by Digimarc corporation so that watermark resist to geometrical transformations. It is possible to reduce computation time and the loss of embedded data by transformation domain since the holographic watermark can be only used to determine the geometrical distortions without additive information. And also, the partial holographic watermark can recover fully the embedded data because of the redundancy of hologram, and it is especially robust to cropping and cutting distortions.

We can recover the embedded bit data using simple computation, which is the Fourier transform of watermarked image multiplied by the reconstructed wave in Eq. (3). Set of the embedded bit data $d(x_o, y_o)$ and the recovered bit data $d(x_i, y_i)$ can be expressed by,

$$d(x_o, y_o) = \sum_{l=1}^{N} d_l(x_o, y_o),\tag{7}$$

$$d(x_i, y_i) = \int_{-\infty}^{\infty} \int_{-\infty}^{\infty} w(x_i, y_i) U_R(\xi, \eta) \exp[j2\pi(\xi x_i + \eta y_i)] d\xi \, d\eta,\tag{8}$$

where N is number of embedding bit data. The Fourier transform of Eq. (8) is reconstructed with three components, which are the recovered real and virtual bit data, and the Fourier spectrum of the content image. We must separate the reconstructed bit data from the Fourier spectrum of the content image that disturbs recovering bit data. We should block a low frequency region using window mask like Fig. 2 and make the bit data recover in the high frequency region since the Fourier spectrum is generally concentrated in a low frequency region. The embedded bit data can be recovered only using window mask without the original content. Fig. 2(b) is watermarked image of the holographic watermark by an embedding image in Fig. 2(a). The recovered image and window mask is shown in Fig. 2(c). The size of window mask depends on the region of the embedding data. We used window mask everywhere except the recovered region in our simulations. To design the size and location of window mask in Fig. 2(c), we determined the coordinate of the recovered bit data using Eq. (5). The bit data consists of multiple binary data stream as "1" and "0" in this experiments so that the holographic watermark can be applied for biometric information and two-dimensional barcode.

      (a)   (b)   (c)

Fig. 2. Extraction of embedding image (a) Embedding image, (b) Watermarking image, (c) Recovery image

As seen in Fig. 3, the holographic watermark can embed and recover multiple bits without the original content image. To show the holographic watermark of ability to embed a great number of bits, 80 bits of Fig. 3(a) have been used as a watermark to be embedded in the content image with 45dB. The start and end pixel points of the embedding bits are (20, 100) and (105, 120), respectively, and a reference and reconstruction point are (1, 129). The holographic watermark of Fig. 3(b) is made by each bit of Fig. 3(a) and then multiplied by weighting value not to distinguish visually from the content image. As seen in Fig. 3(b), the holographic watermark is constructed to have a uniform intensity distribution as a whole by using random phase modulator which can improve the quality of watermarked image and the recovered data. The embedded data is first multiplied by random phase modulator before it is Fourier transformed and then superposed by a reference point. But the recovered data is obtained independently of the random phase modulator. As seen in Fig. 4(d), the recovered bits appeared in different regions that one recovers from (20, 100) to (105, 120) and the other recovers from (238, 159) to (153, 139) according to Eq. (5). One pixel is one bit displayed by "0" and "1" and therefore we can embed the bit data as much as the size of a content image except the size of a window mask of Fig. 2(c). The embedding bit data can be recovered without error in a simulation when the size of window mask is half a content image and under. The embedding capacity of the holographic watermark has the maximum 256×128 bits when a content image is "lena" image with the size of 256×256 like Fig. 3.

(a)   (b)   (c)   (d)

Fig. 3. Holographic watermark using multiple bits (a) Multiple bits(80bit), (b) Holographic watermark, (c) Watermarking image, (d) Recovered bits

But if we can not remove the effect of the twin images, the embedding capacity can not help reducing as much as the size of one image. To embed the more multiple bits, the proposed holographic watermark is realized by an off–axis hologram to re-cover the only one. The field component $|R(\xi,\eta)|^2$ and $|O(\xi,\eta)|^2$ have plane wave travel-ing with respect to the optical axis. These components remain sufficiently to close to the optical axis to be spatially separated from the real and virtual images. A virtual image is multiplied to a linear exponential factor $\exp(j2\pi\alpha y)$ is deflected away from the optical axis at angle 2θ to the left of the hologram. Similarly, a real image is de-flected at angle -2θ from the optical axis to the right of the hologram. In that case the off-axis hologram of Eq. (1) is given by,

$$U_{H_{off}}(\xi,\eta)=O(\xi,\eta)^* R(\xi,\eta)\exp(-j2\pi\alpha y)+O(\xi,\eta) R(\xi,\eta)^* \exp(+j2\pi\alpha y),\qquad(9)$$

where the spatial frequency α of the reference wave is written as,

$$\alpha = \frac{\sin 2\theta}{\lambda f}.\qquad(10)$$

As seen in Fig. 4, an off-axis holographic watermark can embed the more multiple bits and variable forms because the only one image is recovered. To investigate that effect, the payload with 80, 205, and 260 bits were embedded in the content image with the size 256×256 pixels(by PSNR ≥ 45dB). Fig. 4(b), (c), and (d) are the results of the recovered multiple bits without an error.

Fig. 5 is the evaluation of the holographic watermark and spread spectrum meth-ods with PSNR(peak signal-to-noise ratio) and payload when bit-error of the recov-ered bits did not arise. In general, practical watermarking system must implement a compromise between robustness and the competing requirements like imperceptibility and information rate. Increased robustness requires a stronger embedding, which in turn increase perceptibility of the watermark. However, the proposed method is satisfied with the conditions that increase the more embedding without perceptibility. The holographic watermark can embed 1,024 bits with PSNR 39dB and all of the embedded bits also recover without detection error as shown in Fig. 5.

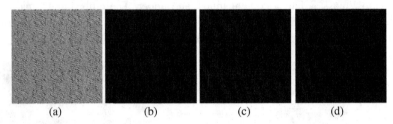

(a)   (b)   (c)   (d)

Fig. 4. Recovered multiple bits from off-axis holographic watermark (a) Off-axis hologram, (b) 80 bits, (c) 205 bits, (d) 260 bits

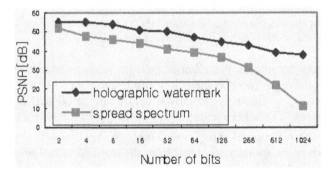

Fig. 5. PSNR vs. number of bits

Considering one random sequence used as one bit with the minimum watermark embedding strength, spread spectrum watermarking for embedding multiple bits can be realized by superposing a several random sequences onto the content image to embed multiple bits [11]. The total amount strength of the conventional spread spectrum method is linearly proportional to the embedded random sequence. For intensity(strength) of the hologram, the light from each point(bit) on the object interferes with the reference wave is to create a sinusoidal fringe with a vector spatial frequency that is unique to that the object point.

4   Simulation Results and Analysis

The digital watermark must be available not only to the more information but also to robustness of the distortions and attacks. The main problems are geometrical transformations. In our case the holographic watermark has to resolve the above problems. To investigate the effect of using the holographic watermark, the holographic watermark with size of 256×256 is given by a binary data, which was evaluated after geometrical transformations. The robustness is usually measured by the BER(bit-error ratio), defined as the ratio of wrong recovered bits to the total number of embedded bits. By changing the orientation of the hologram the diffracted wave can be made to skew horizontally left and right with respect to the vertical axis as shown in Fig. 6. Pixels with different hologram orientations will therefore light up from different angles as the hologram is rotated. Fig. 6(a), (b), (c), (d), and (e) are the rotated holograms that change -60, -45, 45, 0, and 60 degrees, respectively, and Fig. 6(f), (g), (h), (i), and (j) are the reconstructed images from the rotated holograms. To test the holographic watermark for rotation attack, the 8 bit gray scale of "lena" image, 256×256 pixels in size, was watermarked with PSNR 44dB.

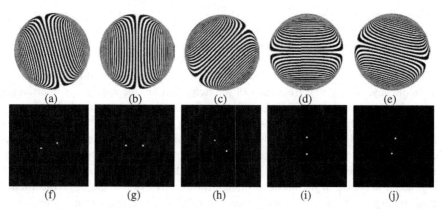

Fig. 6. Reconstructed images from the rotated hologram. Hologram rotation are (a) -60, (b) -45, (c) 0, (d) 45, and (e) 60 degrees. Reconstruction images are (f) -60, (g) -45, (c) 0, (d) 45, and (e) 60 degrees

Fig. 7 is the results of the recovered bits from the holographic watermark that is rotated from 15 to 90 degrees. As shown in Fig. 7, rotating attack may be recognized correctly by gradient of the recovered bits because it is the same as a rotated angle of the watermarked image. However, the modified image shown in Fig. 9(b) has to be reversed to obtain the correct results. Fig. 7(c), (d), and (e) are the recovered bits at different locations, although bit error may be arose from a rotating angle of watermarked image.

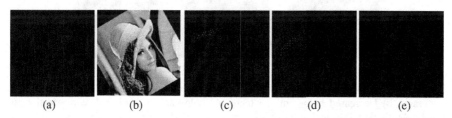

Fig. 7. Rotation attacks. Recovered bits are (a) Input bits, (b) Rotated watermarking image, (c) 15, (d) 45, and (e) 90 degrees in a counterclockwise direction

Fig. 8 shows the recovered bits from a distorted watermarked image after inverse geometrical transform. If the inverse transform brought distorted image to right direction, the embedded bits will be recovered without bit error as shown in Fig. 8(b). Faulty inverse may lead to bit error such as Fig. 8(c).

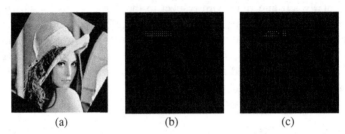

(a)   (b)   (c)

Fig. 8. Recovered bits from the reversed watermarking image (a) Inversed watermarking image, (b) correct recovered bits, (c) incorrect recovered bits

Fig. 9 shows that the diffraction angle of the hologram is determined by the spatial frequency. The spatial frequency of the hologram i.e. the number of interference fringes per mm can be adjusted. This is achieved by changing the angle between the reference and object waves. However, a scaling distortion of the hologram also causes the spatial frequency to change since it is the same as a changing distance between interference fringes. If the original hologram of Fig. 9(a) decreases in size, the number of interference fringes increases with the spatial frequency shown in Fig. 9(b), and a decrease in the hologram magnifies a diffraction angle of reconstruction image of Fig. 9(d). Fig., 9(e) and (f) are the results of reconstruction image from a decrease and increase in the original hologram respectively.

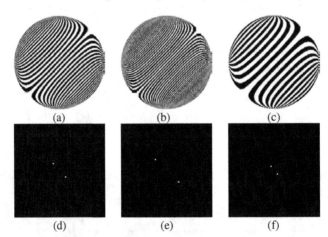

(a)   (b)   (c)

(d)   (e)   (f)

Fig. 9. Reconstructed images for the different spatial frequency of the hologram (a) Original hologram, (b) Decreased hologram, (c) Increased hologram, (d) Original reconstruction, (e) Magnification, (f) Demagnification

Fig. 10 is the result of the embedding bits recovered from a decrease and increase in watermarked images. It is seen in the Fig. 10 that the embedding bits are recovered for different images 256×256(×1, original image), 128×128(×0.5), and 512×512(×2) pixels in size, although the recovered bits have a different distance between twice and a half from 15 pixels. In this way it has been verified that the holographic watermark can still be recovered from the scale distortions of watermarked image. The recovered bits of Fig. 10(b) magnify 30 pixels with a decrease in watermarked image size and Fig. 10(c) demagnifies 7 pixels with an increase in size.

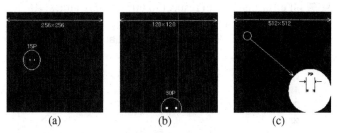

(a)   (b)   (c)

Fig. 10. Recovered bits by (a) original size, (b) demagnification, and (c) magnification of holo-graphic watermark. Sized here to have the same printed dimensions

The scale effects of the holographic watermark can be found from the Eq. (5) de-rived above for bits locations as shown in Eq. (11),

$$ M = |\frac{\partial_{x_i}}{\partial_{x_o}}| = |\frac{\partial_{y_i}}{\partial_{y_o}}| = |\frac{\partial_f}{\partial_{f'}}| = m|1-\frac{f'}{f} \mp m^2 \frac{\lambda_1 f'}{\lambda_2 f}|^{-1} \qquad (12) $$

where m and M are scale factor of the holographic watermark and recovered bit, re-spectively. If m is the demagnification ($m <1$) to which the holographic watermark, then we can see that embedded bits are recovered with magnification as shown in the Fig. 10(b). The holographic watermark is especially to robust to magnification ($m >1$) so that the error ratio of the recovered bits is lower than demagnification.

Fig. 11 is result of the recovered bits that was realized from watermarked images with the various scale distortions of 60~200%. The holographic watermark can be correctly recovered by 90% scale distortion above 40dB. The recovered bits may be seen for 60% scale, although BER increases with a decrease in size. In this way it has been verified that the holographic watermark can still be recovered from the scale distortion.

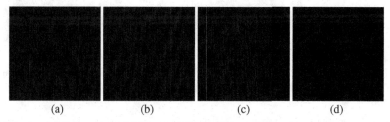

(a)   (b)   (c)   (d)

Fig. 11. Recovered bits with (a) >90% (b) 80% (c) 70% (d) 60% scales in watermarking image size. The size of the original watermarking image is 256×256 pixels

Fig. 12 shows BER of the holographic watermark that was transformed by scaling attack. It was performed on size of 256×256 pixels, 90 bits inserted. This graph allows immediate evaluation of the allowable the scaling attack of the holographic watermark for given BER. It is especially useful in case that BER range is given and corresponding maximal allowable scaling distortion needs to be evaluated. And also, we can see robustness(BER) comparisons for a given visual image quality which depends upon a strength in the holographic watermark. An image of PSNR 39dB may be taken a suitable trade-off between robustness and visual quality, in that case Fig. 13 shows 3.3% bit error under with respect to 60% scaling attack.

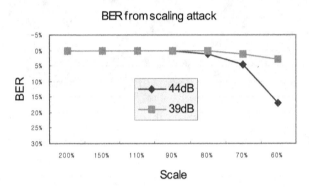

Fig. 12. BER vs. scaling attack for the holographic watermark

The holographic watermark is robust to a cropping distortion because hologram has an abundant redundancy by nature. To investigate the effect of cropping images, watermarked images were cropped from the original images with size of 256×256 pixels. Fig. 13 is result of the recovered bits from watermarked image with a cropping attack. Payload 90 bits were inserted in watermarked image and a visual quality was kept up PSNR 39dB. It is seen in the Fig. 13 that the recovered image may be recognized for partial images 128×128(50%) and 100×100(40%) pixels, respectively, although BER increased with a decrease in image size.

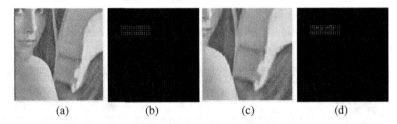

(a)   (b)   (c)   (d)

Fig. 13. Cropping images and recovered bits for payload 90 bits and PSNR 39dB. Image sizes are (a) 128×128(50%) and (b) 100×100(40%) pixels and recovered bits are (c) 128×128 and (d) 100×100

Fig. 14 shows robustness(BER) vs. cropping attacks for a proposed method. It was performed on size of 256×256 pixels, 90 bits inserted. For a given cropping, Fig.

14 can be used in determining the expected BER for a desired visual quality. The images of PSNR 44dB and 39dB were detected 20% and 2.2% bit error, respectively, with the cropped size of 100×100 pixels.

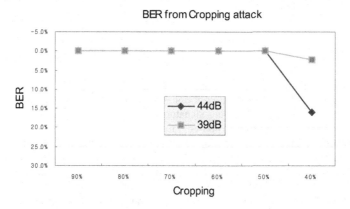

Fig. 14. BER vs. cropping attack for the holographic watermark

5   Conclusion

In this paper we propose a new digital watermarking scheme for copyright protection. Holographic watermark allows multiple watermark recovery without original cover image, even if watermarked image was distorted by lossy compression and generalized geometrical transforms such as rotation, scaling, and cropping. From the theoretical analysis and simulation results, the proposed method is fit for watermarking applications and requirements. The holographic watermark using off-axis Fourier hologram was embedded in the spatial domain and recovered by using inverse Fourier transform of hologram, and it was separated from frequency region of cover image by window-mask without original cover image. For watermark embedding strength, we embedded and recovered maximum 1,024 bits that consist of binary number over PSNR 39dB. As a geometrical robustness we use a BER defined as the ratio of wrong expected bits to the total number of embedded bits. All experiments were performed on the 256×256 pixels, and 8bit gray scale of 'lena'. And also watermark payload was 90 bits with different PSNR 39dB and 44dB. Simulation results showed that our proposed method is very robust to all geometrical distortions not more than 20% when numeric measurement of visual quality indicates by PSNR > 44dB on average. Even 50% distorted image can be recovered without error in all the BER vs. attacks graph if quality illustrates PSNR >39dB. Though this paper is limited in generalized geometrical attacks, the further study to increase the robustness about different attack such as D/A and A/D conversion for off-line protection will be performed in the future.

Acknowledgement

The present work has been supported by the NRL (National Research Laboratory) Project in Korea (2000N-NL-01-C-286).

References

1. I. J. Cox, J. kilian, T. Leighton, and T. Shamoon, "Secure spread spectrum watermarking for multimedia," NEC Res. Insti., Princeton, NJ, Tech. Rep. 95-100, 1995.
2. I. Pitas and T. Kaskalis, "Applying Signatures on Digital Image," Workshop on Nonlinear Signal and Image Processing, pp.460-463, June 1995.
3. K. T. Kim, J. H. Kim, and E. S. Kim, "Multiple Information Hiding Technique using Random Sequence and Hadamard Matrix," Opt. Eng, Vol.40, No.11, pp. 2489-2494, 2001.
4. J. J. K. O'Rauanidh and Thierry Pun, "Rotation, Scale and Translation Invariant Digital Image Watermarking", Signal processing journal, 1998.
5. C. Y. Lin, "Public Watermarking Surviving General Scaling and Cropping: An Application for Print-and-Scan Process", *ACM Multimedia 99*, Orlando, FL, USA, Oct 1999.
6. C. Y. Lin and Shih-Fu Chang, "Distortion Modeling and Invariant Extraction for Digital Image Print-and-Scan Process", *ISMIP 99*, Taipei, Taiwan, Dec. 1999.
7. R. Caldelli, M. Barni, F. Bartolini, and A. Piva, "Geo-metric-Invariant Robust Watermarking through Constellation Matching in the Frequency domain," Proceedings of 7th IEEE ICIP 2000, Vol.II, pp.65-68, Vancouver, Canada, Sep., 2000.
8. C. R. Choi and J. Jeong, "Robust Image Watermarking Scheme Resilient to De-synchronization Attacks," SPIE 2002 Security and Watermarking of Multimedia Contents IV, San Jose, USA, Jan., 2002.
9. D. Gabor, "A New Microscope Principle," Nature, Vol.161, pp.777, 1948.
10. E. N. Leith and J. Upatnieks, "Reconstructed Wavefronts and Communication Theory," J. Opt. Soc. Am, Vol.52, pp.1377, 1962.
11. F. Hartung, J. K. Su, and B. Girod, "Spread Spectrum Watermarking: Malicious Attacks and Counterattacks," in Proceedings of SPIE 3657, Security and Watermarking of Multimedia Cotents, pp. 147-158, 1999.

Hybrid Fingerprint Matching
on Programmable Smart Cards*

Tommaso Cucinotta, Riccardo Brigo, and Marco Di Natale

Scuola Superiore Sant'Anna
{cucinotta,rojelio,marco}@sssup.it

Abstract. This paper presents a hybrid fingerprint matching algorithm combining two heterogeneous schemes, namely the texture-vector and minutiae-based methods. The proposed technique has been designed in order to run on a programmable smart card, with image processing and feature extraction performed on the host, and matching performed by the card device. The two matching algorithms have been carefully tuned in order to achieve an acceptable performance despite the computation and memory constraints. Given the high level of intrinsic security that smart cards already have, and the interactive nature of target applications, the complexity of the problem has been greatly reduced, making such an approach feasible. This is validated by the experimental results we show, gathered from an implementation onto a Java Card device, where acceptable false acceptance and rejection rates are achieved at the cost of a reasonable response time of the device.

1 Introduction

User authentication is one of the most important issues when designing a secure system. Traditional password based solutions, relying on the concept that a user is authenticated by proving knowledge of a secret information, usually offer an unacceptable security level. In fact, the secret information can easily be revealed to (or stolen by) unauthorised users. If the password is not strong, it can also be easily guessed by an attacker. Use of smart cards, along with cryptographic authentication protocols, increases security by requiring a user to prove both possession of a physical card, containing a cryptographic key, and knowledge of a secret information, usually a Personal Identification Number (PIN) protecting the card (two factor authentication). This raises the security level with respect to remote attackers, but still it is subject to the problem of voluntary delegation, or card stealing / PIN extortion. Biometrics based authentication techniques solve this problem, by requiring the user to prove possession of a unique, characteristic property of his own body, such as fingerprints ridges, hand shape, retina, etc... When such a technique is used in conjunction with smart card technology, a high security level is achieved since users are required to prove, at the same

---

* This work has been partially supported by the European Commission within the IST project 2001-34820 ARTIST, and by the MIUR within the 2002 I4002 PA Project.

S. Katsikas, J. Lopez, and G. Pernul (Eds.): TrustBus 2004, LNCS 3184, pp. 232–241, 2004.

time, knowledge of a secret information, possession of a physical token, and possession of their own physical body (three factor authentication), before access to a system is granted.

This work is focused on systems where the authentication mechanism relies on the cryptographic capabilities of the card, and fingerprint verification is used by the card, in addition or alternative to PIN code verification. An alternative target is a secure application running entirely or in part onto a smart card, where the card itself authenticates users. A typical target application is smart card based digital signature, where the non repudiation property, usually established only at a jurisdictional level by dictating card owner responsibilities, can be technically enforced by requiring a biometrics authentication by the card, before the signing operation takes place.

This paper is organised as follows. Section 2 briefly reviews works found in literature related to fingerprint verification. Section 3 features an overview of the proposed technique, with a detailed description of the matching mechanism that has been implemented on the card device. Evaluation results for the proposed algorithm are reported in Section 4. Specific notes about the algorithm implementation are reported in Section 5. Finally, Section 6 draws conclusions and presents possible areas of future investigation.

2   Related Work

In recent years, the problem of merging smart card technology and biometrics for the purpose of authenticating users has gained more and more attention from research and industry altogether. Smart card based authentication has been widely used whenever user authentication was required, though the result has always been the authentication of the plastic card itself, not the user. Biometrics promise a final solution to this problem, achieving an integrated authentication system in which not only a user is authenticated by proving possession of a physical token and knowledge of a secret information, but by showing to the system some unique biological characteristics of its own body.

Correct use of biometrics and smart cards is not as immediate as it could seem at a first glance. Recent works [1, 2] focused on the possible attacks a system integrating such technologies could be subject to. In [2] eight types of attacks to a biometric authentication system are identified, targeted either to the components themselves, or to the communication protocols among them. Recently, the European Union has also focused attention on feasibility of matching-on-card technologies, as in [3], where it is underlined that, in the context of electronic signatures, the possibility of identifying people based on biometric characteristics is of fundamental importance due to the non-repudiation security requirement, and the need for on-card matching is also outlined.

Feature extraction from fingerprint images has been widely studied, as shown in [4], where a good overview is made on the general structure of automatic fingerprint identification systems (AFIS), emphasizing the main challenges such a system has to face with. In [5] the authors demonstrate how an image enhancement algorithm based on Gabor filters can significantly improve the performances of an AFIS thanks to the greater reliability and precision gained by the minutiae extraction process, which leads to a reduced False Rejection Rate (FRR) for a given False Acceptance Rate (FAR). In [6], Prabhakar proposes an innovative approach to fingerprint analysis & matching, based on the use of a Gabor filter bank to extract from the fingerprint image statistical information, which have been proven to degrade much more smoothly with image quality than classical minutiae-based algorithms. This approach has further been developed in [7] in order to achieve comparable performances even in conjunction with small sensors, which offer to the analysis system only a limited portion of the fingerprint. In the same work, the authors opened a relatively new investigation direction inspired from the so called multimodal biometric verification techniques, where multiple kinds of a person biometric characteristics are used at once for the purposes of authentication. Due to the independence between the different kind of biometric information that is matched in such techniques, a combination of them results in a higher performance, as shown in [8].

The specific problem of combining two fingerprint matching algorithms in order to improve performance is addressed in [9], where the authors compare three different ways of combining the scores obtained from distinct matching algorithms (a linear combination, a multiplicative combination and a combination based on the logistic function) and demonstrate that the best performance is achieved with the logistic function.

With respect to previous investigations on hybrid fingerprint matching, the approach which is being introduced in this paper is specifically focused on the problem of implementing such techniques onto programmable smart card devices. It does not aim at achieving the highest possible performance, but achieving an acceptable performance for the cited usage context, while keeping a sufficiently low complexity level so to allow implementation onto a programmable card device. We give an extensive description of the adopted algorithms, and a precise specification of how various parameters have been tuned in the implementation. Furthermore, we present an on-card architecture for the matching algorithm, realised as a consistent extension to the protocol and JavaCard Applet introduced in [10], and report experimental timings gathered from the execution of the proposed algorithm onto a JavaCard device.

On a related note, fingerprint matching on JavaCard devices is not novel, as industrial products already exist based on the same kind of technology, like the one from Precise Biometrics [11]. However, implementation details and extensive description of the experimental setup from which such measurements arise are not available, making it impossible to perform a comparison with other approaches.

3   Hybrid Matching

Our system uses both Prabhakar's fingercode and minutiae information in order to perform a multi modal biometric verification of the user. Both techniques have been split into the two fundamental steps of feature extraction and feature matching. Thus, the live-scanned fingerprint image is first analysed on the host machine in order to extract the features using the two relatively complex feature extraction algorithms; such features are then transmitted to the smart card device, which performs the matching phases of both algorithms, comparing the received features with the templates previously stored into its internal memory during enrollment.

In the following, we report a description of the extraction and matching algorithms adopted for the two techniques.

3.1   Features Extraction and Representation

Fingercode. Fingercode extraction has been implemented following the method described in [6], where an exhaustive description of the algorithm can be found. Briefly, it consists of the following steps (see Fig. 1). First, the fingerprint image is normalised to a constant mean and variance, then a reference point (core) is determined, defined as the topmost point on the innermost upward ridge. A circular region of interest around the core is then tessellated and filtered using eight Gabor filters, tuned over eight different directions. For each of the filtered images, and for each tessel, the intensity absolute deviation from the mean is computed. The complete list of such absolute deviations, normalised in the range [0..255], constitutes the fingercode of the original image.

Fig. 1. Example of Fingercode computation: a *region of interest* is determined around the core, then it is directionally filtered (only vertical filtering is showed), tessellated and intensity absolute deviations (represented in gray scale) are computed.

Minutiae. In order to extract the minutiae from the fingerprint image, we adopted the algorithm supplied by the National Institute of Standards and Technology (NIST) as implemented in the NIST Fingerprint Image Software (NFIS), a public domain software developed for the Federal Bureau of Investigation.

This algorithm can be roughly subdivided into the following phases[1]. First, the gray-scale fingerprint image is reduced to a binary, black and white one, then

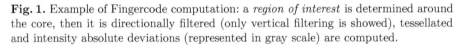

---

[1] For further details the reader is referred to NFIS official documentation, freely distributed by NIST (*http://www.nist.gov*).

analysed in order to find every singular point (bifurcations and terminations) which could be a potential minutia. This operation results in false positives (minutiae detected where none exists), due to low-quality image, cuts, bruises or other noise. Thus, various heuristics are applied to discover and delete such false positives (for example two facing and aligned minutiae at small distance are likely to be due to a cut determining two false terminations). Finally, for each of the remaining minutiae the algorithm outputs the position, direction (defined as the main direction of the surrounding ridge flow) and an index of reliability, determined considering multiple factors such as local image quality and proximity to image borders. Our system excludes from further analysis the minutiae with a reliability index under a given threshold. The others are ordered based on increasing distance from the core, where only the nearest num_m ones, up to a maximum number of $maxMinutiaeNumber$, are considered, so to limit computation requirements for the matching phase.

Let $\{m_i\}_{0 \leq i < num_m}$ denote the set of found minutiae, where m_0 is the fingerprint core. The algorithm builds a graph representation of the minutiae, where each minutia m_i is associated a node n_i in the graph, and the set of outgoing arcs from a node n_i represents the set of minutiae which are considered neighbours of m_i for the purpose of matching. The following algorithm builds the graph:

1. determine the bounding-box of the minutiae set;
2. let ref_i be the number of references to m_i, initially 0;
3. let p be the list of pending minutiae; initially p contains m_0;
4. let c be the list, initially empty, of consolidated minutiae;
5. extract next minutia m_{curr} from p, and add m_{curr} to c;
6. enumerate m_{curr}'s nearest neighbours, given the following restrictions:
   (a) a maximum of max_{neigh} neighbours can be listed, where max_{neigh} is n_c if $m_{curr} \equiv m_0$, n_m otherwise;
   (b) minutiae in c are ignored;
   (c) neighbour's distance from m_{curr} must be in the range $[dist_{min}, dist_{max}]$; we do not accept a neighbour too close because at small distances even light errors in position detection can determine large variations in direction when expressed in polar coordinates; on the other hand we can't accept too far neighbours because at large distances the elastic deformation of finger's skin couldn't be ignored;
7. for each neighbour m_j found
   (a) associate to m_{curr} the corresponding vector (i. e. distance and direction from m_{curr} to m_j and the index j);
   (b) increment ref_j; if $ref_j = max_{ref}$, add m_j to c;
   (c) add m_j to p, if not already present;
8. if p is not empty, continue from step 5.

If $max_{ref} = 1$, the graph becomes a spanning tree touching every minutia in the set; the choice to allow multiple references ($max_{ref} > 1$) to the same minutia is due to the necessity to give the graph enough redundancy, which (as discussed in Section 3.2) reduces the probability of erroneous early abort by the matching algorithm when comparing two corresponding fingerprints. On the other hand, max_{ref} has to be lower than max_{neigh}, otherwise the graph could result in a strongly connected, central cluster of nodes which does not reach outer minutiae[2].

The representation of a fingerprint, as output by the described process, is composed of: the bounding box coordinates; the found minutiae list $\{m_i\}$, including, for each minutia, its Cartesian coordinates (relative to the core), direction and list of vector-distances to its neighbours.

3.2   Matching

Fingercode. Fingercode matching has been implemented as described in [6]: given the two vectors, we compute the sum of absolute differences between corresponding elements and store the result as the score of the process $score_{\text{fc}}$.

Minutiae. The minutiae matching has been inspired by the point-pattern matching algorithm described in [12], with the simplification obtained by computing a common reference point: the core. In the following, we consider two vectors (as defined in Section 3.1, step 7a) $v_1(dist_1, dir_1, i_1)$ and $v_2(dist_2, dir_2, i_2)$ to match given the rotation rot and the tolerance parameters th_{dist}, th_{dir} and th_{angle} when:

$$|dist_1 - dist_2| < th_{\text{dist}}$$
$$|dir_1 - dir_2 + rot|_{360} < th_{\text{dir}}$$
$$|m_{i_1}.dir - m_{i_2}.dir + rot|_{180} < th_{\text{angle}}$$

where $m_i.dir$ denotes the direction of the ith minutia. These three tolerances have been chosen by performing a statistical analysis of pairs of corresponding fingerprints.

The basic task of the algorithm is to find, given the template and the minutiae graphs, a spanning ordered tree touching as many nodes as possible, starting from the two cores (which are assumed to be corresponding by hypothesis) and visiting the graphs only via common arches, i. e. the ones corresponding to vectors matching within accepted tolerance.

The algorithm proceeds as follows:

1. Let T_i and S_i indicate respectively the ith minutia of the template and of the proposed set;
2. let m be the list of matches found, composed of couples of indexes, where the presence into m of the couple (i_1, i_2) means that a match has been detected between T_{i_1} and S_{i_2};
3. let p be a list, initially empty, of pending minutiae;

---

[2] It should be noted that we *do not* guarantee to reach every minutia, but only that the probability of a minutia to be excluded from the graph is sufficiently low.

4. look for the rotation bestRot which gives the maximum number of matches among the two cores' neighbours under tolerances th_{distCore}, th_{dirCore} and th_{angle} (th_{distCore} and th_{dirCore} are less restrictive than their general counterpart to take in account the possible imprecision in core detection); the search has two limitations:
   (a) $|bestRot| < max_{\mathrm{rot}}$ (we assume that the user puts his finger approximately vertically);
   (b) given two rotations rot_1 and rot_2 which give the same number of matches, the lower one (in absolute value) is preferred;
5. for each minutia S_i for which a corresponding T_j was found during previous step, insert (j, i) into m and S_i into p;
6. extract next pending minutia S_{curr} from p and find into m the corresponding matching template minutia T_{corr};
7. for each vector $v_1(dist_1, dir_1, i_1)$ associated to S_{curr} look for a matching vector $v_2(dist_2, dir_2, i_2)$ associated to T_{corr} with rotation $bestRot$ and tolerances th_{dist}, th_{dir} and th_{angle}; for each match found for which (i_2, i_1) is not already into m, add (i_2, i_1) to m and add m_{i_1} to p;
8. if p is not empty, continue with step 5.

Defined $numMin_t$ as the number of minutiae of T lying inside the bounding box of S, $numMin_s$ as the number of minutiae of S lying inside the bounding-box of T, and $numMatches$ as the number of matches found by the algorithm, the score is evaluated as:

$$score_{\mathrm{min}} = 100\frac{numMatches^2}{numMin_t * numMin_s}$$

Matchers' Fusion. Given the two scores $score_{\mathrm{fc}}$ and $score_{\mathrm{min}}$, the overall score is calculated as a linear combination of them:

$$score = \alpha score_{\mathrm{fc}} + \beta score_{\mathrm{min}} .$$

If $score$ exceeds a given threshold th_{score} the system considers the proposed fingerprint to be sufficiently similar to the enrolled one and the match succeeds, otherwise the match fails. Coefficients α and β have been determined with an a posteriori analysis as the ones which minimise the overall Equal Error Rate (EER) of the system.

4   Results

Effectiveness of our verification algorithm has been tested by submitting to it pairs of fingerprint images and by measuring its ability to discriminate between corresponding and non-corresponding ones in terms of FAR/FRR curves.

Tests have been conducted on a database of 55 live-scan fingerprints taken on a group of volunteers, with each fingerprint scan repeated ten times for a total of 550 images. The volunteers were completely unaware of biometrics related technology and scanner use, so they have been subject to a training phase of one minute with visual feedback, so to allow them to understand what was the right position and pressure of the finger for a good scan. Then, they have been asked to pose ten times the finger on the scanner in a natural way.

The obtained images have been analysed and matched in pairs using our algorithm, distinguishing matches between corresponding fingerprints (different images of the same finger) from matches between non-corresponding fingerprints. Figures 2(a) and (b) show the obtained joint (based on minutiae and on finger-code) scores' distributions in the two cases. In the two graphs, the X axis reports the score obtained with minutiae matching, which is higher when a higher number of matching minutiae is detected, while the Y axis reports the fingercode score, which is lower when the live-scan fingerprint is more similar to the on-card template. The same distributions are reported in the 3D plot of Figure 2(c) for convenience.

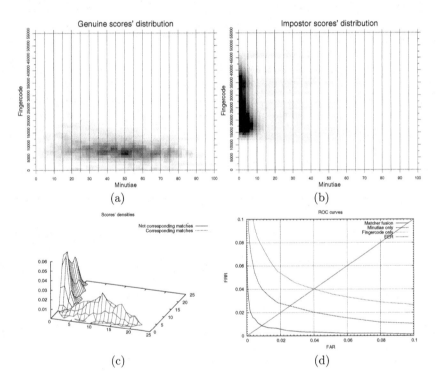

Fig. 2. (a)-(c) Joint score distributions for genuine and impostor matches. (d) ROC curves.

In Fig. 2(d) we compare the Receiver Operating Curves (ROCs) relative to each matcher separately and to their combination. These curves represent the FAR/FRR pairs that are obtained by continuously varying the score threshold of the matching algorithms. As the picture highlights, the hybrid technique results in a considerable increment of performance when compared to the results achieved singularly by the two matchers. In fact, in the hybrid ROC curve, the FRR value, for each possible FAR, is consistently lower than those obtained singularly by the two matchers. Furthermore, while the minutiae based and fingercode matchers obtain, respectively, an EER of about 2.3% and 4%, the combined matcher obtains an EER of about 0.8%. The combined matching algorithm requires an on-board computation time of about 11–12 seconds.

5   Implementation Notes

The described biometric authentication system has been developed, on the host side, as an extension to the MUSCLE Card [13] middleware, and on the card side as an extension to the MUSCLE Card JavaCard Applet. This framework defines a high level API that smart card aware applications can use to access smart card storage, cryptographic and PIN management services in a unified, card independent way. The framework also includes a JavaCard Applet allowing the middleware to use the on-card services by means of the protocol described in [10]. Briefly, the framework allows applications to manage on-board data containers (objects), cryptographic keys, and PIN codes. A security model allows to protect, on a per object and a per operation basis, objects and keys, by means of Access Control Lists (ACLs).

An extension mechanism has been embedded in the framework so to allow applications to enhance the basic protocol and Applet in order to support application specific extensions. Biometrics based authentication has been embedded in this context by allowing the access to on-card resources (e.g. reading an object or using a cryptographic key) only after a successful on-board fingerprint verification. Furthermore, the existing access control mechanism allows, by using ACLs, the possibility to combine the new authentication mechanism with traditional PIN based or challenge-response cryptographic based authentication. The used fingerprint scanner is FX2000 USB, by Biometrika s.r.l. (http://www.biometrika.it), providing a portable development kit and API for access to the acquired biometric data. The development platform has been a RedHat 7.3 Linux system.

6   Conclusions and Future Work

In this paper, a hybrid fingerprint matching mechanism has been introduced, designed with the aim of running onto a programmable smart card. Experimental results showed that, by taking advantage of the simplifications inherent to the application context and using ad-hoc designed data representations, it is possible to realise an on-board hybrid fingerprint matcher with an acceptable performance, even into such scarce-resource devices as programmable smart cards, maintaining reasonable execution times. In a short future, it is scheduled to undertake investigations related to the feasibility of on-board multi modal authentication based on alternative means of biometrics.

References

1. Hachez, G., Koeune, F., Quisquater, J.J.: Biometrics, access control, smart cards: A not so simple combination. In: Proc. of CARDIS 2000. IFIP (2000)
2. Ratha, N., Connell, J., Bolle, R.: Enhancing security and privacy in biometrics-based authentication systems. IBM Systems Journal **40** (2001)
3. Scheuermann, D., Schwiderski-Grosche, S., Struif, B.: Usability of biometrics in relation to electronic signatures. Technical Report GMD-Report-118, GMD - Forschungszentrum Informationstechnik GmbH (2000)
4. Jain, A.K., Pankanti, S.: Automated fingerprint identification and imaging systems. In: Advances in Fingerprint Technology, 2nd Edition. H. c. lee and r. e. gaensslen edn. Elsevier Science (2001)
5. Hong, L., Jain, A., Pankanti, S., Bolle, R.: Fingerprint enhancement. In Sarasota, F., ed.: Proc. 1st IEEE WACV. (1996) 202–207
6. Prabhakar, S.: Fingerprint classification and matching using a filterbank. PhD thesis, Michigan State University (2001)
7. Ross, A., Prabhakar, S., Jain, A.: Fingerprint matching using minutiae and texture features. In: Proceeding of the International Conference on Image Processing (ICIP). (2001) 282–285
8. Ross, A., Jain, A.K., Qian, J.Z.: Information fusion in biometrics. Lecture Notes in Computer Science **2091** (2001) 354–359
9. Marcialis, G., Roli, F., Loddo, P.: Fusion of multiple matchers for fingerprint verification. In: Proc. of Workshop su Percezione e Visione delle macchine, 8vo Convegno dell'Associazione Italiana per l'Intelligenza Artificiale AI*IA02, Siena, Italy (2002)
10. Cucinotta, T., Natale, M.D., Corcoran, D.: A protocol for programmable smart cards. In: Proceedings of the 14th International Workshop on Database and Expert Systems Applications (DEXA'03), Prague, Czech Republic, IEEE Computer Society Press (2003) 369–374
11. Pettersson, M., Harris, M.: Whitepaper: Match-on-card for java cards. Precise Biometrics (2002)
12. Wamelen, P.V., Li, Z., Iyengar, S.: A fast algorithm for the point pattern matching problem. Technical Report 1999-28, Louisiana State University, Dept. of Mathematics (1999)
13. Corcoran, D., Cucinotta, T.: MUSCLE card framework – application programming interface, v1.3.0 (2001)

Protecting ASF Movie on VOD

Ji-Hyun Park, Jeong-Hyun Kim, and Ki-Song Yoon

ETRI(Electronics and Telecommunicatios Research Institute), 161 Gajeong-dong
Yuseong-gu, Daejeon, 305-350 Korea
{juhyun,bonobono,ksyoon}@etri.re.kr

Abstract. Easiness of creating and distributing digital information is increasing
the production of the digitalized movies. However, since digital content is easy
to make copies and it can be distributed through internet which is open to
anyone, the problems in security and intellectual property become important
issues. These problems are occurred at local content saved in users' PC until
recently. Encrypting the full content is one solution to protect saved content.
Streaming content has solved these problems by removing data immediately
after processed. But, recently some hacking tools have been appeared, which
can save the streamed data. So, streamed media is also not free for illegal use
any more. Protecting scheme for streamed content is more complicate because
the streaming server must be considered. If the full content file is encrypted, the
streaming server cannot transmit the content because the encrypted content may
be unknown type to the streaming server. In this paper, we propose a DRM-
based streaming system which can not only protect streamed ASF content but
be easily integrated with existing ASF streaming system. ASF is the multimedia
file format of Microsoft. To explain our system, we describe some related
technology, service architecture, encryption scheme and decryption scheme of
our system.

1 Introduction

Changes in internet and network environment have made it possible to provide high-
quality content services in real time. As demand for digital content is increased,
problems related to intellectual property rights are getting more important. Streaming
service like video-on-demand solved these problems by preventing content from
being saved. But, as the advent of several tools able to save streamed content, the
streamed content is not free from these problems any more. Particularly, if a
streaming system serves high quality digital content, it is easily predicted that the
damages by illegal use will be much greater. Therefore, with security countermeasure
like access control, new technologies to control and manage rights of content are
needed. One of the solutions is DRM(Digital Rights Management)[8,9,11].

To apply DRM to streaming system, an encryption program is required on the
server side, and some modules to play protected content are required on the client
side. DRM should be integrated with streaming system without modifying the
existing streaming server. it means that DRM should be implemented by works to the
content file and the client player. Since commercial streaming systems aim to serve
high quantity data, more processing time is needed to decode and play content in the
client device. The processing time of DRM should be minimized to guarantee the

S. Katsikas, J. Lopez, and G. Pernul (Eds.): TrustBus 2004, LNCS 3184, pp. 242–250, 2004.

quality of streaming. For this reason, minimizing the amount of data to be encrypted is one of the essential factors to design the DRM modules.

In this paper, we propose a DRM-based streaming system which can be easily integrated with existing ASF streaming system as well as protect streamed ASF content. We encrypt ASF files without breaking file format so that it can be sent by Microsoft Media Server. Our encryption scheme provides some encryption options in order not to degrade the streaming performance.

2 Related Works

2.1 Windows Media Rights Manager

WMRM(Windows Media Rights Manager) is the DRM technology of Microsoft for protecting Windows media files. WMRM is an end-to-end DRM system that offers content providers and retailers a flexible platform for the secure distribution of digital media files. It provides tools that can be used to package Windows media files and issue licenses for them[14].

The content packaging, distribution, and licensing process begins with a piece of encoded content. The content packager packages the content as an encrypted Windows media file and then shares the secrets for decrypting and licensing the file with the license issuer. Consumers are then issued a license to play the file, and use it according to the business rules defined for it.

It is the easiest way to protect Windows media files, but it is hard to be customized because it is not an open technology.

2.2 ISMACryp

ISMACryp is the nickname of ISMA 1.0 Encryption and Authentication, which is a cryptographic framework for ISMA 1.0 MPEG-4 streams. The framework is extensible to new media encodings, can be upgraded to new cryptographic transforms, and is applicable to a variety of key management, security, or DRM systems. ISMACryp also defines a default encryption of media streams and authentication of media messages for ISMA 1.0. The main goal of ISMACryp is interoperability at the ISMA receiver with or without cryptographic services[7].

3 Service Architecture

A streaming server sends stream data according to the content file format without respect to whether content is protected or not. The format of the protected content must not be modified in order to be streamed correctly. So, it is required to apply methods which don't break the content format. Such methods can be obtained through analyzing the content format.

To play protected content, information related to decryption should be transmitted from the server to the client. This information includes some important data like decryption keys. Therefore a secure network channel between server and client is needed.

From the end-users' point of view, they want to watch the protected content by the same way as the original content. They won't be willing to do additional actions to watch the protected content. Therefore users' inconvenience should be considered and minimized.

Fig 1 shows our service architecture. Streaming server and client are the existing component of the streaming system. We added ASF protection application and license server to achieve the secure ASF streaming.

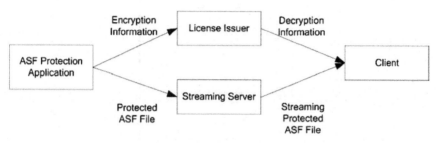

Fig. 1. Service Architecture

The ASF protection application is an application to encrypt ASF file. It encrypts only media data part of ASF files in order not to break the ASF file format. We can select the frame type to be encrypted, or the size of the data to be encrypted. It also sends the information about encryption to the license server. The license issuer manages the information needed to decrypt the protected ASF files. It includes key information, the type of the encrypted media data, the size of encrypted data, and so on. The license issuer sends this information to the legal client. Client includes a media player, a decryption module and a DRM core module. The DRM core manipulates the licenses acquired from the license Issuer. It also manages lots of authentication information securely, and it protects content from being exposed out of our system by authenticating the modules loaded in the client environment[9,13].

As mentioned above, we have some prerequisites to apply the DRM technology on the streaming system as follows. File must conform to common ASF specification. For example, files must have a header object, a data object, and an optional index object. License server must be ready to accept incoming requests from DRM clients and provide necessary information.

4   ASF File Protection

4.1   ASF File

ASF(Advanced Systems Format) means the extensible file storage format developed by Microsoft for authoring, editing, archiving, distributing, streaming, playing, referencing, or otherwise manipulating content. It supports data delivery over a wide variety of networks and is also suitable for local playback[1,6].

An ASF file is organized into sections called objects. There are three top-level objects, a header object and a data object, and an optional index object. The header object contains general information about the file, such as file size, number of streams, error correction methods, and codecs used. Metadata is also stored here. The header object is the only top level object that can contain other objects. The data object contains the stream data, organized in packets. The simple index object contains a list of associated timestamp–key frame pairs that enables applications to seek through a file efficiently. Fig 2 shows the structure of ASF file.

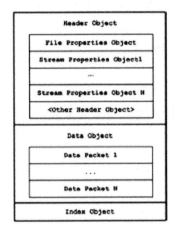

Fig. 2. ASF File Structure

4.2 Encryption Scheme

The DRM system for downloaded content encrypts the full file to protect it[12]. As mentioned above, the streaming server decides the sending data by information of the movie data when it transmits a movie. If the full file is encrypted to protect it, the information needed to read media data will be also modified. It would make the streaming service impossible.

To avoid this problem, we encrypt the only media data not the metadata. Fig 3 shows the detailed structure of ASF file. The data object consists of a lot of data packets. The data packet is the actual packet which is transmitted to the client device during streaming. The data packet consists of error correction data, payload parsing information, payload data, and padding data. The payload data in the data packet have the actual media data. The media data of the identical media object number make one video frame or one audio frame.

To encrypt the media data in the unit of frame, we aggregate media data to make a frame. It can be achieved by merging media data of the identical media object number. Then we encrypt the frame data, and then attach 1 byte to indicate the encryption. It increases the size of the movie file slightly. The encrypted frame data is divided to the same size of original media data except the last. The size of the last media data is increased by 1 since we attach 1 byte data of marking the encryption. Fig 4 shows this process. Some other metadata should be modified because the file size is changed.

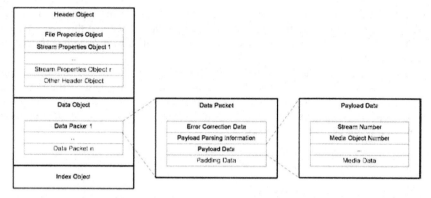

Fig. 3. Structure of Data Object

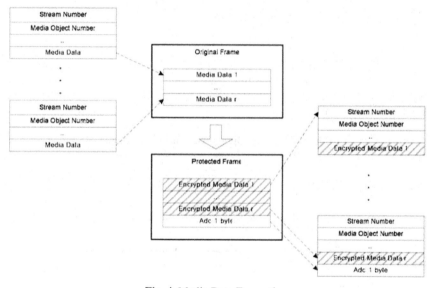

Fig. 4. Media Data Encryption

Video sequence frames can be divided on two distinct categories – key frames and others. Key frames are the essential elements for decoding process as they don't contain any dependency and can be decoded as is.

Thus encryption applied to key frames is sufficient in the way it protects key information for the ASF visual decoder. Files encoded in such way still can be played by any robust ASF player, but most part of visual information is perceived as garbage.

On the playback, the protected content should be processed by our decryption module. In order to redirect playback data flow to our decryption module, we modify the streaming properties object which is in the header object. We overwrite the codec ID with our codec ID, and then save the original codec ID into the codec specific data slot.

Some encryption algorithms are use aligned blocks to encrypt. For example, standard DES[2] uses 64 bit aligned blocks. To encrypt packet, which are not aligned to 64 bit boundary, data must be padded, but this approach changes file size in almost all the cases. Using downsize alignment approach helps to resolve this issue for any packets with size bigger than 64 bits. Obviously for all adequate video frames are much bigger than 8 bytes

Fig 5 shows the structure of the encrypted sample of ASF video. The length of tail is less than 8. We encrypt 8 bytes of the sample data continuously. If the remainder data length is less than 8, we don't encrypt them in order not to change the whole sample size. The tail part includes those data. The encryption byte flag indicates whether the frame is encrypted or not.

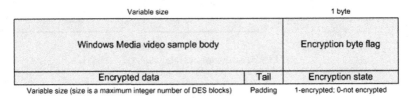

Fig. 5. ASF Video Sample Encryption

Our encryption scheme provides several encryption options. We distinguish the encrypted frame by 1 byte marking flag. This scheme increases file size, but it makes it possible to encrypt media data with several options. Table 1 shows the encryption options of our encryption scheme.

Table 1. Encryption Options Option Type Option List

Option Type	Option List
Media Type	- Video Only
	- Audio Only
	- Both Video and Audio
Video Media	- Key Frames Only
	- All Frames
Range	Time based encryption range

5   Protected File Playback

Decryption is performed by DMO filter based on Microsoft DirectShow technology, i.e. media objects model is used for on the fly media decrypting. In case of manual connection of filter's pin in the player, we can provide internal data flow safety.

5.1   Direct Show

Microsoft DirectShow is architecture for streaming media on the Microsoft Windows platform. DirectShow provides for high-quality capture and playback of multimedia streams[3]. It supports a wide variety of formats, including ASF, MPEG, AVI, MP3, and WAV sound files. It supports capture using Windows Driver Model(WDM) devices or older Video for Windows devices. DirectShow is integrated with other DirectX technologies. It automatically detects and uses video and audio acceleration hardware when available, but also supports systems without acceleration hardware.

DirectShow simplifies media playback, format conversion, and capture tasks. At the same time, it provides access to the underlying stream control architecture for applications that require custom solutions. DirectShow components can be easily extended to support new formats or custom effects.

5.2 DMO

Microsoft DMOs(DirectX Media Objects) are a new way to write data-streaming components. In some respects, DMOs are similar to Microsoft DirectShow filters. Like a DirectShow filter, a DMO takes input data and uses it to produce output data. However, the application programming interfaces for DMOs are much simpler than the corresponding APIs for DirectShow. As a result, DMOs are easier to create, easier to test, and easier to use[5].

Decryption filer should be implemented in the form of DMO since Microsoft's windows media player only allows the DMO type filter when it process WMV(Windows Media Video) codec related movie file.

5.3 Decryption Scheme

Automatic decryption by DMO is possible due the fact that the graph rendering system[4] performs search of the decoder which is capable of decoding media type specified in the respective streams of the media file. For usual video files, that leads to a proper codec being used in the filter graph. But in our case, we can fake the codec ID in such way that we force a player application substitute the standard codec by our custom DMO. That fact alone is insufficient for successful decoding of the video because our codec media data is still compressed after decrypted. To overcome this situation the decryption DMO must restore the original media types for outgoing media streams. It allows the filter graph or the client application to put the original decoder right after our decrypting filter. Fig 6 shows the filter graph of the original movie playback, while fig 7 shows the filter graph of the protected movie playback.

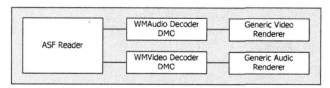

Fig. 6. Filter Graph of the Original Movie Playback

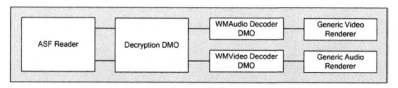

Fig. 7. Filter Graph of the Protected Movie Playback

Fig 8 shows the difference of two types of playback. Fig 8-a is a screen of playing the protected ASF file without decryption. Fig 8-b is a screen of playing the protected ASF file with decryption.

a) Playback without Decryption   b) Playback with Decryption

Fig. 8. Playback Comparison

Playback of protected file requires a player application to obtain all information needed to decrypt source. Therefore the player signals to the DRM core what it intended to handle and for which purpose. Information obtained from DRM core describes media format, meta-information and user rights. For the protected file playback, that data also includes decryption keys.

Before starting playback, the client application invokes the DRM core to ask metainformation. The DRM core can signal whether source requires decryption or any other type of handling. Fig 9 shows the state diagram of the client process.

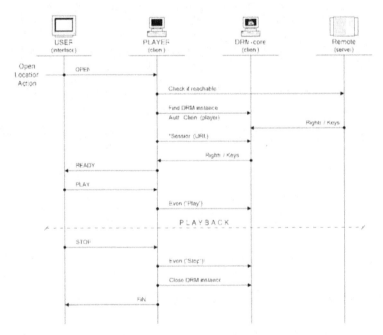

Fig. 9. State Diagram of the Client Process

6 Conclusion

We designed the DRM functions which don't change the ASF file format. We achieve it by analyzing the ASF file format. Decryption key and other encryption parameters are sent to the license issuer simultaneously with encrypting content. The license issuer gives the information to the legal users only. Client can play the protected content using the information received by the license issuer.

Our encryption scheme has several encryption options. We can select the amount of encrypted data size considering the streaming performance. It implies that the more complicated encryption algorithm can be applied without degrading the streaming performance.

We are going to study DRM issues and performance issues related to the streaming. Those include decreasing the DRM overhead, error perception and recovery, and efficient key management for streaming services.

References

1. ASF Specification,
   http://www.microsoft.com/windows/windowsmedia/format/asfspec.aspx
2. "Data Encryption Standard(DES)", FIPS Publication 46-2 (1993)
3. DirectShow, http://www.microsoft.com/Developer/PRODINFO/directx/dxm/help/ds/
   cframe.htm#default.htm
4. DirectX SDK, http://www.microsoft.com/directx
5. DMO, http://msdn.microsoft.com/library/default.asp?url=/library/en-us/wcedshow/html/
   _cxrefdmowrapperfilter.asp
6. http://www.microsfot.com/windows/windowsmedia
7. "ISMA Encryption and Authentication Specification",
   http://www.isma.tv/resources/ techspecs/
8. Joshua Duhl, Susan Kevorkian, Understanding DRM Systems, IDC 2001
9. Junseok Lee, "A DRM Framework for Distributing Digital Contents through the Internet",
   ETRI Journal, Vol.25, No.6 (December 2003)
10. Kenneth Louis Milsted, "Automated Method and Apparatus to Package Digital Content for
    Electronic Distribution using the Identity of the Source Content", United States Patent
    6,345,256
11. Olin Sibert, "DigiBox: A Self-Protecting Container for Information Commerce", 1st
    USENIX Workshop on Electronic Commerce (1995)
12. Seongoun Hwang, "Design and Implementation of a Licensing Architecture for
    Distribution of Copyright-Protected Digital Contents," Telecommunications Review,
    Vol.12, No.5 (October 2002)
13. Windows Media DRM,
    http://www.microsoft.com/windows/windowsmedia/drm/default.aspx

DiffSig: Differentiated Digital Signature for Real-Time Multicast Packet Flows

Namhi Kang and Christoph Ruland

University of Siegen, Institute for Data Communications Systems
Hoelderlin-str. 3, 57076 Siegen, Germany
{kang,ruland}@nue.et-inf.uni-siegen.de

Abstract. We are studying toward several goals necessary to apply digital signature to value-added real time contents to multicast over an insecure and unreliable channel. In this paper we propose a new digital signature framework, called DiffSig, through the first trying to categorize security services that can be achieved by digital signature. DiffSig is able to support equivalent security with smaller key sizes, which results in faster computations and lower transmission overhead. In addition, DiffSig allows a participant to join or leave the communication dynamically.

1 Introduction

Data origin authentication is one of the main goals to deploy secure multicast communication. In unicast communications, this is typically achieved by using message authentication codes (MACs)[1]. In multicast, it is hard to apply the MAC primitive directly owing to the difficulty of key management and the possibility of insider collusion. These shortcomings can be solved by applying digital signatures instead of MAC since only the source is able to bind its identity to the signature. However, there exist critical performance problems when the asymmetric cryptography primitive is employed to packet flows with real time properties.

Both computation and transmission overhead of most regular digital signature schemes such as RSA[2] and DSA[3] are caused by using large key sizes for protecting data in the sense of long-term security. It is too ambiguous to specify how much time is enough for the long-term security, though. It differs depending on the application, the policy or the underlying environment. Herein lies a foundation stone of our idea: to focus on security services rather than on managing cryptographic primitives as previous work did. That is, we focus on the fact that each security service has its own requirements and properties. If a security service needs to resist against attacks only for a short period such as a week or a day, long enough key for one or two decades is apparently overuse. This leads us to build a new conception that it is useful to divide security services into two fold in the case of the real time flows. One is authentication, precisely data origin authentication and the other fold is non-repudiation of origin.

On the basis of this notion, we propose a new digital signature framework, called DiffSig (Differentiated digital Signature), for real time multicast packet

S. Katsikas, J. Lopez, and G. Pernul (Eds.): TrustBus 2004, LNCS 3184, pp. 251–260, 2004.

flows. DiffSig consists of two different digital signature schemes: EP and AP digital signature, shorts for 'Expedited Processing' and 'Assured Processing' respectively. EP signature supports fast real time authentication and AP signature is for achieving non-repudiation of origin. DiffSig is able to offer equivalent security with smaller key sizes in particular.

This paper is organized as follows. The next section discusses previous work and their shortcomings. Section 3 describes the proposed DiffSig framework including our security service category. Following we present deploying issues in section 4 and conclude this paper in section 5.

2 Related Work

Most previous work to support data origin authentication in multicast are divided into two categories: MAC based approaches[4][5] and digital signature based approaches[4, 6–9]. Multicast data origin authentication enable all receivers to ensure that the received data is coming from the exact source rather than it is coming from any member of the group. Therefore, an asymmetric property, which means only the source can generate an authentication information thereafter the receiver is only able to verify the authenticity of the source, is required. To achieve asymmetric property, TESLA[4] uses time asymmetry and asymmetric-MAC scheme[5] uses asymmetric key sets whereas digital signature based schemes use asymmetric key pair between the source and the receiver. From the viewpoint of efficiency, MAC is better than digital signature. However, in the setting of MAC, participants in a group cannot achieve non-repudiation. In some applications, non-repudiation is necessary. An example of such applications is financial information push service such as real time stock quotation. Moreover, it is too difficult to share single symmetric key with multiple communicators in multicast. In this reason, some additional mechanism is required, for example TESLA requires time synchronization mechanism.

Digital signature based approaches provide solutions to the key sharing and the non-repudiation supporting problem of the MAC. In this case, most previous work uses single amortizing signature over several packets to reduce computation and transmission overhead. The conspicuous differences between them are two: the one is the way to set a group of packets for amortizing and the other is the way to achieve the loss tolerant property. However, these schemes are still highly expensive since the essential security of an asymmetric key based scheme depends on a large key. There is no doubt that the length of a key must be increased more and more as time goes by. Recent day, the recommended key size of digital signature standards is ranging from 1024 bits to 2048 bits for short-term and long-term security respectively (see [10] as one of references). Obviously the source should use at least 2048 bits key to support non-repudiation to a financial application. According to our experiments (see section 4), it takes 52.1/1.52 ms to sign/verify a 1024 bytes packet using 2048 bits RSA. It is indeed expensive to adopt to some multimedia applications.

3   Differentiated Digital Signature

3.1   Security Service Category

We categorize security services of digital signature into two folds instead of three nevertheless data integrity is also achieved by digital signature. Data integrity can be encompassed implicitly by both authentication and non-repudiation in our scheme. In this paper, non-repudiation is referred to 'Non-repudiation of Origin' that is intended to protect against a sender's false denial of being both the creator and the sender of the arriving packet. In general multicast, other non-repudiation services [11] such as non-repudiation of delivery, submission, or transport are nearly impossible to support because of the unreliable property. Table 1 shows attributes that are used to classify security services in the case of applying digital signature to real-time applications. The effectuation point indicates the time when a security service is active and the R-T sensitive is defined as a level of real time sensitive. The lifetime means a valid term of security service.

Table 1. Classification of security services

Security service	Effectuation point	R-T sensitive	Lifetime
Authentication with Packet Integrity	*On packet arrival*	*High*	*Instant*
Non-repudiation with Portion Integrity	*On disputing point*	*Very low*	*Long*

In real time application, the authentication procedure should be performed immediately so that the receiver could use the authenticated packet within the predefined buffering time, called playback time. This is because any packet arrived after playback time becomes obsolete even though the packet has been certainly arrived and verified. Moreover, it is useless to maintain the validity of authentication for a long time because as soon as the data has been verified the authentication service becomes meaningless. From the only viewpoint of real time authentication, therefore, the source does not need to use a large key such as 2048 bits in length targeted for long-term security. Additionally, real time packet authentication procedures provide implicitly the integrity of the arrived packets.

On the other hand, non-repudiation has no restriction of real time treating since it is essentially for protecting against denial of the past transaction. It becomes into force after the point of any party's claim. Hence, the receiver does not need to verify non-repudiation immediately on receiving packet. Instead, the validity of the non-repudiation service must remain secure for a long term. To achieve this properly, the key length should correspond to the currently recommended key length for long-term security. Like authentication, data portion (meant sequence of packets) integrity also can be achieved along with non-repudiation.

3.2   DiffSig Framework

DiffSig consists of the EP and the AP digital signature. The EP signature concentrates its attention only on achieving data origin authentication without interfering real time requirements. To do this, the source generates EP signatures using EP keys that are available only for the pre-defined short-time duration. In this paper, the EP and the AP key is referred to as the small and the large key respectively. We note that the EP signature is as strong as a general signature using recommended key length within its validity term. EP signature is however not capable of supporting long-term available non-repudiation since the EP key may be compromised after it's lifetime. Herein lies the main purpose of the AP signature: to supplement incompleteness of EP signature caused by using small keys in the sense of the long-term security.

Both EP and AP signatures of DiffSig use an amortizing signature over several packets to gain efficient processing. EP signatures amortize over all packets in a block and AP signatures amortize over all EP signatures in a container as illustrated in fig. 1. Here, we refer to a block as a set of packets and to a container as a set of blocks. That is, the source performs time consuming signing operations one time per block with the EP key and one time per container with the AP key thereby enabling both the source and the receiver(s) to reduce the amount of computational cost of the signing/verifying procedure.

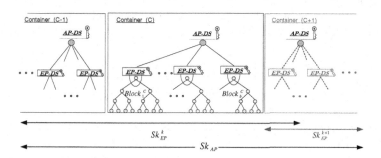

Fig. 1. DiffSig architecture with key lifetime

Fig. 1 illustrates the range of both keys lifetime and how these work together to form a DiffSig as well. The source uses several EP keys such as SK_{EP}^k and SK_{EP}^{k+1} according to its predefined validity term whereas single SK_{AP} can be used all the time during whole session. AP signature should be arrived at the receiver side before the valid lifetime of the short key which is used to generate EP signatures in the same container of AP signature. Thus, two short keys can be overlaid in some duration as like SK_{EP}^k and SK_{EP}^{k+1} described in fig. 1.

In this paper, the EP signature of DiffSig employ the hash tree scheme[7] which is based on Merkle hash[12]. We note that other previous schemes, if it is based on digital signature, also can be easily employed in our EP signature. The main advantage of the hash tree scheme is complete robustness to arbitrary packet loss rather than probabilistic loss tolerant of other schemes such as EMSS[4], argumented chain scheme[8] or SAIDA[9]. The procedures are described in more detail in the following section.

4   Deployment Considerations

4.1   EP Key Selection

In this section we discuss the way to derive a minimum EP key length. It is based on the lower bound of the Lenstra and Verheul's suggestion[13], where they defined IM Y (y) as an infeasible (Million Instructions Per Second) MIPS[1] years for year y to derive the key length. The derived key is computationally equivalent to the same strength offered by the DES in 1982. The cost of 0.5 MMY was considered as secure to resist software attack on DES in 1982. They also considered that the expected processor speed-up according to Moore'r raw and the expected increasing in the budget available to an attacker according to the trend of the US Gross National Product during the period 1982 to year y, such that

$$\text{IM Y (y)} = 5 * 10^5 * 2^{12(y-1982)/18} * 2^{(y-1982)/10} \text{ MIPS-Years.} \quad (1)$$

In addition, to select the length of the conventional asymmetric key system[2], they applied the asymptotic run time L[n][3] of a NFS (Number Field Sieve) combined with the fact that a 512 bits modulus was broken in 1999 at the cost of around 10^4 MIPS year, such that

$$\frac{L[2^k]}{\text{IM Y (y)} * 2^{12(y-1999)/18}} \geq \frac{L[2^{512}]}{10^4}, \quad (2)$$

weher a factor $2^{12(y-1999)/18}$ indicates that the cryptanalytic is expected to become twice as effective every 18 months during year 1999 to year y.

To set the EP key length, we define IAO (X) as an infeasible amount of operations in period X and propose the following intuitive theorem based on equation (1) and (2).

Theorem 1. Let $S = \{x_1, \cdots, x_j : x_1 + \cdots + x_j = X\}$ be a set of sub periods of X, and let k be the length of a EP key. If k meets $L[2^k] \geq 55.6 * 2^{12(y-1999)/18} * IAO(x_i)$, then the length of k is secure enough within x_i, for all $x_i \in S$.

Proof. If a computer operates OPs during period X as the maximum amount of operations, then the computer can operate at most $OPs * (x_i/X)$ in x_i, where x_i is one of sub periods of X. That is, all elements of S have its own IAO (x_i) and the total amount of these must be equivalent to IAO (X), (since $\sum_{i=1}^{j} IAO(x_i) = \sum_{i=1}^{j} IAO(X) * \frac{x_i}{X} = IAO(X)$). Therefore, IAO (x_i) is an infeasible amount of

---

[1] Conventionally, the DEC VAX 11/780 is referred to as a 1 MIPS machine.

[2] In DSA, we consider a size p of finite field $GF(p)$ rather than a subgroup size q.

[3] $L[n, u, v] = e^{(v+o(1))ln(n)^u ln(ln(n))^{1-u}}$, where $u = 1/3$ and $v = 1.9229$ in NFS.

Table 2. EP key length for different periods and its cost(Sign/verify a 1024-bits length data using OpenSSL[14] library on PIII 924MHz PC (millisecond))

Period(x_i)	Year	Month	Week	Day	Hour	1/2Hour
$IAO(x_i)$	$1.88 * 10^{24}$	$1.57 * 10^{23}$	$3.67 * 10^{22}$	$5.15 * 10^{21}$	$2.15 * 10^{20}$	$1.07 * 10^{20}$
Min. bound for theorem 1	$1.05 * 10^{27}$	$8.78 * 10^{25}$	$2.05 * 10^{25}$	$2.88 * 10^{24}$	$1.20 * 10^{23}$	$5.98 * 10^{22}$
Key size (bits)	1108	1008	952	880	772	748
RSA Sign	13.22	10.1	9.53	8.31	6.93	6.25
Verify	0.58	0.49	0.47	0.43	0.37	0.35
DSA Sign	6.14	4.97	4.69	4.29	3.93	3.56
Verify	6.06	4.64	4.45	4.08	3.59	3.12

operations within x_i. Then, we can apply $IAO(x_i)$ to equation (2) since 1 MIPS is equivalent to $3.15 * 10^{13}$ operations, where we approximate $\frac{L[2^{512}]}{10^4}$ to $1.75 * 10^9$. □

As an example, IMY (2004) (=$5.98 * 10^{10}$ MIPS) is secure untill end of year 2004 according to equation (1). Thus we can regard $1.88 * 10^{24}$ as the IAO (year) in 2004. Thereby we can deduct a proper EP key length for any sub period as described in table 2. If a day is determined as a sub period, the source can use 880-bit key to sign an EP signature. This EP signature offers the same security level for a day as does a 1108-bit key for this year and a 2054-bit key for the next two decades.

4.2   EP Digital Signature

We employ the hash tree scheme[7] for EP signature. Consider the following scenario and notations: A *source* wish to send a packet flow to its group denoted $GR = \{U_u | u = 1, \cdots, v\}$. Packet flow is divided into several containers and c^{th} container consists of d blocks indexed with b and b^{th} block consists of q packets indexed with p. EP_b and $EPKey = \{SK_{EP}^k, PK_{EP}^k | 1 \leq k \leq l\}$ denote EP signature for b^{th} block and k^{th} EP key pair respectively, where l is the total number of keys to be used for a session. H_T^b and $\{H_{Sp}^b\}$ denote the top hash value of the tree and Sibling hash value set on the path from p^{th} packet to the top of the hash tree of the bth block respectively, and $r = \{true, false\}$ is the verification result set. The EP signature procedures are as follows.

<u>Protocol EP DS:</u>
Each block b, For $1 \leq b \leq d$
1)*Source* constructs authentication hash tree
2)*Source* then generates $EP_b = Sign(SK_{EP}^k, H_T^b)$
3)*Source* $\rightarrow GR : [Packet^1, \{H_{S1}^b\}, EP_b], \cdots, [Packet^q, \{H_{Sq}^b\}, EP_b]$
Upon arrival at $U_u :: Packet^p$ is authentic if and only if $r = true$
4) Check whether it is the first arrival among packets in a block b
4.1) First: calculate H_T^b and then compute $r = Verify(PK_{EP}^k, H_T^b, EP_b)$
4.2) No: compute r, if the integrity of $\{H_{Sp}^b\}$ is valid, then $r = true$

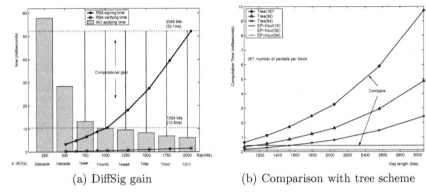

(a) DiffSig gain   (b) Comparison with tree scheme

Fig. 2. Time efficiency of DiffSig (experiment conditions are same with table 2)

The left side of fig. 2, (a), shows that the cost of a general digital signature scheme depends on the key length whereas DiffSig depends on the lifetime of the deriving EP key. In order to show an apparent efficiency, we compare signing time between the EP signature of which $IAO(x_i)$ period is hour and the hash tree scheme in (b) of fig. 2. Here, the number inside round bracket of legend indicates the number of packets per block. In the case of transmission overhead, if 1024 and 2048 bit RSA is employed for example, each packet is able to gain 252 and 1276 bits respectively since 772 bits is used for generating the EP signature.

4.3   AP Digital Signature

The role of the AP signature consists of two parts. One is providing non-repudiation and the other is managing EP keys since the lifetime of the EP key is short. Firstly, we describe the non-repudiation aspect of the AP signature. Non-repudiation is not time sensitive, hence the source does not need to transmit AP signatures along with every packet. We denote AP_c and $APKey$ as the AP signature for c^{th} container and a AP key pair respectively. Non-repudiation is performed as follows.

Protocol AP DS :: Non-repudiation:
Each Container c, For $1 \leq c \leq e$, where e is the total number of container:
1)*Source* generates $AP_c = Sign(SK_{AP}, H(H(EP_1^c)|| \cdots ||H(EP_d^c)))$
2)*Source* $\rightarrow GR : [H(EP_1^c), \cdots, H(EP_d^c), AP_c]$
Upon arrival at U_u :: Portion of flow is valid if and only if $r = true$
3)Replace corresponding parts of $[H(EP_1^c), \cdots, H(EP_d^c), AP_c]$ with U_u's own set Y (see Fig. 3 for example, we refer to X and Y as an EP signature sub set transmitted before and after the joining respectively.)
4) Compute $r = Verify(PK_{AP}, H((set\ X)||(set\ Y)), AP_c)$
5) Portion of flow is authentic if and only if $r = $ true

The source should not transmit AP signature once at the end of the session, but rather transmit periodically at every boundary of a container. If an AP signature is transmitted once, every receiver cannot leave from the group until the session is over, and the source should store all EP signatures of the session. Furthermore, it is insecure owing to the possibility that the source might become dishonest. A dishonest source may use the fact that almost all EP keys are already expired at the finishing time of the session. In this reason, a participant can leave the communication at the boundary of any container.

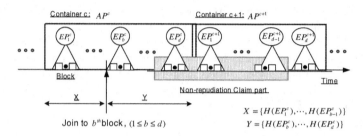

Fig. 3. Simple example

Fig. 3 illustrates an example to show how to achieve non-repudiation with allowing dynamic joining/leaving property. Consider, a participant join to a group during sending time of cth container thereafter he claims the non-repudiation of some portion of the packet flows. In this example, the joiner did not receive all EP signatures of the cth container, namely $(X||Y)$ in fig. 3, that are fed into an AP_c signing function, but he can verify an AP_c based on the following theorem 2.

Theorem 2. Let $EP = \{EP_b | b = 1, \cdots, d\}$ be a set of whole EP signatures in a container, where $X \cup Y = EP$, and let $h{:}D \to R$ be a collision resistant hash function. Then finding a collision on Y of EP to forge an AP signature is much difficult than finding a general collision (namely, $h(d_s) = h(d_t)$, where $d_s, d_t \in D$ and $s \neq t$).

Proof. Let E_1 is the event that an attacker can forge an AP signature and let E_2 be the event that an attacker finds a collision pair $(X||Y)$ and $(X||Y)'$ of points in D and let E_3 be the event that an attacker finds a collision on Y (say $(X||Y')$ or $(X'||Y')$). The probability of E_1 is that

$$Pr[E_1] = Pr[E_2] * Pr[E_3|E_2] = Pr[E_3]. \tag{3}$$

$Pr[E_2]$ is regarded as the same case with general hash collision such that

$$Pr[E_2] = Pr[h(d_a) = h(d_b)] = Pr[E_3] + Pr[E_3^c]. \tag{4}$$

Therefore, we conclude such that

$$Pr[E_1] = Pr[E_3] \leq Pr[h(d_s) = h(d_t)], \tag{5}$$

where the equality is met if the size of set X is multiple of hash block size (say 512-bit block). □

Second role of the AP signature is the EP key management that is necessary because an attacker is able to start key searching trial as soon as the key information is open to the public. EP key distribution can be performed by three different ways: the first way is periodic sending at the beginning of a block, the second way is using an advertisement such as web-based advertising and the third is hybrid way where the source combine the first and the second way to gain bandwidth efficiency. In the setting of the first way, the source should transmit same EP key multiple times but it is easy to manage the secure session. The receiver can join at the beginning of every block, say periodic-time joinable property. The second way provides any-time joinable property but the source should update the following EP key carefully. Finally, in the setting of the hybrid way, the source uses an advertisement during the lifetime of the EP key and transmits the next EP key on the point of expiration of the current EP key. The EP key management procedures using hybrid way are as follows.

Protocol AP DS :: Short Key Management:

Key generation (Off-line):

1)$Source$ specifies $l = (SessionTime)/(keyLifeTime)$

2)$Source$ generates l EP key pairs, $EPKey$

3)$Source$ signs public EP keys, $Sign(SK_{AP}, PK_{EP}^k)$, for $1 \leq k \leq l$

Upon expiration of the current EP key (say (SK_{EP}^k, PK_{EP}^k)) (On-line):

4)$Source$ loads new key pair: $(SK_{EP}^{k+1}, PK_{EP}^{k+1})$

5)$Source \rightarrow GR : [PK_{EP}^{k+1}, Sign(SK_{AP}, PK_{EP}^{k+1})]$

Upon arrival at U_u :: PK_{EP}^{k+1} is authentic if and only if $r =$ true

6)Compute $r = Verify(PK_{AP}, PK_{EP}^{k+1}, Sign(SK_{AP}, PK_{EP}^{k+1}))$

5   Conclusion

We show that it is greatly useful to divide security services into two folds and then generate two different signatures for each fold according to the property of services. This notion allows DiffSig to use a smaller key so that a group user can verify the authenticity of data origin efficiently. We also show that how to deduct a proper key size for authentication and how to support dynamic membership changing of multicast group.

References

1. S. Kent and R. Atkinson. Security Architecture for the Internet Protocol. IETF RFC2401, Nov. 1998.
2. RSA Laboratories. PKCS #1 v2.1: RSA Cryptography Standard. Jun. 2002.
3. U.S. National Institute of Standards and Technology. Digital Signature Standard (DSS). Federal Register 56. FIPS PUB 186, Aug. 1991.
4. A. Perrig, R. Canetti, J. D. Tygar and D. Song. Efficient Authentication and Signing of Multicast Streams over Lossy Channels. IEEE Security and Privacy Symposium, 2000.

5. R. Canetti, J. Garay, G. Itkis, D. Micciancio, M. Naor and B. Pinkas. Multicast Security: A Taxonomy and Some Efficient Constructions. Infocom'99, 1999.

6. R. Gennaro and P. Rohatgi. How to Sign Digital Streams. Lecture Notes in Computer Science, vol. 1294, pages 180-197, 1997.

7. C. K. Wong and S. S. Lam. Digital Signatures for Flows and Multicasts. In Proc. IEEE ICNP '98, 1998.

8. P. Golle and N. Modadugu. Authenticating streamed data in the presence of random packet loss. NDSS'01, pages 13-22, Feb. 2001.

9. Jung Min Park and Edwin K. P. Chong. Efficient multicast stream authentication using erasure codes ACM Trans. Inf. Syst. Secur. 6(2):258-285, 2003.

10. U.S. National Institute of Standards and Technology. Recommendation for key management. Special Publication 800-57, draft Jan. 2003.

11. ISO/IEC 13888-1. Information technology-Security techniques-Non-repudiation-Part 1: General. ISO/IEC JTC1/SC27, 1997.

12. R. Merkle. Protocols for public key cryptosystems. In Proceedings of the IEEE Symposium on Research in Security and Privacy, pages 122-134, Apr. 1980.

13. Arjen K. Lenstra and Eric R. Verheul. Selecting cryptographic key sizes. Journal of Cryptology 14(4):255-293, 2001.

14. OpenSSL Project. http://www.openssl.org/.

Large-Scale Pay-As-You-Watch
for Unicast and Multicast Communications*

Antoni Martínez-Ballesté, Francesc Sebé, and Josep Domingo-Ferrer

Dept. of Computer Engineering and Maths, Universitat Rovira i Virgili
Av. Països Catalans 26, E-43007 Tarragona, Catalonia, Spain
{anmartin,fsebe,jdomingo}@etse.urv.es

Abstract. This paper addresses the problem of pay-as-you-watch services over unicast and multicast communications. For each communication model, we present two solutions, non-verifiable and verifiable, depending on the existence or non-existence of trust between the source and the receiver(s). In verifiable schemes, the source obtains a proof of correct reception by the receiver(s); in non-verifiable schemes, receiver non-repudiation is not guaranteed, so there must be a trust relationship between source and receiver(s). While solutions for unicast pay-as-you-watch can be based on existing technologies, novel algorithms based on aggregation and multisignatures are needed and presented here to overcome implosion in multicast pay-as-you-watch.

Keywords: Pay-per-view systems, multicast, electronic payments.

1   Introduction

Several multimedia services consist of a customer or a set of customers who are interested in a certain content (say audio or video streams). In most of these services, the customer must nowadays pay for receiving or accessing the content. For instance, in current digital TV platforms, a flat monthly rate is paid to subscribe to a basic package of channels and services. Two different payment methods can be used to pay for the events not included in the flat rate:

- *Pay-per-view.* The content is viewed *after* the customer has paid. The customer pays for the whole piece of content. Thus, if she wants to stop watching anytime, she is losing a part of her money. This is the most common scheme used in current PayTV platforms for special events such as football matches, film premieres, etc.
- *Pay-as-you-watch.* Small payments are performed as contents are being streamed from the server to the customer. Pay-as-you-watch (or pay-as-you-listen) seems to be an option that fits better the customer needs. Successive payments can be performed every minute, for example. If a customer switches her player off, she has only paid for the minutes viewed so far.

* This work has been partly supported by the Spanish Ministry of Science and Technology and the European FEDER fund under project TIC2001-0633-C03-01 "STREAMOBILE".

S. Katsikas, J. Lopez, and G. Pernul (Eds.): TrustBus 2004, LNCS 3184, pp. 261–268, 2004.

1.1   Contribution and Plan of This Paper

Our paper deals with pay-as-you-watch, both for *unicast* (one-to-one communication) and *multicast* (one-to-*n* communication, usually with $n \gg 1$) transmission. For each communication model, we present two solutions, non-verifiable and verifiable, depending on the existence or non-existence of trust between the source and the receiver(s). In verifiable schemes, the source obtains a proof of correct reception by the receiver(s); in non-verifiable schemes, receiver non-repudiation is not guaranteed, so there must be a trust relationship between source and receiver(s). While solutions for unicast pay-as-you-watch can be based on existing technologies, novel algorithms based on aggregation and multisignatures are needed for multicast pay-as-you-watch in order to overcome the implosion problem resulting from many content receivers sending simultaneous payment to a content provider.

In Section 2, non-verifiable and verifiable pay-as-you-watch in a unicast scenario are discussed. Section 3 deals with non-verifiable and verifiable pay-as-you-watch problem in a multicast scenario. Finally, conclusions are summarized in Section 4.

2   Pay-As-You-Watch in Unicast Communication

In unicast communication, the receiver directly establishes a session with the content provider (source). This is the distribution architecture currently used in most commercial pay-per-view services over the Internet. Unicast seems to be the most versatile option, because the subscriber can request a content at any time. Its main drawback is its lack of scalability on the server side: the server must have huge computing and communications resources to be able to service a large number of simultaneous unicast communications. Even with a large investment in hardware and bandwith, a peak in the number of unicast subscribers may result in service denial or degradation.

Some significant initiatives in unicast content distribution are CinemaNow [CinNw], Movielink [MovLn], Europe Online [EurOn] and NDS [NDS], etc. Payment in those services is based on a combination of flat rate user subscription and advance pay per view for special events.

Let us consider a method for pay-as-you-watch in unicast communications. A first and easy solution for implementing a pay-as-you-watch service is to assume an agreement between the content provider and a telecommunications carrier; the buyer is then charged by the carrier for the time she has been enjoying the service and the carrier transfers payment to the content provider. Due to the universal and free access inherent to Internet, the aforementioned carrier-provider scheme does no longer work. On the Internet, there is no carrier (or there are many of them), so contents should be paid directly to the provider as they are being received.

2.1   Non-verifiable Unicast Solution

A non-verifiable pay-as-you-watch solution is one in which the provider obtains no proof of correct content reception by customers. Even without such a proof, a unicast provider is aware of the content received by each customer. The reason is that the content is sent using individual connections. Therefore, the provider can charge the customer for the minutes she has received. Thus, *the non-verifiable unicast solution consists of the provider metering the contents sent to each customer and thereafter billing the customer accordingly.*

The main drawback of non-verifiable systems is the need for trust between provider and customers:

- On one hand, the customer must trust the service provider: the customer must believe that the service provider will not charge her for contents she has not received.
- On the other hand, the provider cannot prove a subscriber is receiving a certain content. In this way, a dishonest customer could repudiate having received a certain content. After repudiation, the dishonest user could claim her money back and/or redistribute the received content without being punished.

2.2   Verifiable Unicast Solution

Since the number of simultaneous unicast customers is limited by the provider's outgoing bandwidth, it is highly unlikely that the number of customers is so large that the provider is swamped by the incoming flow of customer payments. Therefore, a pay-as-you-watch scheme can be put in place where the customer pays in real-time as she is receiving the content.

The transaction costs of standard electronic payments are usually considered too high for small amounts such as those required for real-time payment of small time slots. These transaction costs can be split into communication and computation costs, the latter being caused by the use of complex cryptographic techniques such as digital signatures. Micropayments are electronic payment methods specifically designed to keep transaction costs very low. In most micropayment systems in the literature, computational costs are dramatically reduced by replacing digital signatures with hash functions. This is the case of PayWord and Micromint[Riv95], where the security of coin minting rests on one-way hash functions.

In [Dom02], we proposed a verifiable pay-as-you-watch scheme based on PayWord. A prototype system offering that service is available at [Str04]. The operation of that system can be sketched as:

1. The customer subscribes to the service.
2. The service provider certifies the customer key.
3. The customer generates a PayWord chain and signs the root.
4. As the content is being served to the customer, several payments are requested by the provider. Each payment requires each customer to send a coupon, *i.e.* a piece of the PayWord chain, to the service provider.
5. If the customer stops paying, the provider pauses sending the stream.

3   Pay-As-You-Watch in a Multicast Scenario

Multicast content distribution [Mill99] is a solution to overcome the lack of scalability of unicast communications.

Multicast consists of one source sending the same content to a set of n receivers, where usually $n \gg 1$. The main goal of multicast is to prevent the source from having to send the same content once for each customer: the content is replicated and distributed over a multicast tree, formed by multicast routers or active network nodes. In order to organize the distribution of the content, multicast sessions are advertised and interested customers join the multicast group for the upcoming session.

This approach is less versatile than the aforementioned unicast distribution: a group of customers must watch or listen to the same content at the same time. Thus, multicast distribution is suitable for large scale live events or near-on-demand video services.

In the near future, most multimedia delivery services are likely to operate in multicast mode to send content over the Internet. Given that a large audience is possible, collecting real-time payment (pay-as-you-watch) from all customers may result in a bottleneck at the source or payment collector. This bottleneck, known as the *implosion problem* [Qui01], arises in any communication from n parties to one party (in our case from the the multicast customers to the multicast provider).

3.1   Non-verifiable Multicast Solution

In a multicast scenario, the source is not aware of the identity of all receivers [Fen97]. Thus, in principle, multicast pay-as-you-watch faces an intrinsic problem, because the provider needs to know how long each customer has been receiving the content. In encrypted multicast communications [MSEC03], the content is encrypted under a symmetric session key known only to the set of registered receivers. When a customer registers to join the session, a rekeying procedure is performed so as to let newcomer learn the (new) session key. In the same way, a rekeying procedure is performed when a customer leaves the current session: a new decryption key must be generated so that it is only known to the remaining receivers.

When a customer is interested in registering to a multicast session, she must request the decryption key. In this way, the source/provider knows exactly the moment at which the customer starts receiving the content. On the other side, the customer can disconnect without notifying the source. Hence, in a subscription-based service, customers must periodically confirm that they stay connected. This many-to-one confirmation communication must be private and authenticated and, unfortunately, can lead to implosion problems at the source. To remedy this, a scheme for secure reverse transmission of bits from the leaves (receivers) to the root (source) of a multicast tree was presented in [Dom04] which avoids the implosion problem.

A Protocol for Many to One Bit Transmission. By using the protocol in [Dom04], a set of u users, with $u \gg 1$, send a bit of information to the source. This protocol provides secrecy and authentication, by means of symmetric cryptography. In order to avoid implosion, bits are aggregated by intermediate nodes of the multicast tree as they are sent up to the source of the tree. This aggregation operation of data packets inside the network requires the support of the network infrastructure in terms of processing resources. Active networks [Psou99] allow information to be handled in the core nodes of the network.

The protocol can be summarized as follows:

Protocol 1 (Many-to-one bit transmission)

1. The source generates a set of $2u$ intervals $[I_i^{min}, I_i^{max}]$, for $i=1$ to $2u$, which are sent to the users.
2. Let $\boxplus$ be a homomorphic addition, *i.e.* if $\boxplus$ is performed on two encrypted values, the ciphertext corresponding to the addition of cleartexts is obtained. The parameters for using $\boxplus$ are multicast to users.
3. In order to collect one bit from every user:
   (a) The source multicasts a challenge message v, which is used by the users to choose values $s_u^0 \in [I_u^{min}, I_u^{max}]$ and $s_u^1 \in [I_{u+1}^{min}, I_{u+1}^{max}]$ representing, respectively, bit values 0 and 1.
   (b) User u sends to her parent router in the multicast tree (the one she gets the multicast stream from) a message M_u containing s_u^0 or s_u^1, depending on the value of the bit she wants to send.
   (c) Intermediate routers generate a message $M_{desc} = M_1 \boxplus \cdots \boxplus M_d$, where d is the number of child nodes of the router, and sends M_{desc} up to their parent router.
   (d) Finally, the source obtains an aggregated message M from which she is able to efficiently retrieve all values s sent by the users.

In our approach, if a user/customer sends any of her secret values s_u^0 and s_u^1, it means that she is still online. This is useful for the source/provider to learn that the customer must be billed till at least the moment of receiving the last s_u^i. However, note that the provider does not obtain any proof, *i.e.* she could not convince a third party, that the customer is correctly receiving the multicast content. So a scheme where keepalive bits are sent using Protocol 1 is non-verifiable.

3.2   Verifiable Multicast Solution

As mentioned before, the main barrier to using traditional micropayment schemes for fee collection in multicast environments is the implosion problem. Nevertheless, due to the increase in the computational power of processors and the advances in digital signatures techniques, it is no longer obvious that the computational cost of a digital signature is still unaffordable for micropayments [Mic02].

By using verifiable payment subscription, the source can prove that a certain customer has received a certain portion of content. On the other hand, a customer cannot deny having received the content (non-repudiation).

Our proposal is secure and scalable. It is based on the concept of multisignature [Bol03]. Multisignatures allow any subgroup of a group of entities to jointly sign a document in such a way that any verifier is convinced that each member of the subgroup participated in the signature.

Definition 1 (Computational Diffie-Hellman problem (CDH)). The CDH problem consists of finding $h = g^{\log_g u \cdot \log_g v}$ given three random elements $\{g, u, v\}$ of a group.

Definition 2 (Decisional Diffie-Hellman problem (DDH)). The DDH problem consists of deciding whether four elements $\{g, u, v, h\}$ in a group satisfy $\log_g u = \log_v h$.

Definition 3 (Gap-Diffie-Hellman group). A Gap-Diffie-Hellman (GDH) group is one in which the CDH problem is hard but the DDH problem is easy.

In [Bol03], a multisignature scheme is proposed which can be built over any Gap-Diffie-Hellman (GDH) group. We next recall that scheme.

Protocol 2 (GDH multisignature)

1. *Key generation.* Let G be a GDH group and g a generator of G. In order to generate her public-private key pair, a customer U chooses a random positive integer x_u (her private key) and publishes $y_u = g^{x_u}$ (her public key).
2. *Signature computation.* In order to sign a message m, a customer U computes her signature as $sig_u = \mathcal{H}(m)^{x_u}$, where $\mathcal{H}$ is a one-way hash function.
3. *Signature verification.* This signature is verified by solving the DDH problem over the elements

$$\{g, y_u, \mathcal{H}(m), sig_u\}$$

If the answer to the DDH problem is yes, then the signature is accepted as valid.
4. *Multisignature computation.* Given a customer U_1 with a public-private key pair (y_{u_1}, x_{u_1}) and a customer U_2 with a public-private key pair (y_{u_2}, x_{u_2}), a multisignature of U_1 and U_2 on a message m is computed as follows:
   (a) U_1 computes $sig_{u_1} = \mathcal{H}(m)^{u_1}$
   (b) U_2 computes $sig_{u_2} = \mathcal{H}(m)^{u_2}$
   (c) The multisignature on m is then computed as

$$sig_{u_1,u_2} = sig_{u_1} \cdot sig_{u_2}$$

5. *Multisignature verification.* The multisignature can be verified by solving the DDH problem over the elements

$$\{g, y_{u_1} \cdot y_{u_2}, \mathcal{H}(m), sig_{u_1,u_2}\}$$

If the answer to the DDH problem is yes, then the multisignature is accepted as valid.

The generalization of the above multisignature computation and verification to a set of n customers is straightforward. Next, we propose a scalable solution whereby the multicast source/provider can collect a proof that all customers registered in a multicast session have received a specific piece of content.

Protocol 3 (Aggregation using multisignatures)

1. *Customer registration.* In our proposal, we require each customer U_i to have a public-private key pair (y_{u_i}, x_{u_i}). The public key must be certified by a trusted certification authority.
2. *Payment request.*

   (a) The source generates a message m specifying the content, the time slot and the amount of money to be paid. This message m is multicast to the set of registered users who are currently receiving the content.
   (b) Upon reception, customers check the content of m for correctness and sign it. That is, customer U_i computes $sig_{u_i} = \mathcal{H}(m)^{u_i}$ and sends it up to her parent router in the multicast tree.
   (c) Intermediate routers check the correctness of the received signatures, aggregate them by generating a multisignature on m and send the aggregated signature up to their parent router in the multicast tree.
   (d) Upon reception of the final multisignature, the source checks its correctness.

Some remarks on Protocol 3 are in order:

- The final multisignature received by the source can be used to prove to a third party that a specific subset of customers signed the receipt and the payment corresponding to the content described in m. Thus Protocol 3 results in a verifiable solution for pay-as-you-watch multicast transmission.
- In case one of the customers leaves the group or fails to send a valid signature, a new rekeying process will be performed so that the failing customer is excluded from knowledge of the new session key.
- The size of the multisignature does not increase when aggregating signatures. This makes our proposal scalable, because the source will not be imploded by reception of a final aggregated signature which has the same size as the individual customer signatures.

4   Conclusions

We have presented in this paper several approaches to pay-as-you-watch transmission, both in unicast and multicast scenarios. For both scenarios, we have proposed non-verifiable and verifiable solutions. In a non-verifiable solution, the content provider does not obtain any proof that the customer has correctly received a specific piece of content; thus, a trust relationship between customers and provider is needed. Verifiable solutions are more versatile in that they can be implemented in the absence of trust.

In the case of unicast, existing technology can be adapted to produce both non-verifiable and verifiable solutions. Content metering and subsequent billing yields a non-verifiable scheme. Standard micropayments can be used to construct a verifiable scheme.

In the case of multicast, innovative protocols are required to overcome the implosion problem caused by a huge number of real-time micropayments being sent by customers to the multicast provider. The protocols we have proposed rely on aggregation of information at the intermediate multicast routers. If the aggregated information is not signed, we obtain a non-verifiable scheme; if it is signed, the resulting scheme is verifiable. In particular we have shown how to efficiently aggregate signed information using multisignatures.

References

[Bol03] A. Boldyreva, "Threshold signatures, multisignatures and blind signatures based on the Gap-Diffie-Hellman-Group signature scheme", in *Int. Workshop on Theory and Practice in Public Key Cryptography-PKC'2003*, LNCS 2567, Berlin: Springer-Verlag, pp. 31-46, 2003.

[CinNw] CinemaNow, http://www.cinemanow.com

[EurOn] Europe Online, http://www.europeonline.com

[Dom02] J. Domingo-Ferrer and A. Martínez-Ballesté, "STREAMOBILE: pay-per-view video streaming to mobile devices over the Internet", in *Proceedings of the 13th International Workshop on Database and Expert Systems and Applications (DEXA'2002)*, Los Alamitos CA: IEEE Computer Society, pp. 418-422, 2002.

[Dom04] J. Domingo-Ferrer, A. Martínez-Ballesté and F. Sebé, "Secure Reverse Communication in a Multicast Tree" in *Third International IFIP-TC6 Networking Conference - NETWORKING 2004*, LNCS 3042, Berlin: Springer-Verlag, pp. 807-816, 2004.

[Fen97] W. Fenner. Internet Group Management Protocol, Version 2. RFC 2236, November 1997.

[Mic02] S. Micali and R. L. Rivest, "Micropayments revisited" in *Topics in Cryptology - CT-RSA 2002*, LNCS 2271, Berlin: Springer-Verlag, pp. 149-163, 2002.

[Mill99] C. K. Miller, *Multicast Networking and Applications*. Reading MA: Addison Wesley, 1999.

[MovLn] MovieLink, http://www.movielink.com

[MSEC03] Multicast Security Working Group (MSEC WG). http://www.securemulticast.org

[NDS] NDS, http://www.nds.com

[Opp02] R. Oppliger, *Security Technologies for the World Wide Web (2nd Edition)*. Norwood MA: Artech House, 2002.

[Psou99] K. Psounis, "Active networks: Applications, security, safety and architectures", *IEEE Communication Surveys*, vol. 2, no. 1, pp. 1-16, 1999.

[Qui01] B. Quinn and K. Almeroth, "IP multicast applications: challenges and solutions", Internet RFC 3170, Sept. 2001. http://www.ietf.org

[Riv95] R. Rivest and A. Shamir, "PayWord and Micromint: Two simple micropayment schemes", Technical Report, MIT LCS, Nov. 1995.

[Str04] http://vneumann.etse.urv.es/streamobile

Reducing the Communication Overhead of an Offline Revocation Dictionary

Jose L. Muñoz, Jordi Forné, Oscar Esparza,
Josep Pegueroles, and Esteve Pallarès

Technical University of Catalonia (Telematics Engineering Department)*
1-3 Jordi Girona, C3 08034 Barcelona, Spain
{jose.munoz,jordi.forne,oscar.esparza,josep,esteve}@entel.upc.es

Abstract. A Public Key Infrastructure (PKI) is required to securely deliver public-keys to widely-distributed users or systems. The public key is usually made public by war of a digital document called Identity Certificate (IC). ICs are valid during quite lang periods of time (usually up to several years). However, there are circumstances under which the validity of an IC wust be terminated sooner than assigned and thus, the IC needs to be revoked. The Revocation Dictionary (RD) can be defined as the cryptographic structure that contains the status data about the revoked certificates of the PKI domain. Three basic operations can be performed over the RD: add status data, remove status data and request the RD to tell us whether certain status data is contained by the RD or not. The last operation is called "status checking" and it is relevant to the PKI performance. In this paper we propose an efficient war of implementing a RD that can be distributed offline and that minimizes the communication overhead of the status checking process. The statistics of the status checking are used, like in the Huffman algorithm for source coding, for building an unbalanced hash tree that minimizes the length of the RD response.

1   Introduction

A Public Key Infrastructure (PKI) is required to securely deliver public-keys to widely-distributed users or systems. The public key is usually made public by way of a digital document called Identity Certificate (IC). The PKI is responsible for the Identity Certificates (ICs) not only at the issuing time but also during the whole life-time of the certificate. An IC has a bounded life-time: it is not valid prior to the activation date and it is not valid beyond the expiration date. Typically, the validity period of an IC ranges from several months to several years. In this context, certificate

---
* This work has been supported by the Spanish Research Council under the project ARPA (TIC2003-08184-C02-02) and the European Research Council under the project UBISEC (IST-FP6 506926).

S. Katsikas, J. Lopez, and G. Pernul (Eds.): TrustBus 2004, LNCS 3184, pp. 269–278, 2004.

revocation can be defined as *"the mechanism under which an issuer can invalidate the binding between an identity and a public-key before the expiration of the corresponding certificate"*. Thus, the existence of a certificate is a necessary but not sufficient evidence for its validity, the PKI needs to provide its end users with the ability to check, at the time of usage, that certificates are still valid (not revoked). This feature is commonly known in the PKI as the status checking.

The Revocation Dictionary ($\mathcal{RD}$) can be defined as the cryptographic structure that contains the status data about the revoked certificates of the PKI domain. The master copy of the $\mathcal{RD}$ for a set of certificates is updated by a Trusted Third Party (TTP)[1] called "issuer". The update process must reflect the revocations and expirations (if a certificate has expired it makes no sense to store revocation information about it). The $\mathcal{RD}$ issuer is also responsible for making publicly available the status data. Usually, the end entities that want to perform a status checking do not have a straight connection to the issuer, they get the status data from intermediate entities instead. In this sense, the issuer can distribute the $\mathcal{RD}$ using two kind of intermediate entities (see Figure 1).

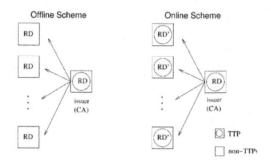

Fig. 1. The Offline Scheme versus the Online Scheme

The intermediate entities used for online distribution are known as *responders* and they are TTPs that can provide their own cryptographic evidence for the status data they produce. In other words, responders can change the underlying cryptographic structure of the $\mathcal{RD}$ received from the issuer. On the other hand, the intermediate entities used for offline distribution are known as *repositories*. Repositories are not TTPs and

---

[1] The CA that issued a certain certificate is usually the one who is in charge of distributing the status data of this certificate, but in general this function can be delegated to an independent TTP.

therefore they cannot change the $\mathcal{RD}$ received from the issuer, that is, a repository is a merely booster.

In this paper we propose a cryptographic structure for the $\mathcal{RD}$ that can be distributed offline and provide an efficient status checking. Our structure uses the statistics of the status checking, like in the Huffman algorithm for source coding, for building an unbalanced hash tree that minimizes the length of the $\mathcal{RD}$ response.

The rest of the paper is organized as follows: in Section 2 we present the related work. In Section 3 we discuss why we choose offline revocation based on a hash tree. In Section 4 we present the cryptographic structure of our system and some practical aspects that must be taking into account for its implementation. Finally, we conclude in Section 5.

2 Related Work

In this Section we present in short the main structures proposed to build a $\mathcal{RD}$ (for further information you are referred to the particular references).

Offline Distribution. The simplest structure to build a $\mathcal{RD}$ is a signed "black" list that includes all the identifiers (serial numbers) of all revoked but not expired certificates issued by the PKI domain. There are several standards based on this idea, below we mention them.

Traditional Certificate Revocation List (CRL) is the most mature offline system. CRL is part of X.509 [10] and it has also been profiled for the Internet in [2]. A CRL is a digitally signed list of revoked certificates where for each entry within the list the following information is stored: the certificate serial number, the revocation reason and the revocation date.

Delta-CRL (D-CRL) [4] is an attempt of reducing the size of the CRLs. A Delta-CRL is a small CRL that provides information about the certificates whose status have changed since the issuance of a complete list called Base-CRL.

In *CRL-Distribution Points* (CRL-DP) [4] each list contains the status information of a certain subgroup of certificates and each subgroup is associated with a distribution point. Each certificate has a pointer to the location of its distribution point.

The *Certificate Revocation Tree* (CRT) [6] and the *Authenticated Dictionary* (AD) [9] are both based on balanced hash trees [7]. The hash tree allows content to be retrieved in a trusted fashion with only a small amount of trusted data. The content is stored in the leaves of the hash tree but only the root of the tree is trusted (this structure is further discussed in the next Section).

Online Distribution. Online schemes usually use the responder's signature over the status data as cryptographic evidence. Notice that end entities are not required to be aware of the backend infrastructure used to collect the revocation information and maintain the responder's local database[2]. The most popular online protocol used by responders is the *Online Certificate Status Protocol* (OCSP) [8] that has been proposed by the PKIX workgroup of the IETF.

3   Why Offline Revocation Based on Hash Trees?

At first sight it is clear that offline systems are more robust than online systems in the sense that it is more complex to maintain the level of security of a responder than of a repository: a responder has to be in contact with end entities, but at the same time, it has to protect its private key against intruders. Next, we informally discuss some attacks to the online and offline schemes and their possible countermeasures.

- *Masquerade Attack:* An attacker could attempt to masquerade a trustworthy issuer or a trustworthy responder. Countermeasures: On the one hand the End Entities must verify that the status data has been issued using the certificate of the trustworthy issuer or the trustworthy responder. On the other hand the trustworthy entities must protect the private key or keys associated with the certificate or certificates used to issue the status data. Obviously, the less number of TTPs in the system, the less is the probability of having a private key compromised.
- *Response Integrity Attack:* An attacker could modify part or the whole of a response sent by legitimate repository or responder. Countermeasures: This attack cannot be successfully carried out if the response is verified according to the procedure of each particular system.
- *Replay Attack:* An attacker or a malicious repository could resend an old (good) response prior to its expiration date but after the contents have changed. Countermeasures: Decreasing the validity periods of the responses will decrease the window of vulnerability[3].
- *Denial of Service (DoS) Attack:* An attacker could intercept the responses from a legitimate repository or responder and delete them or the attacker could delay the responses by, for example, deliberately

---

[2] The responder database is usually updated by means of a CRL or requesting other responders.

[3] Notice that decreasing this period may lead the revocation system to scalability problems.

flooding the network, thereby introducing large transmission delays. Countermeasures: The only way to prevent this attack is to introduce redundancy of repositories/responders in the system. Notice that it is easier and more secure to introduce new repositories (non-TTPs) than responders (TTPs). Therefore, it is much easier to protect an offline system against DoS attacks than do the same for an online system.

The previous discussion shows the many benefits that offline distribution presents. However, it introduces significant communication overhead in the status checking and this hinders its development in bandwidth-constrained environments (such as m-commerce).

Next we analyze the communication overhead introduced by each system depicted in Section 2. The size of the response provided by an online responder can be simply expressed as $C_{online} = S$, where S can be approximated by the size of a digital signature. In the case of a CRL the size can be expressed as $C_{CRL} = S + n\mathcal{E}$, where $\mathcal{E}$ is the size of a list entry and n is the number of revoked certificates that includes the list. In the case of balanced hash trees [7] we need to describe in more detail how they work in order to give an expression for its communication cost. A sample balanced hash tree is depicted in Figure 2.

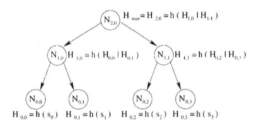

Note: h is a OWHF

Fig. 2. Balanced Hash Tree.

We denote by $N_{i,j}$ the nodes within the tree here i and j represent respectively the i-th level and the j-th node. We denote by $H_{i,j}$ the cryptographic value stored by node $N_{i,j}$. Nodes at level 0 are called "leaves" and they represent the data stored in the tree. In the case of revocation, leaves represent the set Φ of certificates that have been revoked: $\Phi = \{s_0, s_1, \ldots, s_j, \ldots, s_{n-1}\}$. Here s_j is the data stored by leaf $N_{0,j}$. Then, $H_{0,j}$ is computed as (1)

$$H_{0,j} = h(s_j). \tag{1}$$

Here h is a One Way Hash Function (OWHF). To build the tree, a set of k adjacent nodes at a given level i; $N_{i,j}$, $N_{i,j+1}$, ...,$N_{i,j+k-1}$, are combined into one node in the upper level, node that we denote by $N_{i+1,j}$. Then, $H_{i+1,j}$ is obtained by applying h to the concatenation of the k cryptographic variables (2)

$$H_{i+1,j} = h(H_{i,j}| H_{i,j+1}| \ldots | H_{i,j+k-1}). \tag{2}$$

At the top level there is only one node called "root". The $\mathcal{D}$igest of the tree is defined as the H_{root} value and a validity period signed by the issuer. The $\mathcal{P}ath_{s_j}$ can be defined as the set of cryptographic values necessary to compute H_{root} from the leaf s_j.

Example. Let us suppose that a certain user wants to find out if s_1 belongs to the sample tree of Figure 2. Then $\mathcal{P}ath_{s1} = \{H_{0,0}, H_{1,1}\}$ and the response verification consists in checking that the $H_{2,0}$ computed from the $\mathcal{P}ath_{s_1}$ matches $H_{2,0}$ included in the $\mathcal{D}$igest

$$H_{root} = H_{2,0} = h(h(h(s_1)|H_{0,0})|H_{1,1}). \tag{3}$$

Notice that the hash tree can be pre-computed by a TTP and distributed to a repository because a leaf cannot be added or deleted to the $\mathcal{RD}$ without modifying H_{root}[4] which is included in the $\mathcal{D}$igest.

The sample tree of Figure 2 is a binary tree because adjacent nodes are combined in pairs to form a node in the next level ($k = 2$). In general, the communication cost of a Balanced k-ary Hash Tree (B-kHT) can be expressed as

$$C_{B-kHT} = \mathcal{S} + \mathcal{H}(k-1)\lceil log_k(n)\rceil. \tag{4}$$

Here $\mathcal{H}$ is the size of a hash value. It can be also formally demonstrated that the minimum communication costs for a balanced k-ary hash tree are reached when $k = 2$ [5]. The size of a membership response from a $\mathcal{RD}$ containing n elements can be summed up as $\Theta(1)$ for online signature systems, $\Theta(n)$ for CRL systems and $\Theta(log_k(n))$ for balanced hash trees.

---

[4] To do such a thing, an attacker needs to find a pre-image of a OWHF which is by definition computationally infeasible.

4   Unbalanced Binary Hash Tree

Despite the good behavior of balanced hash trees compared to CRLs, they have higher communication costs than online systems which is still a problem in bandwidth-constrained environments. For instance, we have developed and published a protocol[5] in ASN.1 for a system based on a balanced hash tree and we have observed that for a population of 1.000 revoked certificates, the response of the balanced hash tree doubles the size of the online response (using our implementation of OCSP).

The system we propose uses the statistics of the status checking for building an unbalanced hash tree. The idea is to provide shorter paths for the leaves that have the higher request rates. This structure minimizes the average length of the membership response provided by the $\mathcal{RD}$ compared to balanced hash trees.

The unbalanced hash tree performs better than the balanced hash trees when the membership of certain elements of the dictionary is verified more frequently than other elements. In the case of revocation this might happen in many scenarios, for instance, in the Business-to-Consumer scenario (B2C) where status data of the servers' certificates is requested more often compared to clients'. Anyway, in the worst case (the request rate is equiprobable for all the data contained by the tree) our approach leads to a binary balanced tree.

Next we outline the algorithm[6] that builds the hash tree. Let us assume that Π_i is the probability for membership of element s_i to be requested, then

1. Line up the set of elements by falling probabilities Π_i.
2. The two elements with least probabilities are combined to generate a new node as explained in the previous Section. The new node (a internal tree's node) now is considered to have a probability the sum of probabilities of the two elements.
3. Go to the first step until a single node which probability is 1 is generated. This element will be the root of the tree.

Figure 3 shows the resulting Unbalanced binary Hash Tree (U-bHT) for four elements s_0, s_1, s_2, and s_3, with $\Pi_0 = \frac{1}{8}$, $\Pi_1 = \frac{1}{4}$, $\Pi_2 = \frac{1}{8}$, and $\Pi_3 = \frac{1}{2}$. Then, the average communication cost for the sample unbalanced tree is

---

[5] If proceeds, the reference of such publication will be included in the final version.

[6] The algorithm we use to build the unbalanced binary tree is equivalent to the one used by Huffman in the binary coding [3].

$$C_{U-bHT}^{sample} = S + (\mathcal{H}\frac{1}{2} + 2\mathcal{H}\frac{1}{4} + 3\mathcal{H}\frac{1}{8} + 3\mathcal{H}\frac{1}{8}) = S + 1,75\mathcal{H}. \qquad (5)$$

While the communication cost for the binary balanced tree (with four elements) is

$$C_{B-bHT}^{n=4} = S + \mathcal{H}log_2(4) = S + 2\mathcal{H}. \qquad (6)$$

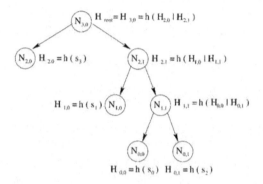

Fig. 3. Sample Unbalanced binary Hash Tree (U-bHT)

The number of cryptographic nodes of the $\mathcal{P}ath$ "P" is equivalent to the number of bits of the Huffman binary coding, which according to [3], can be bounded by

$$-\sum_{i=0}^{n-1} \Pi_i log_2 \Pi_i < P < -\sum_{i=0}^{n-1} \Pi_i log_2 \Pi_i + 1. \qquad (7)$$

Therefore, the communication cost of the U-bHT can also be bounded by

$$S - \mathcal{H}\sum_{i=0}^{n-1} \Pi_i log_2 \Pi_i \leq C_{U-bHT} \leq S - \mathcal{H}(\sum_{i=0}^{n-1} \Pi_i log_2 \Pi_i + 1). \qquad (8)$$

According to a well-known result in Information Theory, C_{U-bHT} reaches its maximum for $\Pi_i = 1/n$. Thus, in the worst case our system behaves like the binary balanced hash tree

$$P|_{\Pi_i=1/n} \approx -\sum_{i=0}^{n-1} \frac{1}{n} log_2 \frac{1}{n} = log_2(n). \qquad (9)$$

At this point, there are still several aspects that should be considered for an implementation[7], such as:

– *Data stored by the leaves.* If leaves store the serial numbers of revoked certificates, then the leaves must be ordered to prove that a given certificate is not revoked [9]. As in the unbalanced tree adjacent leaves do not contain consecutive serial numbers, a sequence of statements is more practical for the unbalanced tree. A statement is a condition on the serial numbers of the certificates and on which CA issued them. Below we show a sample statement literally taken from [6]

$$s_j : \quad CA_x = CA_2 \quad and \quad 156 \leq X < 343 \tag{10}$$

which means that the certificate with serial number $X = 156$ issued by CA_2 has been revoked, while the certificates with serial numbers from $X = 157$ to $X = 343$ (both included) issued by CA_2 have not been revoked. Notice that the statement defines the status information of a range of certificates independently of its position within the tree.

– *Starting Up.* Before building the initial tree, we must know the probability of each leaf of the tree. Usually, when the system starts up, these probabilities are not known. In this case, the leaves can be considered equiprobable, leading to a balanced tree. Later, adaptive algorithms can be used to learn the actual probability of each leaf through statistical monitoring (for this purpose, counters in the repositories can be used to inform the issuer).

– *Tree Updating.* When a certificate has been revoked or when a revoked certificate reaches the end of its documented life-time, the status data must be updated. The tree is periodically rebuilt to include updated data and the rebuilding process is performed according to the collected statistics.

5   Conclusions

In general, offline systems are more robust than online systems. However, offline systems have higher communication overhead than online systems. Among the offline systems, those based on hash trees have the lowest communication overhead. In this paper we have proposed an efficient way of implementing a Revocation Dictionary ($\mathcal{RD}$) based on a binary hash tree that minimizes the communication overhead of the status checking

---

[7] The system presented in this paper is not only a theoretical proposal but it is also currently being developed inside a Java test-bed for certificate revocation.

process. In the proposed system, the statistics of the status checking are used, like in the Huffman algorithm for source coding, for building an unbalanced hash tree that minimizes the length of the dictionary's response. The system performs better than balanced hash trees when the status of a subset of certificates is verified frequently (B2C scenarios, where status data of the servers' certificates is requested much more often than regular clients, can take advantage of the proposed system).

On the other hand, if status checking rates are similar for all certificates our approach leads to a binary balanced tree which is the best option among the balanced trees. Although our research is focused on certificate revocation, this work may be applied to other problems that require an authenticated dictionary like certificate generation (see Certificate Verification Tree [1]), time stamping, etc. Finally, as future work, the problem of the potential increase in the costs for updating the tree should be addressed.

References

1. I. Gassko, P.S. Gemmell, and P. MacKenzie. Efficient and fresh certification. In *International Workshop on Practice and Theory in Public Key Cryptography (PKC2000). Lecture Notes in Computer Science*, pages 342–353. Springer-Verlag, 2000.
2. R. Housley, W. Ford, W. Polk, and D. Solo. Internet X.509 Public Key Infrastructure Certificate and CRL Profile, 1999. RFC 2459.
3. David Huffman. A method for the construction of minimum-redundancy codes. *IRE*, 40(9):1098–1101, 1952.
4. ITU/ISO Recommendation. X.509 Information Technology Open Systems Interconnection - The Directory: Autentication Frameworks, 2000. Technical Corrigendum.
5. H. Kikuchi, K. Abe, and S. Nakanishi. Certificate revocation protocol using k-Ary Hash Tree. *IEICE Transactions on Communications*, 8:2026–2032, 2001.
6. P.C. Kocher. On certificate revocation and validation. In *International Conference on Financial Cryptography (FC98). Lecture Notes in Computer Science*, number 1465, pages 172–177, February 1998.
7. R.C. Merkle. A certified digital signature. In *Advances in Cryptology (CRYPTO89). Lecture Notes in Computer Science*, number 435, pages 234–246. Springer-Verlag, 1989.
8. M. Myers, R. Ankney, A. Malpani, S. Galperin, and C. Adams. X.509 Internet Public Key Infrastructure Online Certificate Status Protocol - OCSP, 1999. RFC 2560.
9. M. Naor and K. Nissim. Certificate Revocation and Certificate Update. *IEEE Journal on Selected Areas in Communications*, 18(4):561–560, 2000.
10. ITU/ISO Recommendation X.509. Information technology Open Systems Interconnection - The Directory: Public Key and Attribute Certificate Frameworks, 1997.

Breaking Down Architectural Gaps in Smart-Card Middleware Design*

Tommaso Cucinotta, Marco Di Natale[1], and David Corcoran[2]

[1] Scuola Superiore Sant'Anna, Pisa, Italy
[2] Identity Alliance, Austin, TX

Abstract. This paper presents an open and modular middleware for smart cards, interoperable across multiple card devices, and portable across various open platforms. The architectural design is centred around the definition of a smart card API that allows protected access to the storage and cryptographic facilities of a smart card. The proposed API allows partitioning of a smart card driver architecture into a lower *card-dependent* level, that formats and exchanges APDUs with the external device, and a higher *card-independent* level, that uses the API for implementing more sophisticated interfaces. The proposed architecture, along with a set of pilot applications such as secure remote shell, secure web services, local login and digital signature, has been developed and tested on various platforms, proving effectiveness of the new approach.

1   Introduction

Security of applications and services is becoming an increasingly important issue to be addressed since the early stages of the design and development of complex software systems. In order to achieve an adequate level of security while exchanging information or running transactions onto an open network, such as the Internet, cryptographic mechanisms need to be used. Cryptography enabled services guarantee that only authorised entities can access sensitive data or valuable services when cryptographic keys are properly managed by all parties.

Smart card (SC) technology is, among others, an enabler for guaranteeing the secure management of cryptographic keys. Card devices have a high degree of trustworthiness, for many reasons: a card owner always has physical control of the card; on-card architecture is very simple, hence on-board code and logic can be easily made functionally correct; SC hardware is designed to be tamper-proof, so that it is very hard and expensive to try to recover contained data by physical inspection. Smart cards are sufficiently powerful to perform cryptographic operations on-board, without any need to reveal cryptographic keys to the outside world. These operations are only allowed after a proper user identity verification, through the use of Personal Identification Numbers (PINs), or even biometrics information.

---

* This work has been partially supported by the European Commission within the IST project 2001-34820 ARTIST, and by the MIUR within the 2002 I4002 PA Project.

S. Katsikas, J. Lopez, and G. Pernul (Eds.): TrustBus 2004, LNCS 3184, pp. 279–288, 2004.

Even if smart cards have been widely adopted and supported on proprietary platforms, they are not being used on open platforms due to the lack of open solutions. On these systems, open source libraries and applications allow the use of cryptography for data protection, but the achieved security level is strongly limited because of the use of software-only cryptography. SC technology typically features a "proprietary" approach in which every manufacturer deliberately deviates from standards in order to give its products some added functionality and to link its customers to the company as long as possible. Standard APIs for interoperability do exist [1, 2], but only a few vendors provide their implementation on open platforms, and for only one or a limited set of devices. This situation discourages smart card integration and has the consequence of an overall reduction in the use of smart card devices, hindering the development of their potential in increasing security of computer applications and services.

As a result, computer systems based on open platform are especially subject to be overpopulated with cryptographic keys that are managed in software and stored onto hard-drives, possibly protected by weak passwords quickly chosen by careless users. The MUSCLE[1] Card middleware, which is being introduced in this paper, constitutes a step toward openness and simplification in smart card middleware design and implementation.

The paper is structured as follows. The next section introduces common concepts about SC middleware and makes an overview of other open architectures for smart cards. Section 3 introduces the proposed architecture and features an overview of the new API. Finally, we draw our conclusions in Section 4.

2   Background on Smart Card Middleware

The world of smart cards is characterised by various card-reader (serial, PS/2, USB, wireless) and card device (storage only, crypto-enabled, GSM-enabled, programmable) types. In spite of the effort made by standard organisations [3, 4], card devices have many restrictions and non standard filesystem structures.

The simplest way of increasing an application or system security through the use of smart card technology is by delegating management and use of one or more cryptographic keys to the card device. For PKI applications, one or more public key certificates can be stored on the card for easing mobility of the card among various physical locations. This is usually achieved through common, high-level, application programming interfaces that support on-card operations in a manner that is independent of the card and reader devices.

Two APIs that have been defined for this purpose are PKCS#11 [1] by RSA Labs, and PCSC [2], Part 6, by the PCSC Workgroup. Such high level APIs are made available to applications through a smart card middleware that requires various drivers to be installed on the system, depending on the actual reader and card devices that are going to be used. A generic smart card middleware architecture is depicted in Figure 1(a).

---

[1] Movement for the Use of Smart Cards in a Linux Environment.

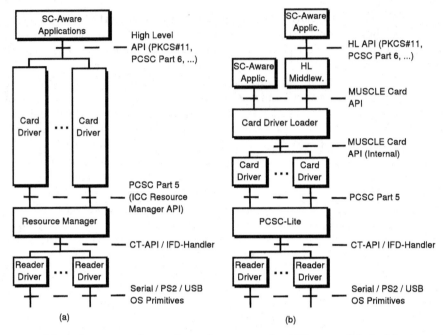

Fig. 1. (a) Architecture of a traditional smart card middleware. (b) Architecture of the proposed smart card middleware.

At the bottom layers, a resource manager component is required for managing the SC readers that are available on the system, and making their services available to higher level components, in a way that is independent of the hardware connected to the system. This is done through the PCSC ICC Resource Manager interface [2, Part 5], which provides function calls for listing the available readers, querying a reader about the inserted card(s), enabling or disabling the power to an inserted card, and establishing an exclusive or shared communication channel for data exchanges with a card. The reader driver takes care of translating the requests into the low-level Protocol Data Units (PDUs) to be transmitted to the reader through the low level serial OS primitives. Reader drivers implement the CT-API or the PCSC IFD-Handler API [2, Part 3, Appendix A], and the resource manager translates calls to the PCSC Part 5 interface to the appropriate lower level API calls. The higher software stack performs data exchanges through command APDUs compliant to the ISO T=0 or T=1 protocols [5].

The top level component of the middleware is traditionally a monolithic component, provided by card vendors, that implements the PKCS#11 or PCSC Part 6 interfaces. These APIs have calls that allow the application to locate, manage and use cryptographic keys and public key certificates that are available on the card. The card driver translates such requests into the appropriate lower level ISO T=0 or T=1 command APDUs to be exchanged with the card. Typically, it supports a range of similar card devices provided by the same vendor. Furthermore, it must comply with the higher level API, what requires additional tasks to be performed in the component, such as session management and transaction handling. Such tasks are quite similar in the driver implementations provided by different vendors, where the only changes regard the specific way information is exchanged with the card by means of APDU exchanges. This is why we investigated on the possibility of introducing a further abstraction layer, breaking the traditional driver architecture through the use of a middle-level API.

In fact, our architecture has a lower level (LL) driver, which formats and exchanges command APDUs with the card device, and a higher level (HL) one, which performs the additional management tasks required for the compliance with the higher level interface. This is done through the introduction of a middle-level API, clearly identifying the boundary and commitments of the two sublayers. As it will be shown in Section 3, the main benefit of such an approach is that it is possible to write the HL-API-specific management code only once. Interoperability among card devices is achieved by writing, for each card, a different LL driver implementing the common middle-level API.

2.1   Related Projects

The OpenSC [6] project provides a library and a set of utilities for accessing ISO 7816 [3] and PKCS#15 [7] compliant card devices. It provides a good set of middleware components, as well as modules for their integration within widely used secure applications, constituting an effective solution for integration of ISO 7816-4 and PKCS#15 compliant, pre-formatted devices. Though, various cards exist today with custom, proprietary APDUs for filesystem management, which adhere to ISO 7816-4 only in a read-only fashion, and/or do not respect the PKCS#15 standard for managing information about the on board cryptographic material. Such devices cannot be directly supported within this architecture, especially on the side of card-personalisation.

The SecTok [8] project provides a library for the management of files onto an ISO 7816-4 compliant device. It does not support cryptographic functionality of the devices, thus it cannot be used in the context of cryptographic smart cards.

The Open Card Framework (OCF) [9] is a Java based development platform for smart card development. It aims at reducing dependence among card terminal vendors, card operating system providers and card issuers, by the adoption of a consistent and expandable framework. The core architecture of OCF features two main parts: the CardTerminal layer, providing access to physical card terminals and inserted smart cards, and the CardService layer, providing support for the wide variety of card operating systems. OCF is a promising framework for smart card integration within Java applications. Despite the modular and expandable design, its main limitations are due to the lack of support of some readers due to the way I/O is managed at the lowest levels of the architecture, and the inherent difficulties and overhead needed in order to access such functionality from programs written in different programming languages than Java.

The GPKCS#11 project [10] aims at providing support functionality that ease the development of a PKCS#11 driver for cryptographic tokens. Unfortunately, the project lacked detailed documentation about its features, and it has not been maintained since year 2000.

The Common Data Security Architecture (CDSA) [11] is an open standard introducing an interoperable, multi-platform, extensible software infrastructure for providing high level security services to C and C++ applications. It features a common API for authentication, encryption, and security policy management. As far as smart card technology is concerned, the CDSA standard supports external cryptographic devices through the use of PKCS#11 modules, while the overall architecture is designed and focused around higher level security services, such as certificate and CRL management, verification of signatures, authentication, and others.

The architecture that is being introduced in this paper, at the authors' knowledge, is the only open architecture completely modular that allows multiple heterogeneous devices to be supported through the implementation of a common lower level API, which exposes sufficient functionality needed by most PKI applications since the time of issuing of the card by a CA, up to the final use of the device by applications. The efforts needed for the implementation of such drivers is limited, with respect to the full implementation of one of the well known standards for smart cards, such as PKCS#11 or PCSC level 6. Still connectivity with such standards is possible through the implementation of the higher level API through the MUSCLE Card API, what can be done in a separate module, and once and for all.

3   Proposed Architecture

The middleware architecture of the MUSCLE Card project is shown in Figure 1(b). At the bottom layers, the PCSC-Lite project provides an open and stable daemon for managing the SC-related hardware resources of the PC (e.g. serial/USB ports, connected readers). Various readers are supported through reader drivers, most of which open source, implementing either the CT-API or the IFD-Handler interface. Devices connected to serial and PS2 ports need to be already connected when the daemon starts, while USB devices can be plugged at run-time, provided that the drivers are installed onto the system.

At the above layer, independence from the card is achieved by using a common API. Specifically, the Card Driver Loader, at the time the card is inserted, identifies the inserted device through the Answer To Reset (ATR) bytes, then loads dynamically the driver that can manage the card. Differently from traditional approaches, in which higher level APIs such as PKCS-11 or PCSC Level 6 are implemented by card drivers, in the proposed architecture a card driver implements a simpler API (see Section 3.1).

The API exposes basic storage, cryptographic and access control functionality to the host machine, independently of the kind of card device the host is using. This interface is inspired by the protocol introduced in [12], in that most function calls are directly mapped into the APDUs of the protocol. This layer has been implemented in various card drivers for card devices that are different in architecture and nature. Examples are Schlumberger Cyberflex Access 32K and Gemplus 211/PK cards, two programmable cards based on the JavaCard platform; the Schlumberger Cryptoflex 16K card, which exposes a set of ISO 7816-4 APDUs for filesystem management, and custom commands for cryptographic operations; the US Department of Defence (DoD) card, which exposes a custom data model. Details on the proposed API follow in the next subsections. On top of our API, further application and middleware layers have been developed. Specifically, an open source PKCS-11 module, mapping the PKCS-11 API calls into the appropriate sequences of MUSCLE Card API function calls, has been developed.

As an alternative, applications can directly use the proposed API in order to talk to smart card devices at a lower level, and take advantage of the exposed functionality, like access control mechanisms based on multiple PINs or other authentication means. The API has been directly used for embedding smart-card technology into a set of target applications, within the Smart Sign project (http://smartsign.sourceforge.net): a command line digital signature application (sign-mcard), a variant of the OpenSSH software (openssh-mcard). A PAM [13] module has been directly developed using this API, allowing smartcard based user authentication for applications using PAM on Unix like systems, like the Unix login. Finally, a CSP module for Windows platforms has also been developed, integrating functionality of the exposed architecture into applications like MS Outlook, Internet Explorer and Windows login.

3.1   MUSCLE Card API Overview

This section features a technical overview of the proposed API. The discussion is focused on the introduction of the API main features, and explanation of the main design choices behind its development. The complete API specification [14] is available for download at the URL: *http://www.musclecard.com*.

Objectives and Design Choices. Main aim of the API design is to provide higher layer software components with an open, simple, card independent framework which exhibits sufficient generality to meet the requirements of a multitude of target applications, including digital signature, secure e-mail, secure login, secure remote terminal and secure on-line web services, both PKI based and not.

These requirements have been identified in having a means of generating, importing, exporting, and using cryptographic keys on the card. Another requirement is to have a means of creating, reading, and writing generic data on the card in generic "containers". This is useful, for example, to store on the card a public key certificate associated with a private key. Access to some of these resources needs to be granted only after host application and user authentication.

The result is a simple and light interface that has been proved to be effective in allowing integration of smart card technology into secure applications, as shown by our sample application cases. The API design allows future extensions, like the use of alternative key types or authentication mechanisms, as proved by the biometrics extensions that have recently been added [15].

The API does not address sophisticated card services that might be needed by specific applications. Multi-key digital signatures and authentication schemes may need specific functionalities to be provided through the use of multiple cards. These applications can still benefit from the exposed middleware by extending it with the required functionality, given the open nature of the project.

The set of functions available in the proposed API is summarised in Table 1. API functionality has been divided into 5 general function sets, giving access to one or more of our middleware class of services, namely: session management, data storage, cryptographic key management, PIN management, access control, and a set of miscellaneous further functions. In the following, we provide detailed information on the intended use of the various API calls.

Table 1. MUSCLE Card API function set

Session mgmt	ListTokens, EstablishConnection, ReleaseConnection
	WaitForTokenEvent, CancelEventWait, BeginTransaction, EndTransaction
Data storage	CreateObject, DeleteObject, ListObjects, WriteObject, ReadObject
Cryptography	GenerateKeyPair, ComputeCrypt, ImportKey, ExportKey, ListKeys
PIN mgmt	CreatePIN, ChangePIN, UnblockPIN, ListPINs
Access ctrl	VerifyPIN, GetChallenge, ExtAuthenticate, GetStatus, LogOutAll
Miscellaneous	WriteFramework, GetCapabilities, ExtendedFeature

Session Management. The API has a minimal set of functions allowing the enumeration of connected readers and inserted smart cards, and management of the connections to the card devices. Establishment of a connection to a card device is a prerequisite for the use of any of the other functions of the API. Specifically, the `ListTokens` function is able to enumerate readers connected to the system, readers which have a card inserted, along with the type of inserted device, and the list of all supported card devices in the system. Furthermore, an application is able to block and wait until a card insertion or removal by using the `WaitForTokenEvent` function. Once a card is inserted into a reader, the `EstablishConnection` and `ReleaseConnection` functions allow to reset the device and prepare it for subsequent commands. When connecting to a card, it is possible to select either exclusive or shared access to the card. In the latter case, it is possible to acquire an exclusive lock on the device with a call to the `BeginTransaction` function, and release it with the `EndTransaction` function.

Data Storage Services. Our middleware allows the definition of simple containers for applications' data called *objects*, identified by means of a string identifier (OID). Access control is enforced on a per-object and per-operation basis, distinguishing among create, read, write and delete operations (more details will be given later). The data storage services suffice for the target applications cited in the beginning of Section 3.1, by allowing them to store, retrieve and manage data onto a card in a secure and controlled way.

The `CreateObject` function allows creation of an empty object on the card, providing the object name, size and access control list (see forward for details about this). The same information may be visioned by applications for all existing on card objects through subsequent calls to the ListObject function. Reading and writing of data to and from objects is performed, respectively, through the ReadObject and WriteObject functions. Execution of these functions may be restricted on a per-object and per-operation basis. The API specification does not define specific object contents, leaving the applications total freedom on what to store onto a card, like user private information, application specific data or public key certificates. As far as the card storage capacity is concerned, the interface specification gives only a view of the total available memory on the device, through the GetStatus function.

Cryptographic Services. The API allows up to 16 keys to be managed on the card, identified by means of a numeric key identifier. A full key pair can be stored by using two key identifiers. Key types are those provided by the Java Card 2.1.1 API: RSA, DSA, DES, Triple DES, Triple DES with 3 keys. The interface is designed to allow further key types in the future. Operations provided on cryptographic keys are import/export from/to the host, computation of cryptograms, and listing of keys. All key operations except key listing are allowed only after proper host application or user authentication. The API allows key pairs to be directly generated on board guaranteeing the private key is not exposed outside the card. In this case the public key can be obtained with a call to ExportKey, right after the key pair generation. When a key pair is created on-board, the host application specifies under what conditions subsequent reading, overwriting and use operations are allowed for each of the keys in the pair. The same rules can be specified when importing a new key from the outside world.

Security Model and Access Control Enforcement. A simple Access Control List (ACL) based model is defined to protect on-board objects, allowing operations to be performed only after proper host application and user authentication. This may be performed by means of a PIN code verification, a *challenge-response* cryptographic authentication protocol, or a combination of both methods. Furthermore, the API has been designed to allow future support for other identification schemes, like fingerprint verification. Access rules for on-card resources are specified by using the concept of *identity*. This term refers to one of several authentication mechanisms that host applications and users can use to be authenticated to a smart card. Identities, PINs, and cryptographic keys are referred to by means of numeric identifiers. Different types of identity are defined: identities n.0-7 are labelled as *PIN-based* and are associated, respectively, with PIN codes n.0-7; identities n.8-13 are said *strong* and are associated, respectively, with cryptographic keys n.0-5 for the purpose of running challenge-response cryptographic authentication protocols; identities n.14-15 are *reserved*[2].

A successful run of any of the authentication mechanisms causes the *log in* of the associated identity, in addition to identities already logged in. The use of multiple identities allows a host application to switch to a higher security

---

[2] The fingerprint verification mechanism recently developed uses identity n.14.

level that grants access to more of the card's capabilities, as it runs additional authentication mechanisms. Furthermore the *LogOutAll* command allows a host application to return back to the unauthenticated security status.

An ACL specifies which identities are required to grant access to each operation of each object or key. Object operations are *read, write* and *delete*. Key operations are *overwrite* (either by means of regeneration or by means of import), *export*, and *use*. An ACL associated with an object or key is specified by means of three Access Control Words (ACW), each one relating to an operation. An ACW consists of 16 bits. Each bit corresponds to one of the 16 identities that can be logged in. An all-zero ACW means that the operation is publicly available, that is a host application can perform it without any prior authentication. An ACW with one or more bits set means that all of the corresponding identities must be logged in at the time the operation is performed. An all-one ACW has the special meaning of completely disabling the operation, independently of the connection security status. This is useful to disable reading of private keys.

PIN Management Services. Functions have been defined for PIN management, allowing to create, verify, change and unblock PINs. Specifically, the *CreatePIN* function allows to create a new PIN on the card, provided that the transport PIN has already been verified, and the *ListPIN* function allows listing of the existing PIN codes. Up to eight PIN codes are allowed in principle to be created onto a single card, though the actual maximum number depends on the underlying device, and may be queried by using the *GetCapabilities* function. The *VerifyPIN* function allows verification of a PIN code, and, if successful, logs in the corresponding identity. Finally, the *ChangePIN* function may be used to change the current PIN value, and the *UnblockPIN* function to unblock it after it blocked due to several verification tries with the wrong code.

Extensibility. Our middleware allows connectivity to smart card devices at a lower level than the one that is usually required for the implementation of standard PKCS#11 or PCSC interfaces. The set of functionality that is exposed to applications has been voluntarily kept small, in order to achieve a simple API. Particular attention has been paid to extensions that could be needed in the future. In order to allow such extensions to be performed without compromising the previously developed software, the middleware has versioning built into it. The version information is available through the *GetStatus* command, by means of *minor* and *major* version numbers.

Card Specific Behaviour. The API which has been just introduced provides a unified means, for higher level middleware components as well as applications, to access the described smart card services in a unified, card-independent way. However, it must be noted that only a JavaCard device with the MUSCLE Card Applet on-board is able to support the full set of functionality available through this API. Each specific card generally supports only a subset of such functionality. The API provides, through the *GetCapabilities* function, a means for querying what features are supported by the particular device that is connected to the system.

4   Conclusions

In this paper we described an open middleware for smart cards, which is highly modular due to the adoption of a new interface layer that abstracts from the specifics of a card. Such interface has been designed to support minimal functionality needed by applications that use smart card devices to manage cryptographic keys and other kind of data, e.g. public key certificates. In the proposed middleware architecture, a traditional smart card driver is split into two sublayers: the lower level one focuses on abstracting the specifics of each single device; the higher level one implements a standard interface, such as PKCS#11, still leaving the applications freedom to use the lower level interface, if needed. For example, a smart card aware, biometrics enhanced, application can directly use the middle level interface for using added functionality. Development of target PKI enabled applications proved effectiveness of the new approach.

References

1. RSA Laboratories: PKCS-11 version 2.1.1 Final Draft: Cryptographic Token Interface Standard. (2001)
2. PCSC Workgroup: Interoperability Specification for ICCs and Personal Computer Systems. (1997)
3. International Standard Organization: ISO/IEC 7816-4/7/8/9: Information technology - Identification cards - Integrated circuit(s) cards with contacts - Parts 4, 7, 8, 9. (1995)
4. GSA: Government Smart Card Interoperability Specification: Contract Modification. (2000)
5. International Standard Organization: ISO/IEC 7816-3: Information technology - Identification cards - Integrated circuit(s) cards with contacts - Part 3. (1989)
6. Kirch, O.: OpenSC - smart cards on linux. In: Proc. of the 10th International Linux System Technology Conference, Saarbruecken, Germany (2003)
7. RSA Laboratories: PKCS-15: A Cryptographic Token Information Format Standard. (1999)
8. Center for Information Technology Integration (CITI), University of Michigan: Sectok library and applications. (2001)
9. OpenCard Consortium: OpenCard Framework General Information Web Document. second edn. (1998)
10. TrustCenter: gpkcs11 - GNU PKCS#11 implementation. (2000)
11. The Open Group: Common Security: CDSA and CSSM, Version 2.3. (2000)
12. Cucinotta, T., Natale, M.D., Corcoran, D.: A protocol for programmable smart cards. In: Proc. of DEXA 2003, Prague, Czech Republic (2003)
13. Samar, V., Schemers, R.: Request for comments 86.0: Unified login with pluggable authentication modules (PAM) (1995)
14. Corcoran, D., Cucinotta, T.: MUSCLE Card API, version 1.3.0. (2001)
15. Brigo, R.: Protecting smart card access by on-board biometrics verification. Computer Engineering Thesis. University of Pisa (2002)

On the Security of the Lee-Hwang Group-Oriented Undeniable Signature Schemes

Guilin Wang, Jianying Zhou, and Robert H. Deng

Infocomm Security Department (ICSD)
Institute for Infocomm Research (I²R)
21 Heng Mui Keng Terrace, Singapore 119613
{glwang,jyzhou,deng}@i2r.a-star.edu.sg
http://www.i2r.a-star.edu.sg/icsd/

Abstract. Undeniable signature is an intriguing concept introduced by Chaum and van Antwerpen at Crypto'89. In 1999, Lee and Hwang presented two group-oriented undeniable signature schemes with a trusted center. Their schemes are natural generalizations of Chaum's zero knowledge undeniable signature scheme proposed in 1990. However, we find that the Lee-Hwang schemes are *insecure*. In this paper, we demonstrate five effective attacks on their schemes: four of them are *insider universal forgeries*, in which one dishonest member (maybe colluding with a verifier) can get a valid signature on any chosen massage, and another attack allows a dishonest member to prevent honest members from generating valid signatures. We also suggest heuristic improvements to overcome some of the problems involved in these attacks.

Keywords: undeniable signatures, digital signatures, cryptographic protocols.

1 Introduction

Undeniable signature is a special kind of digital signature in the sense that the validity of an alleged signature cannot be verified without the cooperation of the signer. Since in such schemes the verifiablity of signatures is only limited to designated verifiers, undeniable signatures have been suggested to construct electronic commerce schemes, and fair exchange protocols etc.

The concept of undeniable signature was first proposed at Crypto'89 by Chaum and van Antwerpen [1]. Followed by this pioneering work, Chaum proposed a zero-knowledge undeniable signature scheme in [2]. Later, at Auscrypt'92, by combining the two concepts of undeniable signature and group-oriented signature [5, 6], Harn and Yang proposed the concept of *group-oriented undeniable signature* [11], in which *only* when all members in an authorized subset of a given group operate collectively, they can generate, confirm or deny a signature on behalf of the group. If the authorized subsets are all subsets of t or more members of a group with n members, then it is called a (t,n) *threshold undeniable signature scheme*. In a *secure* (t,n) threshold undeniable signature

S. Katsikas, J. Lopez, and G. Pernul (Eds.): TrustBus 2004, LNCS 3184, pp. 289–298, 2004.

scheme, even if $t - 1$ colluding dishonest members (maybe colluding with a verifier) cannot generate, confirm or deny a signature.

In [11], Harn and Yang also designed two concrete threshold undeniable signature schemes: $(1, n)$ scheme and (n, n) scheme. However, Langford pointed out that their (n, n) scheme only has a security of 2-out-of-n, because any two adjacent members can generate a valid threshold signature on any message [15]. Later, Lin et al. presented a general (t, n) threshold undeniable signature scheme [18], but it is also subjected to Langford's attack. To overcome Langford's attack, Lee and Hwang constructed two group-oriented undeniable signature schemes with a trusted center [16] by naturally generalizing Chaum's zero-knowledge undeniable signature [2] to group-oriented environment.

In this paper, we present a security analysis of the Lee-Hwang schemes [16] by demonstrating five attacks: one attack on signing protocol, two attacks on confirmation protocol and another two attacks on denial protocol. Under reasonable assumptions, our attacks are simple, straightforward, and effective. In these attacks, four of them are *insider universal forgeries*, in which one dishonest member (maybe colluding with a verifier or the designated combiner) can get a valid signature on any chosen massage, and another attack allows a dishonest member to prevent honest members from generating valid signatures. In addition, we suggest heuristic improvements to overcome some of the problems involved in these attacks.

The rest of this paper is organized as follows. Section 2 reviews the Lee-Hwang schemes. Section 3 presents five attacks on their schemes, and Section 4 proposes some heuristic improvements. Section 5 discusses related work. Finally, the conclusion is given in Section 6. The full version of this paper [28] also addresses a design problem in their generalized group-oriented undeniable signature scheme.

2   Review of the Lee-Hwang Schemes

The Lee-Hwang schemes [16] consist of a trusted center TC, a designed combiner DC [1] and a group of n members U_i ($i \in A = \{1, 2, \cdots, n\}$). In this section, we only review the (t, n) threshold undeniable signature scheme. For the details of the generalized scheme, please refer to the original paper [16].

2.1   System Setup

The trusted center TC first determines the following public parameters:

- P, p : two large primes, such that $P = 2p + 1$.
- α: an element of order p in $\mathbb{Z}_P$.
- $H(\cdot)$: a collision free one-way hash function[2].

---

[1] DC is an untruthful entity [19, 17].

[2] In order to guarantee the order of overwhelming part of $H(m)$ is p, it is required [16] that if the order of $H(m)$ mod P is $P - 1$, then let $H(m)^2$ be the digest of a message m. Because this processing does not affect the discussion here, we will simply use $H(m)$ as the digest of the message m.

- l: a security parameter (e.g. $l = 1023$).
- x_i: n public values, each x_i is associated with the member U_i such that $x_i \neq x_j$ if $i \neq j$ ($i, j \in A$).

After that, the TC selects a secret random number S from $\mathbb{Z}_P$ as the group private key, and a random polynomial $f(x) \in \mathbb{Z}_P[x]$ of degree $t - 1$ such that $f(0) = S$. Then, the TC privately sends the share $s_i = f(x_i)$ to the member U_i as his secret key, and publishes $Y = \alpha^S \bmod P$ as the group public key.

2.2   Signing Protocol

Any t members U_i ($i \in B$, $|B| = t$ and $B \subseteq \{1, 2, \cdots, n\}$) can generate a threshold undeniable signature on any message m as follows.

(1-1) Each U_i calculates his partial undeniable signature $z_i = H(m)^{s_i C_{Bi}} \bmod P$, where the Lagrange coefficient C_{Bi} is determined by

$$C_{Bi} = \sum_{j \in B, j \neq i} x_j / (x_j - x_i) \bmod p.$$

Then, U_i sends z_i to the designed combiner DC.

(1-2) Upon receiving t partial undeniable signatures, the DC computes the threshold undeniable signature Z on message m by

$$Z = \prod_{i \in B} z_i \bmod P \; (= H(m)^{\sum_{i \in B} s_i C_{Bi} \bmod p} \bmod P = H(m)^S \bmod P).$$

2.3   Confirmation Protocol

If t members U_i ($i \in B$) in the group agree to verify an undeniable signature pair (m, Z), then the verifier V and these t members execute the following confirmation protocol cooperatively.

(2-1) V chooses two random numbers $a, b \in_R \mathbb{Z}_p$, computes the value $W = H(m)^a \alpha^b \bmod P$ and sends W to each member in B.

(2-2) After receiving W, each U_i ($i \in B$) selects a number $k_i \in_R \mathbb{Z}_p$, and computes the value $K_i = \alpha^{k_i} \bmod P$. Then, all K_i are broadcasted so that all members in B can compute the following value R_1:

$$R_1 = W \prod_{i \in B} K_i \bmod P \; (= W \prod_{i \in B} \alpha^{k_i} \bmod P = W \alpha^{\sum_{i \in B} k_i} \bmod P).$$

Moreover, U_i computes and broadcasts the following value $R_{2,i}$

$$R_{2,i} = R_1^{s_i C_{Bi}} \bmod P.$$

Up to this, the DC (and any member) calculates the following value R_2

$$R_2 = \prod_{i \in B} R_{2,i} \bmod P \; (= R_1^S \bmod P).$$

At last, R_1 and R_2 are sent to the verifier V.

(2-3) V reveals the values of a and b to each member U_i in B.

(2-4) Each member in B checks whether $W \equiv H(m)^a \alpha^b \bmod P$. If it does hold, then the value $k = \sum_{i \in B} k_i \bmod p$ is revealed to V.

(2-5) V accepts (m, Z) as a valid signature pair if and only if the following two equalities hold:

$$R_1 \equiv W\alpha^k \bmod P, \quad R_2 \equiv Z^a Y^{b+k} \bmod P.$$

2.4   Denial Protocol

Any t members, U_i $(i \in B)$, can convince a verifier V that an alleged signature pair (m, Z) is not generated by the group. For this goal, the following denial protocol is run between these t members and V [3].

(3-1) V randomly selects two numbers $q \in_R [0, l]$ and $c \in_R \mathbb{Z}_p$, then computes and sends $E_1 = H(m)^q \alpha^c \bmod P$ and $E_2 = Z^q Y^c \bmod P$ to each member in B.

(3-2) All members in B cooperate to find the value of q by trial and error. Then, each U_i $(i \in B)$ chooses a random integer d_i and sends $blob(d_i, q)$ to V as his commitment to q [4].

(3-3) V reveals the value of c to each member in B.

(3-4) Each member U_i in B checks whether the following two equalities hold:

$$E_1 \equiv H(m)^q \alpha^c \bmod P, \quad E_2 \equiv Z^q Y^c \bmod P.$$

If they do hold, then each U_i sends back d_i to the verifier V.

(3-5) V opens all $blob(d_i, q)$ to check whether all the committed values are equivalent to q. If yes, V believes that (m, Z) is not generated by the group.

3   Five Attacks on Lee-Hwang Schemes

In [16], Lee and Hwang claimed that less than t members in their threshold scheme, or t_r members in the generalized scheme, cannot generate, confirm or deny a group-oriented undeniable signature. However, this is not true. We identify five attacks on their schemes: In the first attack, against signing protocols, one dishonest member can prevent honest members from generating valid signatures; in the other four attacks, against confirmation and denial protocols, one dishonest member (maybe colluding with the DC or a verifier V) can generate a valid signature on any chosen message. So, these later four attacks are insider universal forgeries, which should be avoided in a secure multiparty digital signature scheme [19].

---

[3] In practice, if $l = 1023$, then the denial protocol could be repeated twice to restrict the chance of cheating less than one in a million, or 10 times to reach a security level of $1/2^{100}$.

[4] $blob(d_i, q)$ means that the value of q is committed by d_i [2, 16].

In the following attacks, for convenience but without loss of generality, we always assume U_1 is dishonest and $B = \{1, 2, \cdots, t\}$. Sometimes, the success of an attack needs the help of the DC or a verifier V, i.e. in this case, the DC or V is also dishonest. This is reasonable because the DC and V are untruthful entities in the system. Here, we only describe attacks on the Lee-Hwang threshold undeniable signature scheme. Similar attacks can be applied to their generalized group-oriented scheme.

3.1   One Attack on Signing Protocol

[Attack 1]. In the signing protocol, no method is provided to verify the validity of each partial signature z_i. So dishonest member U_1 may cheat others by publishing a false $\bar{z}_1$ instead of true z_1. Then, using his valid partial signature z_1 and other published valid partial signature z_i [5], he can compute the valid threshold undeniable signature Z on message m by the following equation.

$$Z = \prod_{i=1}^{t} z_i \bmod P \; (= H(m)^S \bmod P).$$

But the DC, other group members and the expected receiver of the valid signature on message m can only get an invalid signature $\bar{Z}$ on message m by the following equation

$$\bar{Z} = \bar{z}_1 \cdot \prod_{i=2}^{t} z_i \bmod P.$$

Once U_1 obtains the valid signature pair (m, Z), he keeps it secretly, and reveals it to a relevant party when it is favorable to him/her. This unexpected receiver may provide (m, Z) to the group for verification. Group members cannot deny the validity of such a signature pair, because it is indeed valid. The essence of this attack is that dishonest member U_1 (maybe colluding with the DC) successfully prevents other members from generating valid signatures without any penalty, because no mechanism is provided to identify the cheaters.

3.2   Two Attacks on Confirmation Protocol

In these two attacks, it is assumed that t members in B agree to verify a valid signature pair (m, Z) for a verifier V. Then, the dishonest member U_1 (maybe colluding with the verifier V) can get a valid undeniable signature $\bar{Z}$ on an arbitrary message $\bar{m}$ selected by himself.

[Attack 2]. In this attack, U_1 colludes with a verifier V. Before attacking, they have chosen a message $\bar{m}$. Then, V selects two random numbers a and b, and computes $W = H(m)^a \alpha^b \bmod P$ normally. Member U_1 sets $\bar{K}_1 = H(\bar{m}) a^{k_1} \bmod P$, although each other member U_i $(i = 2, \cdots, t)$ honestly chooses k_i and computes

---

[5] If only the DC knows the values of these valid z_i's, we assume the DC colludes with U_1 and reveals these values to him.

$K_i = \alpha^{k_i} \bmod P$. After $\bar{K}_1$ and all K_i are broadcast, the following $\bar{R}_1$ and $\bar{R}_2$ are calculated:

$$\bar{R}_1 = W\bar{K}_1 K_2 \cdots K_t \bmod P \; (= W\alpha^{k_1 + \cdots + k_t} H(\bar{m}) \bmod P),$$

$$\bar{R}_2 = \bar{R}_1^S \bmod P \; (= Z^a Y^{b + k_1 + \cdots + k_t} H(\bar{m})^S \bmod P).$$

Then, $\bar{R}_1$ and $\bar{R}_2$ are sent to V and V reveals a and b to each member in B. Each member in B checks and finds that W has the right form since the verifier prepared $W = H(m)^a \alpha^b \bmod P$ properly. According to the confirmation protocol, $k = k_1 + k_2 + \cdots + k_t \bmod p$ will be sent to V. Using the values of a, b and k, U_1 and V obtain the signature $\bar{Z}$ on message $\bar{m}$ by the following equation

$$\bar{Z} = \bar{R}_2 / (Z^a Y^{b+k}) \bmod P \; (= H(\bar{m})^S \bmod P).$$

[Attack 3]. In this attack, under the assumption that U_1 publishes the value K_1 last, he can get a valid threshold undeniable signature on any chosen message $\bar{m}$. The details are described as follows.

When U_1 has received W from V and all K_i from U_i ($i = 2, 3, \cdots, t$), he computes and broadcasts his value $\bar{K}_1$ as follows

$$\bar{K}_1 = H(\bar{m})(WK_2 \cdots K_t)^{-1} \bmod P.$$

Then, the following value $\bar{R}_1$, instead of R_1, will be calculated:

$$\bar{R}_1 = W\bar{K}_1 K_2 \cdots K_t \bmod P = H(\bar{m}) \bmod P.$$

Followed by this value $\bar{R}_1$, $\bar{R}_2 = \bar{R}_1^S \bmod P = H(\bar{m})^S \bmod P$ will be produced. Then, $\bar{R}_1$ and $\bar{R}_2$ are sent to V. As a response, V sends a and b back to each member in B. Up to this, U_1 gets a valid signature pair $(\bar{m}, \bar{R}_2)$.

In the step (2-4), U_1 has the following two choices: (1) He selects a random number $k_1 \in_R [0, p-1]$ and reveals it to other members; (2) He disrupts the confirmation protocol by telling other members that he lost the value of k_1 with a reasonable excuse. In the first case, V will fail in step (2-5) with probability of $(p-1)/p$. But in the second case, possibly, the protocol will be conducted again and at this time U_1 behaves honestly. Anyway, from the above attack, U_1 gets a valid undeniable signature $\bar{R}_2$ on message $\bar{m}$ selected by himself.

If U_1 cannot access the value of $\bar{R}_2$, he will also succeed in this attack in collusion with the DC or a verifier V to get $\bar{R}_2$.

3.3   Two Attacks on Denial Protocol

In these two attacks, it is assumed that t members in B agree to deny an alleged signature pair (m, Z) for a verifier V. Then, the dishonest member U_1 (maybe colluding with verifier V) can get a valid undeniable signature pair $(m, \bar{Z})$ or $(\bar{m}, \bar{Z})$, where $\bar{m}$ is an arbitrary message selected by himself.

[Attack 4]. In [16], no details were given on how to find the value of q in the denial protocol by trial and error method. A straightforward method, which is used in [2,9], is to compute the values of $E_1^S \bmod P$ and $H(m)^S \bmod P$ by using the signing protocol, then all members in B find the value of q from the following equation by trial and error:

$$E_1^S / E_2 = (H(m)^S / Z)^q \bmod P.$$

However, by exploring this method, a valid signature $\bar{Z} = H(m)^S \bmod P$ on message m is generated, so each member (and the DC) knows its value. Therefore, U_1 (or any dishonest member of them) may keep this signature privately or reveal it to a third party which has interest in it. In some scenarios, members in B are unwilling to generate the signature of message m.

[**Attack 5**]. In this attack, U_1 colludes with a verifier V to get a valid signature on any chosen message $\bar{m}$. For this sake, V prepares $E_1 = H(\bar{m}) \bmod P$ and $E_2 = Z^q \alpha^c \bmod P$. When all members in B generated E_1^S by using the signing protocol, U_1 knows that this value is the valid signature $\bar{Z}$ on message $\bar{m}$, i.e., $\bar{Z} = E_1^S \bmod P = H(\bar{m})^S \bmod P$. In step (3-3), verifier V disrupts the denial protocol with some reasonable excuse. Then, possibly, the denial protocol will be repeated and at this time V behaves honestly. Generally, it would be unreasonable to assume that the denial protocol will not be conducted again only because a verifier erroneously sends a wrong value.

4   Improvements

In the attack 1, the problem is that when a signature Z is generated, *neither* the DC *nor* any member in B knows whether Z is a valid signature on message m. Using knowledge proofs for discrete logarithms [3,22], each member in B can convince others to believe that his partial signature is generated properly. However, to prevent one dishonest member executing the knowledge proof protocols on behalf of an illegal verifier [7], cryptographic commitment schemes [21] or designated verifier proofs [13] should also be used. Otherwise, blackmailing problem [12,14] will arise. At the same time, each member should check whether Z is identical with the product of all z_i, $i \in B$. If this is not the case, the DC can cheat honest members by publishing a false Z which is not equivalent to the product of all z_i.

The kernel problem in attacks 2 and 3 is that a dishonest member can use a value of K_i without knowing the value of k_i such that $K_i = \alpha^{k_i} \bmod P$. To overcome this problem, some standard techniques, like knowledge commitments or discrete logarithm knowledge proofs [3,25], could be employed in the confirmation protocol.

The reason for the success of attacks 4 and 5 is that values of the form X^S, i.e. $E_1^S \bmod P$ and $H(m)^S \bmod P$, are generated in order to find the value of q by trial and error. A direct countermeasure is not to generate these values in the process of finding q. Unfortunately, we have no idea to solve this problem at the moment.

Finally, please note that it is easy to eliminate the trusted center in the Lee-Hwang schemes since the distributed key generation protocol for discrete-log cryptosystems in [10] can be used directly in this setting. However, the point is that our attacks also apply to this improved threshold undeniable signature scheme.

5   Related Work

In [19], Michels and Horster discovered some attacks against several multiparty signature schemes. Their attacks are in common that the attacker is an *insider*, i.e., a dishonest group member, and the protocol will be disrupted. In fact, our attack 3 is inspired by their work.

In [20], based on Schnorr's signature scheme [23], Michels and Stadler proposed an efficient convertible undeniable signature scheme in which confirmation protocol and denial protocol are combined together into a verification protocol, and furthermore, they extended their scheme to a (t, n) threshold undeniable signature scheme. Since they used techniques of verifiable secret sharing for discrete logarithms [21] and their verification protocol has a different structure, the attacks presented here cannot be applied to their scheme.

Base on the first undeniable RSA signature scheme [9] and Shoup's threshold RSA signature [25], Wang et al. presented a threshold undeniable RSA signature scheme in [27]. Our attacks presented here cannot be applied to this scheme either because discrete logarithm knowledge proofs [3, 25] are used to verify the validity of partial signatures and no values of the form X^d are calculated, where d, similar to the value of S in the Lee-Hwang schemes, is the signing key in [27].

6   Conclusion

In this paper, we demonstrated five effective attacks on the Lee-Hwang group-oriented undeniable schemes [16]. Four of these attacks are insider universal forgeries, in which one dishonest member (maybe colluding with a verifier or the designated combiner) can get a valid signature on any chosen massage, and the remainder allows a dishonest member to prevent honest members from generating valid signatures but no mechanism is provided to identify the cheaters. To overcome some of the problems involved in these attacks, heuristic improvements were also suggested. However, how to solve the problem in the denial protocol is still open. At the same time, the Lee-Hwang schemes have one strong limitation: group members cannot be deleted efficiently. Furthermore, as pointed out in [19], heuristic improvements cannot guarantee the security of a repaired cryptosystem. So, threshold cryptosystems should be designed as provably secure [26, 8]. These problems would be considered in the future research.

References

1. D. Chaum and H. van Antwerpen. Undeniable signatures. In: *Crypto'89, LNCS 435*, pp. 212-216. Springer-Verlag, 1989.

2. D. Chaum. Zero-knowledge undeniable signatures. In: *Eurocrypt'90, LNCS 473*, pp. 458-464. Springer-Verlag, 1991.
3. D. Chaum and T.P. Pedersen. Wallet databases with observers. In: *Crypto'92, LNCS 740*, pp. 89-105. Springer-Verlag, 1993.
4. I. Damgård and T. Pedersen. New convertible undeniable signature schemes. In: *Eurocrypt'96, LNCS 1070*, pp. 372-386. Springer-Verlag, 1996.
5. Y. Desmedt. Society and group oriented cryptography: A New Concept. In: *Crypto'87, LNCS 293*, pp. 120-127. Springer-Verlag, 1988.
6. Y. Desmedt and Y. Frankel. Threshold cryptosystems. In: *Crypto'89, LNCS 435*, pp. 307-315. Springer-Verlag, 1990.
7. Y. Desmedt and M. Yung. Weakness of undeniable signature schemes. In: *Eurocrypt'91, LNCS 547*, pp: 205-220. Springer-Verlag, 1991.
8. P.-A. Fouque and D. Pointcheval. Threshold cryptosystems secure against chosen-ciphertext attacks. In: *Asiacrypt'01, LNCS 2248*, pp. 351-368. Springer-Verlag, 2001.
9. R. Gennaro, H. Krawczyk, and T. Rabin. RSA-based undeniable signature. In: *Crypto'97*, pp. 132-148. Springer-Verlag, 1997.
10. R. Gennaro, S. Jarecki, H. Krawczyk, and T. Rabin. Secure distributed key generation for discrete-log based cryptosystems. In: *Eurocrypt'99, LNCS 1592*, pp. 295-310. Springer-Verlag, 1999.
11. L. Harn and S. Yang. Group-oriented undeniable signature schemes without the assistance of a mutually trusted party. In: *Auscrypt'92, LNCS 718*, pp. 133-142. Springer-Verlag, 1993.
12. M. Jakobsson. Blackmailing using undeniable signatures. In: *Eurocrypt'94, LNCS 950*, pp.: 425-427. Springer-Verlag, 1994.
13. M. Jakobsson, K. Sako, and R. Impagliazzo. Designated verifier proofs and their applications. In: *Eurocrypt'96, LNCS 1070*, pp. 143-154. Springer-Verlag, 1996.
14. D. Kügler, and H. Vogt. Marking: a privacy protecting approach against blackmailing. In: *Public Key Cryptography (PKC'01), LNCS 1992*, pp. 137-152. Springer-Verlag, 2001.
15. S.K. Langford. Weakness in some threshold cryptosystems. In: *Crypto'96, LNCS 1109*, pp. 74-82. Springer-Verlag, 1996.
16. N.-Y. Lee and T. Hwang. Group-oriented undeniable signature schemes with a trusted center. *Computer Communications*, 22(8): 730-734. Elsevier Science, May 1999.
17. C-M. Li, T. Hwang, and N-Y. Lee. Threshold-multisignature schemes where suspected forgery implies traceability of adversarial shareholders. In: *Eurocrypt'94, LNCS 950*, pp. 194-204. Springer-Verlag, 1995.
18. C.-H. Lin, C.-T. Wang, and C.-C. Chang. A group-oriented (t, n) undeniable signature scheme without trusted center. In: *Information Security and Privacy (ACISP'96), LNCS 1172*, pp. 266-274. Springer-Verlag, 1996.
19. M. Michels and P. Horster. On the risk of discruption in several multiparty signature schemes. In: *Asiacrypt'96, LNCS 1163*, pp. 334-345. Springer-Verlag, 1996.
20. M. Michels, and M. Stadler. Efficient convertible signature schemes. In: *Proc. 4th Workshop on Selected Areas in Cryptography (SAC'97)*, pp. 231-244. Ottawa, Canada, 1997.
21. T.P. Pedersen. No-interactive and information-theoretic secure verifiable secret sharing. In: *Crypto'91, LNCS 576*, pp. 129-140. Springer-Verlag, 1992.
22. T.P. Pedersen. Distributed provers with applications to undeniable signatures. In: *Eurocrpt'96, LNCS 547*, pp. 221-242. Springer-Verlag, 1996.

23. C.P. Schnorr. Efficient signature generation for smart cards. *Journal of Cryptology*, 1991, 4(3): 161-174.
24. A. Shamir. How to share a secret. *Communications of the ACM*, 1979, 22(11): 612-613.
25. V. Shoup. Practical threshold signatures. In: *Eurocrypt'00, LNCS 1807*, pp. 207-220. Springer-Verlag, 2000.
26. D.R. Stinson and R. Strobl. Provably secure distributed Schnorr signatures and a (t, n) threshold scheme for implicit certificates. In: *ACISP'01, LNCS 2119*, pp. 417-434. Springer-Verlag, 2001.
27. G. Wang, S. Qing, M. Wang, and Z. Zhou. Threshold undeniable RSA signature scheme. In: *Information and Communications Security (ICICS'01), LNCS 2229*, pp. 220-231. Springer-Verlag, 2001.
28. G. Wang, J. Zhou, and R. H. Deng. Cryptanalysis of the Lee-Hwang group-oriented undeniable signature schemes. Full version of this paper, available at http://eprint.iacr.org/2002/150/, Sep 2002.

Author Index